PERFECT HOSTAGE

PERFECT HOSTAGE

A Life of Aung San Suu Kyi

JUSTIN WINTLE

HUTCHINSON
LONDON

Published by Hutchinson 2007

2 4 6 8 10 9 7 5 3 1

Copyright © Justin Wintle 2007

Justin Wintle has asserted his right under the Copyright, Designs
and Patents Act 1988 to be identified as the author of this work

First published in Great Britain in 2007 by
Hutchinson
Random House, 20 Vauxhall Bridge Road,
London SWIV 2SA

www.randomhouse.co.uk

Addresses for companies within The Random House Group Limited can be
found at: www.randomhouse.co.uk/offices.htm

The Random House Group Limited Reg. No. 954009

A CIP catalogue record for this book
is available from the British Library

ISBN 9780091796518 (Hardback)
ISBN 9780091796815 (Trade paperback)

The Random House Group Limited makes every effort to ensure that the papers
used in its books are made from trees that have been legally sourced from
well-managed and credibly certified forests. Our paper procurement policy can be
found at: www.randomhouse.co.uk/paper.htm

Typeset by Palimpsest Book Production Limited,
Grangemouth, Stirlingshire

Printed and bound in Great Britain by
Mackays of Chatham PLC, Chatham, Kent

for Pawongduen, Khun Nat and Supinya Klangnarong

CONTENTS

PART TWO: The Daughter

PART THREE: Sixteen Months

PART FOUR: The Political Madonna

ILLUSTRATIONS

Picture Credits

2, 3, 6, 7, 10, 13, 16, 22, 24–28, 41, 42 © Justin Wintle. 1, 8, 15, 18 Courtesy of Dr Kosuke Mizuno and the Centre for South-East Asian Studies, Kyoto University. 4, 5, 19, 29, 31, 34, 37 Author's collection. 9, 12, 20, 35 Private collection. 11 Courtesy of Dr Shankar Acharya. 14, 17 Photograph courtesy of U Kyaw Win. 21, 33 Courtesy of Martin Morland. 30 Courtesy Dr Margaret Stearn. 32 © Cartoonnews International Syndicate. 23 Photograph by Sandro Tucci – *Sunday Times* / Black Star Inc. 36 Courtesy of ALTSEAN. 38. Courtesy of Aung Zaw and *The Irrawaddy* magazine. 39 Courtesy *The Independent*. 40 Official UN photograph

PRINCIPAL BURMESE PERSONAE

Aung Gyi: Army officer and co-founder of the NLD

(Bogyoke) Aung San: Independence leader and father of **Aung San Suu Kyi**

Aung San Lin: The younger of **Aung San Suu Kyi's** two brothers

Aung San Oo: The elder of **Aung San Suu Kyi's** two brothers

Aung San Suu Kyi: Leader of the National League for Democracy; 1991 Nobel Peace Prize winner

(U) Aung Shwe: Acting chairman of the NLD following **U Kyi Maung's** arrest in October 1990

Ba Maw: Nationalist leader who became Burma's puppet dictator during the Japanese occupation of 1942-45

Ba Win: Aung San's eldest brother and early political mentor

(Daw) Khin Gyi: Aung San Suu Kyi's maternal aunt married to communist leader **Than Tun**

(Daw) Khin Kyi: Aung San Suu Kyi's mother

Khin Nyunt: Head of Military Intelligence and confidante of **Ne Win**; ousted in 2004

Khun Sa: Shan warlord and narcotics trader

(U) Kyi Maung: Former army officer, founder member of the NLD and its acting chairman following the arrest of **U Tin Oo** in July 1989

(Thakin) Kodaw Hmaing: Writer and leader of the pre-war patriotic *Dobama Asi-ayone*

(Bo) Let Ya (Hla Pe): Close colleague of **Aung San** and one of the 'Thirty Comrades'

Ma Than É: Expatriate employee of the UN and **Aung San Suu Kyi's** mentor in New York

Maung Aye: Army general and member of Burma's military junta since 1992

(Dr) Maung Maung: Lawyer; President of Burma from 19th August to 18th September 1988

Min Ko Naing: Student leader who came to prominence in 1988; leader of the ABSDF

Mindon: penultimate Burman king who created Mandalay

Ne Win: Army general who seized power in 1962

(U) **Nu:** Close colleague of **Aung San** and Burma's first prime minister following independence

(U) **Pandita:** Buddhist master (*Hsayadaw*) of the *Vipassana* school of meditation

Rewata Dhamma: The first among several monks who offered **Aung San Suu Kyi** instruction in Buddhism

Sanda Win: Ne **Win**'s favourite daughter

(U) **Saw:** Right-wing nationalist politician responsible for **Aung San**'s assassination

Saw Maung: Army general and titular head of state from 18th September 1988 until April 1992

Saya San (Hsaya San): Leader of an anti-colonial rebellion in the early 1930s.

Sein Lwin: Army officer and **Ne Win** loyalist; President of Burma from 29th July until 12th August 1988

(Dr) **Sein Win:** Cousin of **Aung San Suu Kyi** and leader of Burma's democratic government in exile

(**Thakin**) **Soe:** Leader of the Red Flag communists

Than Shwe: Army general; head of state since April 1992

Supayalat: King **Thibaw**'s queen

Than Tun: A leader of the White Flag communists married to **Khin Gyi**

(U) **Thant:** Secretary-General of the United Nations 1961-71

Thibaw: the last Burman king, dethroned by the British in 1885

(U) **Tin Oo:** Former general and first chairman of the National League for Democracy

(U) **Win Khet:** Founder member of the NLD and creator of the NLD-LA

Win Thein: Student bodyguard of **Aung San Suu Kyi** who walked before her at Danubyu

(U) **Win Tin:** Writer and journalist; founder member of the NLD imprisoned since 1989

GLOSSARY (INCLUDING ACRONYMS)

Like Chinese and Thai, Burmese is a 'tonal' language, employing pitch and voice quality to distinguish five different syllable types. The weighting of Burmese vowels does not therefore correspond exactly to their English equivalents, so that transliteration is at best an approximation. With regard to consonants, some anomalies persist, the most common being *ky* and *gy*. *Ky* is pronounced 'ch', so that phonetically Aung San Suu Kyi becomes Aung San Suu Chee. *Gy* is pronounced 'j', rendering Aung Gyi as Aung Jee. It should also be noted that *-one* is pronounced as in English 'bone' or 'cone', and *oke* is pronounced as in 'broke'. *Bogyoke* is therefore Bojoke, or thereabouts.

ABFSU	All Burma Federation of Student Unions
ABSDF	All Burma Students' Democratic Front
ADB	Asian Development Bank (United Nations)
AFPFL	Anti-Fascist People's Freedom League
AIR	All India Radio
ALTSEAN	Alternative ASEAN Network
Arahanta	Lit. 'to be worthy of deserving'; in Burmese Buddhism, one who has reached the final stage of spiritual progress
Arhat	The quality of being worthy of deserving; one who has attained enlightenment
ASEAN	Association of South-East Asian Nations
BBC	British Broadcasting Corporation
BCP	Burmese Communist Party; *see* CPB, the more common acronym
BDA	Burmese Defence Army
BIA	Burmese Independence Army
BNA	Burmese National Army
Bo	Leader, commander

Bodhisattva	In Theravada (Hinayana) Buddhism, the term used to denote a future Buddha. In Mahayana Buddhism, the term used to denote an enlightened being who delays his (more rarely her) entry into *Nirvana* by helping others
Bogyoke	Great leader; general
BSPP	Burma Socialist Programme Party
Burrifs	Shortened form of Burma Rifles
CIA	Central Intelligence Agency (USA)
CPB	Communist Party of Burma (more rarely BCP, Burmese Communist Party)
CRDP	Committee for the Restoration of Democracy in Burma
CRPP	Committee Representing the People's Parliament
CSEAS	Centre for South-East Asian Studies (Kyoto University)
DAB	Democratic Alliance of Burma
Daw	Honorific applied to an older woman
DEA	Drugs Enforcement Administration
Do-bama Asi-ayone	Lit. 'We Burmese Association'
DPNS	Democratic Party for a New Society
DVB	Democratic Voice of Burma (broadcasting station)
Eingyi	Upper garment worn by Burmese women
EU	European Union
Galon	Mythical bird well equipped to destroy *naga*
Gautama	Alternative name for the Buddha, derived from his original name Siddharta Gautama
GCBA	General Council of Burmese Associations
Gainggyoke	Provincial Buddhist abbot, equivalent to a bishop
Guomindang	Chinese nationalists, opposed to Chinese communists. *Kuomintang* in the older spelling, sometimes abbreviated to KMT
Hinayana	The 'Lesser Wheel' school of Buddhism, derived from the Pali for 'elders', as distinct from *Mahayana*, the 'Greater Wheel'. Also known as *Theravada* Buddhism
Hluttaw	Council; assembly; parliament
Hsayadaw	Venerated Buddhist monk; also *Sayadaw*
Hti	Gold finial in the form of a stylised umbrella that graces a *stupa*
IMF	International Monetary Fund (United Nations)
Jataka	A story drawn from the Buddha's previous births/lives
Jinglee	A homemade dart-like weapon usually made from the spokes of a bicycle wheel
Kala	Derogatory term used to describe foreigners, especially Indians and Europeans
Kamauk	Broad-rimmed hat traditionally worn by peasant farmers
Kanji	Unit of the Japanese written language
Kempeitai	Japanese military police
KIA	Kachin Independence Army

KIO	Kachin Independence Organisation
KNDO	Karen National Defence Organisation
KNLA	Karen National Liberation Army
KNPP	Karenni National Progressive Party
KNU	Karen National Union
Ko	Honorific applied by younger men among themselves
Kyat	Burmese monetary unit (singular and plural)
Kyun	Slave
Lathi	Wooden stick used by the Burmese police and other security forces
Lawkatat	'Liberal' curriculum offered by Buddhist monastic schools; literally 'worldly knowledge'
Longyi	The Burmese sarong, worn by both men and women
Lon Htein	Lit. 'security control': paramilitary security force deployed by the military regime against civilians
Ma	Honorific applied to younger women
Maung	Honorific applied to young males
MEHS	Methodist English High School
MI	Military Intelligence, more properly MIS, Military Intelligence Service
Metta	(Pali): 'loving-kindness'; consideration for others
Min	King
Minlaung	Royal pretender
Mujahin	Islamic holy fighter; mujaheddin
Myanmar	The name given to Burma by SLORC in 1989: more formally, Myanmar Naing Ngan – 'Union of Myanmar'
Myochit	Patriot
Myothugyi	Local chief; lord
Naga	Mythical serpent-dragon
Naingandaw Adipati	Lit. 'Great National Leader', the title adopted by the wartime fascist leader Dr Ba Maw
Nat	In Burmese animism, a spirit
NCGUB	National Coalition Government of the Union of Burma
Ngapi	Fish-paste
NHK	Japan's public broadcasting service
NLD	National League for Democracy
NLD-LA	National League for Democracy – Liberated Area
Nirvana	The final state of enlightenment sought by Buddhists
NUP	National Unity Party
Paya	Burmese pagoda, temple; or, the Buddha
PDP	U Nu's Parliamentary Democracy Party
PLA	U Nu's Patriotic Liberation Army; China's People's Liberation Army
PNO	Pa'o National Organisation
Pongyi	Buddhist monk
PVO	People's Volunteer Organisation
Pwe	festival

Pyat lei pyat	Lit. 'four cuts': a strategy used by the Tatmadaw to weaken insurgency groups
Pyatthat	A miniature tiered pavilion used to ornament a gateway or a monastery roof
Pyithu Hluttaw	People's assembly or council; parliament
Red Flags	The lesser of two Burmese communist groups formed after the War. See White Flags
RGH	Rangoon General Hospital
RUSU	Rangoon University Student Union
Sangha	Order of Buddhist monks; priesthood
Satyagraha	Indian: lit. 'force born out of truth'
Sawbwa	An hereditary Shan prince
SEAC	South-East Asia Command
Shutsu jin shiki	(Japanese): ceremony conducted for the benefit of troops departing for a war front
Shwe Pyidaw	Golden Land
Sila	In Buddhism, moral discipline
SLORC	State Law and Order Restoration (or Restitution) Council
SOE	Special Operations Executive (British)
SPDC	State Peace and Development Council
Stupa	The bell- or dome-like structure at the centre of a pagoda, often housing sacred relics and other treasures
Tat	Army
Tatmadaw	The national army
Thakin	Lit. 'master', equivalent to Indian *sahib*: originally applied to the British, but adopted by Burman nationalists in the pre-war period
Theravada	See above: *Hinayana*
Thingyan	Annual water festival or *pwe*: for many the high point of the Burmese calendar that also marks the beginning of the Burmese year. Held during April
Thanaka	A yellow paste applied to the faces of women and children partly as a cosmetic, partly as a sun shield, made from sandalwood
Thathameda	Tax on wealth
Thathanabaing	Buddhist patriarch or 'high abbot'
Thoke-thin-ye	Burmese tradition of removing rivals by complete elimination
Thwe-thauk	Ritual pledge
Tipikata	Lit. 'three baskets' in Pali: the sacred texts of Hinayana (Theravada) Buddhism; in Sanskrit *tripitaka*
U	Honorific applied to older men
UDP	Unity and Development Party of Thakin Soe
UN	United Nations
UNDP	Union Nationals Democracy Party; United Nations Development Programme
UNESCO	United Nations Educational, Scientific and Cultural Organisation

UNFAO	United Nations Food and Agriculture Organisation
UNHCHR	United Nations High Commission for Human Rights
UNLD	United Nationalities League for Democracy
UNSC	United Nations Security Council
USDA	Union Solidarity and Development Association
UWSA	United Wa State Army
Vipassana	A school of Buddhist meditation
VOA	Voice of America
White Flags	Main post-1945 Burmese communist group
Wungyi	Minister
Wunthanu	Lit. 'racially faithful ones', used by some Burmans
Yama	Hell
YMBA	Young Men's Buddhist Association, derived from the YMCA, Young Men's Christian Association
Yoma	Mountain range
Zata	Natal horoscope

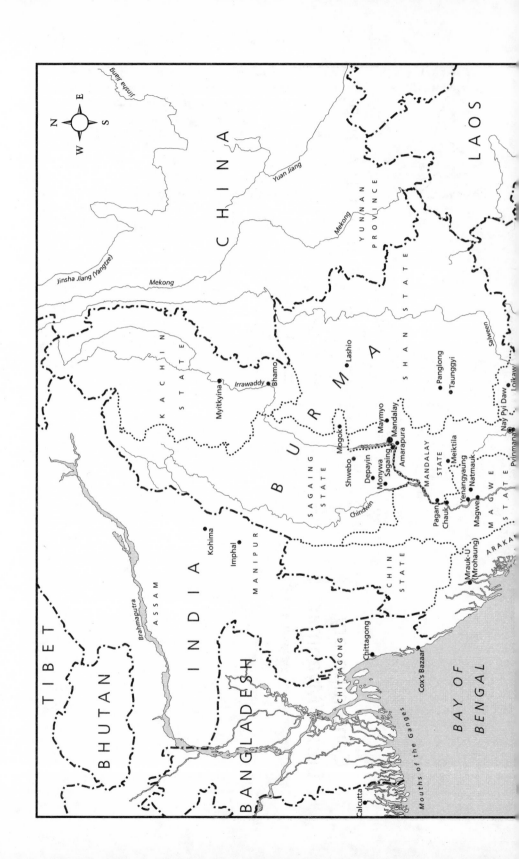

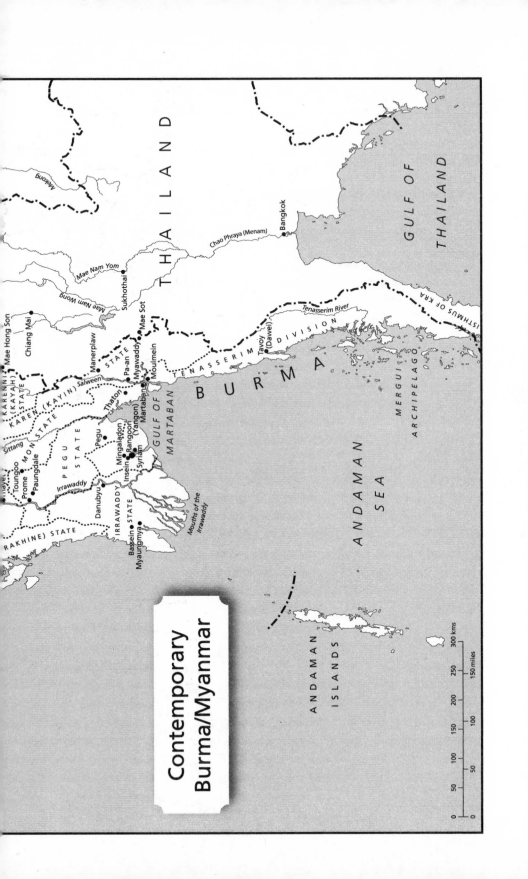

Contemporary
Burma/Myanmar

They hate her because they fear her. A whole army is afraid of a single woman. They are at a loss over how to deal with her.
An anonymous diplomat, quoted in *The Times*, 30th January 1993

Biographers are inescapably at the mercy of the material at their disposal and of events and insights which shape their judgement.
Aung San Suu Kyi, *Aung San* (1984)

PROLOGUE

'IT happened before first light,' she told me, 'when the village was still asleep.' Soldiers of the Tatmadaw – Burmese Army – began setting fire to the huts. Woken by their dogs, most managed to escape the flames, but some did not. Because the huts were made of wood, bamboo and thatch, they burned easily and quickly. Flames danced against the sky, bounced off the hillsides, echoed in the trees.

As the villagers scrambled from their dwellings, some shrieking, others with their loose nightclothes on fire, three girls were seized by the soldiers and raped at gunpoint in front of their families. A father who tried to intervene was shot dead. So was one of the girls' aunts. Another woman, stripped naked, had her breasts cut off, and then they thrust a bamboo stem – or it may have been a *lathi*, a stick used as a cudgel by those who wear uniforms in Burma – into her vagina.

Everyone who had survived the conflagration was herded together and force-marched five or six miles through the forest to where army trucks awaited them. Bundled aboard like cattle, they were driven along a dirt track through the hills until they reached a makeshift encampment ringed with barbed wire. There they began their new lives the same day, as unpaid construction workers on a new road being speared through the lower-lying jungle. Shackled with chains, they had become, in the space of a few short hours, less than slaves.

Seven months later Wah Lay escaped with two of her friends. All three belonged to the Karen people, one of the larger among Burma's many ethnic minorities. Using the sun as their signpost, they made their way eastwards, heading for the relative safety of Thailand, avoiding roads and well-worn paths for fear of coming face-to-face with Tatmadaw patrols. With no provisions they foraged the undergrowth for food, eating whatever roots, berries and greenery they thought safe. Within a week all three had severe stomach pains, and soon afterwards fever. Before they could reach the border, both of Wah Lay's companions died. She survived.

'I don't know why,' she said. 'Maybe it's what God wanted.'

To get to Thailand had taken Wah Lay the best part of a month. As soon as she had managed to cross the narrow Moei river, she collapsed unconscious. She came to three days later in a hospital in Mae Sot, an edgy, lawless border town awash with refugees, aid workers, corrupt policemen and spies. When she was sufficiently recovered she was taken to Wang Kha refugee camp, where 7,000 other Karens who had fled Burma were cooped up in an insecure settlement close enough to the frontier for Burmese artillery shells sometimes to sweep through their midst at night; the Tatmadaw gunners aimed level, to maximise havoc.

Wah Lay used the word 'God' because she had been brought up a Christian, like many other Karens. When she was taken captive, a silver crucifix she wore around her neck had been ripped off by a Burman soldier, cutting into her flesh. But others at the camp were Buddhists and Muslims. In Burma no one religion can protect the individual from the vengeance of the military.

When she talked to me, in April 1999, Wah Lay had been at Wang Kha more than a year. She was thirty-seven years old, and had lost three children, as well as her husband, in a previous assault. Her account conformed with others I had either heard at first hand, or had read in a burgeoning body of reports compiled by myriad relief agencies and human-rights groups. Burma's military regime was running amok, carrying out a programme of systematic oppression against many of the ethnic minorities who, comprising around 35 per cent of the population, inhabit Burma's resource-rich uplands.

To get its hands on such resources, and to assert its xenophobic authority, the regime was either killing or relocating thousands upon thousands of Karens, Karennis, Mons, Chins, Kachins, Shans, Rakhines, Rohingyas and others of the country's non-Burman peoples. By 1999, some half-million 'tribals' had escaped to Thailand. Of these, 120,000 were corralled in twenty-odd refugee camps strung along the Thai–Burmese border. Others had gone westwards, to Bangladesh and India, and a handful northwards into China.

Sometimes when the Tatmadaw carried out a raid, villagers were not even taken to a labour camp, but simply dumped at the end of an unfinished road and left to fend for themselves in inhospitable terrain. And in case any of the displaced straggled back to the remains of their homes, the army sowed the surrounds with landmines. Nor were acts of individual atrocity, such as Wah Lay described, uncommon. Rape, mutilation and killing were routine, overseen by Tatmadaw officers.

According to one report, half the remains of two different women were discovered tumbling in a cement mixer many miles from the scene of their murder. Sometimes a man, a woman or a child was shot for no better reason than that a soldier had a rifle in his hand and a bullet in the breach. Sometimes grenades were tied to victims' necks, then exploded. Bodies were chucked into gullies and ravines like so much refuse. Or they might be left lying on the ground where they had died, for the Asian vulture and other predators of human flesh to claw, pick and nibble at.

Yet the guerrilla armies that fought the government were not so clean, either. They too planted landmines, and sometimes supported themselves by trading opium, heroin and amphetamines. At Wang Kha refugee camp, the first thing that struck me was how Christians, Buddhists and Muslims kept themselves apart. Even under extreme duress, they wanted to have as little as possible to do with each other.

Just how unwholesome Burma is only became apparent to me when, in 1998, I began visiting the refugee camps in Thailand. I quickly learned that it was not just the ethnic minorities who were suffering. A military dictatorship installed by General Ne Win in a *coup d'état* as long ago as 1962 was also brutalising significant numbers of the majority Burman people themselves.

Another scandal that excited the concern of human-rights agencies was the fact that many of the soldiers participating in the Tatmadaw's activities were only boys – kids snatched from the slums of Rangoon, Mandalay and other Burmese conurbations and press-ganged into service without either their parents' consent or knowledge. Given a uniform and rations – but, until they were older (if they lasted that long), no pay and no continuing education – they were being deployed (and continue to be deployed) as porters, jungle-beaters and frontline targets in the army's interminable montagnard campaigns against insurgents.

Similarly, many Burmans as well as non-Burman Burmese had been coerced into joining labour gangs, to work unpaid on new roads, railways, bridges, dams and pipelines, or in coal and jade mines, which are part of the junta's schemes of survival and self-enrichment. In Burma – seemingly a permanent fixture on the UN's list of ten least-developed nations – all but the topmost brass are oppressed. As well as its large army, out of all proportion to national security needs, the regime maintains pervasive domestic-surveillance networks that keep a watchful eye on everyone: not Big Brother so much as a secondary army of ever-watchful Little Brothers.

The driver of your taxi, the man selling lottery tickets or cheroots at the street corner, the woman who sits beside you in a tea-house, the over-friendly monk at a Buddhist pagoda or the neighbour you have known for twenty years – any or all of these may be a government informer. And then there is the infamous 'Form 10', which obliges every citizen – if one may use that word – to make a detailed report of any guest who has stayed overnight in his or her house. Permits must be sought for a TV satellite dish, mobile telephones are priced out of the reach of most, and only a very few are allowed access to the worldwide Internet – not that many Burmese can afford a personal computer. The media are tightly censored and, at the first sign of student unrest, colleges and universities are shut down; or, if not shut down, restricted to the children of proven junta loyalists – young men and women whom the ruling generals hope will become tomorrow's obedient technocrats. As one senior UN official in Bangkok put it to me, Burma is a country 'where just to turn your head can mean imprisonment or death'. Even foreign visitors who have done nothing amiss may find themselves on the wrong end of a quick beating at the hands of the government's uniformed or plain-clothed thugs. No dissent, or hint of dissent, is tolerated.

Yet so much of what goes on in Burma passes unnoticed in the international press. It is a difficult country to report, just as, because of its size and varied terrain, it is a difficult country to police in the way the regime would like. Although, for the sake of hard currency, it has, since 1996, opened up to carefully managed large-scale tourism, foreign journalists and their ilk are perennially unwelcome. If they are found to have slipped into Burma, they are put on the first plane back to Bangkok, their notebooks, laptops and cameras confiscated. Instead, news about Burma leaks out in dribs and drabs, like spurts of scalding water from an antiquated central-heating system. Only through the perseverance and dedication of a small number of expatriate media agencies and ill-funded relief organisations staffed by refugees outside Burma, and the courage of their own informers inside the country, putting their liberty and sometimes their lives at risk for the sake of truth and exposure, is something like a steady narrative maintained.

Without a regular flow of dependable, non-partisan information about it, any country can go to the dogs unseen. A regime that is oppressive can get away with almost anything, provided it too maintains its own kind of vigilance. But with Burma other factors kick in. The long and vividly captured conflict in Indochina – Vietnam, Cambodia and Laos, on the other side of Thailand – satiated interest in South-East Asia for a generation; and, since Saddam Hussein's invasion of Kuwait in 1991, world media attention has concentrated on the Middle East, especially following 9/11. For all the talk of 'globalisation', international news-gathering was as selective in 2005 as it was in 1985 or 1965. Just as it took ten years and more for the outside world to appreciate the enormity of what went on in China during the Cultural Revolution, so we are only now beginning to understand the enormity of what has gone on in Burma. Perhaps if the ruling junta had actual plans to develop nuclear weapons, we would be more alert. But the irony is that, when it comes to weapons of mass destruction, Burma's generals and lieutenant-colonels are doing (and have been doing) far more damage on the streets of our cities than Saddam could ever have done. Burma is second only to Afghanistan as a producer and exporter of heroin – a trade the US government asserts has mainly fallen into the hands of those who, in any decent society, should be combating it: the country's rulers. Similarly, to the dismay of Burma's neighbours, the military appear to condone the production and distribution of tens of millions of amphetamines each year.

Why bother to make a dirty bomb when a syringe is all it takes? Yet short of an internal implosion or direct intervention, and all the moral qualms that direct intervention evokes, it is hard to see things changing fast.The USA has, since 1997, applied economic sanctions – as, belatedly, the EU has begun to. But quite apart from the doubtful efficacy of such initiatives – they hurt the oppressed at least as much as those who oppress them, the argument goes – the Burmese junta has greatly benefited from changes that have occurred in neighbouring China. There, following Deng Xiaoping's economic reforms of the 1980s, a new breed of aggressive entrepreneur has emerged, in the main no more concerned with human rights than their stubbornly communist predecessors, but willing to do business with any pariah state that does not threaten China's security.

Since 1988 Burma has procured more than $3.5 billions' worth of arms from China. It has also imported armaments from the Russian Federation, India, Pakistan and Israel, amongst others. It belongs to ASEAN (Association of South-East Asian Nations, the regional trading bloc), and has strong trading ties with Japan and South Korea as well as with Thailand, Malaysia, Singapore and, increasingly, India. In fact, the junta can get all the goods and know-how it needs much closer to home than either Europe or North America. Western sanctions therefore, even if they were properly enforced, are at best window-dressing – the politics of indecision.

And so Burma stays stuck in the mud. It is a country where a majority live in constant fear: for their property, for their jobs (if they have one), for their health, for the well-being of their loved ones and for their own continuing existence. Education – the key to prosperity in any modern nation – is, outside Burma's military academies, especially backward; and the torture of perceived dissidents is routine. Only a small minority – politically neutral entrepreneurs as well as loyal servants of the regime and its leaders – may expect a reasonable lifestyle, while those at the very top (the generals and their cronies) live in considerable luxury. But these too must survive on their wits and their nerves. Periodically, thrown into turmoil by its own inner feuds and tensions, the junta purges itself, and nobody really knows when he or she won't be carted off to serve an indeterminate sentence in one of Burma's many and abhorrent jails.

A bleak and, some would say, hopeless state of affairs. But just because of that, the figure of Aung San Suu Kyi, winner of the 1991 Nobel Peace Prize, shines with peculiar intensity: a woman considered by many the best (and even only) hope Burma has.

Because of her, Burma is not forgotten. By some she is called the Titanium Orchid, for her qualities of steadfast endurance, commitment to principle and personal grace. In Burma itself she is known more simply as 'The Lady', said in English for fear of being overheard saying her actual name. Yet up until 1988, Aung San Suu Kyi was, for her own people, known only as an expatriate seemingly unconcerned with their plight. Once in a while her photograph appeared in state-run newspapers, while to the world at large she scarcely registered.

By nature a deeply private individual, she had spent her entire adult life abroad, making only fleeting visits home. She was married to an Englishman, Dr Michael Aris, and lived with him and their two teenage boys in England. Prior to her marriage she worked for the United Nations in New York. But then her life, and the lives of those around her, turned topsy-turvy. At the end of March 1988 she received a telephone call telling her that her mother, Daw Khin Kyi, very much a person in her own right in Burmese circles, had been taken to Rangoon General Hospital and was gravely ill. At once Aung San Suu Kyi packed a suitcase and boarded an aeroplane. But it wasn't just a mercy flight. She and Dr Aris had often talked of the day she might have to return to Burma. Both now sensed that day was upon them.

Two elements converged. On the one hand there were Aung San Suu Kyi's formidable personal attributes. On the other was the bald fact of her parentage. Her long-dead father, Aung San, was not just a great Burmese patriot, but *the* great Burmese patriot – the man who had, with the greatest difficulty, steered Burma towards independence from British colonial rule in the immediate aftermath of the Second World War. And it was because she was Bogyoke Aung San's daughter that Suu Kyi had primed herself to one day play some or other significant role in her country's affairs.

For many centuries, until the advent of the British, 'Burma' (but never the whole of it) had been ruled by kings and queens and princes. Now, in an hour of desperation, the Burmese turned to Aung San Suu Kyi as the nearest they had to a royal personage. But this only aggravated the military regime. The generals feared to touch her, but the more she spoke out for human rights and democracy, the less secure they felt, until, on 20th July 1989, they placed her under house arrest.

And there she is again today: a woman in her early sixties with only a maid to fetch what she needs; isolated from her friends, and above all isolated from her children; her residence, at 54 University Avenue beside Inya Lake in the north of the capital, a crumbling colonial villa surrounded by an unkempt garden full of weeds and a perimeter wall of faded pink. For neither house arrest, nor isolation, nor a spell of actual imprisonment in one of the world's most ghastly jails, nor threats to her life, nor failing health, nor persistent vilification at the hands of the Burmese media – she's a 'traitor', a 'whore', a 'drug addict', a 'communist', a 'CIA-agent', a 'profiteer', an 'imperialist stooge', a 'Western fashion girl', a 'political stunt princess' – has persuaded her to accept what has always been on offer: her freedom, on condition that she leaves her native land for good.

Thus has been created the best-known prisoner of conscience presently alive. In the narrow gallery of modern saints her image stands out, and it is commonplace to hear Aung San Suu Kyi likened to Nelson Mandela, Martin Luther King, even Mahatma Gandhi, whose philosophy of non-violence she has assiduously espoused.

The book that follows tells Aung San Suu Kyi's story and, inseparable from it, the story of both her father General Aung San and of Burma itself. For the most obvious of reasons, it has been written without Aung San Suu Kyi's consent or participation. Out of courtesy, a letter was written to her and attempts were made to deliver it. Whether it ever got through is not known. But that has not deterred me: indeed, it may be more appropriate for there to be some distance between someone as political as Aung San Suu Kyi and her biographer.

A letter was also written (and hand-delivered) to the Burmese ambassador in London, asking for contact with the SPDC (State Peace and Development Council), as the junta currently styles itself. To this too there has been no reply. Should the regime feel I have misrepresented it, it has only itself to blame. It was given the opportunity to put its case, but declined to field a spokesman.

But many others have given freely of their time to assist my researches: full acknowledgements will be found immediately after the main body of this book. Like all responsible writers about Burma, I have refrained from identifying those Burmese informants who might otherwise suffer at the hands of their government. Some non-Burmese informants also asked that their names be withheld.

I have also followed convention by sticking to 'Burma' in preference to 'Myanmar': the name given to Burma by SLORC (the State Law and Order Restoration Council) in 1989. Outside South-East Asia, the country is still best known as Burma. Many refuse to use the word Myanmar because, in their view, there is no good reason to respect the whims of an illegally constituted government.

The reader's attention is drawn to the distinction employed between 'Burmese' and 'Burman'. The latter, whether as noun or adjective, refers to Burma's core population. 'Burmese' denotes the wider national identity, anything to do with Burma as a whole and all its varied peoples.

Chinese names are transliterated using the Pinyin method, though I have made an exception of Chiang Kai-shek, who (since few outside mainland China know him as Jiang Jieshi) retains his older Wade-Giles spelling. But wherever appropriate variant spellings (including the renaming of many Burmese towns and cities by the junta) are given in parentheses.

Justin Wintle, London, 2007

PART ONE

LAND AND FATHER

I

AT THE SHWEDAGON

I do not think there is a word for evil in Buddhism. I think this is something you must ask real Buddhist scholars. But we speak of ill will, we speak of ignorance, we speak of greed, but we don't speak of evil as such. There is no evil, just stupidity.

Aung San Suu Kyi, in conversation with Ivan Suvanjieff,
Rangoon, August 1995

AUNG San Suu Kyi became a public figure, and a woman to be reckoned with, on a specific day at a specific time in a specific place. Even though she was not yet politicised in any radical sense, on the late morning of 26th August 1988 she mounted a temporary rostrum in the grounds of the gold-encrusted Shwedagon pagoda that presides over Rangoon and addressed a crowd variously estimated at between 300,000 and one million individuals. As a result of this speech she emerged as the active figurehead of an oppressed people; and her face – fine-boned and pale, but graced with dark eyes of beguiling intelligence and intensity – attracted the attention of even greater audiences from the pages of the international press.

She was aged forty-three. A bare six months beforehand she was to all intents and purposes nothing more (though nothing less) than the wife and companion of a well-respected English academic living in Oxford, with some academic ambitions of her own and four short books to her credit, and with two time-consuming adolescent sons to rear.

She wore, as she often did, traditional Burmese dress: a close-fitting white top, or *eingyi*, half-sleeved and rising to the neck; a quietly colourful patterned Burmese sarong, or *longyi*; and simple sandals: apparel well suited to her diminutive, slender figure.

Contrary to myth, this was not her first public address. Two days earlier she had spoken briefly at another, smaller gathering at Rangoon's General Hospital, mainly to confirm that she would be speaking at the Shwedagon. It was word of this that brought out the huge crowd. From the late afternoon of the 25th the citizenry of Rangoon began making its way to the Shwedagon, some walking four or five miles to be there. Others arrived by bus, truck, motor car and bicycle, from the surrounding townships and further afield. Many thousands, determined to get as close as possible to the wooden stage from which she would speak, camped out all night, bringing with them rice-cakes and water, cushions, blankets and – indispensable in the hot, rainy season – umbrellas, though mercifully the lowering clouds that hung over the city forbore to break.

Some arrived a full eighteen hours before Aung San Suu Kyi herself appeared. Although the pro-democracy rally had been flagged, and talked about, for more than a week, it was the surprise, almost last-minute decision of Aung San Suu Kyi to speak that turned what already promised to be a memorable occasion into the biggest people-event Burma had yet known.

Her trump card was already in place on the platform: a giant portrait of the great Bogyoke (pronounced boh-joke, meaning 'big leader', or thereabouts), Aung San – not just her deceased father, but also the martyred father of Burmese independence and of the modern nation. Few knew what Aung San Suu Kyi stood for, or what she might say. But by simple virtue of being Aung San's daughter, it was scarcely imaginable she would disappoint. Such was the mood of yearning and anticipation that she could have recited a laundry list and still her every word would have been applauded.

The whole country was in turmoil. In March and April 1988 the military government had cracked down hard against protesting students. Then, at the beginning of the second week in August, it cracked down even harder against the people at large. Three thousand or more civilians, young and old, as well as not a few Buddhist monks, had been gunned down or hacked to death by the regime's soldiery on the streets of Rangoon, Mandalay and other Burmese conurbations.

A year later, similar numbers were butchered in Beijing's Tiananmen Square. Given that China's population is twenty-five times the size of Burma's, the hurt done to Burmese families was proportionately so much greater. Yet the Burmese people refused to be cowed, as perhaps too many were in the People's Republic. They continued their overwhelmingly peaceful protests, with the result that the army 'returned to barracks'.

As early as 15th August a seasoned British journalist, Michael Fathers, who had covered the long-drawn-out war in Vietnam, reported in *The Independent* that 'government in Burma has come to a halt'. Though few could have known it at the time, the return to barracks was a calculated stop-gap measure only, a chance for the Tatmadaw to regroup before reimposing itself on the nation with greater ruthlessness than ever before. But in that last week of August 1988 it seemed that anything might happen: complete restoration of the democracy that the dictator General Ne Win had kicked into touch in his 1962 coup; or utter meltdown, with all the further horrors that might entail.

When she spoke, Aung San Suu Kyi did not explicitly offer herself as a leader to oppose the generals; nor did she indulge in crude rabble-rousing. Quite deliberately, she projected herself as someone who sought reconciliation between all the disparate elements of Burmese society that were at loggerheads with one another – the beleaguered, fractious ethnic minorities included. She praised the rebellious students for their commitment and courage, but did not swing full-square behind them. She made an impassioned plea for the restoration of democracy, yet insisted that the army still had its part to play. The Tatmadaw was, after all, in large measure her father's creation, and she knew that not all Burma's problems – ongoing communist insurgency, for example, or the activities of Khun Sa and other 'opium warlords' in the north-east – could be solved by words alone.

In keeping with this level-headed, dispassionate approach, Aung San Suu Kyi avoided both the bludgeoning rhetoric of overstatement and the wimpish ambiguities of understatement. With five microphones attached to an improvised frame in front of her, she read a prepared text, written in impeccable, but slightly stilted, Burmese. From the outset of her public career it was possible to detect something of the governess about her: she would speak her mind, but be fair to all.

In a strange way, she projected herself as a sort of oriental Mary Poppins. Those who were well acquainted with her knew her skittish humour and her capacity for laughter; but 'on duty', such qualities were not just rationed, they were banished. And at the Shwedagon, Aung San Suu Kyi was very much on duty, for her people and for the nation her father had envisioned. On either side she was flanked by unarmed student 'bodyguards'. Also on the dais were several older members of her circle, who had various axes of their own to grind; and discreetly at the rear were her husband Michael Aris and their holidaying boys, Alexander and Kim.

It took a while for the crowd to still, even after Aung San Suu Kyi had stepped onto the dais. Monks wielding canes moved among the people, tapping the more noisy on the shoulders.

'Reverend monks and people!' she at last began, drawing the most respected strand of Burmese society into her purview; then, after paying tribute to the students who were at the forefront of the democracy movement, she begged a minute's silence, to remember the many victims of the regime's violence.

Advocating a 'multi-party democratic system' as the only acceptable cure for Burma's woes, she next introduced herself, momentarily going on the defensive. 'A fair number of people,' she said, were unacquainted with her 'personal history'. It was true, she admitted, that she had spent most of her life abroad, and that she was married to a foreigner – hardly qualifications for a patriot, in the average Burman's eyes. But it was not true that she knew nothing about Burmese politics. 'The trouble is,' she said, 'that I know too much.'

Again, Aung San Suu Kyi invoked her father's shade. She reminded everyone how selflessly and assiduously Aung San had worked to bring about Burma's independence; but also how it had been his intention to withdraw 'from power politics altogether' once his aims were realised.

'I could not,' she declared, in the most widely quoted part of her speech, 'as my father's daughter remain indifferent to all that is going on. This national crisis could in fact be called the second struggle for national independence.'

No clearer statement of Aung San Suu Kyi's readiness to involve herself in Burmese affairs could have been made. If necessary she was prepared to give up everything else in her life, but only for as long as it took to set matters aright. She steered clear of invective, and refrained from making personal attacks on any of the generals in power. She was at pains to save the army's face. Properly disciplined, the Tatmadaw was a national asset, 'a force in which the people can place their trust and reliance'.

'Let me speak frankly,' she continued, her voice rising. 'I feel strong attachment to the armed forces. Not only were they built up by my father; as a child I was cared for by his soldiers.'

This took some by surprise, especially the handful of foreigners present, who knew Burma only as a country crushed by its military, as a bulletocracy. Yet, with bloodstains still visible on Rangoon's streets, it was essential, if change was to occur, for both the army's commanders and its rank-and-file to be won over.

What Aung San Suu Kyi wanted was a military wholly answerable to a civilian government, which in turn would be answerable to the people. Throughout her speech she reiterated the need for 'unity' as well as 'discipline'. Yet she also took the opportunity to distance herself from some older dissidents, many of whose reputations were badly tarnished. 'There are some veteran politicians,' she said, 'who wish to help me in various ways. I have told such politicians that if their object is to obtain positions of political power for themselves, I would not support them in any way.'

In other words, she wished to make plain from the outset that she was, and would be, nobody's puppet, nobody's stooge.

Many times the crowd applauded Aung San Suu Kyi as she spoke – at least those who could hear her. Some held up video cameras and cassette tape-recorders. At the end the applause was loud and long. But there are doubts as to how well or carefully she was listened to. The tannoy system used that day was hardly state-of-the-art electronics, and here and there were bawling babies and wailing children. For many, it was not what 'Daw' (as she had now to be called) Aung San Suu Kyi said that mattered, but the chance to lay eyes upon the Bogyoke's offspring, from however far away.

Yet for the woman at the centre of it all it was an extraordinary feat. To speak in front of not hundreds, not thousands, not tens of thousands, but hundreds of thousands – far more in fact than Aung San had ever addressed at a single sitting – took rare determination and self-composure. Unlike her English husband, Suu Kyi was not even equipped with the experience of lecturing regularly at universities. As Aung San's daughter, it would have been enough simply to appear on the stage and let the seasoned politicians (who, over the preceding weeks, had been urging her to speak out) do the business. She would still have helped the cause of liberty in Burma.

But that was not her way. Three months later she told another journalist, Roger Matthews, in characteristically laconic manner, 'I was not really nervous. I did not have time to be. I was far more worried about actually getting there because of the terrible difficulty in getting through the tremendous crowds. Just to arrive on the platform was the most tremendous relief. But I can't say I would describe it as an enjoyable experience.'*

As a very young girl – so the story goes – Suu Kyi was, like many small children the world over, afraid of the dark. But she refused to submit to her fear. Steeling herself, she crept downstairs in the dead of night in the family home a mile or so from the Shwedagon and stayed in the dark until her fear was overcome, then returned to her bed and slept.

Situations lay ahead that would be much sterner tests, an assassination attempt included. But behind her, metaphorically as well as literally, was the figure of Aung San.

Among the small books she had published was a brief, somewhat idealised biography of her father. His ideas, and in particular the idea that Burma must become a fully functional democracy that would embrace all its varied peoples, were also hers.

The portrait of Aung San behind her on the stage was a devastating juxtaposition: the delicate, middle-aged, but still beautiful woman dwarfed by the blown-up eminence of the national patriarch to whose memory even the dictator Ne Win and his fellow generals regularly paid homage.

There was the added poignancy that forty-two years before, in January 1946, Aung San himself had delivered a keynote speech to the people at the Shwedagon, close to where Aung San Suu Kyi was standing, at a time when Burma's independence from British rule had yet to be assured. In the popular imagination, long cauterised by the excesses of a heartless regime, it seemed as though a saviour had arrived. Where – through no great fault of his own, but because of a hail of assassins' bullets – Aung San had failed to deliver a lasting resolution, was it possible that Aung San Suu Kyi would succeed in righting Burma's wrongs and end the interminable nightmare that constituted its modern, and not-so-modern, history?

*Financial Times, 24th October 1988

II

THE *SHWE PYIDAW*

> *When China sneezes, the Irrawaddy floods.*
> Burman proverb

THE cynic would say that 'Burma' (or for that matter 'Myanmar'), as outlined in the contemporary atlas, does not exist, and never has, in the sense of being a peaceable homogenous whole. At no point has any one ruler or government wielded unchallenged authority over the whole of that body of land bound to the west by India and, latterly, Bangladesh; to the north by China; to the east by Laos and Thailand; and with a lengthy coastline arched around the north-eastern corner of the Bay of Bengal, more locally the Andaman Sea, backing onto the Indian Ocean.

At best a degree of harmony has prevailed among a moiety of the various ethnic components that make up Burma, but never for very long. Ironically, and disconcertingly for the critics of colonialism, the British came closest to establishing overall order, for a decade or two during the middle years of their imperial rule. It was also the British who were chiefly responsible for giving Burma its present shape, its agreed international boundaries. But even they chose to leave some of the mountainous 'frontier areas' – kept separate from 'ministerial Burma' – well alone. The threat of insurrection was never far below the surface; and the borders with China were not finally defined until after the British had left. Even the great Aung San could not persuade all the peoples of Burma to come unambiguously under the one umbrella. Some recalcitrant Karens refused to join his proposed Union of Burmese

Peoples, while the assent of other important ethnic-minority groups was given only conditionally.

Yet this has not prevented at least the upper strata of the Burman people from subscribing to a somewhat fanciful national history stretching back in time far further than actual evidence allows – a history that Aung San himself sometimes evoked. Keenly dismissive of jingoistic nationalism as he was at other times, in his Shwedagon speech of 20th January 1946 he said:

Imperishable memories rise in our mind today as we stand on this sacred ground covered by the mantle of twenty-five centuries spread out from the holy ground of the Shwedagon Pagoda. Imperishable memories of the countless thousands who have participated in the endless march of history, of untold sacrifices and matchless deeds of heroism and valour wrought by giants of old and new rising ever to the call of historic destiny and the unquenchable and invincible spirit they have bequeathed to us as their richest legacy. We must, for a moment, bare our heads and bow to those dead and mighty, and we shall vow to them that we too in our time will lift ourselves to their heights and make ourselves worthy of their shades and the heritage they have handed down to us. Our nation shall live again!

Many myths have grown up around 'Burma' and its past. At their heart is the legend of Burma as the 'Golden Land' – the *Shwe Pyidaw* – which to this day is used by the military regime to promote controlled tourism to parts of the country that it aspires to rule in its entirety. The epithet was first used by the people of India, who called those lands east of Bengal *Suvarnabhumi* (which also translates as 'Golden Land') from perhaps as early as the second century BC. But it remains unclear just what it was that the Indians considered 'golden'. Either there were already some dazzling Buddhist pagodas, or at least temples of an indeterminate faith, or the Indians had in mind some other kind of riches.

Then, as now, three important rivers – the Chindwin and Sittang as well as the Irrawaddy, each sourced in the eastern Himalayas – watered a large, fertile plain that drained into the Andaman Sea. There were extensive forests of teak, ebony and ironwood, the premium building materials of the day, and in the horseshoe of high mountains surrounding the plain were valuable minerals: gold, silver, copper, iron, lead and (soon of particular interest to the Chinese) jadeite, the most valued type of jade. Rubies and sapphires from *Suvarnabhumi* were also prized for their quality, and off the southern coast pearls could be had by the hatful.

In modern times world-class deposits of zinc and wolfram (essential to the manufacture of some modern weapons) have been discovered, as well as deposits of oil in Burma's 'hot dry' central region, where the annual rainfall rarely exceeds twenty inches, and copious supplies of offshore gas.

Who inhabited the Burmese flatlands before and at the beginning of the first millennium is largely conjectural. It seems there were a number of distinct centres of civilisation, influenced by the two mature, primary civilisations that have long impacted on Burma's development: India and China. But although there are strong traces of Indian culture at this time, including the remains of Vedic shrines and early Buddhist stupas, ethnically the vast majority of today's Burmese have their origins in later migrations from southern China and, more particularly, Tibet, the ultimate source of the Burman language.

The earliest-known literary reference to Burma occurs in the *Geography* of the second-century AD Romano-Greek-Egyptian astronomer Ptolemy, for whom 'Further India' was a place of cannibals. Within another hundred years, Chinese writers too began taking an interest in Burma, though the kingdom of Lin Yang noted by them otherwise remains a mystery. But beyond dispute is the emergence of another 'Irrawaddy' kingdom, or at least city-state, made up of the Pyu people, centred on Sri Ksetra ('Field of Glory') near the modern township of Prome, and sometimes described as 'proto-Burman'. The puzzle about the Pyu state, however, is that while a handful of later inscriptions indicate a strong relationship between the language spoken by its citizens and that of the Burman people proper, archaeological excavations have revealed that Sri Ksetra was highly Indianised, Vishnu being worshipped as much as (or even more than) the Buddha.

The Pyu state seems to have come to an abrupt end *circa* 832, when it succumbed to incursions by the T'ai people (forebears of, *inter alia*, today's Thais), emanating from the powerful kingdom of Nanchao in south-western China. Only after its collapse did those we know as Burmans begin arriving in Burma in significant numbers: a migration that was just one of a long series of regional displacements caused by the steadily expanding Chinese imperium, lasting from well before the formal founding of the Chinese empire by the megalomaniacal First Emperor Qin Shihaungdi in 221 BC at least until Mao Zedong's Cultural

Revolution of the mid-1960s, when a fresh wave of emigrants from China sought safety and sanity elsewhere.

While the main body of the Burmese peoples arrived in Burma from Yunnan down the three main river corridors of the Chindwin, the Irrawaddy and the Sittang, and also perhaps from the mountain-bound Salween to the east, there was another well-established people already resident in Tenasserim – the long finger of Burmese territory stretching down the eastern side of the Andaman Sea – and in parts of the Irrawaddy basin. These were the Mons, the 'western' half of the Mon-Khmer race believed to have come originally from Mongolia. While the eastern half, the Khmers, created the civilisation of Angkor Wat in Cambodia, their Mon cousins, before colonising what the British were to call Lower Burma, had first set up in neighbouring Siam (Thailand).

For centuries the Burmans and the Mons fought bloody wars, first for control of the Irrawaddy delta and the middle reaches of the Irrawaddy river valley, then for control over each other. But between wars the Mon-Burman interface could be mutually stimulating. Significantly, the Mons already enjoyed extensive cultural and commercial relations with India, and with Ceylon (Sri Lanka), facilitated by a well-developed seaborne trading network around the rim of the Bay of Bengal. That Theravada (or Hinayana, 'Lesser Wheel') Buddhism became Burma's principal religion is presumed to be the product of both these interactions.

As more and more Burmans entered Burma's lowlands, and births swelled their numbers, so they began to prevail – over the Mons, and over others who stood in their way. And in time they too built an extraordinary city that eclipsed anything that had preceded it in Burma; that indeed rivalled Angkor Wat; and that lends substance to the idea of a *Shwe Pyidaw*.

Even today Pagan (pronounced Pa-garn) impresses mightily. Either at dawn or just before dusk the visitor climbs hundreds of steps to the upper galleries of one of its bigger Buddhist pagodas and gazes out north, east and south across an endless vista of other pagodas, a seemingly infinite sea of individually styled giant ornamental beehives of varying hues – white, russet-red and occasionally gold – caught by the rising or sinking sun. To the west meanders the Irrawaddy – at this point albeit far closer to Mandalay than to Rangoon – still a mile-wide belt of sometimes silver, sometimes blue, sometimes ochre water, not unlike the lower reaches of the Nile, with its dry-season sandbars and high, treeless banks, but in all seasons the elongated wellspring of life, of prosperity.

Nowhere else on the planet exhibits such an extensive physical testimony to a creed or ideology concentrated in one site. Yet what the visitor sees at Pagan is less than half of what once existed there. Around 2,000 pagodas have survived more or less intact, some of truly massive size, so that to visit each would take many months. But at its height the city boasted upwards of 4,000. Gone too is Pagan's kingly citadel, a non-religious complex of mainly wooden palaces, offices, warehouses and barracks constructed by the riverside and responsible for administering what Burmese history books call the 'First Burmese Empire'.

Officially Pagan (or Bagan, as it is nowadays called) was founded in 849, though like many ancient foundation dates this is not accepted by every modern scholar. It seems a little early, even given an unquestionable Burman capacity for self-assertion. Perhaps the Burmese did set up a village or small township there sometime in the mid-ninth century; or perhaps there was already a town or village on the same spot, which the Burmans commandeered for themselves by force of arms. What is never contested is that, during the course of the eleventh century, Pagan emerged as a powerful and resplendent polity; or that this was largely the inspiration of King Anawrahta.

Anawrahta would be high on the list of Aung San's 'giants of old', just as today he is beloved of Burma's ruling generals, who are anxious to validate their own claims to embody the traditions and continuities of Burmese history. If legend – and such fetchingly romantic narratives as *The Glass Palace Chronicle* (*Hman-nan Raza-windaw-gyi*, compiled in the 1820s) – is to be credited, Anawrahta came to the throne through single combat with a rival claimant in 1044. During his reign, lasting until 1077, he brought the western region of Arakan, where another Burman kingdom already existed, under his sway, established some sort of authority over the Shan plateau in the north-east of the country and campaigned in Siam. It has even been claimed that Anawrahta's eastern campaigns reached as far as Cambodia and prevented Siam falling permanently under Khmer domination. For the future of Burma, however, his more signal victories appear to have been over the Mons to the south, especially the Mon kingdom of Thaton.

According to tradition, once Anawrahta had established his rule at Pagan, a Buddhist monk called Shin Arahan began urging him to embrace Theravada Buddhism. But there were no copies of the sacred *Tipikata*

– the 'three baskets' of Buddhist scriptures written in Pali – at Pagan. There were thirty copies at Thaton, however, and Anawrahta determined to have at least one for himself. Emissaries were duly dispatched in 1057. When the King of Thaton refused to accommodate Anawrahta's desire, the Burman monarch gathered an army, marched south and seized all thirty copies, then sent them to Pagan on the backs of no fewer than thirty white elephants – the white elephant being the rare, prized symbol of any Burmese (as also Siamese or Thai) monarch's legitimacy. He is also supposed to have persuaded many of Thaton's master-craftsmen to return with him to Pagan, while other less fortunate Thatonites, driven from their homes, were enslaved.

So began two centuries of splendour, during which the great majority of Pagan's pagodas (or *payas*) were raised. Not only kings, but high-ranking nobles sought merit, expiation of their sins of violence and an assurance of their posthumous reputations by raising monuments to the good lord Buddha, whose peculiarly godless teaching promised a state of eternal serenity (*nirvana*) to those who adopted his demanding, yet compassionate discipline.

The heart of the city belonged to the royal citadel, protected on three sides by high, Chinese-style stamped-earth walls, and on the fourth by the waters of the Irrawaddy. But the pagodas, spread out over thirty square miles and more, and tended by tens of thousands of monks and pagoda slaves living in monasteries between them, were built of brick, then covered with stucco. Many contained sacred relics, even (supposedly) hairs and toenails of the Buddha himself, as well as priceless Buddha images, paintings and other treasures.

Visiting Pagan was an important rite of passage undertaken by all the king's subjects, no matter how far from Pagan they lived – though for most, since Burman settlements tended to be riverine, the Irrawaddy provided easy access. Above all, Pagan gave the early Burmans not only an enduring sense of collective identity, but also pride and a feeling of superiority over the wild tribes who inhabited the surrounding mountains. As the city became renowned both for its wealth – derived from its pivotal position on a flourishing Sino-Indian trade route – and as a centre of Buddhist learning at a time when Buddhism was being driven out of its native India, Pagan's denizens luxuriated in a militarily potent self-belief.

Thanks to Anawrahta and his successors, the Burman army grew into something to be feared, at least on the South-East Asian mainland. But it did not deter more powerful aggressors from further afield; and in the thirteenth century Pagan fell victim to its own, widely fabled success.

Genghis Khan – every inch Alexander the Great's equal as a conqueror – and his murderous hordes wreaked havoc throughout central Asia and eastern Europe. Nor did his death in 1227 more than momentarily staunch the flow of Mongol rapacity. First his sons, then his grandsons, carved out four great khanates. Among them was virtually the whole of China, finally subjugated by Kublai Khan in 1279.

Like his grandfather, Kublai was possessed of restlessness and insatiable ambition. The image of a wanton, sedentary and corpulent potentate wallowing in grandeur, conveyed in Samuel Taylor Coleridge's celebrated poem, only fits his final years. As an old man (he lived to be eighty), Kublai wore slippers made from the skin of an exotic Korean fish and was carried in a litter borne by four elephants. But in his prime he was an energetic warrior whose victories matched Genghis's; even in his dotage the idea of fresh expeditions beckoned.

Having brushed aside China's vastly civilised but militarily supine Song dynasty, Kublai imposed his authority on both Tibet and Manchuria, and might have conquered Japan had his fleets not been destroyed by violent storms. Undeterred, he switched his attention to Vietnam, which was overrun by a Mongol army in 1281. Six years later it was Burma's turn.

Kublai had already demanded tribute of Pagan's ruler, the vicious King Narathihapate – the usual prelude to a Mongol onslaught. When Narathihapate refused to comply, instead seizing and beheading Kublai's envoys and then launching forays into Chinese territory, the Mongol emperor decided he had the necessary pretext for invasion.

Among the spies sent ahead to reconnoitre Pagan was, if the Italian's own account is to be believed, Marco Polo, who claimed in his *Travels* to have been a close and trusted confidant of the 'Tartar emperor'. Whether Polo actually reached Burma, or merely regurgitated some tale he had heard as, languishing in a Genoese jail, he dictated his memoirs to Rusticello of Pisa, is debated. But if Polo was being truthful, then he was probably the first and last European to see Pagan (referred to by its Chinese name of Mien, being a corruption of Mranmar, the origin of 'Myanmar') in all its glory.

Tantalisingly, Polo offers only an anecdotal snapshot:

There once lived in this city a rich and powerful king. When this king came to die, he commanded that above his tomb or monument there should be erected two towers, one of gold and one of silver, such as I will describe. One tower was built of fine stones and then covered with gold, a full finger's breadth in thickness, so completely that it appeared as if made of gold only. It was fully ten paces high and of a width appropriate to its height. In form it was circular, and round the whole circuit were set little gilded bells which tinkled every time the wind blew through them. The other tower was of silver and was built on the same plan as the golden one and of the same size and structure. This structure was designed as a token of the king's greatness and for the sake of his soul. And I assure you that the towers were the fairest to be seen in all the world and were of incalculable value.*

For Kublai Khan, even such a brief report might have kindled his rapacity. Although too old to lead his horsemen any more, the promise of untold spoils inspired him to dispatch an army, under the command of his grandson Prince Yesu Timur, in 1287.

Already a terrified Narathihapate had fled his capital, and serious revolts had broken out among the Mons, Rakhines (Arakanese) and Shans. With devastating precision, the Mongol army stormed down the upper Irrawaddy, brushed aside such disorganised Burman forces as it encountered, entered Pagan, forced its inhabitants to flee for their lives, looted it of every valuable they could lay their hands on, razed the royal citadel, then abruptly turned heel and returned to China, their baggage trains laden with booty.

So at least runs the Chinese-Mongol version of events. In Burman chronicles, although Pagan was indeed sacked, Burman guerrilla tactics forced the Mongols to abandon any idea of colonising the kingdom of Pagan; and their return to China was imposed upon them by harrying manoeuvres.

Either way, although Theravada Buddhism survived as the principal religion, and cultural matrix, of the Burman people, and although Pagan remained the centre of a greatly damaged kingdom for some decades to come, militarily and economically the 'First Empire' was finished; and the 'Golden Land' plunged into a darkness from which it has never fully recovered.

Yet there was another side to Pagan. Eyeing even those pagodas that have survived, today's visitor may reasonably ask: how exactly were such monuments erected in a pre-industrial age? Though no records survive, the answer has to be through involuntary and slave labour, just

* See Marco Polo, *The Travels*, trans. Ronald Latham (1958)

like the Pyramids, the Great Wall of China, the Athenian acropolis and the Coliseum. There was no other way. It was as though every cathedral in medieval Europe had been sited in a single small county – an economic impossibility unless the bulk of the labour was unpaid.

The regime-approved guide will tell you differently. 'We built Pagan ourselves,' he says, 'we the Burman people, out of our love for Buddha.' But as soon as his back is turned and he is out of earshot, a gainsayer whispers to the traveller; 'Your question is good. In eight hundred years nothing much has changed.'

III

AFTER THE MONGOLS

Burma is a narrow country; even the mainland is little more than a vast valley, a river basin running north–south, with hills to east and west. Its written history is that of the valley, not the hills, for only the plains were civilised, the hills were illiterate and have no history.

G.E. Harvey, *British Rule in Burma 1824–1942* (1946)

THE Mongol assault on Pagan gave the lie to any supposition that, with its apron of high mountains, Burma is immune to attack by a major land force. Whether to the west, north or east, the mountains are penetrable by a series of passes, as innumerable migrating tribes and clans discovered. However hazardous such passages may be, they do not constitute impossible barriers. As the Japanese again demonstrated in the Second World War, they provide would-be aggressors with corridors of access when they are not vigorously defended.

In the wake of the sack of Pagan, the Burmans found themselves with a new enemy, making their hold on Burma's flatlands distinctly precarious.

As well as attacking Burma and Vietnam, the Mongols destroyed the centuries-old kingdom of Nanchao, in 1253. Although the T'ais had already begun expanding southwards, it was this event that triggered a major knock-on migration. At first those who chose not to come under Mongol-Chinese rule settled in the Menam basin, creating a dazzling bijou state around Sukhothai, the first capital of Siam; but soon some turned westwards, taking advantage of Pagan's disarray.

Some T'ais, known as Shans, had already settled in Burma's great north-eastern upland plain, which eventually became known as the Shan plateau. Towards the end of the thirteenth century, led by warrior princes, they began arriving in significant numbers. In particular a family of princes, or *sawbwas* (the Burman corruption of the T'ai-Shan *saopha*), called the 'Three Brothers', challenged the Burmans head-on. Pagan was again sacked, possibly with even greater ferocity, in 1299.

Unlike the Mongols, the Shans, as well as some other T'ai peoples, came to stay. Sometimes supported by the Siamese, and sometimes in league with the rebellious Mons and Rakhines, they vied for final hegemony over central Burma for close on three centuries. Even when the Burmans eventually reasserted themselves, Shan *sawbwas* proved difficult and tricky customers. Indeed, perhaps because every Shan prince thought of himself as a ruler subject to none other than himself, the Shans finally failed to implement permanent authority over a much wider area of Burma than 'Shanland'. Soon enough they quarrelled among themselves.

Until the middle of the sixteenth century there was no clear winner in the prolonged, three-cornered struggle between the Burmans, Mons and Shans. But then two Burman strongmen – Tabinshwehti and (arguably the finest of all Burman warrior rulers, or 'giants of old' in Aung San's phrase) Bayinnaung – stepped forward to found the 'Second Empire'.

In 1551 Bayinnaung reduced the Mon capital at Pegu (Bago). Four years later he captured the predominantly Shan city of Ava, which became the Burman capital. But his victories, convincing as they were, told only half the story. Other migrant groups had been trickling into Burma from China and Siam. Though they could not make headway in the flatlands – the central plains, the Irrawaddy valley and the narrow coastal strip of Tenasserim – they colonised great swathes of the uplands.

Today the number of 'ethnic minorities' to be found in Burma is hotly disputed by ethnologists: some say there are just ninety, others up to twice that number. Much depends on whether a particular language is held to be a language in its own right or a dialect of another. What is not in dispute is the existence of several discrete main groupings: the Shans, of course (who make up Burma's biggest minority), then the Karens, the Karennis, the Chins and the Kachins and, up against the Indian border, the erstwhile head-hunting Nagas. Added to this list should be the Mons, even though they may fairly claim to have resided in Burma longer than anyone else; and, in Arakan, Buddhist Rakhines and Muslim Rohingyas, migrants from Bengal.

For anthropologists, Burma's ethnic congestion has long been a generous research laboratory. Every minority and sub-minority has its own costumes and customs. Some, like the celebrated Padaung in the Shan-Karenni hinterlands, or 'Long-necks' – Padaung women famously have their necks encased in copper coils from around the age of seven – have also caught the attention of photojournalists and camera-happy tourists. But for anyone wanting to rule the whole of Burma, the minorities present an enduring challenge. Fiercely independent, some minorities – especially those regarded by the Burmans as inferior breeds fit only to be slaves – resist control by waging an exacting guerrilla warfare from their highland fastnesses, so that yet again Burma's torque of mountains, far from affording protection and fostering a sense of common identity, has been an abiding source of friction and disunity.

Yet on another, genetic reading Burma exemplifies the ability of people from different ethnicities to mix and integrate. From time immemorial incursive warfare meant, at worst, slaying the menfolk and seizing the womenfolk, for the purposes of sexual pleasure and reproduction. Less dramatically, individuals of different ethnicities have sometimes simply fallen in love. Although in the remoter reaches of the mountains there may be groups who have retained relative genetic 'purity' from the time their ancestors entered Burma, it is questionable how many 'pure' Mons there are – or, for that matter, 'pure' Burmans.

Similarly, although the contemporary state of Burma is, administratively, parcelled into seven 'Burman' divisions, and seven states each named after one of the larger 'minorities' (see map on pp. xviii–xix), many non-Burmans can be found in the former, just as many Burmans can be found in the latter. The Karens especially, though their 'state' is to the east, lying against the Thai border, can be found throughout the Irrawaddy delta, while in the lowlands of the upper Irrawaddy basin Shans are ubiquitous.

In Rangoon – Burma's capital until 2005 – Burmans barely make up a majority, while in Mandalay it is estimated that some 40 per cent of the second city's present inhabitants have Chinese blood. For the traveller, it is invariably instructive to find out something about the lineage of those encountered. 'My father is Lisu, but my mother is Wa' or 'My grandmother was a Burman, but my grandfather was English' – and so forth. But for most Burmese, ethnicity is arbitrarily determined by the paternal bloodline. And in Burmese history the 'race card' has too often been played for whatever quick advantages of prestige and power it may confer.

The 'Second Burmese Empire', or Toungoo Dynasty, lasted a shade over three centuries before it too came unstuck. Well before the eighteenth century the court at Ava, outwardly conservative, had fallen prey to corruption, venality and family feuds within the royal circle. Burma's rulers no longer took to the saddle, but preferred to stay at home, surrounded by slaves, eunuchs and concubines. Court hierarchies, court etiquette and the kingdom's sumptuary laws, determining who could wear what, were elaborate, restrictive and ultimately self-defeating. Nor did it help that, by tradition, the senior queens (up to four of them) were chosen from among the king's half-sisters.

Beyond the court, the land was governed by an antiquated feudal system. At the bottom were the villages, clustered around the Irrawaddy like grapes on the vine, which produced the foodstuffs essential to the sustenance and comfort of a carefully graded nobility and gentry. Each village was under the authority of a headman, but he in turn was answerable to some feudatory master, either appointed by the court as a mark of royal favour or enjoying a hereditary title of his own; up and down the entire social chain, 'squeeze' was operated – those above extorting everything they could get from those below.

For perhaps a majority of Burmese living at this time, the court at Ava was a distant charade. Old kings went, new kings came, princes squabbled and queens and princesses intrigued. Of greater importance were the seasons, the health of crops, a calendar rich in festivals, or *pwe*. Overarching local life and binding communities together, whether out in the boondocks or within a city or township district, was the local pagoda. Buddhism not only furnished an explanation for the inequalities of life – you are what you are because you were what you were in a previous life – but set the moral pattern, told people what they should and should not do, and provided the rudiments of social welfare, all at a very modest 'voluntary' cost. Dressed in their brown, orange or yellow robes, Buddhist monks, or *pongyi*, provided at least an elementary education. Literacy was unusually high for a pre-industrial society, and a distinctive Burman literature evolved.

The most common fears were drought, crop failure, famine and an array of tropical diseases – deadly malarial fevers among them. But side by side these was the fear of some fresh war breaking out, when royal

officials would come storming by, demanding that men of fighting age
perform their obligatory military duty.

Hardly a decade passed when heavy fighting did not erupt in some
quarter of the kingdom. But as the eighteenth century unfolded, warfare
became, once again, continuous and endemic.

There were four main theatres. In the south, sensing that the Toungoo
dynasty had become enfeebled beyond repair, the Mons reasserted
themselves. In 1740 they proclaimed their independence, setting up
a rival court at Pegu. Three years later they seized Syriam, the port
across the river from Rangoon (then but a village known as Dagon),
slaughtering its inhabitants. In the north-west, the Hindu Indian state
of Manipur, led by the warlock Gharib Newiz, began making incursions
into Burmese territory; while to the north the Chinese, who under
the Qianlong emperor sought to turn Burma into a vassal state,
launched a series of blistering cross-border raids. Finally, to the east,
the Burmans' long-standing rival, Siam, keen to annex as much of
Tenasserim as it could, showed itself willing and able to profit from
any weakness.

Matters came to a head in 1749. Gharib Newiz arrived before the
walls of Ava just as the Mons began advancing upstream from the delta.
Although he failed to breach the city's defences, the Mons did so
towards the end of the dry season in April 1752. The last Toungoo
monarch, his senior queen and selected retinue were banished to Pagan,
and Ava itself was burned to a cinder.

For a second time Burman aspirations to rule over all Burma had
crumbled. Yet Ava's foes reckoned without Burman resilience. The Mon
Revolt and the exertions of Gharib Newiz only served to clear the stage
for the third, most potent, Burman empire. Even as the smoke drifted
over the ruins of Ava, a former *myothugyi* (chief) of Shwebo and official
of the court, Alaungpaya, assumed the mantle of strongman. Rallying
what was left of the Burman army, and raising fresh recruits, he first
cleared the Burman heartland around the confluence of the Irrawaddy
and Chindwin rivers, and then, as his forces matured, orchestrated a
counter-offensive so devastating that the Mons would never again
mount a credible challenge to Burman power. Three years of bitter
fighting culminated, in May 1757, in the destruction of Pegu. Syriam
was reoccupied, and so too was Dagon, renamed Yangon (Rangoon),
'End of Strife'.

Alaungpaya next turned his wrath on Manipur, which was not just taught a lesson by him, but briefly annexed in 1759. But his own nemesis awaited the following year. Leading an army into Siam, he was badly injured when an ill-mounted cannon crushed him beneath the walls of the Thai capital Ayutthaya. At once Alaungpaya's generals called a halt to the campaign. The king himself died soon after being carried back across the Burmese border, without reaching Shwebo, his chosen capital. However, he left behind a resurgent Burman throne, a new dynasty (the Konbaung), and in Naungdawgyi, Hsintyushin, Singu and Bodawpaya successors each minded to pursue Burman hegemonism. Arakan was once more brought within the Burman pale, and fractious Shan princes were obliged to renew payment of an annual tribute.

More satisfyingly still, three attempted Chinese invasions were repulsed. Ayutthaya, the Siamese capital, was destroyed, and with it seemingly the very existence of Siam, in 1767. Never before had Burman rulers enjoyed such fortune and influence. The capital was moved back to Ava, so that for the next hundred years central Burma became known as the 'Kingdom of Ava', and for once the word 'empire' seemed to fit. Yet the fruits of cherished victories lasted barely two generations. Alaungpaya and his sons, and his grandson Bagyidaw, were destined to become the last of the 'giants of old'.

Just as the Burmans had regrouped after the calamities of the 1740s and early 1750s, so now the Siamese, or Thais, recovered their vim. Under a leadership that gave birth to the Chakri Dynasty, a new capital – what became Bangkok – was built near the mouth of the Chaophraya river in the Menam basin, and further Burman attacks were beaten off. At home the usual local rebellions resurfaced. And Bodawpaya, seizing the throne in 1782 and holding it until his death in 1819, soon exhibited all the symptoms of a tyrant, albeit a most religious tyrant.

During the earlier part of his reign he implemented such strict observance of Theravada Buddhist precepts that even his Burman subjects groaned under the punishments and exactions meted out upon them. The smallest infringements of rules that were never intended to be more than guidelines for a healthier, purer way of life were met with fines, imprisonment, even execution. And an ambitious programme of pagoda-building and other 'public' works resulted in unprecedented levels of forced labour among even the king's supposedly 'free' subjects.

But the greater failure was one of intelligence and understanding. The Third Empire was carved out of what was becoming a most backward part of East Asia. The Konbaung kings took little account of European colonial aggression, fast approaching their own doorstep.

If European curiosity about Burma began with Marco Polo at the end of the thirteenth century, it was soon followed by the attention of other Italian merchant adventurers in the fourteenth century, notably one Nicolo di Conti. Such men, however, travelled mainly overland, and their ambition was limited to the acquisition of personal riches. A more potent threat emerged with the seafaring Portuguese. In the wake of Vasco da Gama's celebrated voyages of discovery, a strong trading colony was established at Goa, in India. Then in 1511 Alfonso de Albuquerque seized Malacca on the Malayan mainland, and with it control of the sea-trade between the Indian Ocean and the South China Sea, through the eponymous Strait of Malacca.

Where the Portuguese went, the Dutch, the English and eventually the French followed. The governing principle of European commercial expansion was that trade should not be an option for the heathen inhabitants of far-off lands, but an absolute requirement. If native potentates and merchants refused to concede this point by persuasion or treaty, then it was thought legitimate to use force.

The arrival of European trading vessels on the horizon portended that sooner or later political and military pressure would be applied: not an altogether hopeless state of affairs, except that nowhere was Asian weaponry anything near a match for European arms. That, after all, was what the 'round-eye' white men were best at: manufacturing newfangled weapons and building ships that could withstand the longest, most arduous journeys.

Smarter local rulers noticed this, and began bartering trading rights in commodities that the Europeans wanted. Gems and spices, later teak and other woods good for repairing and even making stout fighting vessels *in situ*, were exchanged for flintlocks, muskets and cannon, and for the services of men trained in their use.

In Burma, at the end of the sixteenth century, Felipe de Brito, a Portuguese adventurer operating out of Goa, offered his services as a mercenary to the King of Arakan. Skilfully he carved out a small fiefdom for himself, based on Syriam, the delta port that controlled much of the Burma trade.

De Brito rode his luck for fifteen years, until in 1613 the Burmans stormed Syriam and subjected the *kala* interloper to a gruesome death, by slow-working impalement. Among the Portuguese, however, de Brito was something of an anomaly. Although Portugal had founded vast colonies in South America, in the East it preferred to create well-fortified trading entrepôts. Goa was one example; Macao, off China's coast, another.

The English (later the British) pursued a more eclectic approach. Although they too sometimes strove for 'simple' trading stations – Hong Kong, for instance – when these did not work, or local rulers imposed unacceptable restrictions, they became greatly more ambitious, annexing entire territories and nations. Out of this was born what became the British Raj. The whole Indian subcontinent was subjugated to the rule of men born 6,000 or so miles away. But, in the first instance, it was not the British (or even the English) Crown that undertook such ventures. Rather it was the East India Company, a joint-stock enterprise founded in 1600, which gave rich Englishmen opportunities to accumulate yet more wealth. The risks were significant – ships and their cargoes could founder, or just disappear – but the rewards could be magnificent. As the East India Company grew, it offered a chance for England's younger sons not just to have adventures in far-flung places, but to get rich themselves in the Company's employ.

Compared to the Company, the modern multinational, so often disparaged as the engine of Western 'economic imperialism', is a weak-kneed, lily-livered creature. From the beginning it was understood that the Company's ships should carry fire-power and if need be, a platoon of fighting men. That was the way – the only way – to do business in hostile climes. So a young man with a smattering of education could prove himself as both soldier and trader.

It might as well have been called the Eat India Company. From small beginnings, the Anglo-British spread across the subcontinent, from north to south and back again, and eastwards into Bengal, fuelled by (as well as avarice) a constant rivalry with other 'powers': the Netherlands, of course, but also France, which somewhat late in the day started dreaming of an eastern empire.

The decisive engagement occurred at Plassey, on the banks of the Bhagirathi, on 23rd June 1757, when the luckless Nawab Siraj-al-Dawla (Suraja Dowlah), backed by the French but undermined by financial and political chicanery, was defeated by Robert Clive (later Lord Clive of India). But Plassey did not put an end to France's oriental aspirations. In the long-drawn-out Napoleonic Wars at the end of the century, both the Company and the British government became aware that France was meddling in Indochina, where indeed it eventually made colonies of Laos and Cambodia as well as Vietnam.

As the Company consolidated its hold on Bengal, it was inevitable that tensions would develop with the neighbouring Kingdom of Ava. In the past several attempts had been made to open up a Burma trade, but with no enduring success. As the French began muscling in on South-East Asia, it was only a matter of time before the British made a more concerted effort.

So besotted was the Burman throne with its own new-found image of unlimited glory and foudroyant power that it did not grasp the danger until too late.

IV

THE SALAMI WARS

[I]t is of primary importance to allow no other European power to insert itself between British Burmah and China. Our influence in that country ought to be paramount. The country itself is of no great importance. But an easy communication with the multitudes who inhabit Western China is an object of national importance.

Lord Cranborne, writing to Sir John Lawrence,
Governor-General of India, 1867

THE British did not take Burma in one fell swoop. Rather they sliced away at it, fighting three separate wars, the first beginning in 1824, the last ending in 1885. The first was the most treacherous, and almost ended in fiasco. An initial expeditionary force of 11,000 mixed British and Indian troops had to be supplemented by 29,000 more. Of the 15,000 men who died, more than 13,000 succumbed to malaria and other tropical diseases. (Among those who experienced fierce hand-to-hand combat was Captain Frederick Marryat, RN, of *Mr Midshipman Easy* and *Children of the New Forest* fame.) There was also uncertainty as to whether the expedition was simply punitive or whether the objective was to create a protectorate.

For decades the long border between India (including Bengal) and Burma had been a flashpoint. If the East India Company was dismayed by Burman actions in Manipur and Assam – the one again subjugated by Bodawpaya towards the end of his reign, the other occupied by his successor Bagyidaw in 1823 – then the Burmans were equally dismayed by the East India Company's apparent collusion with rebels in Arakan.

No diplomatic solution seemed possible. The government in Calcutta tried repeatedly to maintain a representative (usually called the Resident) at the Court of Ava, to guard and promote its interests, but each time the mission failed. Either the representative's duties were obstructed, or he was expelled or humiliated beyond endurance. Like the Chinese emperors, the kings of Ava expected foreigners especially to abase themselves in their presence. Nor did the hubris of the Burmese monarchs end there. Having for some years had secret contacts with the French, in 1810 King Bodawpaya blithely instructed his ministers to tell one Captain Manning that if the English cared to petition him, then he would send an army to Europe and put an end to Napoleon Bonaparte, provided the King of England personally rendered homage afterwards.

The following year relations were again strained as a maverick refugee from Arakan, Chin Byan, assembled a guerrilla army in the forests of Bengal, then seized the principal Arakanese city of Mrohaung. Bodawpaya at once concluded that Chin Byan had the clandestine backing of Calcutta. The British denied this, but when, to prove their point, they endeavoured to capture Chin Byan once he had been driven out of Arakan, they were unable to hunt him down. Nor did King Bodawpaya's death in 1819, ending a reign that stretched back thirty-seven years, ease the situation. King Bagyidaw was even more determined to flex the Burman muscle. Ava's finest commander, Thado Maho Bandula, was appointed Governor of Assam. Forced back into Burma by a colonial army now prepared, after many years of distractions elsewhere in India, to give the Kingdom of Ava its full attention, General Bandula was next appointed Governor of Arakan.

News soon reached Calcutta that Bandula was amassing an army of invasion that would strike at Bengal. Indeed, King Bagyidaw had given him a pair of golden handcuffs. Once Calcutta had fallen, Bandula was to march immediately to London – wherever that might be – and apprehend King George III, who was to be brought back to the king's new capital at Amarapura ('Immortal City') in the golden handcuffs, to prostrate himself before the throne. Accordingly the government of India declared a state of war. As Bandula advanced across the border, the British struck from the sea: predictable, one might have thought, of a proven maritime power, but evidently something that had not occurred to either King Bagyidaw or his advisers.

Early in May 1824 a British fleet made up of warships and troop transports occupied Rangoon with no difficulty at all. But then the troubles began. Sir Archibald Campbell's force reckoned without the weather. Almost immediately monsoon rains set in, and for the next half-year the British and their Indian auxiliaries found themselves marooned where they had landed. The war-plan was to advance from Rangoon up the Irrawaddy until Amarapura was reached and occupied. However, not only did the rains make the rivers difficult to navigate and the unroaded land impossible to traverse, but anticipated support from the fractious Mons failed to materialise.

It became harrowingly obvious that Campbell's supplies – of food and materiel as well as of men – were wholly inadequate to the task. Meanwhile the citizens of Rangoon, already beginning to prosper as a commercial centre, had been evacuated by Bagyidaw's agents on pain of death. The king's fear was that some Burmese might regard the British as liberators. Rangoon's inhabitants were corralled into jungle camps, where they too suffered the inclemencies of the season.

The longer Campbell was holed up in Rangoon, the easier it was for the Burmans to regroup. Having been taken wholly by surprise, they now harried British detachments sent out to forage the countryside. Strangely, Bandula was not permitted to continue his advance into Bengal, which must have caused the British even greater embarrassment. Instead he was ordered to use his army to block any advance up the Irrawaddy.

By tradition Burman armies avoided pitched battles on their own ground. Their generals preferred to build well-fortified stockades, from which their troops could mount lightning assaults on an enemy with relative impunity. Bandula dug in at Danubyu, a township on the western bank of the Irrawaddy some 200 miles upstream from Rangoon. As the rains eased off in October, the British prepared to advance. In December two small Burman forces sent to impede their progress were brushed aside, and by the end of March 1825, the British arrived before Danubyu. Campbell decided to attack Bandula's cleverly designed fortress, but in the event there was no contest. On 1st April Bandula was struck by a rocket fired over Danubyu's outer defences and died instantly. Bereft of a beloved and fearless leader, Bandula's several thousand soldiers abandoned Danubyu and dispersed under cover of darkness.

Bandula's death was the critical moment in the First Anglo-Burmese War. Although the British bore superior arms, historically Burman fighters had often displayed formidable tenacity. With a second rainy season around the corner, Campbell's campaign might easily have devolved from a logistical shambles into a military catastrophe, comparable with what happened seventeen years later in Afghanistan, when an entire expeditionary army was annihilated in hostile terrain. But the weakness of the Burman order of battle, as perhaps of all Burmese power structures, was that too much depended on one individual. There was no disciplined chain of command to cope with the loss of a commander.

After Danubyu, Campbell's men hunkered down at Prome until the monsoon passed, then advanced steadily towards the Burman capital, pausing only as successive attempts were made to broker a ceasefire. Only when in February 1826 the British reached Yandabo, within striking distance of Amarapura, did Bagyidaw at last cave in. To avoid the indignity of a *kala* army entering his capital, he agreed to concede to the British Arakan and Tenasserim, where a separate campaign had been fought. He further agreed not to meddle any more in Assam and Manipur, to pay an indemnity equivalent to one million pounds, and that henceforward a British Resident should be permitted to maintain an office befitting his station at his court. Conversely, a Burman embassy would be opened in Calcutta, to facilitate better relations in the future.

Had Campbell pressed ahead, two more costly wars might have been avoided. As his military secretary on the campaign, Major J.J. Snodgrass, recorded in *The Burmese War 1824–1826*, there was a tangible air of disappointment among the British officers: 'we were only three marches from the capital of the despot, the source from which the war and all its lengthened miseries had sprung, and from the primary cause of so much suffering and bloodshed, and it was not in the nature of a British soldier to turn his back upon the Golden City, the supposed riches of which we had hoped to share, without some feelings of regret'.

Despite the return of Rangoon to Burman rule, the Treaty of Yandabo was a bitter affront to Burman *amour propre*. The Kingdom of Ava may have been reduced by just two outlying provinces (one of which, Arakan, was only questionably part of 'Burma' anyway), but the loss of so much seaboard meant less control over maritime trading, with consequent economic damage. The treaty was therefore to be abrogated as soon as circumstances and resources permitted, and war resumed. Yet there were difficulties. While trade with Manchu-governed China was fast expanding, the returns were insufficient to underwrite an aggressive stance towards the British in India. Moreover, much of Burma's not inconsiderable wealth was dedicated to maintaining the court at Amarapura in the style tradition dictated.

The king, luxuriating in such titles as Lord of the White Elephants, Ruler of All Umbrella-Bearing Chiefs and Lord of the Universe, had, in addition to his palace guard, a personal retinue of 1,000 men and women charged with satisfying his every want. Several senior princes and other grandees also maintained lavish courts, either at the capital or in the provinces of which they were the governors.

Nothing much could be done about Arakan and Tenasserim, but on other particulars of the treaty the court prevaricated. In September 1826 Calcutta dispatched John Crawfurd, an erstwhile Governor of Singapore and something of an orientalist, as Resident to Amarapura, instructing him to secure a further trade or commercial treaty. But Crawfurd's reception was similar to that of previous envoys. When finally granted an audience with Bagyidaw, he had to undergo the familiar degradations. Obliged to walk the full length of the palace's 'eastern' wall, he had also to close his very English umbrella. He was further required to remove his shoes in the royal presence, which he flatly refused to do. As punishment he was kept waiting for more than two hours, and the treaty eventually offered him was nowhere near what the Company expected. Meanwhile, the king's ministers ducked and weaved in the matter of paying the agreed indemnity. Finally Crawfurd threw in the towel: 'hopeless and disgusted' by the attitude of those with whom he was supposed to negotiate, he returned to India.

A major stumbling block was what the term 'Resident' meant. In British eyes, a Resident was something higher than an ambassador, a proconsul even, someone tasked with securing an informal protectorate. For King Bagyidaw, the title was simply an irritant.

More progress was made by Crawfurd's successor, Henry Burney, nephew of the celebrated English novelist Fanny Burney. He was more sensitive than Crawfurd, perhaps because as a major of the Bengal Infantry he was used to adjusting to the ways of the 'native'. For a while he won Bagyidaw over. For eighteen months the two men got on famously, discussing books and boats, guns and horses together. But in 1831, much like his counterpart George III of England, the Burman king began exhibiting signs of madness. Burney's good work was fast undone. First Bagyidaw's unsympathetic senior queen grasped the reins of power. Then, in 1837, when it became clear that Bagyidaw was wholly deranged, his brother Tharrawaddy, hostile to everything the British stood for, seized the throne. The usual bloodbath of loyalists to the outgoing regime threatened to follow. Five ministers of state were summarily executed. Burney intervened with threats of dire consequences to protect other potential victims, with the result that he was frozen out of court life. No longer able to fly the flag in Amarapura, he too returned to Calcutta.

The third Resident appointed to the court of Ava in accordance with the terms of the Treaty of Yandabo fared even worse. Colonel Richard Benson, also of the Bengal Infantry, was treated with calculated contempt. The ground floor of the living quarters assigned to him flooded as soon as the monsoon rains arrived, in May 1839. In July, his health broken, he beat an ignominious retreat, and Calcutta more or less abandoned any idea of high-level representation at Amarapura.

All that could be done was watch and wait. That Tharrawaddy was blighted by the same mental deficiencies as his brother – doubtless induced by the incestuousness of Burmese royal marriages – offered some hope, since it was widely understood that sooner or later he too would have to go. In 1845 his own sons decided to restrain their father, making him a prisoner in his palace, a sort of house arrest. But when he died in 1846, his successor proved a reactionary of the worst sort. Over the next two years the newly enthroned King Pagan ordered the deaths of some 6,000 supposed enemies. He had little aptitude for diplomacy, and even less for the cares of government. Besotted with his harem, and an inveterate gambler, he allowed his ministers and governors to behave much as they pleased.

From a British-Indian perspective, Burma had become dangerously destabilised. That rebellion flared up inside the country was perhaps tolerable; but that Burman power-mongers should be perceived as aiding and abetting anti-British insurgency in Tenasserim and Arakan was not. 'Honest' British traders, determined to expand a still-modest Burma trade, were too often treated roughly, not just in Amarapura, but also in Rangoon. Another war became a racing certainty.

In 1851 two British sea captains were apprehended in Pegu, on a trumped-up charge of murder. They would not be executed, it was insinuated, if a handsome indemnity was paid. For the then Whitehall-appointed Viceroy of India, Lord Dalhousie, such a demand, however carefully concealed, was tantamount to blackmail. In an age of Palmerstonian 'gun-boat' diplomacy, he dispatched HMS *Fox*, accompanied by two vessels belonging to the East India Company, to Rangoon under the command of Commodore Lambert. But for once gun-boat diplomacy did not deliver. Although, under pressure, the offending Burman Governor of Pegu, Maung Ok, was dismissed, his replacement was no more sympathetic to British demands, and Lambert found himself getting nowhere very slowly. Without seeking further orders from his superiors, he used his warship to blockade Rangoon port. When a few loose shots were fired in its direction, he devastated Rangoon's defences with sweeping broadsides.

Lambert could, and perhaps should, have been court-martialled, for exceeding the orders given him. Dalhousie, though, backed his man, even though privately he conceded that Lambert had overreacted. An ultimatum demanding fresh reparations was delivered to Amarapura. When the deadline passed, on 1st April 1852, the British-Indian war machine swung swiftly to. Before the month was out both Rangoon and Martaban, another important Burmese port, were occupied, followed by Bassein. Come mid-May, the rains set in. But Dalhousie and his two commanders, Lambert and General Godwin, had learned the lessons of the First Anglo-Burmese War. This time around, to the chagrin of the opposing Burman generals, every attention was paid to the details of supply and healthcare. No reinforcements were needed, and few men died of disease.

The initial success of Dalhousie's expeditionary force created an acrimonious debate. Just what were the goals of this latest Burmese escapade? To teach the errant Burman a lesson, or to annex the entire country? Both in Calcutta and London there was no shortage of hawks urging the latter course. Dalhousie himself was more cautious. When the rains stopped, he ordered his forces to advance on Prome, which fell to Godwin in November, and with it (effectively) the entire province of Pegu.

Now the British had command of all 'Lower Burma', a swathe of territory extending unbroken from Bengal to far down the Kra isthmus, and with it the Irrawaddy delta. For Dalhousie that was enough. While it was within his grasp to take the whole country, he reasoned that it would be more trouble than it was worth. With no sea-ports left, the Kingdom of Ava would have no choice but to respect the imperatives of British trade. To have gone the whole hog would have been to overburden an already stretched administration in India.

In December 1852 the annexation of Lower Burma was formally asserted in Calcutta, and later in London. The Second Anglo-Burmese War was over. British-Indian casualties had been light, though amongst them was Rear-Admiral Henry Austen, the surviving brother of Jane Austen, then in his seventies and the epitome of English pride, as also of English prejudice.

In the short term Dalhousie's caution proved salutary. The second British-Indian advance up the Irrawaddy threw the court of Ava into utter confusion and sparked a revolution. All along there had existed a faction, grouped around a junior prince, Mindon, that was better versed about the wider world than any preceding generation. These courtiers had urged King Pagan to avoid provoking war and negotiate peaceably with Calcutta. When hostilities had commenced, Mindon and his closest supporters had fled the capital.

By December 1852 a state of civil war prevailed in 'Upper Burma' – one reason why Pagan's military response to Dalhousie's strike force was so feeble. However, the situation was resolved early in 1853. The forfeiture of Pegu made it clear to a majority of the Hluttaw, Council of State, that Mindon had been right, and the king wrong. In a bloodless coup Pagan was deposed and Mindon was offered the throne.

Unlike his predecessors, King Mindon did not celebrate his accession to power with a massacre of innocents. Instead he immediately freed such Europeans as languished in Amarapura's dreadful jails, and persuaded two Italian priests to act as intermediaries between himself and Arthur Purves Phayre, newly appointed Commissioner of Pegu by Dalhousie. Phayre, who had a better knowledge of Burma than any previous Englishman, and who spoke the Burman language (*Bamar*), tried to persuade Mindon to acknowledge the annexation of Pegu province in a new treaty. But Mindon had no intention of going down in history as the monarch who signed away half the kingdom. He was also apprehensive that such an agreement might fuel further insurrection. Yet in other important respects the two men saw eye-to-eye. With other problems to attend, both wanted an amicable, constructive relationship.

In 1855 Phayre himself, escorted by 400 armed men, journeyed upstream to Amarapura, where he was received by a Burman ruler who for once exuded charm and common sense, and who did not insist that Phayre remove his footwear. Phayre was impressed by Mindon's desire to bring about modernising reforms. It was noted that the king was a thoughtful, scholarly individual who had a deep commitment to his Buddhist faith. Like many other junior princes, he had spent his adolescence inside monasteries, and at one point had been ordained into the *Sangha*, or Buddhist monkhood. In a new-found spirit of mutual interest, fresh trade terms were agreed in 1862, following a second visit by the Commissioner. There would no longer be any customs barriers between British and Avan Burma. It was further agreed that, for the purposes of navigation, the Irrawaddy should be regarded as an open highway.

Thus was a *modus vivendi* sorted. The Kingdom of Ava would continue to receive its essential supplies of rice and *ngapi* (a kind of fish-paste, another staple of the Burman diet) from the Irrawaddy delta without having to pay through the nose, while teak, sesame seeds, silk and other commodities would flow south into the ready hands of British merchants. These arrangements, together with the opening of the Suez Canal in 1869, more than halving seaborne journey times between the Far East and western Europe, transformed Rangoon into a major port.

For the government in Calcutta – Lower Burma was incorporated into the Indian province of Bengal – Mindon's attitude was welcome news. Although Pegu had been swiftly overrun, it was a good three years before it was finally pacified, and there were further outbreaks of unrest in Tenasserim. But of far greater concern were unfolding events in India itself. In 1857 half the country rose in revolt, called the Indian Mutiny by English historians, but the Great Uprising by their Indian counterparts. Only in the later stages of Mindon's reign did cracks begin to appear in the façade of his relatively liberal regime, at least in British eyes. Among Burmans, Mindon has always been regarded as a near-perfect sovereign who pointed Burma in the right direction while retaining its distinctive traditions.

The most important of King Mindon's reforms, carried out by his brother the Kanaung Prince and a senior minister known as the Kinwun Mingyi, was the introduction of the salaried official to replace the old, hopelessly compromised system of appanage, whereby court appointees and hereditary office-holders were given fiefdoms to farm as best (or as unscrupulously) they could. A new general tax (the *thathameda*), based on actual wealth and ability to pay, was designed to replace the age-old practice of 'squeeze'. But if these and other measures suggested a modernising tendency, it soon emerged that the court's taste for spendthrift opulence had not been exorcised. Nor was there yet any move towards moderating the absolutist powers of the Burman throne.

Seven years into his reign, in 1860 King Mindon abandoned Amarapura as his capital and ordered his court to relocate to a newly created citadel at Mandalay, a few miles further up the Irrawaddy. The cost was prohibitive, the more so since the king simultaneously embarked on a costly pagoda-building programme. This included the Kuthodaw Paya and its 729 marble steles, each housed in a mini-stupa of its own, upon which were engraved the entire *Tipitaka*.

Such undertakings were scarcely unique. Creating a new capital had often been undertaken by Burmese rulers. It was one way of marking a new beginning, of underscoring that the Lord of the White Elephants was worthy of his multiple titles. Similarly the creation of many new pagodas, as well as earning Mindon personal 'merit' against his future reincarnation, reasserted the throne's claim to be the defender of the Buddhist faith. But to achieve these things meant a continuation of traditional patterns of slave, forced and corvée labour. Mandalay fast became a fabled city of the East, captured in the English poet Rudyard Kipling's famous 1892 lines:

> On the road to Mandalay,
> Where the flyin'-fishes play,
> An' the dawn comes up like thunder outer
> China 'crost the Bay.*

But raising Mandalay cost the Burmese people dear.

The high point of Mindon's reign came in 1871, when only the Fifth Buddhist Council ever was convened at his court. This drew monks, abbots and worshippers from those countries where Theravada Buddhism was practised – Ceylon, Siam, Laos and Cambodia – as well as smaller numbers from Vietnam, China, Japan and even Tibet. The humiliation of Ava's defeat in 1852 was in some measure vanquished. By arrangement with the Commissioner of Pegu, a gleaming new umbrella-like gold finial, or *hti*, was placed atop the Shwedagon in Rangoon, again at exorbitant expense.

The great Buddhist gathering signalled where Mindon's real heart lay. The reforms of the earlier part of his reign were not supplemented by further modernisations. Instead, the kingdom slipped back into its erstwhile lethargy. Familiar problems resurfaced. To the intense irritation of the British Chamber of Commerce in Rangoon, free trade between

---

* Rudyard Kipling, 'Mandalay', 1892

the two Burmas was stymied by the enforcement of royal monopolies in key commodities, notably rubies, mined in great profusion at Mogok. Then in 1875 royal protocol again became an issue. Sir Douglas Forsythe, heading up a British mission to Mandalay, declined to remove his shoes in the royal presence, with the full backing of his superiors in Calcutta. Thereafter British influence at Mindon's court waned. Meanwhile it transpired that Mindon's ministers had dealings with France, now firmly established as an expanding colonial power in Indochina. This was particularly threatening, since the long-term strategy of both European powers was to control and develop overland trade routes into southern China, particularly the resource-rich province of Yunnan.

When Mindon died in 1878, Britain's worst fears came true. In 1866 the Kanaung Prince – the heir apparent to the throne – had been assassinated and, rather than nominate another successor, Mindon let the matter rest. When, suffering from acute dysentery, he took to his deathbed, there was some hope that he would be succeeded by the moderate Nyaungyan Prince. But the Kinwun Mingyi, the most powerful of Mindon's ministers, realising that reform could once again be put on the agenda, had other ideas. He wanted a puppet on the throne: the relatively unknown Thibaw Prince.

Fearing that there was a plot against his life, the Nyaungyan Prince and a younger brother took refuge in the British Residency. Instead of handing the princes back to the court, the Resident had them smuggled to Rangoon, whence they were shipped to Calcutta. Mindon expired, and the pusillanimous Thibaw was enthroned. But where the Kinwun Mingyi had miscalculated was in his choice of 'Second Queen' for the twenty-two-year-old Thibaw. Supayalat (nicknamed Soup Plate in Rangoon) was not just pretty: she was vicious to the bone and had a natural aptitude for intrigue. Finding ready allies among a reactionary clique of senior army men, she saw to it that Thibaw appointed several like-minded ministers.

In February 1879, Supayalat orchestrated a slaughter of potential rivals for the Crown, along with their wives and children. In the first wave of killings some eighty of Thibaw's relatives were dispatched, among them eight brothers and half-brothers. The royal prisons filled up fast, those inside them shackled and tortured. The Kinwun Mingyi survived the massacre, but henceforward his influence was severely trimmed.

In Burma such post-succession purges had been commonplace. King

Bodawpaya, for instance, is thought to have done away with eighty-three princes and princesses at a single sitting, in 1789. But ninety years later times had changed. The lurid goings-on in an upriver oriental court were no longer distant and speculative. A telegraph wire connected Mandalay to Rangoon and, via Rangoon, to Europe. In the London *Times* and other Western newspapers reports demonising Thibaw and his abhorrent queen accumulated. In Rangoon the Chamber of Commerce made hay out of Mandalay's misfortunes, its members rubbing their hands in expectant, greedy glee.

Was there not a moral case for regime change? The Prime Minister Lord Salisbury thought so, his Foreign Secretary Lord Randolph Churchill thought so, and even Queen Victoria considered intervention 'inevitable'. But still a pretext was needed, one of those little triggers that set history in motion, to spur the Cabinet and the Viceroy of India into decisive action.

The beginning of the end of the Burman monarchy came in August 1885. A leaked letter revealed that, through his agent in Mandalay, the French Foreign Minister, Jules Ferry, had promised Thibaw's government arms. At the same time the Bombay Burma Trading Corporation, a British enterprise with offices in Rangoon, was, in the minds of members of the Chamber of Commerce, being quite unjustly penalised for exceeding its teak-logging quota apropos a concession it leased from Mandalay near Pyinmana, on the Sittang river. A fine of £146,656 imposed by a royal law court was not only unmerited, but out of all proportion to the alleged infringement.

Colonel (later Sir) Edward Sladen, formerly British Resident in Mandalay during the reign of King Mindon, submitted a strongly worded report to his masters in Calcutta urging immediate annexation – a report swiftly forwarded to Westminster. 'Not only are the interests of our own province seriously affected by anarchy and misrule in upper Burma,' Sladen wrote, 'but the interests of humanity are infringed by the continued excesses of a barbarous and despotic ruler.'

Battle plans for an attack on Mandalay had already been drawn up in 1878. They included provisions to requisition river steamers belonging to the Irrawaddy Flotilla Company, the most successful of several companies vying to take advantage of the 1862 'open waterway' initiative. No matter that, under duress, the French government had withdrawn its agent (a shadowy gentleman by the name of Monsieur Hass), an ultimatum was delivered direct to Thibaw's court on 30th October 1885. Either (amongst other demands) the Burman government dropped its suit against the Bombay Burma Trading Corporation or it faced the consequences. Thibaw – believing, in an alcoholic stupor, that his kingdom was, with the acquisition of better weapons than it possessed in 1852, invulnerable to attack, and that war would give him the opportunity of driving the British out of Burma altogether – refused to back down. By standing his ground he would 'gain for us the notable result of placing us in the path to the celestial regions and to Nirvana, the eternal rest'.

But the British had more powerful weapons. On 14th November a task force commanded by General Sir Henry North Dalrymple Prendergast, comprising barges and steamers requisitioned from the Irrawaddy Flotilla Company and spear-headed by two gunboats, the *Irrawaddy* and the *Kathleen*, began its journey northwards. At strategic points the river had been fortified with gun emplacements, overseen by an Italian engineer in Thibaw's pay, but these the British howitzers, mounted on the 'flats' (as the barges were called), easily destroyed. Signor Comotto also failed to halt Prendergast's advance by sinking some of the king's own ships in his path. Instead, realising he was about to be taken prisoner during the campaign's first engagement at Thayetmyo, he bolted so quickly that he left behind documents that told the British everything they needed to know about the defences he had designed.

In places there was a manful resistance, but time and again Burman forces melted away or surrendered, preferring Prendergast's promised leniency to the febrile wrath of Thibaw and his paramour, if they returned home defeated. The same timorousness, combined with inadequate communications, prevented accurate reports of Prendergast's progress being laid at Thibaw's feet. Mandalay was gearing up to celebrate a tremendous victory. Only when the far-off thunder of British guns was heard in the capital, on 25th November, did the dismal truth set in.

Queen Supayalat climbed the ornate spiral watchtower of her husband's palace and fainted when she saw the broad expanse of the Irrawaddy strewn with enemy boats. Had Thibaw had an ounce of pluck and abandoned Mandalay, he might have caused endless trouble in the maquis, if only as a resistance figurehead. As it was, he was either too indolent, or too scared of the revenge his own people might exact, to flee his citadel – although many others did just that. Too late a royal messenger was sent downstream bearing a letter of truce. At first light on 28th November British and Indian troops landed on the foreshore, accompanied by a regimental band. A long column of soldiers marched musically past Mandalay's pagodas, markets, shops and go-downs towards the citadel three miles away, soon to be renamed Fort Dufferin, after the then Viceroy of India.

Colonel Sladen, there for the kill, had already gone ahead. Without removing his shoes he entered the Hall of Audience, where he found Thibaw reclining next to Supayalat on his Lion Throne. The king asked, then begged, for a few days' respite, but Sladen, acting under instructions, granted him only twenty-four hours. Thibaw and Supayalat gathered together such valuables as they could and retired to a summer pavilion within the palace enclosure. Next afternoon – by which time, much to the dismay of the task force's booty-hungry officers, the palace had been quietly stripped of its most precious portable contents by its former female servants – Prendergast himself arrived, to take the formal surrender of the kingdom. The king and queen, along with Supayalat's mother, Sinpyumashin, and a handful of still-loyal retainers, were carried to the river in bullock carts and put on board the steamer *Thoreah*. The only pause came when Supayalat, placing a cheroot between her lips, requested the soldiers escorting her for a light.

The *Thoreah* manoeuvred into midstream for the night, lest anyone should attempt a rescue, then set sail for Rangoon at dawn on the 30th. Thibaw and Supayalat were conveyed to the far side of India, there to endure guarded exile at Ratnagiri. Only after Thibaw's death in 1916 was Supayalat permitted to return to Burma, where she survived for another twenty years under virtual house arrest in a Rangoon bungalow – according to *The Times* (20th December 1916) 'a pathetic old lady, strangely different from the feline personality who had dominated Thibaw in the tragic days before the monarchy came to its sudden inglorious end'.

Perversely, when she too passed on, a private citizen denuded of all her titles and most of her assets, the crowds turned out in their thousands to attend her funeral. In November 1885 the crowds in Mandalay had behaved rather differently. Though they too turned out in great numbers, and lined the city's sun-baked streets to watch the royal couple's ignominious departure, there was an eerie satisfaction on many of their faces. A few hurled stones at the imperial soldiers, but most simply watched in silence. The British may not have been greeted with unequivocal joy, but there was unmistakable relief that a tyrant and his succuba had been sent packing.

V

BRITISH BURMA

Why, of course, the lie that we're here to uplift our poor black brothers instead of to rob them. I suppose it's a natural enough lie. But it corrupts us, it corrupts us in ways you can't imagine. There's an everlasting sense of being a sneak and a liar that torments us and drives us to justify ourselves night and day. It's at the bottom of half our beastliness to the natives. We Anglo-Indians could be almost bearable if we'd only admit that we're thieves and went on thieving without any humbug.

George Orwell, *Burmese Days* (1934)

BY the time Aung San was born, in February 1915, the year before Queen Supayalat came home, Burma in its nominal entirety had been a British colony for thirty years.

There was talk, before Mandalay was occupied, of replacing Thibaw with a compliant puppet king (the Nyaungyan Prince was the obvious candidate); but that would have left too much to chance, and so annexation was preferred: not directly to the British Crown, but to its 'jewel', the Raj in India, created in the wake of the Indian Uprising, when the moribund East India Company, creaking under the burden of its accumulated responsibilities, was finally wound up.

Formal annexation of the kingdom of Ava was declared on 1st January 1886 – Foreign Secretary Lord Randolph Churchill made it his 'New Year's present' to his queen, Victoria. This offered Burman dignity a double affront. Divided administratively between 'Burma Proper' (or 'Ministerial Burma', essentially wherever Burmans formed a majority) and the 'Frontier Areas' (the ethnic-minority uplands), Burma was not even to be a colony in its own right but a division of Bengal.

Up until 1890 central Burma especially seethed with unrest. Resistance groups, numbering between half a dozen and several hundred men, and operating either out of the jungle or out of villages and townships not yet under British control, caused Burma's upcountry administrators endless anxiety. There was a long series of bloody scuffles that required the costly deployment of 32,000 colonial troops and 8,000 military police.

Insurgency spread to the Irrawaddy delta itself, which the British had ruled since the early 1850s. For a few months, between the end of 1886 and the beginning of 1887, it was touch and go whether Burma could be held. Only by dealing ruthlessly with the captured ringleaders – shot or hanged without trial – was 'rebellion' crushed. The British, perennially upset to have their righteous authority challenged, dismissed the insurgents as 'dacoits', mere bandits and gangsters of the kind they had long encountered in the backwaters of India. And some were just that. But many were not. Some belonged to the Burman aristocracy. Having already experienced a diminution of their status under the reforms instituted by Mindon and the Kanaung Prince, members of the Burman nobility grasped that under British rule they would have no influence at all. Others were monks, the venerable as well as novices, who took to the stick and the gun because they felt the only world that mattered was under imminent threat of extinction.

For a few years 'Upper' Burma was quite as lawless as Colonel Sladen had claimed it was under Thibaw. The upshot was that the new colonial masters as a class (there were always individual exceptions) developed a deep-seated mistrust of the Burman character. Even George Orwell, that paradigm of dissident English liberal-socialist opinion, was not above reproach in this regard.

Born in 1903 in India, with unacknowledged Burman relatives in the family, Orwell joined the Imperial Civil Service after leaving Eton, and served five years in the colonial police between 1923 and 1927, rising to the rank of District Commissioner in his last posting, at Katha in the far north. *Burmese Days*, the novel he wrote about his experiences there, first published in the United States in 1934, delivers a coruscating and classic portrait of bloody-minded colonial administrators carrying out their duties with no regard at all for 'local' sensitivities. Yet at Rangoon Station, in a fit of pique, Orwell the ex-public-schoolboy once gave a disrespectful Burman boy an on-the-spot thrashing with his cane.

Conversely, many British in Burma admired and cherished some of the 'tribals', among them the Shans, the Chins, the Kachins, the Karennis and, especially, the Karens. All these peoples, as well as the Nagas in the north-west, whom the British left almost entirely to their own devices, bore a historic grudge against their Burman counterparts, who had so often ridden roughshod over them. So they welcomed the British, who showed little inclination to fully invest their traditional homelands beyond stationing the odd District Officer in their midst, for the purposes of liasing with the colonial government in Rangoon and collecting a few taxes that never approached the extortionate amounts demanded by the Konbaung monarchy.

The aim was to administer the Frontier Areas at as small a cost as possible – let sleeping dogs lie, and all of that. Thus the Shan states – those fifty-odd petty princedoms ruled by their *sawbwas* – remained intact. But more than that, the willingness of Christian Karens particularly to cooperate with the British led to them being preferred above their Burman counterparts. As in India, the colonial hierarchy looked to groom dependable 'natives' to help run the country. Such men and women could, after all, be paid far less than the white man, and still be grateful for it; and it was one way of integrating Burma within the Raj. Some Burmans, too, were co-opted into the colonial regime, but never in proportionate numbers. Partly this was the decision of the British, partly it reflected an unwillingness among Burmans to recognise the colonial authority by serving it. Either way, employment patterns reinforced Burman resentment. Having ruled the roost for so long, it was humiliating to have to look up to those whom the Burman was culturally conditioned to look down upon.

Equally upsetting to the Burman was the arrival of a corps of Indian civil servants, brought in to apply the skills they had acquired in Calcutta, Delhi, Madras and Bombay. Indian judges gave rulings according to Indian colonial law; Indian bureaucrats prepared tax schedules; and Indian policemen arrested Burman miscreants. If the idea was to make Burma a part of the Raj, the Raj was made a part of Burma. 'What we gave Burma was not a government but an administration,' wrote G.E. Harvey, an officer of the Indian Civil Service, in his 1946 book *British Rule in Burma 1824–1942*. 'Political direction, so far as there was any, came from the Indian government, with the British parliament in the dim background.'

And then, on the coat-tails of Indian civil servants, came the hated *chettyars*, Indian money-lenders well versed in driving their mainly

peasant clients into debt, then seizing their land to create large estates
of which they became the absentee landlords. Ironically, they prospered
because Burman money-lenders were, if anything, even more rapacious.
There was, too, a significant influx of Chinese: coolies to work in British
factories and plantations, and merchants and businessmen heading for
Rangoon. The country was being overrun not just by one set of foreigners,
but by many.

It was galling to Burman nationalists that Rangoon was made the capital
of all Burma, for Burmans comprised far less than half the city's
population. Yet, vividly cosmopolitan, Rangoon now put Burma on the
map as never before. As an international port and commercial centre
it easily outshone Bangkok and rivalled Singapore. Along its waterfront
sprouted a line of grand edifices, among them the Customs House and
the famous Strand Hotel. Away from the river the British laid out several
landscaped parks, including the Zoological Gardens, and created the
Royal (Kandawgyi) and Victoria (Inya) Lakes. As the new century
gathered momentum, the city became a favoured stopping place for
cruise liners and a choice watering hole for the moneyed globetrotter.

If the heart of Rangoon belonged to the Sule Pagoda, and if the soul
of Burma was, as ever, enshrined in the Shwedagon, reputed to have
been founded soon after the Buddha's death in the fifth century BC, the
Buddhist faith was challenged by both Anglican and Catholic cathedrals,
as well as by dozens of smaller churches and mosques. Other kinds of
facility arrived as well – an athletics stadium and a race track, for
example, Rowe's the celebrated department store, and a string of
colonial clubs, the Pegu Club taking pride of place. And, later, a plethora
of cinemas, and Burma's first aerodrome, at Mingaladon, close to the
principal cantonment of the Anglo-Indian military.

Long before the runway at Mingaladon was laid, the British built
Rangoon Railway Station, a splendid four-towered colonial extravaganza
that epitomised the advent of at least one aspect of the Industrial
Revolution. As early as 1889 a rail track all the way to Mandalay was
opened. This formed the backbone of a burgeoning rail network that
connected all the main centres of Burmese commerce: Bhamo in the far
north-east, along the 'China Road', Bassein in the west, Moulmein and
Mergui in the south. And once the railways had been built, motor roads
followed. As in India, Malaya, Australia and Africa, the British were
adept at furnishing a modern infrastructure.

These were high-calibre engineering feats that reflected the purpose of Britain's presence, which was first and foremost to exploit Burma economically. Well before the fall of Mandalay, the Irrawaddy delta had begun its transformation into the world's leading 'rice basket', eventually exporting three million tons of top-quality grain a year, much of it to Europe via the Suez Canal. Tobacco and rubber plantations followed. But the flagship enterprise was the Burmah Oil Company, established in 1886, which developed oilfields at Chauk, Yenangyaung and elsewhere. Although the First World War provided a massive boost to Burmese oil production, to help keep the Royal Navy fuelled, even by 1913 it was hitting an annual 200 million gallons.

There were other add-on benefits, necessary for the smooth running of Burma Ltd: a post and telegraph system linking all the country's main towns and cities; the introduction of modern banking methods; and a judiciary that, though never ideally impartial towards 'the native', was widely regarded, in respect of civil litigation certainly, as superior to anything that had gone before. Significantly, many well-to-do Burmans studied for the Bar, learning their trade at the Inns of Court in London. Law was a profession that remained open to them, and brought with it both respectability and a promising income.

Burmans also qualified as doctors trained in Western medicine, as architects and as teachers, both at college level and in the secularist 'government schools' that the British introduced to ensure a supply of literate workers for their corporatist ambitions. A Burman middle class emerged that was not dependent on the 'vertical' patronage systems that had dominated Konbaung culture.

However much the imposition of colonial rule rankled, British Burma could appear, to the casual observer at least, a progressive success story, compared to what had gone before. There were, too, humanitarian gains, not least the eradication of slavery.

Slavery in Burma had long been of two kinds. On the one hand were war captives, forced to do whatever their captors wanted – though such was the quantity of these in earlier times that, allowed to marry, they were often settled in their own villages, adding to Burma's ethnic diversity, once they had been granted manumission. In this category were 'pagoda slaves', prisoners of war donated to pagodas and monasteries for work on their agricultural estates, freeing the monks to spend more time attending their pastoral duties, or in prayer and meditation. On the other hand were 'bondsmen' and 'bondswomen', individuals who entered a state of more or less absolute servitude to pay off accumulated debts, or to earn their impoverished parents a longed-for windfall.

Slavery of both sorts was ended by the British, as were excessive involuntary labour and the routine use of torture in Burmese prisons. Although, in times of emergency, the colonial authorities indulged in 'extra-judicial killings', and individual cases of beatings (and worse) in colonial police stations were not unknown, there was a real increment in respect for human rights. Ideally at least, the rule of law became impersonal; while further down the line, following the pattern set in India, limited democratic power-sharing with indigenous political leaders was instituted between the two world wars.

Whether such changes would have occurred anyway, regardless of British intervention, is open to conjecture. As well as political and tax reforms, King Mindon's reign had witnessed a surge of factory-building in and around Mandalay. From these beginnings there might have flowed a more thoroughgoing programme of modernisation, as eventually happened in neighbouring Siam – another monarchical Buddhist state that never became a European colony, but in due course became a functioning democracy. Yet Siam (Thailand) was blessed with a peculiarly responsible line of kings, the Chakri Dynasty. Mindon's patchwork reforms apart, there is scant reason to suppose Burma's pre-colonial rulers capable of behaving with the same resolve.

Even so, the British may have done Burma a disservice by arbitrarily getting rid of its throne, however rotten it appeared both to the outside world and to many of its own subjects. With the throne went an entire societal matrix that held at least the Burman people together. As in Thailand, in time this might have furnished a broader cohesion.

Among the 'native' institutions profoundly damaged by the British was a close intimacy between government and the Buddhist *Sangha*, or Order of Monks. After 1886 the surviving *thathanabaing* – the patriarchal 'high abbot' of Burmese Buddhism, loosely analogous to the Archbishop of Canterbury, with provincial *gainggyoke* under him – was allowed to continue in his post until his death in 1895, but was not replaced. The colonial administration made no determined effort to dismantle Buddhism in Burma – the pagodas, monasteries and monastic schools, so long the mainstay of education there, were left alone. But Buddhism as a source of governmental legitimacy, as well as sometimes formal rebuke, was accorded no special privileged status.

That too was an affront to Burmese Buddhists. But in the matter of religion, the Raj in Burma unwittingly went one step further. Unlike the Spanish and Portuguese conquistadors in the Americas, the British were first and foremost simple mercantilists. In their assault upon Mandalay there was none of Christopher Columbus's homage to God. Even so, just because Lord Dufferin, Prendergast & Co. were nominally Christian, they were blind to whatever antics their collared brethren might get up to, with enduringly divisive results.

The British occupation of Burma enabled droves of Christian missionaries to go to work in the Burmese uplands, although the earliest of these arrived some ten years before the first Anglo-Burmese War and was not even an Englishman. Adorinam Judson – a resourceful, muscular and uxorious American Baptist – landed in Rangoon in 1813. As he quickly discovered, few Burmans could be persuaded or cajoled to succumb to the blandishments of Christ. They were altogether at ease with their 'idolatrous' Buddhist faith. Setting up shop in the river port town, described by Judson as an 'unspeakably filthy village', he tried enticing converts by running Christian meditation classes, but in six years managed only one submission. The hill peoples, though, were another proposition entirely. Many still practised animism, the worship of local spirits and deities, in Judson's eyes hardly a religion at all. Where were their temples? Where was their church? Where their hope? Where their discipline? They were ripe for God's picking.

Intriguingly, some – the Karens, the Karennis, the Kachins and the Lisu – entertained a belief in a 'Lost' or 'Golden' Book: something their ancestors had possessed in a dim distant past, but which had mysteriously vanished. Brandishing their bibles, it was easy for Judson and those who followed him, from the American Board or the London Missionary Society (and later Catholic missionaries as well) to convince the tribals that their Book was not lost after all, but was now being wondrously restored to them.

Learning their language, Judson targeted the Karens, who subscribed to a creation myth similar to that of Genesis. They expressed belief in a big god called Y'wa, which for Judson was synonymous with Yaweh (Jehovah). Conceivably the Karens had, at some point during the tortuous migrations that eventually brought them to Burma, come into contact with Nestorians, a Christian sect that, driven out of Syria, established a mission in China in 635. (Among later oriental Nestorians was Sorghaghtani Beki, the multi-talented mother of Kublai Khan, though

Kublai himself was a Tibetan Buddhist.) Judson encountered little difficulty in arousing the Karens' interest and soon made his first Karen convert: Ko Tha Byu, a genuine dacoit wanted by the Burman government for thirty murders.

Repentant and amazed after hearing Judson preach the gospel in his own tongue, Ko Tha Byu himself became a missionary. He set about making converts, some of whom also became missionaries, both among the Karens and among the Chins and Kachins. By the time the thrice-married Judson died, in 1850, an estimated 10,000 hill people had been baptised.

Whole swathes of Burma's uplands, as well as some ethnic communities in the lowlands, were Christianised during the period of British rule, and today there are still Western missionaries operating out of Thailand. Few of the pioneering missionaries, however, asked themselves how their intervention (which was cultural as well as religious and inevitably acquired political overtones) was justified. They were so certain of the truths they disseminated that there could be no reasonable challenge to their activities. They might on occasion make mistakes and misjudgements in the field, but their mission was underwritten by no less an authority than the Creator of All Things. They belonged to God's Expeditionary Force.

The long-term fall-out has been, for hundreds of thousands of Burmese uplanders, calamitous. Once the Burman people regained ascendancy, in the wake of Independence in 1948, and a military government was installed in 1962, the tables were turned a second time. Too often Christians were discriminated against simply because of their religion.

But it was not just the introduction of a usually evangelical version of the Christian religion that the colonisation of Burma promoted. Whether British, French, Dutch, Belgian, Portuguese or German, nineteenth-century European imperialism was riddled, from top to toe, with political disjunction.

At 'home', governments were becoming progressively liberal and democratised. In London, from the Great Reform Act of 1832 onwards, power began passing to the people, at least in vociferous theory. But in the colonies, people power was considered anathema by many of those sent to administer them.

The two worlds could not be kept apart, however. From their very 'oppressors', as also from missionaries, the subject peoples of Asia learned about 'self-determination', amongst other rights. Liberation and patriotism fused, though in different ways in different territories under different leaders. In Vietnam, Ho Chi Minh hitched his wagon to a militant blend of Marxism-Leninism and Maoism. In India, Mahatma Gandhi, delving deep into the roots of his own culture, chanced his all on the moral superiority of rational pacifism. In Dutch Indonesia, Ahmad Sukarno, playing the charismatic card for all it was worth, devised a strange hybrid of populism and dictatorship. And in Burma ...

In Burma there was Aung San – 'Rough Hands', as he was known to some of his compatriots, but no less effective for that.

VI

SATURDAY'S CHILD

Politics means your everyday life. You, in fact; for you are a political animal, as Aristotle long ago declared. It is how you eat, sleep, work and live, with which politics is concerned. You may not think about politics. But politics thinks about you.

Aung San, speaking at the Shwedagon, 20th January 1946

EVEN as a small boy Aung San was a handful. He was not naughty in the way other children can be, but (like his daughter) he could be supremely stubborn. If he didn't get his way he would sulk; if that didn't work he would assay a hunger strike.

He was the last-born of U Pha and Daw Su, two solid citizens of Natmauk, a township in Burma's 'central hot dry zone' in modern Magwe Division, which was connected to both Mandalay and (more distant by a factor of two) Rangoon by rail, though it was not on the main north–south highway, or for that matter within easy striking distance of the Irrawaddy.

Historically, Natmauk had strong associations with the court of Ava. Aung San himself claimed, in the briefest of self-portraits written towards the end of his life, that his 'ancestors were rural gentry and patriots'. Although there is no evidence that his family suffered any severe hardship when he was growing up, life was not easy, either. But for the British conquest, Aung San might have followed his forebears to Mandalay, to serve the Burman government and perhaps rise to lofty heights. As it was, his best-known forebear, U Min Yaung, was a local hero. Appointed the *myothugyi* (chief) of Myolulin, a township near Natmauk, by King Thibaw, he was among the first to take up arms against the British following the fall of Mandalay. But he paid for his rebellion with his life. Eventually captured, he was at once decapitated.

U Min Yaung was Aung San's great-uncle on his mother's side, or more precisely his maternal grandmother's cousin – the word 'uncle' never being applied with technical rigour by the Burmese. The grandmother in question, Daw Thu Zar, would often regale her favourite grandchild with the legend of U Min Yaung, so that from his cradle Aung San was imbued with the spirit of revolt and independence. He was also, in his own words drawn from an autobiographical fragment found after his death, 'rather fond of music and dance, especially drums. I would be tapping a table or anything that can be tapped.' In the same fragment, Aung San recounts how as a child he was susceptible to flattery. 'Once on a visit with my parents to a village 10 miles away and stopping at the headman's hut, I was addressed by a boy of the same age as "Captain". That pleased me so much that I gave him a fistful of white jaggery every time he addressed me thus.'

Of his parents, it was the mother, Daw Su, who made the running. U Pha, socially inferior to his wife, was a scholarly man, even though he came from farming stock. By nature taciturn in the extreme, he was singularly ill equipped to be an advocate or 'pleader' in local and divisional law courts, his chosen profession. He did not have many clients. In sharp contrast, Daw Su was outgoing and manifestly capable, the way so many Burmese women are. She it was who ensured a respectable income, managing such assets as the family had and making sure the land it owned turned in a comfortable annual profit.

Aung San was preceded by eight other children – five brothers and three sisters. Three of them (two brothers and one sister) died, either in infancy or early childhood, and between Aung San and his nearest sibling was a gap of four years. He was therefore very much a parental afterthought, and because of that was especially cherished, to the point of being pampered.

The day of his birth, 13th February 1915, was a Saturday. An astrologer forecast in his *zata* (natal horoscope) that Aung San would achieve great eminence and live for 120 years. Initially he was given the name Maung Htein Lin. But this was scarcely used. Instead, within the family and then outside, he was called Aung San, even though he had not been born on a Sunday, the only day of the week that, by tradition, warranted the use of the letter A in the first of however many given names.

The usual explanation of this astrologically high-risk departure from convention is that one of his older brothers, Aung Than, thought it would be convenient if his baby brother's name rhymed with his own. Curiously, if this were so, Aung Than was prescient, for it soon became a Burmese fashion for children of the same parents to have like-sounding names, the better to circumvent the impractical fact that, except among Muslims and one or two other lesser minorities, in Burma family names are not mandatory, making it so much harder to identify relatives or assemble genealogies.

The boy was blessed with neat, regular features, and the same concentrated gaze that was to mark out Aung San Suu Kyi. Though destined not to grow tall, Aung San was a handsome, slightly feminine-looking male whose features would one day lend themselves to the iconography of the Burmese state.

To begin with it was feared that the young darling of the family had been born dumb. Aung San did not begin talking until he was almost four. Later he made up for this deficiency by launching sometimes into impromptu speeches that might last hours. When he was not so minded he could lock up completely – moody silences that were to become a part of his legend.

Aung San was a sickly child, with a history of skin disease. But he quickly learned to turn even this to his advantage, refusing medication unless it was accompanied by extra pocket money, which on one occasion he used to purchase a packet of cheroots. Daw Su, finding her son pulling these apart in his room, gave the offending tobacconist a good dressing down, and the tobacconist in turn threatened to give the boy a good hiding. Aung San did not return to the shop, but persuaded one of his brothers to make his purchases for him.

Throughout his life Aung San was able to command the loyalty and respect of those older than himself, and subordinate them to his will. When, in his final months, he presided over a cabinet in Rangoon, all its members were his seniors. But as a child, the same ability held him back for a while. Until he was nearly eight he refused to go to school, even though his brothers and sisters had started when they were five. His parents simply indulged his obstinacy.

In Natmauk, 'school' meant attending lessons at a monastery. There was no 'National School' of the sort introduced in the early 1920s.

However, monasteries supplied two kinds of elementary education: traditional instruction in Buddhism, and a more liberal curriculum called *lawkatat*, or 'worldly learning'. Both offered classes in reading and writing Burmese, but only the latter included such disciplines as mathematics.

What seems to have changed Aung San's mind about opting out of education was the sight of his brother Aung Than prancing around the neighbourhood on a white pony, dressed in the fine, flowing robes of a prince prior to having his head shaved. As in Thailand and Laos, it is customary in Burma for males raised in the Buddhist faith to enter a monastery for at least a few weeks during adolescence. To become a 'novitiate' is both a rite of passage and citizenship training Theravada-style. At least once in their lives young men must practise humility, obedience and abstinence from every human temptation.

To have a son to send to a monastery to become a novitiate reflects well on any family and demands a celebration. In Natmauk this meant the son being paraded around town as though he were a prince, in the few hours before he lost his liberty. Evidently the sight of his brother having so fine a time on a 'dancing pony' fired the boy Aung San's imagination. Perhaps too there was confusion in his young mind, filled with his grandmother's stories about U Min Yaung and other worthy patriots. Did not great leaders also ride about on horseback?

Aung San ran to his mother and told her that he too wanted to become a novice. Daw Su, seizing the moment, replied that there was no problem. But first he must learn to read and write, and that meant going to school.

Once enrolled at the U Thaw Bita Monastery *lawkatat* school, Aung San made rapid progress. By the age of thirteen he had not only caught up with his fellow pupils, but was overtaking them, regularly coming top of class and skipping two grades in the process. As a pupil he was diligent as well as fast-learning, and addicted to books. But there was one thing Aung San could not learn at the U Thaw Bita Monastery, and that was English – in colonial Burma considered a prerequisite for anyone who wanted to get on in life. Already more interested in what he might be able to read in English than in English as a means to self-advancement, Aung San clamoured to attend the National School at Yenangyaung, thirty or so miles away, where his eldest brother Ba Win had become a teacher (and would become headmaster).

At first Daw Su and her husband U Pha were loath to let him go.

He was too young to leave home, and too frail. It would also be costly. Aung San's response was to stop taking food. When this had gone on for a day or two, his parents relented. Placed in Ba Win's care, Aung San was on his way to Yenangyaung in 1928. That Yenangyaung was no ordinary provincial town was implicit in its name, which means 'smelly water'. It was at the heart of Burma's booming oil-extraction industry, and so a place where the weight and character of British rule were more keenly felt than elsewhere, and political currents ran deep. Oilfield workers received good pay, relative to other sectors, but security was tight.

The National Schools were established in the wake of the first of a long series of student protests that erupted in Burma at regular intervals during the course of the twentieth century, against British rule to begin with, and later against the military regime instituted by General Ne Win in 1962.

Once the 'dacoit' insurgency of 1886–7 had been suppressed, Burma was for a generation largely quiescent. During the Great War of 1914–18 the colony even provided four battalions, to fight alongside British troops against a crumbling Ottoman empire in Mesopotamia. All four, however, were made up of uplanders – Karens, Chins and Kachins: tough, resilient, resourceful men who, like the Gurkhas of Nepal, responded well to military discipline and took pride in wearing the imperial uniform.

The Burmans did not enlist, and were not encouraged to. Although after the war some Burman units were formed, they were never more than a minority within the colonial Burma Army. More readily Burmans joined the colonial police, the better to preserve at least a semblance of self-regulation within their own communities. But beyond that there was, generally, a reluctance among Burmans to identify too closely with the occupying power. Rather – often with a great deal of acrimony between its rivalrous leaders – a nationalist movement slowly gathered momentum.

Initially it was Buddhist monks and their younger protégés who took the lead, as advocates of 'cultural nationalism', so often a prelude to something more robust. Some called themselves *wunthanus*, 'racially faithful ones'. At the turn of the century several patriotic Buddhist clubs were formed, in Moulmein, Mandalay, Bassein and other towns and cities. In 1906 these coalesced as the YMBA (Young Men's Buddhist

Association), consciously modelled on the YMCA (Young Men's Christian Association) – that 'born-again' self-improvement movement founded during a meeting of young evangelicals in the churchyard of St Paul's Cathedral in London in 1844.

For a decade the YMBA remained a somewhat nebulous, rarefied affair, mainly middle-class and with close ties to a reviving interest in Burman history and Burman literature. But in 1916 the YMBA shifted into the political arena. Sponsoring an 'All Burma' conference of Burmese Buddhists at Rangoon's Jubilee Hall (built to commemorate Queen Victoria's Diamond Jubilee of 1897), the Association brought an old skeleton out of the cupboard. The colonial British never removed their shoes when entering the precincts of a pagoda. Such disrespect was not only sacrilegious; it symbolised the subjection of the Burman people.

The revival of the 'shoe controversy' (which, in a different context, had so bedevilled Anglo-Burman relations in the nineteenth century), was both serious in itself and emblematic of a wider disaffection. In effect, Buddhism – the very essence of Burman existence – had become disestablished. Although the deliberations of the 1916 conference had little impact on the colonial administration, they caught the attention of the Burman public, sparking the first anti-colonial massed rally in the capital.

Burman nationalism was back on the agenda, confirmed four years later when the YMBA, amalgamating with other patriotic organisations that had sprung up in the interim, re-created itself as the General Council of Burman Associations, or GCBA. This time around, however, the leading lights were not monks or professors, but English-trained lawyers, among them U Chit Hlaing, a native of Moulmein, and U Ba Pe, editor of the Rangoon-based *Sun*, the first English-language newspaper run by Burmese.

It was against this background that the student protests of 1920, strongly supported by the GCBA, exploded. As in India, the British needed a steady flow of literate natives to serve as clerks in Burma. As the colony developed, there was a need for some properly trained individuals. But there was a reluctance to concede that education was an end or a right in itself. The monastery schools were left alone, but as regards the core Burman population – in the ethnic hinterlands there were any number of missionary schools – no great effort was made to raise educational standards, except in the main conurbations. By 1920 there were only two colleges in the entire country. One was Rangoon College, which had grown out of the Rangoon Government High School, founded in 1873. The other was the American Baptist College, also in Rangoon, later called Judson College and sometimes disparagingly known as the 'Karen College'.

In 1920 Sir Reginald Craddock, the Lieutenant-Governor of Burma (still an annexe of India), proposed creating Rangoon University. This would be done by affiliating the American Baptist and Rangoon Colleges. But Craddock's plan was definably elitist. The blueprint for Rangoon University was the University of Calcutta, which in turn had been modelled on the residential English Oxbridge (Oxford and Cambridge) pattern. Only those students whose families could afford big fees were to be admitted; and the syllabus was to be limited to a narrow spectrum of the 'humanities'.

Craddock's scheme was met with derision and a series of damaging strikes, prompted by the students of Rangoon College. In December 1920 they staged a well-publicised 'camp-out' at the Shwedagon pagoda. It took time, but a University Amendment Act of 1924 delivered what the students and the GCBA wanted. Admission to Rangoon University was to be based on ability, not just wealth, and its curriculum was correspondingly broadened, to include technical and scientific subjects. Further, and just as crucially, the Rangoon University contretemps led to the creation of the National Schools. If it was right that those Burmese youths with the most aptitude should attend university, then it was also fair that, around the country, such youngsters should be identified through a 'modern' educational system at secondary level, subsidised (but not governed) by the colonial state.

Although the GCBA had been instrumental in achieving these gains, it was the students who claimed the victory, and with it a prominent and abiding role in the politics of patriotic nationalism. But other factors were involved. Within two years the united front implicit in the GCBA split into two main factions, between the followers of U Chit Hlaing and U Ba Pe. The majority followed U Chit Hlaing, who argued passionately in favour of 'Home Rule' (already the terminology of Irish nationalism was impinging upon Burmese affairs): Burma should be completely divorced from India and given as much autonomy as possible, in the hope that this would lead to full independence. A minority sided with the more 'moderate' U Ba Pe, who urged that Burma should stick with India, if only because – thanks to the left-leaning but tolerated

Congress Party there – anti-colonial politics had reached a far more advanced stage than in Burma. By tagging along, Burma might hope to recover its autonomy sooner rather than later.

At the heart of the split within the GCBA was the matter of 'dyarchy'. Following the Mutiny, or Great Uprising, of 1857, the British had slowly recognised that India was, in the long term, ungovernable except through some kind of power-sharing with Indians themselves. The art was to restrict such power-sharing to a bare minimum. Key areas of decision-making – foreign policy, defence, taxation and macro-economic management, for example – should remain firmly under British control. But, if it helped diffuse colonial antagonisms, then by all means, through a complicated apparatus of partly elected advisory councils, allow Indians to have a say in such matters as educational and health-care provision, agricultural management, forestry and urban planning.

In 1917, as a result of the Montagu-Chelmsford Report, Britain had accepted the 'self-government' of India as a legitimate long-term goal, but at the same time neatly avoided setting out any timetable for a more meaningful transfer of power. Dyarchy was formally introduced into India in 1919. Because Burma was still part of India, some of the new 'reforms' necessarily filtered through to Rangoon. A Government of Burma Act, 1921, provided for an advisory Executive Council, some of whose members should be native Burmese. Then in 1923 Burma became a full gubernatorial province of India, no longer subordinate to Calcutta, with a predominantly elected 103-member Legislative Council to 'assist' the appointed Governor (as the former Lieutenant-Governor now became). From this was extracted a smaller, streamlined Executive Council.

By its nature, dyarchy was ambivalent. Although it introduced some of the trappings of democracy into Burma – the electoral franchise was notably liberal for its times, the vote being given to all adults, women as well as men, aged eighteen or over – there was no disguising the fact that the Governor always had the final say in determining policy. Conversely, no sensible Governor would strive too hard to introduce policies that were opposed by a majority on the Legislative or Executive Councils.

Hence the division within the GCBA, with some feeling that to go along with dyarchy as constituted by the British was merely a form of surrender; others that it offered at least some way forward, in the face of *force majeure*.

This mixed response to dyarchy played into student as well as British hands. Soon enough, 'Burmese politics' devolved into heated arguments, and not a little mutual mud-slinging, between the two rival camps of U Chit Hlaing and the '21 Party' of U Ba Pe, which did little or nothing to advance the cause of independence.

There was one man, however, who saw through them both and resorted to armed rebellion.

Saya San (Hsaya San) was a former monk and sometime teacher, who had joined the GCBA at its inception, but left it in 1928. Claiming direct descent from the founder of the Konbaung Dynasty, King Alaungpaya – both were natives of Shwebo – and possessed of a temperamental, charismatic character, he raised support among the peasantry and younger monks of the upper Irrawaddy delta, proclaiming it his intention to hurl the British back into the sea whence they had come.

On 21st December 1930, Saya San threw down the gauntlet on a hill outside Tharrawaddy. The forces he had raised he called the Galon Army – the *galon* being, like the Indonesian *garuda*, a mythical eagle equipped to overcome and destroy the evil *naga*, or serpent-dragon, now represented by the *kala* British. For the next two years Saya San's adherents wreaked havoc in what had once been Lower Burma, even though Saya San himself was captured, then executed, as early as November 1931. By the time his rebellion was finally crushed, with the assistance of Karen soldiery, 3,000 of his followers had been killed, while another 8,000 languished in jail.

At the time the British dismissed the Saya San Uprising as something manic and archaic. Like the Chinese Boxer Rebellion of 1898–1900, it seemed to smack of oriental millenarianism. Those who participated in it wore amulets and other charms they mistakenly believed would render them immune to bullet and artillery shell alike. They indulged in seemingly incomprehensible rituals and incantations, and their bodies were tattooed with all manner of bestial symbol. But while about Saya San there was undoubtedly a misplaced grandeur of haughtiness, ordinary Burmans responded to his call-to-arms for entirely convincing reasons. Maurice Collis, the author of many informed books about South-East Asia and its history, who was serving in Burma at the time of the uprising, was among the few who grasped, however faintly, its real import. In *Trials in Burma* (1937) he wrote: 'The peasants rose because that was their way of expressing the national dislike of a foreign government. Every man and woman in Burma wanted to get rid of the English [*sic*] government, not because it was oppressive or lacking in good qualities, but because its policy was pro-English instead of being pro-Burman.'

Another trigger of the revolt was the burden of colonial taxation, combined with the predations of Indian *chettyars* and a slump in rice prices induced by the worldwide Great Depression. Tellingly, when Saya San and other 'rebels' were put in the dock during what amounted to a show trial, the two lawyers who pleaded their cause most forcefully, Dr Ba Maw and U Saw, rapidly became major figures in the Burmese political firmament. The losers were the two factions of the GCBA. Although each expressed sympathy with Saya San's aims, and secretly raised funds to feed and supply the Galon Army, neither unambiguously threw in its lot with him. Sensing how the rebellion would end, they declined to join him in the field.

For a younger, up-and-coming generation of Burman patriots, such pusillanimity was unwelcome. Saya San was quite as much a heroic revolutionary as he was a traditional *minlaung*, or royal pretender.

Saya San's rebellion coincided with the two years Aung San spent at the National School in Yenangyaung. Ba Win, his eldest brother charged with looking after him, was a full fourteen years older and performed his duties well. Taking Aung San into his household, he assumed the role of a wise father, enforcing discipline, but also encouraging open talk about Burmese affairs. Like many other National School teachers, Ba Win took a close, partisan interest in national politics. In all probability he was a formative influence on Aung San, instilling in his gifted younger brother that sense of selfless public duty that was to shape his career.

That Aung San was gifted was already becoming apparent. In 1930 he took a nationwide 'pre-high-school' examination, set by the government and applied in both National and monastic schools, and came out top. As a result he was awarded a scholarship, valued at ten *kyat* a month for three years, designed to help him through the last three grades of secondary education.

True to form, Aung San completed his studies at the National School in Yenangyaung in just two years. In 1932 he matriculated with an A grade, with distinctions in both Burmese literature and Pali, the formal language of Burmese Buddhism. These precocious successes did not affect his monthly stipend, which he was allowed to carry forward with him to Rangoon University. He also carried forward a rapidly maturing sense of political commitment. In Yenangyaung, as well as editing the school magazine, he was an eager participant in the school debating club. As even Aung San Suu Kyi was to acknowledge in her brief life of her father, *Aung San of Burma*, 'the style of his delivery was uninspiring', but 'his conviction and the thoroughness with which he prepared any subject he tackled earned him a reputation for eloquence'.

An example of such thoroughness, and of his growing commitment, occurred when he volunteered to defend the motion that 'The country is better than the city'. While for some this might have been an invitation to wax lyrical on the joys of a bucolic existence, Aung San turned it into an opportunity to eulogise all those Burmans who, though born and raised in the sticks, had rendered the nation great services. At the close of his schoolboy speech, he broadened his scope to include such famous country hicks as Abraham Lincoln. The aspiring pupil had done his homework. Aung San also availed himself of any opportunity to attend political meetings and rallies in Yenangyaung town, and developed an ability to mimic those he heard, not always with an intent to flatter. He joined the school student union, and constantly urged fellow members to devote themselves unstintingly to the national cause. But he was not always remembered kindly. Often gauche and unsocial, from adolescence onwards he seldom suffered fools gladly, and even his teachers considered him difficult, for all his academic promise. When, at the end of the summer holidays in 1931, his father U Pha died, Aung San had of necessity to delay his return to Yenangyaung. As his brother Aung Than later recorded in a sketch memoir, when Aung San was quizzed by the then headmaster as to why he had not come back for the start of term, he replied it was because his father had been taken ill. When asked if his father had recovered, he answered brusquely, 'He is dead.'

As Aung San sometimes stated after he had achieved national prominence, in an ideal world he would have preferred to pursue a life of scholarship and detachment; but, given the condition Burma was in, to have done so would have been an abrogation of his responsibilities as part of a young elite. He never made any bones about coming from a relatively privileged background. Unlike Mao Zedong or Pol Pot, both of whom pretended to have climbed from the bottom of the social pile, he did not attempt to conceal his origins. He was determined to use whatever advantages he enjoyed for the common good.

In a speech delivered to a meeting of the East and West Association at the City Hall in Rangoon in August 1945, Aung San remarked, with some bitterness, that 'Part of the [Burmese middle class] became rich and joined the British imperialist side as officials, rice-millers, brokers, merchants, money lenders, absentee landlords, etc.' Such a path seems never to have been contemplated by Aung San himself. Nor, from perhaps as early as his Yenangyaung days, and coached by Ba Win, did Aung San hold any brief for conflating politics and religion. During the 1920s and 1930s two Buddhist monks, U Ottama and U Wisara, were at the forefront of the nationalist awakening. Both were imprisoned by the British for their outspokenness at public gatherings; and inside jail both went on hunger strike to gain their release. Such actions commanded the respect and love of a majority of the Burman people, as Aung San conceded in his 1945 City Hall address: 'When the Rev. Ottama, who was the Buddhist priest leader in those days, thundered "Craddock: go back!" to Sir Reginald Craddock who was the Lt Governor of Burma at that time, all people thrilled to the marrow of their bones to hear such bold talk from their brave leader.'

But while privately Aung San adhered to the religion of his forefathers, acquiring much of his moral compass from that faith, the vision he had for his country was secularist from the outset.

In the years after Yenangyaung, Aung San would toy with an array of political creeds and fashions, Marxism and fascism among them. Essentially he was a left-leaning pragmatist, for whom the liberation of his countrymen from the stranglehold of foreign domination took precedence over any particular dogma.

In this respect he was not unlike the young Ho Chi Minh, twenty-five years Aung San's senior. Determined to rid Vietnam of the French, Ho was eventually driven into the embrace of communism. Without Chinese and then Soviet support, he was powerless to overcome his foes. But in the immediate aftermath of the Second World War, Ho was more open-minded. Unsuccessfully, he tried to enlist the backing of US President Harry Truman for his nationalist movement.

For Aung San too, tough choices lay ahead. In another Burmese age, he might have entered the Buddhist *Sangha* just as much as he might have entered royal service, and bowed his way towards venerability. In her short biography, Aung San Suu Kyi tells us that while at Yenangyaung 'the sorrow of his father's death had filled him with a desire to become a monk'; and that when he first went to Rangoon he 'apparently conceived a great admiration for an Italian Buddhist monk, U Lawkanada'. That

– despite an obvious appetite for scholarship and learning – he did not become a monk defined the youthful Aung San, just as it defined some other young Burmese he now encountered at Rangoon University. Until the British were expelled, any non-political aspiration should be laid aside.

VII

FROM CAMPUS ODDBALL TO NATIONAL HERO (AGED 20)

I should like to know English better, and perhaps even take a shot at the examination of the Indian Civil Service. After I pass I could throw the job away, as Subbhas Chandra Bose did, and go into politics. Then the country as well as the Government would look up to me for my education as well as my dedicated purpose.

Aung San, 1936, in Bo Tun Hla, *Bogyoke Aung San*

THE Saya San Uprising crushed, and the economy slowly recovering, for close on four years the colonial government in Burma was able to relax. More businesses were getting started, more schools and colleges were opening, and increasingly Burman Burmese – in the towns and cities at least – seemed to understand that it was better to swim with the 'English' tide than against it. In the Legislative Council there were some fractious members, but usually they bored each other to death with interminable diatribes, U Ba Pe setting a record on the 6th and 7th of May 1933, when he rose to his feet in the chamber at Government House and spoke for forty hours non-stop. Even Rangoon University, the scene of those untoward disturbances in 1920, had apparently been tamed. When Aung San enrolled there for a combined BA course in literature and languages (including Pali) in September 1932, the majority of students were compliant and well heeled. The university, as it was intended to, offered them the chance to rise above the common ruck, to get on in life. A bit of hard work now, a little (but not too much) interim seriousness, and the clever cat would get the cream.

The year before Aung San's arrival the university authorities – in effect the Governor of Burma's office, since the Governor was the *ex officio* Chancellor – had authorised the setting up of a Student Union, and this was bedding down well. Those students elected to be its officers came mainly from the 'smart set', young Burmese who dressed in Euro-American clothes, aped European manners and, if they could afford it, ate European food – a pathology of voluntary cultural displacement endemic in the Far East of the 1920s and 1930s, in non-colonial as well as colonial societies.

Since 1920, Rangoon University had expanded considerably, with several new faculties that occupied a generous, leafy 450-acre site on the western side of Lake Victoria (Inya Lake), well away from the city centre. Students from outside the capital were housed in campus dormitories during term time, and fees were around £50 a year. This was a considerable amount for most Burmese, but half of all students attending the university received bursaries and scholarships, so that higher education was affordable.

Most of the teaching staff were European, predominantly English and Scottish, and the ethos was similar to that of an English public school. Staff expected to be addressed as 'Sir' (more rarely as 'Madam'), and failure to comply with such etiquette could result in instant rustication. There was an unwritten code, amounting almost to systematic complicity, that those students who kowtowed to the authorities could expect to do better than those who did not. Examinations were set internally, not by an external board. Teachers noticed 'model' students, and would pull strings for them once they had graduated.

At first, the Union confined its activities in the main to organising sporting and social events, though, critically, it also hosted debates. Although it had been in part established to provide students with a forum for airing their grievances, not unlike the Legislative Council, it was expected that any dissent should end there.

In September 1932 Aung San was just seventeen, one of the youngest students at Rangoon University. Having shone at Yenangyaung National School, with all the benefits of being looked after by his brother Ba Win, he found himself just one among 2,000. Nor did the majority of his contemporaries share his nationalist enthusiasm. Taken into the 'Pegu' dormitory, he struggled to make friends. He had no time for the easy, feckless banter of student life, for small talk or idle 'hanging around'.

A rude rebuff awaited him during his first term, when he attended a debate sponsored by the Union. Held at the time of a nationwide election to the Legislative Council, the motion was a topic dear to Aung San's heart: that monks should not directly involve themselves in politics. The motion was proposed by Aung San's own brother, Aung Than, then a senior at the university. When discussion was thrown open to the floor, Aung San rose to give a speech he had prepared meticulously beforehand. The trouble was that the proceedings were conducted in English, and although the student from Natmauk had always done well at written English, he had never been taught by a native English speaker and his pronunciation of English words was barely comprehensible. Worse, Aung San looked a shambles. He wore his hair long, and his clothes were torn and dirty. This was not because he could not afford something decent to wear, but because appearances were of little consequence to him. He preferred to spend his money on books and going about town to attend talks and meetings, sometimes getting himself into trouble for arriving back at the campus after curfew. Those who got to know him at Rangoon University later remembered how he seldom washed his clothes, but wore them until they were unbearably soiled. Then he would borrow cleaner clothing from such friends as he had.

Withing moments of launching into his maiden speech at the Union the 'jeers and catcalls'* began. In front of him, Aung Than cringed with embarrassment.

Aung San was undeterred. He continued saying what he had to say until he had reached the end. Cleverly, he interspersed Pali phrases between his English, instead of Burman, so that if anyone was following him they would appreciate that he knew whereof he spoke. He was not against Buddhism – far from it. But those monks (and there were many) who openly supported this or that candidate standing for the Legislative Council not only demeaned themselves, in Aung San's view, but betrayed the intrinsically apolitical principles of their faith.

He persisted in having his say in other debates, however hostile the reception, and nearly always spoke well beyond the allotted time-limit. Inevitably, such behaviour marked him out as an eccentric. Nor did his behaviour away from the debating floor modify people's opinion. The tall, bespectacled Hla Pe – known to history as Let Ya, a *nom de guerre* adopted by him in 1941, and subsequently one of Aung San's closest

* See Aung San Suu Kyi, *Aung San* (1984)

comrades in the Burmese struggle for independence – recalled how as a student Aung San 'would often sit for hours, deep in his own thoughts. Talk to him, and he might not respond.'* Other contemporaries had similar recollections. Mya Sein commented how Aung San 'spoke loudly in short stilted sentences, either in Burmese or in English, with emphasis and a self-styled finality'; while the writer Dagon Taya found him 'crude, rude and raw', with time for nothing other than an obsessive interest in politics.†

Aung San himself was never concerned with what others thought of him, though he recognised the need to improve his presentation if he was to make headway as an activist in the cause of his people. He worked hard at his English. More than once he was caught declaiming the speeches of such celebrated British statesmen as Disraeli and Gladstone amongst the campus bushes. Even as a teenager, he was sufficiently savvy to grasp that some of the future's battles would have to be fought using the English tongue. Addressing, haranguing and educating ordinary Burmese in the only language most could understand was crucial; but so too was the expression of a coherent Burmese position in words that would be understood at Government House, or in Delhi and London.

He was an oddball, but an oddball of high purpose and relentless dedication. Only the cinema exercised any hold over him – as a young man Aung San was an avid movie-goer. Girls did not interest him, or sporting activities, or drunken partying with other students, or going to the theatre or music nights. Already he had committed himself single-mindedly to a cause that, to the last breath of his life, he would never let go.

Little by little Aung San impressed himself on those among his fellow students who shared his nationalistic enthusiasm. A small but definable group of assertive patriots at the university included Hla Pe (Let Ya). But it was not until the monosyllabically named Nu – destined, as U Nu, to become Burma's first post-independence Prime Minister – arrived on the scene that the group made headway in persuading a significant number of others to take a more pro-active stance.

Nu had already graduated from Rangoon University, taking an arts degree in 1929. Eight years Aung San's senior, he was born in 1907, a

* See Maung Maung ed., *Aung San of Burma* (1962)
† Ibid.

native of Wakema township in the heart of the Irrawaddy delta. In 1934 he returned to the campus to study law. In contact with Ba Maw and U Saw, the lawyers who had defended Saya San, Nu was president of the All-Burma Youth League, a body that had come into being as a result of student protests in Mandalay at the threatened closure (for cost-cutting reasons) of Mandalay College. He also had connections with the *Do-bama Asi-ayone*, 'We Burmese Association', set up in 1931 by Ba Thaung and Luy Maung, two patriotic politicians who were candidates during the 1932 Legislative Council elections.

Although to begin with the British did not take the *Do-bama Asi-ayone* at all seriously, it became one of the most effective anti-colonial movements in the period immediately prior to the Second World War. Famously, if with no great degree of formality, its leading members became known as *thakins*, or 'masters', a word previously reserved for officers and ranking officials in the British administration, much as *sahib* was used in India. By hijacking the soubriquet for their own purposes, young patriots not only cheekily 'made a point' – it was Burmans who should be masters of Burma – but openly declared their opposition to the government.

The title of *thakin* was earned, not ceremoniously conferred. You became a *thakin* when those around you began calling you one. But once merited, the title stuck and had the added lustre of being confined to a relatively narrow time-frame, 1931–42. Many of those who came to the forefront in mid-century Burma could justly boast that they were, or had been, *thakins*, Thakin Nu and Thakin Aung San being celebrated instances. After the war, however, there were no new *thakins*.

Nu had the same reservations about Aung San (who quickly joined the Youth League) as others. He was an awkward misfit, his character quite unlike Nu's own, which was gregarious, sympathetic and full of Burmese charm. But once the two young men understood that their aims were identical, a close friendship formed. Within months of Nu's returning to university at the start of the 1934–35 academic year, they were working together. Once this was seen, Hla Pe/Let Ya and others looked afresh at Aung San. Increasingly they were swayed by the subtlety of his arguments, drawn from an unusually eclectic reading of history and politics. They also appreciated his willingness to put in long hours organising and networking.

A significant development at this time was the appearance of several book clubs in Rangoon, which spared their members the full expense of having to purchase the books they wanted. Not all were serious-minded, but some (including one initially funded from the royalties of an immensely successful title written by Saya San) deliberately promoted mainly Western works of radicalism translated into Burmese, offering quite different fare from what could be found in the somewhat conservative (not to say censored) university library.

The best known was the *Nagani* ('Red Dragon') book club, founded in 1937 by a group that included the celebrated writer and *Do-bama* leader Thakin Kodaw Hmaing, as well as Nu. A more literary-minded individual than Aung San, Nu nurtured an ambition, never realised, to become 'the George Bernard Shaw of Burma'. Red Dragon published a dozen or so titles a year up to the outbreak of war with Japan. Among these were Shaw's polemical writings, John Strachey's *Theory and Practice of Socialism* and works by the prominent Indian communist Manabendranath Roy. Overall, the character of Red Dragon's list was Fabian and internationalist.

It was through the book clubs that for the first time Burmese readers became familiar with the writings of Marx, Engels, Lenin and other communist ideologues. Equally, Marxism was only one among several diets on offer. The English utilitarian John Stuart Mill's classic account *On Liberty* was also circulated, providing theoretical variety and choice.

Like most young idealists studying at college, Aung San swung pointedly to the left, just because the left – something entirely new to the Burmese mind – challenged the existing order. But he was not naïve about this. In so far as Marxism indicated a possible pathway for regaining Burma's independence, it demanded to be taken seriously. Whenever the independence movement stalled, Aung San would move closer to Marxism-Leninism, and later suspicions that he was a communist-manqué were not without substance. But he found something lacking in the communist creed. Its strident, atheistic 'materialism', characterising politics as the outcome of economic structures and economic activity and little else, was at odds with his inherited moral values. Marx & Co. furnished a pertinent critique of 'imperialism', the great sin of the British, but failed to accommodate the overarching humanity (let alone spirituality) of Buddhism.

If Nu assumed the leadership of the band of radical students that included, amongst others, Ko Ohn and an Indian Muslim intellectual, M.A. Rashid, during the course of 1935 Aung San came to be regarded as the clique's principal analyst. He had the sharpest brain, and he was the most methodical. In the long term, his critical scrutiny of competing ideologies may have been the decisive factor in preventing communism from becoming the mainstream of Burmese politics (as it did in China and Vietnam). Had he unambiguously embraced Marxism, he might have taken a whole generation with him. Instead he gravitated, albeit haltingly, towards a form of democratic socialism that he thought best suited to all the peoples of his country.

The more immediate task was to wrest control of the Rangoon University Student Union (RUSU), to ensure that the next generation of alumni went out into the greater Burmese world (and perhaps beyond) with their hearts and minds set on the right course. Throughout what the British persisted in calling the spring and summer of 1935 (in reality Burmese seasons follow an altogether different pattern), Nu, Aung San and the others worked assiduously to ensure a favourable result at the upcoming Union elections at the beginning of the next academic year.

Because of Nu's prominence in the All-Burma Youth League, he had already been elected vice-president of the Union, and used this position in debates and other meetings to advance his group's agenda. But each member of the group sounded out his fellow students individually, urging them in one-to-ones to take Burmese politics seriously and think about Burma's future.

It was this intensive grooming that won the day. It did not occur to those 'model' students who stood against Nu and his comrades that, in the face of a dedicated opposition, equal efforts were required. It was not enough to be captain of this or that sport to succeed in the ballot. There was a real battle to be fought. Nu was elected president of the Rangoon University Student Union. Elected to its committee, Aung San was given the responsibility of editing the Union's magazine, *Oway*.

In Burmese *oway* is onomatopoeic. It expresses the cry of the peacock, a traditional symbol of Burma that the Student Union had adopted as its emblem. Much later, towards the end of the century, the peacock would be incorporated into the flags of the All Burma Federation of Students Unions (ABFSU), the dissident All Burma Students' Democratic Front (ABSDF) and the National League for Democracy (NLD), co-founded by Aung San's daughter Suu Kyi.

Buoyed up by his electoral success, but refusing to let it go to his head, Aung San made the best possible fist of his stewardship of *Oway*.

Rather than turn it into a narrow agitprop publication of the victorious faction, he made it a broad-spectrum forum, stimulating debate about Burmese politics and culture. To this end he sought contributions from outside the university. His scoops included essays by well-known and popular Burman writers, among them Thakin Kodaw Hmaing. But he also solicited the views of more open-minded 'colonialists' such as J.S. Furnivall, a former civil servant and author of two books about Burma that did not shamelessly toe the imperialist line. As a result, the latest edition of *Oway* became an eagerly anticipated event among Burma's intelligentsia. Even the *Rangoon Gazette*, a semi-official publication, noted the aplomb with which Aung San had grasped the editorial nettle. But it was not just a matter of improving circulation. From the outset of his political career, Aung San saw the need to promote multilateral dialogue. Keenly aware of how fragmented Burma was, inclusivity (not exclusivity) became his game. Confronting the colonial authorities was unavoidable perhaps; but confrontation could only succeed if it had a broad backing amongst the people.

At last, but still precociously, Aung San was beginning to make a name for himself. The twenty-year-old began writing articles and essays for one or two of Burma's leading English-language periodicals: *World of Books* and *New Burma*. At the beginning of 1935 his degree examination was just three months away, but his energies remained focused on extracurricular activities, principally helping U Nu organise the Union's political agenda. This involved managing a series of guest speakers in the debating hall to talk up anti-colonial themes, among them Dr Ba Maw, U Saw and U Ba Pe. In addition he was busy nurturing contacts with younger activists outside the university.

One of these, Than Tun, a square-faced somewhat truculent young man, was enrolled at Rangoon's main teacher-training college. Already a committed Marxist, he quickly became another close companion. They attended meetings together and would sometimes talk late into the night. However, neither had any inkling where their friendship would lead: marriage to a pair of sisters, followed by a falling-out that was to have profound consequences for Burma.

As the 'cool' dry season readied to make way for the 'hot' dry season, the university authorities began getting nervous about a definable upsurge in student disquiet. Among grievances being openly aired was the high failure rate that usually attended degree examination results. But whose fault was that? Were standards unrealistically high? Or was it because the teachers were failing in their duties? Some students were slackers, but most were not.

It would take just one spark to start a fire, and this Nu provided. On 31st January 1936 he accused a senior university official of immorality. Or, to be precise, of visiting one of Rangoon's many back-street brothels. The issue was not one of simple sexual dalliance. How could the British claim to be so decent (as invariably they did) when they colluded in the physical abasement of young Burmese women?

High-level talks were held between the principal, J.D. Sloss, and Government House. Such incidents had to be handled cautiously. But it was intolerable that a Burmese student should challenge his white superior in such a way. And so three weeks later, on 21st February, judgement was handed down. Nu was expelled from the university.

There was no need for the Union to consider its response, for already another depth-charge was in the offing. Even as Nu was packing his bags, the latest edition of *Oway* rolled off the press. In it was an article purportedly written by the 'King of Hell' (*Yama-min*) entitled 'A Hell Hound at Large', which repeated the charge levelled by Nu, but in more vivid language. The 'Hell Hound' in question was 'a devil in the form of a black dog', 'a base object of universal odium and execration', a 'pimping knave with avuncular pretensions to some cheap wiggling wenches from a well-known hostel' covered with 'buboes and ulcers due to errant whoring', fit only to be 'sentenced to eternal damnation for churlishness, treachery, ruffianism, pettifogging, etc.'

The same article delivered a barely veiled attack on Sloss. Although he was not named, it was implied that the principal was equally culpable for not disciplining a university employee who behaved so badly.

Aung San did not write the piece – that honour belonged to a fellow student, Nyo Mya – but as the editor of *Oway* he was immediately hauled into the principal's office. Sloss demanded the name of the writer. Aung San refused point-blank to give it to him, and Sloss wasted no time in ordering his expulsion too, on 24th February.

Now there was uproar on the campus. The Union committee, convened hastily on the same day, considered what form of protest would be most effective. The following day a 'mass meeting' of students was called. Speaker after speaker stood up to denounce Sloss's actions. A 'strike' was called. Participating students should boycott lectures and refuse to sit any exams.

Up to one-third of Rangoon University's 2,000-odd students joined in. When the university gates were closed on them, they set up a 'strike camp' at the hallowed Shwedagon pagoda. Nu was elected president of a 'supreme' committee, and Aung San its secretary.

The switch to the Shwedagon, although partly induced by the authorities, was a masterstroke. Within days, a matter of student discipline had seized the whole of Rangoon's Burman community. The Burmese press was unanimous in defending the students' action, especially Aung San's principled refusal to divulge his contributor's identity. Here at last was someone of integrity, prepared to stand up full-square to the British. Various papers ran profiles of the student leaders, but it was always Aung San who had the edge in column inches.

Soon the Shwedagon camp grew in size, swelled by other students from Mandalay and elsewhere, and by sympathisers who had nothing to do with any university or college. Well-wishers streamed in from all around, bringing the 'strikers' money and food. Across Rangoon, 'native' white- and blue-collar workers either began underperforming or failed to show at their workplace. And people stopped buying British manufactured goods.

A more brutal regime would have sent in the troops. Instead, the Governor agreed in March to set up a government committee to investigate the student's grievances. Students should be represented on the University Council; they should not be punished for minor infringements of the university's rules and regulations; no action should be taken against those students who had responded to the strike call; such students should be allowed to sit their exams at a later date; the power of expulsion should be removed from the principal's hands; the University Act itself should be amended; and so forth. The Governor agreed to set up another committee, to look into ways of amending the University Act that was, in effect, Rangoon University's charter. Significantly, it was Aung San who was appointed the sole student representative on this second committee. While there was no question that he was one of the main ringleaders of what some now called the 'student revolt', it was tacitly acknowledged by the authorities that he would bring with him the voice of reasonableness.

The strike continued until the middle of the second week of May. A revised examination schedule was agreed, and none of the protestors would be expelled, rusticated or otherwise disciplined. Nu and Aung San were reinstated and, most satisfyingly of all, Sloss was prevailed upon to resign. In his place a Burman, U Pe Maung Tin, was appointed principal of Rangoon University.

This last 'concession' was hailed as a tremendous victory. It was not the first time in Burma that student power had prevailed, much less the first time in the Far East. In May 1919 student demonstrations in Beijing had famously forced the republican government of China to dismiss two senior and unpopular ministers, amid scenes of widespread violence and sympathetic industrial action – a pandemonium that had been closely monitored by resident British officials. The 1936 Rangoon students' strike was a better-tempered affair. Nonetheless, U Nu, Aung San and their comrades had demonstrated that collective action produces results.

Not all the students' demands were met, but enough for them to be able to hold their heads up high. In making concessions, the colonial government put on its usual graceful face. But behind closed doors it had been severely rattled. With their long experience in India, the British knew how such incidents could easily lead to wider unrest. In future the likes of Nu and Aung San would have to be watched with the utmost vigilance.

VIII

'1300': THE YEAR THAT NEVER WAS

To be a subject nation is like someone lost in a forest after midnight in a waning moon ... Even in my sleep, I used to cry in anger over the lack of freedom of my country.

Aung San, 'The Struggle for Burmese Independence',
in *Bama Khit* (Burma Era), 1st August 1943

DESPITE the amnesty offered to the striking students, Aung San did not sit his degree examination in 1936. His politicking had badly interrupted his studies, so he waited until 1937. His BA secured, he then followed Nu's example and re-enrolled at Rangoon University to take a law degree. The authorities hoped that he could be brought within the pale of legitimate activity by giving him the opportunity to pursue an 'establishment' career. But at the end of the academic year, in mid-1938, he failed the first part of the new course. Again, too many other things had been on his mind.

This time he threw in the academic towel, and with it any plans to sit the Civil Service examinations, which he had briefly considered as a way of undermining the 'system' from within. Writing to his mother in Natmauk, Aung San said he would not be coming home for the long vacation, but had decided instead to 'enter politics' – as though, for the last three years, he had been squatting idly on the sidelines.

Much had happened in the interim. Formally, the biggest change to affect Burma resulted from a Government of Burma Act, shunted through the British Parliament in 1935 by Stanley Baldwin's Conservative administration. As with India, where the Congress Party had orchestrated nationwide pressure against the imperial mandate, Burma was to be granted a degree of self-government, as from 1st April 1937. It was even to have its own native Prime Minister, presiding over a native cabinet. But still it was a halfway house. Although the legislation allowed for a bicameral parliament in Rangoon, forty out of 132 seats in the legislative Lower House (House of Representatives) were earmarked for special ('communal') interest groups, among them Indians, Chinese, Karens and representatives of industry – that is, British business concerns. Further, the Governor's veto remained intact. Although some ninety-one departments were allocated to Burmese control, creating endless opportunities for corruption and with it a rapid disillusionment with parliamentary politics, regulation of the military, foreign affairs and national taxation were to be 'reserved' to the colonial authority. The ethnic Frontier Areas were also excluded from the Act's provisions.

The *thakins* of the *Do-bama Asi-ayone* attacked the Act from the beginning, dismissing it as a means of perpetuating dyarchy. Come 1st April 1937, a group of students from Rangoon University, Nu amongst them, burned the Union Jack on the steps of the High Court. Even so, elections held in 1936 ahead of the implementation of the new constitution (Burma's first) were keenly contested and attracted a tolerable turn-out. The *Dol-bama Asi-ayone*, under the guise of the *Komin Kochin* ('Own King, Own Kind') party, entered the contest late. With little by way of grass-roots organisation, it won a bare two seats, on the back of 100,000 votes. Dr Ba Maw, together with his *Sinyetha* ('Poor Man's') party, fared rather better, winning sixteen seats in the House. A blatant demagogue who promised voters unrealistic tax cuts, sweeping land reforms and free education for all, Ba Maw skilfully exploited divisions within such other parties as won some seats, and put together a coalition that duly enabled him to become Burma's first 'elected' Prime Minister.

For Aung San, Ba Maw's success was an irrelevance. Though in his own way Ba Maw could be counted a patriot, his demagoguery did not yet extend to a serious engagement with progressive ideas, and he made too many compromises with the colonial regime. Moreover the man was unconscionably vain, as indeed were other seasoned Burman politicians such as U Saw. Only full Burmese independence and the removal of every vestige of British rule mattered to Aung San. Yet, ever the realist, he did not overestimate his own hand. However much he may have thought truth and justice were on his side, he knew he was still a minor fish and that there was everything to play for. The important thing was to maintain the momentum of the student movement.

During the earlier part of 1937 Aung San threw himself into the creation of an All Burma Student Union, which, thanks largely to his efforts, held a first conference at Mandalay in April. At the same time he encouraged student activists to go out amongst the people and meet peasants and workers, not just to promote the cause of independence, but to listen to and learn from them.

At the end of the year Aung San saw himself re-elected as secretary of the Rangoon University Student Union, with M.A. Rashid (a Muslim intellectual) becoming president: an arrangement that entirely suited Aung San, who at this stage preferred the role of hard-grafting back-seater. Before he finally left the university, Aung San moved into the Union building, taking his bedding with him. He had already left 'Pegu' dormitory after a clash with its warden about his late nights, and transferred to another whose Burmese warden was more understanding. It made better sense to Aung San if he lived where he worked. Asked one day why he had not rigged up a mosquito net, he replied that since he was a revolutionary, and must therefore sooner or later expect a spell of imprisonment, it was only appropriate that he toughened up.

At the end of April 1938 he gave the keynote address at the second All Burma Student Union conference, convened at Bassein. In it, he delivered a stinging attack on British educational policies. Far from advancing the cause of education in Burma, he declared, the colonial authority was holding the nation back. Students should therefore prepare themselves 'physically as well as mentally' for a long campaign to achieve their rights.

This was the closest Aung San had yet come to intimating that armed struggle might become a necessity, though he was careful not to employ those actual words.

In the Burmese calendar April 1938 marked the beginning of a new century. Lasting until April 1939, '1300' was to go down in Burmese history as 'The Year of Revolution'.

Trouble first flared up at the end of August. Not for the first time there were race riots in Rangoon, fuelled by escalating rice prices. The import of low-paid Indian and Chinese workers, particularly at the docks, had long been a grievance among the capital's Burmese labour force.

There had been 'communal unrest', as the British chose to call it, in

1930, when scores were left dead. Now downtown Rangoon erupted again, and the unrest spread to other parts of the city, with even greater casualties on both sides. There was a spate of arson attacks, mainly against shops owned by Indian Muslims, and much looting. Nor, it was claimed, did the colonial security forces – police and troops – intervene swiftly enough to restore order.

The *Do-bama Asi-ayone*, the driving force of the independence movement, kept out of these disturbances. Towards the end of the year, however, it played a major role in supporting – even orchestrating – a fresh wave of anti-British protests.

By then Aung San was firmly embedded in the *Do-bama* leadership. Once he had made up his mind to quit Rangoon University, in line with his expressed desire to 'enter politics', he joined the *Do-bama Asi-ayone* as being the most likely platform to effect change. And he persuaded Nu to come with him. Although Nu had had many dealings with the Association, he had been reluctant to commit himself to any one party. But, with characteristic incisiveness, Aung San put it to him: did he want to become a *thakin,* or did he want to remain a *kyun* – a slave – for the rest of his life?

At the time of their joining there was a split within the *Do-bama Asi-ayone*. A majority of members, loyal to Thakin Kodaw Hmaing, favoured increased militancy and radicalisation. The minority followed Ba Sein, who was characterised as a moderate and therefore accused of being a collaborator, though he was not. The two leaders were not in fact so far apart politically. But there was a degree of the personal rivalry that has long bedevilled Burmese politics, and which was eventually to cost Aung San his life.

At the heart of such rivalry is the cult of the 'big man', universal enough perhaps, but affecting non-Burman as well as Burman Burmese more than most. As one leading dissident of the 1990s put it to me, 'The decision every ambitious Burmese must make is not whether to betray his leader, but when.'

Aung San, who always eschewed assuming the airs of the big man, even after he had become the national leader, chose to attach himself to Kodaw Hmaing, a former monk as well as writer, whose commitment to independence and socialism was as voluble as it was passionate. For his part, Kodaw Hmaing recognised the younger man's exceptional qualities. 'Thakin' Aung San was appointed general secretary of the majority *Do-bama Asi-ayone*, with Nu its treasurer. With Kodaw

Hmaing's full backing, they worked together to turn the Association into a fully functional party, with representatives in all Burma's main towns and cities. What had started as a jest at the expense of the British became a political force of real magnitude.

Aung San's labours bore fruit towards the end of the same year, 1938. In all three of Burma's main oilfields – at Yenangyaung, Chauk and Magwe – discontent among the Burmese workforce was rife. Wages had not kept pace with inflation, and working conditions were deteriorating. In November a strike was called, and by the beginning of December 1,000 oil workers had begun a long march towards Rangoon. Simultaneously, 20,000 agricultural labourers, angered by the refusal of either the colonial authorities or Ba Maw's cabinet to protect their interests against unscrupulous landlords and money-lenders, assembled at different points in Pegu to begin their own march on the capital. And as if this two-pronged protest were not enough, 3,000 students came out on the streets in sympathy.

The British reacted vigorously. Road blocks were mounted to halt the marchers, and many ringleaders were arrested – a relatively easy procedure as the British had taken care to improve their intelligence-gathering. Although some of the oil workers, and some of the peasants, did reach Rangoon, they were only a fraction of the numbers who had set out. But it did not end there. On 13th December there was a massed student rally at Rangoon University, followed by a noisy but non-violent demonstration outside the Secretariat building in the heart of Rangoon a week later.

The police moved in with their batons, and beat one student so violently that he died in hospital two days later, on 22nd December. Abruptly the Burmese 'revolution' had its first martyr. Aung Gyaw had never been a prominent activist, but his death created a furore.

Although the demonstration outside the Secretariat was broken up, it was quickly followed by others, not all of them so peaceable, and with increasing numbers of younger monks participating. Thousands of high-school pupils staged a classroom walk-out to show their solidarity. At Mandalay on 10th February 1939 the colonial police, no longer willing to restrict their crowd-control methods to the odd baton charge, opened fire on a large gathering at the Aindawya pagoda. Seven monks, nine protestors and one child were killed; many more were wounded.

Throughout these disturbances the hand of the *Do-bama Asi-ayone*, and in particular of Aung San, was felt. Although when he joined the

Association, Aung San relinquished his positions in both the Rangoon University Student Union and the All Burma Student Union, his *de facto* leadership of the student movement continued unchallenged. It may therefore be assumed that it was Aung San who coordinated the nationwide student actions in support of the strikers, just as it was Aung San who created a Labour Organisation from within the Association, which provided food, shelter and other forms of sustenance to strikers and marchers.

For his efforts, Aung San was briefly imprisoned. As it became clearer that the colonial authority had no intention of offering any further significant concessions, the *Do-bama Asi-ayone* announced, on 18th January 1939, that if necessary force could, and should, be used to topple the government. As in 1936, a protest camp had been set up at the Shwedagon pagoda. There, students and *thakins* mixed, exchanging ideas and plans; and there, on 23rd January, the police arrived in numbers. Aung San was among several arrested and taken away to the main colonial jail at Insein, a Karen township several miles to the north of the city. He would, he was told, be tried for treason, which potentially carried the death penalty. But fifteen days later he was released without charge. The *Do-bama Asi-ayone* had astutely announced, on 3rd February, that its 'headquarters' were now to be found at Insein. Then, on 6th February, such members of its executive committee as remained at liberty issued a resolution calling for nationwide demonstrations to protest against the detentions. Aung San was set free the following day. The British had no intention of creating a national martyr whose name, unlike Aung Gyaw's, was widely known. Not since the Saya San Uprising of 1931 had the situation been so tense.

Aung San himself was at liberty again when the Mandalay massacre took place. Like millions of his fellow countrymen, he was stunned by the callous action of the colonial police. Aung Gyaw's death could have been interpreted as a tragic mishap, but to gun down unarmed protestors, holy men amongst them, was something else entirely.

On 12th February 1939 Dr Ba Maw was forced to resign as Prime Minister, after losing a vote of no confidence in the legislature. His administration had, all along, been an inglorious affair. His government had singularly failed to provide either popular leadership or a channel of constructive communication to the Governor (Sir Archibald Douglas Cochrane).

In the week preceding Ba Maw's ousting his mock-funeral had been staged in Rangoon, to the delight of hundreds of 'mourners'. However, Ba Maw's resignation was not a prelude to a more resourceful, pro-nationalist government. After the inevitable coalition haggling, he was replaced by the ineffectual U Pu; and within days Ba Maw had rejoined the cabinet, as Minister of Forests.

On the face it, nothing had changed. Come April 1939 and the beginning of the Burmese year of 1301, the British still ruled the roost, and potentially destabilising troubles had been seen off. The Burman population might desire independence, but did not have the means to gain it, while the non-Burman population remained for the most part quiescent and cooperative. Elsewhere in the world, however, there were other developments that would soon transform the situation not just in Burma, but throughout Asia, rendering European colonies there finally untenable.

IX

DESPERATE TIMES, DESPERATE REMEDIES

In political matters Aung San was a bundle of obsessions that would flare out most unexpectedly, but on account of their very intensity those rages could not last very long; a nervous exhaustion would follow quickly and send him into almost a stupor or a sulk. That was his strength as well as his weakness in a crisis. It was also this that made it confusing to deal with him at times, unless of course you had come to know him and waited for him to exhaust himself, and then he was often easy to handle, as the Japanese discovered before their defeat became certain.
Ba Maw, *Breakthrough in Burma: Memoirs of a Revolution* (1968)

JAPAN, hitherto a highly cultured but inward-looking island-nation that for centuries steered clear of any international involvement, had, in the most dramatic fashion, entered the geopolitical arena.

In the latter stages of the nineteenth century, following the 'Meiji Restoration' of 1868, Japanese reformers had understood that the only way to withstand the tide of European imperialism was to imitate it and industrialise. As early as 1905 Japan shocked the West by destroying a Russian fleet in the Strait of Tsushima using modern warships. A few months beforehand it had also defeated a Russian land army at Mukden (modern Shenyang) in Manchuria, north-eastern China.

The war with Russia began with a surprise attack on the Manchurian port of Lushun (then called Port Arthur), where a squadron of Russian naval vessels was anchored. For decades the 2,000-year-old Chinese imperial throne had been tottering towards its final collapse of 1911–12. The 'Great Powers', which now included the United States, had wasted no opportunity to make inroads on the Chinese economy. Famously, the British had led the way, using opium grown in India to open up Chinese markets. But although rivalry between Western powers was often cut-throat, there was an understanding that no one power would attempt to seize all of China for itself. Instead, business was conducted through a series of 'treaty ports' dotted up and down the long Chinese coastline, each having an 'international concession' where Chinese law did not apply, and where Americans, French, Germans, Russians and Italians as well as British warily rubbed shoulders.

The Japanese had other ideas. Having already taken possession of Korea, in 1931 they seized the whole of Manchuria – originally the homeland of the Mongolian Manchus, who, as the Qing Dynasty, ruled over China from 1644 until the birth of the Republic of China in 1912. But Manchuria (or Manchukuo, as the Japanese called it) was only the prelude to a greater ambition, which was to annex the whole of China.

The Japanese conquest of China proper began in 1937, with the occupation of first the capital Beijing (Peking) in July, then Shanghai in August. In December, Nanjing (Nanking) was overrun. An estimated 200,000 Chinese civilians were massacred.

That the Japanese were able to advance so swiftly had something to do with Western apathy, but much more to do with China's internal disarray. Despite some economic and social successes, the Republic had never truly established itself. Up until 1928 much of the former empire was crippled by infighting between opportunist warlords, while after 1928, although the leader of the Guomindang (Nationalist) party, Chiang Kai-shek (Jiang Jieshi), virtually put an end to warlordism, he found himself locked in mortal combat with a new force in the land, the Chinese communists. Chiang thought the communists a greater threat than the Japanese, whom he dismissed as 'dwarf-pirates'. Instead of building up Chinese defences around Beijing after the loss of Manchuria against further Japanese incursions, he committed his forces to a long and debilitating campaign aimed at dislodging the communists (the 'local pirates') from their mountainous 'base areas'. Nor, as 'Generalissimo', was Chiang able to maintain his popular following. The regime over which he presided was habitually corrupt, with well-canvassed connections to China's criminal underworld and its mafia-like Triads.

The winners, in the short as well as the long term, were the communists, from January 1935 led by the charismatic and tactically brilliant Mao

Zedong (Mao Tse Tung). Under Mao's direction, the Chinese Communist Party wasted no time declaring Japan to be the national enemy, and made several well-publicised efforts to form a united front with Chiang Kai-shek's Guomindang. The communists successfully projected themselves as the anti-corruption party, and created a huge following among China's hundreds of millions of peasants.

Chiang suffered defeat after defeat, both on the battlefield and politically. Yet, supported by the West (most of all the United States), he managed to cling on. Whereas the Japanese had little difficulty in sweeping down China's populous eastern seaboard, occupying every major city, the vast interior of China was a different proposition. From late 1938 Chiang was able to establish a new headquarters, at Chongqing, in the landlocked, western province of Sichuan. Despite their every effort, the Japanese were unable to dislodge him. But to survive vigorous aerial bombardment by the Japanese, he needed continuous supplies of weapons and other war materiel. Because the Japanese enjoyed air superiority over China, and had gained control of most of its rail and road networks, this meant looking in another direction: India. But to reach India meant creating a supply line through the neighbouring province of Yunnan, and through Burma.

So was born the 'Burma Road'. Construction began in 1938. The plan to connect Chongqing to both Assam and Rangoon would inexorably draw Burma into hostilities. For the Japanese knew that if they could cut the Burma Road, then Chiang was finished. And the way to do that was to annex Burma itself.

The Japanese were politically as well as militarily audacious. In November 1938 they declared it their intention to create a 'Greater Co-prosperity Region' throughout East Asia. Playing on the nationalist aspirations of those peoples who had come under Western domination, they promised independence. This was demonstrably a fiction. Four years earlier they had installed the 'last Emperor', Puyi, who as a boy had been bundled from his throne during the Chinese republican revolution of 1911, as the emperor of Manchukuo. In reality he was nothing more than a Japanese pawn, with no actual power of any kind. Yet it was a fiction that some of the 'oppressed' peoples of East Asia, among them a growing number of Burmans, willingly subscribed to. Despite reports of horrors committed in Nanjing and other Chinese communities ravaged by Japan – women subjected to multiple rape, men tied to stakes for bayonet practice – it was difficult for them to believe that fellow orientals could treat each other with the measured contempt meted out by Europeans.

At the same time it was becoming clearer by the day that Europe itself was also heading for war. Germany had lost out badly to its European competitors in the headlong rush to acquire overseas territories. Up until a process of 'unification' masterminded by Count Otto von Bismarck in the mid-nineteenth century, Germany had subsisted as a patchwork of electorates and smaller principalities without a coherent foreign policy. It had therefore suffered economic disadvantage, being unable – unlike Britain, France, Holland and others – to rely on cheap raw materials from distant places and ready-made colonial markets for its manufactured goods.

Germany attempted to achieve parity during the Great War of 1914–18, but defeat left it inherently unstable. In these circumstances Adolf Hitler and his National Socialist (Nazi) Party persuaded the German people that the way forward was a fascist programme that combined extreme militarism with a surrender of social liberties and a recidivist racism – features that were not only emulated by the Italian dictator and Hitler's ally Benito Mussolini, but were copied in Japan of the 1930s.

Remote as these developments were from the Irrawaddy river system geographically, in an era of rapidly accelerating economic and political exchange it could only be a matter of time before their impact was felt by all Burmese.

When the annual conference of the *Do-bama Asi-ayone* met at Moulmein in April 1939 there was an air of despondency and self-recrimination. Some senior *thakins* openly attacked the twenty-four-year-old Aung San, accusing him of high-handedness in his dealings with others. Aung San made no attempt to rebut such criticism. Instead he spoke about the likelihood of war in Europe, and urged his comrades to adopt a policy of non-cooperation with the British as and when hostilities commenced – unless the British first agreed to give an assurance that independence would be granted once the coming war was over. While some thought he was being overly imaginative, he was nevertheless re-elected as the Association's general secretary.

At the time Aung San was living at the *Do-bama Asi-ayone*'s headquarters, a small office in Yegyaw Street, just as he had previously lived in the Student Union building at Rangoon University. Apart from small fees from freelance journalism and editorial work for underfunded

Burmese publications, he had no income to speak of and was obliged to rely on gifts from friends. His appearance was as scruffy as before. He did not always feed himself well, and in Yegyaw Street he was sometimes mistaken for an errand boy. His immediate aim was to continue building up *Do-bama* as a viable mass party. Yet, like others amongst his close associates, he was exercised by questions of long-term strategy. Was there in fact any chance that the British could be persuaded to surrender power by peaceful means? Was there any way that what he would later, in a speech delivered at the City Hall in Rangoon on 29th August 1945, call the 'thin democratic façade' erected by the British might be exploited to overcome the entrenched bureaucracy they had also brought with them?

Like other radicals of his own and later times, Aung San believed that the real enemy was the capitalist system itself, with its global extension, its hunger for resources and raw materials, and its willingness to subjugate entire nations that were economically less developed. But following the failures of '1300', it was perhaps inevitable that he should look at all the options, and adopt an even more militant stance. It was not that Burmese nationalists, especially the students, hadn't tried hard; they hadn't tried hard enough.

In this mood, Aung San reconsidered the liberationist credentials of Marxism. Together with sympathisers such as Hla Pe (Let Ya), Thein Pe Myint and Ba Hein, on 19th August 1939 he set up a new group meeting, in Barr Street, that some historians have identified as the precursor of the Burmese Communist Party, if not its actual origin. Again, Aung San was appointed general secretary. There is no evidence, however, that the group did anything other than discuss topical issues within a framework of Marxist ideology. No attempt was made to link up with either the Soviet Communist Party or its Chinese counterpart. Nor did it prepare any propaganda for dissemination among the 'proletariat'. Its only 'international' dimension was with Indian communists, who were the group's inspiration. Thein Pe Myint had spent some time studying in India, and through his connections the well-known Bengali communist B. N. Dass, on a visit to Rangoon, addressed an early meeting.

At the same time, under Aung San's influence, the *Do-bama Asi-ayone* adopted a definably Marxist iconography. The hammer-and-sickle was incorporated into its flag, and the image of a peasant walking into a bright, sunlit future became a fixture on *Do-bama* posters and publications. But the Barr Street group soon disbanded. Aung San was the first to drop out: not necessarily because he had lost heart in Marxist prescriptions – his attitude towards communism remained ambivalent until a few months before his death – but because, in line with his own predictions, on 3rd September Britain declared war on Germany, in the wake of its invasion of Poland. It was no time for partisan politics, the more so since eleven days earlier Hitler and Soviet leader Josef Stalin had signed a non-aggression pact.

Aung San's response to the outbreak of war was to create a 'Freedom Bloc' that, modelled on Subhas (Subash) Chandra Bose's Bengali 'Forward Bloc', was designed to bring a broad spectrum of Burmese nationalists under a single umbrella. Setting aside whatever reservations he had about the man, Aung San called at once on Dr Ba Maw, whose *Sinyetha* party was still the largest patriotic grouping in the Rangoon parliament. Ba Maw agreed to Aung San's proposal, on the understanding that he would be the compact's designated leader. As early as 6th September the Freedom Bloc issued a preliminary manifesto, reputedly drafted by Aung San himself in under two hours. Its message was that while the Freedom Bloc was staunchly 'anti-fascist', 'both ruled and rulers must fulfil their duties'. The British could count on Burmese support in their war against Hitler, but only if they first consulted with the elected Burmese parliament, and only if they gave a guarantee of post-war independence.

Significantly, Aung San did not approach U Saw, the other leading parliamentary patriot, who had broken with Ba Maw in April 1939 to form his *Myochit* ('Patriot') party. U Saw was in the vanguard of those Burmese politicians who looked to Japan for inspiration and a resolution of Burma's quest for independence. Under his proprietorship the *Sun* newspaper regularly extolled the 'new politics' propagated by Japan, and published translated extracts from Hitler's *Mein Kampf*.

Aung San did not consider U Saw an appropriate bedfellow. His greater concern, however, was the response of the colonial authorities, and in particular the negative response of the latest Governor of Burma, Sir Walter Booth. Far from accepting that there was a *quid pro quo* on offer, Booth took the view that the Freedom Bloc's proposal was tantamount to blackmail. By simple virtue of being a British colony, Burma too was at war with Germany (and with Mussolini's Italy). There was therefore no need to consult with the Rangoon parliament, let alone contemplate any 'deal'. Anyone who advocated otherwise was a traitor to the Empire.

Booth was supported by Prime Minister U Pu, who resisted Aung San's attempts to persuade him to join the Bloc: proof, if one were needed, that at this stage even Burman attitudes towards the British were divided. But in January 1940 U Pu went one step further, openly encouraging the Governor to use his 'constitutional powers' to crush Aung San's alliance. U Saw, a member of U Pu's cabinet, gave his tacit assent, at the same time attacking the *thakins* for their extreme left-wing views.

Not for the first time Aung San found himself marginalised. The colonial government was just not amenable to dialogue, at least with the *Do-bama Asi-ayone*. The time for talking was over. But it was one thing to advocate armed struggle, quite another to make it a reality. The only practical solution – if the movement was not to be permanently sidelined – was somehow to acquire arms from at least one of Britain's ideological enemies.

In March 1940, having already written the Freedom Bloc's manifesto, Aung San prepared a new manifesto for the *Do-bama Asi-anyone*. Much of its language was distinctly Marxist, as was its praise for the Soviet Union. Calling for a 'free independent people's democratic republic', it also demanded the 'democratic dictatorship of the proletariat and peasantry', as well as the 'abolition of landlordism, and free distribution of lands to middle and poor peasants with a view to the ultimate nationalisation and modernisation of all lands'. The same applied to Burma's industry and banks. At the same time Aung San urged full equality for women, freedom of conscience and religious worship and 'cultural autonomy for the minorities'.

The last was of some significance. As its name suggests, the *Do-bama Asi-ayone* was a decidedly Burman affair. But now for the first time Aung San openly recognised that any political settlement must take the 'ethnic' peoples into account, otherwise there could be no lasting peace. 'Cultural autonomy' was vague – a fudge even – yet it shows Aung San thinking in whole-picture terms.

Of equal significance, the manifesto proposed a 'constitutional assembly', to determine how a free and independent Burma should be governed. While the *Do-bama* might have its own ideas on this, Aung San saw that without a genuine consensus, arrived at through an elected assembly, even self-government would be dictatorial.

Finally the manifesto turned to the war. Declaring that 'Burma and the world form one organic link', Aung San wrote: 'We cannot contemplate even for one moment the question of participation in the present imperialist war for the freedom of another country so long as we are not allowed freedom of action in such [a] matter.'

This task done, Aung San set off for India with Than Tun and some other *thakins*. The purpose of this first trip abroad was to meet the leadership of the National Congress Party, attend its annual conference at Ramargh, and foster international solidarity among those opposed to imperial rule. Among those he encountered were Mahatma Gandhi and Jawaharlal Nehru, but not Subhas Chandra Bose. The most militant of the Indian nationalists – Gandhi called him the 'patriot of patriots' – Chandra Bose was (with Japan's support) busy raising an army to fight the British.

Aung San and his *Do-bama* delegation took time out to visit India's main cities and sites. In his brief 'Self Portrait' he describes how 'we visited Gaya, Benares, Allahabad, Agre, Delhi, Peshawar, [the] Khyber Pass, Lahore, Amritsar, Ahmedabad, Bombay and Calcutta'. Returning to Burma, he resumed campaigning for independence, at the same time joining a secretive Burma Revolutionary Party, led by Thakin Mya. He also served for a few weeks on the governing body of Rangoon University, as the students' representative. But to his dismay, the colonial authorities now invoked an emergency Defence of Burma Act, allowing them to detain anyone suspected of dissident activity. One by one they started rounding up the *thakins*.

Aung San saw to it that he was placed on the wanted list. At the beginning of June he addressed a gathering in the Irrawaddy delta township of Zalun. As he was speaking, a policeman slipped him a note warning him not to refer to the Chins. In the Chin uplands trouble had broken out following rough treatment of fractious tribal leaders by the British. Aung San paused, then told his audience that he had been asked to remind everybody about the Chin situation. A warrant for his arrest was issued immediately afterwards, with a charge of sedition attached. A princely reward of five rupees was offered for information leading to his capture.

Students protested at the issue of the warrant, but to no avail. Aung San was now a marked man, obliged to lead a fugitive existence, moving from one friend's house to another and from one township to another, up and down the country, his face carefully hidden beneath a hat.

Over the coming weeks scores more *thakins* were arrested and placed in 'preventative detention', usually without charge. Among them were Thakin Nu, Aung San's closest ally, and Thakin Soe, a passionate, violin-playing Marxist who would later play a major role in the Burmese communist movement. Both were sent to the maximum-security prison at Insein, where, with other Burmese intellectuals, they ran what was later nicknamed Insein University. Soe gave instruction in Marxism-Leninism. Nu, ever the literary man, taught English and lectured on Shakespeare.

Also arrested, on 26 July, was Dr Ba Maw, who had, earlier in the year, resigned his seat in the House as he sensed more could be achieved, both for Burma and for himself, by agitating outside of the legislature. At once a court was convened, in Mandalay, and Ba Maw was sentenced to a year's imprisonment on the grounds of sedition.

Aung San had no intention of joining his colleagues in prison. What would be the point? What most needed to be done could only be done outside Insein. But he knew the net was closing on him, and he needed all his wits to remain at liberty. When he could, he met other *thakins* still at large, insisting that armed resistance was now the only way forward. Fine, they replied: but where are the arms? Aung San would answer that if dacoits could lay their hands on rifles and grenades – and dacoity was still a headache for the British outside the main urban centres – then so could he. Yet he knew they had a point. A few guns and grenades might make life difficult for the British, but were unlikely to bring them down. Only a well-trained guerrilla army could do that, but as well as weapons and trainers, it required funds.

But there were no funds. By arresting so many of the *thakins*, the British had all but smashed the *Do-bama Asi-ayone*. Donations were reduced to a mere trickle because there was hardly anyone left to collect them. For a decade Aung San had given his all to the cause of Burmese independence, but he was no nearer realising his goal than he was at the outset.

Early in August 1940 he secretly convened a larger meeting. The solution, he proposed, was to send someone abroad to seek foreign support. He had in mind China: either Chiang Kai-shek's Guomindang government in Chongqing or Mao's communists in the northern province of Shaanxi. Again Aung San's comrades agreed, but – since it was his idea – only if Aung San himself volunteered to undertake the mission. He readily assented, on condition that he had a free hand in making such contacts and agreements as he saw fit. As no one had a better plan, Aung San was given the go-ahead.

Just getting out of Burma presented a major challenge. The quickest way to reach China was overland, but all the border crossings in northern Burma were closely watched. Nor was there any chance of buying a commercial air ticket, since Mingaladon airport too was under tight surveillance. In any case, that would be too costly. Instead, together with another *thakin* from Syriam, Hla Myaing, and assuming the name Tan Luang Shaung, Aung San boarded a Norwegian-owned cargo vessel, the *Hai Lee*, bound for Amoy (modern Xiamen, Fujian province) on 8th August.

The two young men had to work their passage as deckhands during what was a stormy twenty-day voyage. Aung San spent most of the time feeling sea-sick, and at one point passed out on a pile of coconuts. All that the beleaugured *Do-bama Asi-ayone* had been able to give them was a paltry 200 Indian rupees – by today's value, considerably less than US $1,000. With this they were expected to raise a force that would humble what was still the world's largest empire. Nor was Amoy the ideal launching pad for such a quest. A Treaty Port since 1842, its chief claim to fame was that it had once been a principal conduit for the opium trade. Although by 1940 its grandeur was faded, it was still full of spies and smugglers, and it was nowhere near Chongqing, and even further from Shaanxi.

For more than two months Aung San and Hla Myaing shared a room in the cheapest lodgings they could find in Amoy's International Settlement – although Japan now controlled Fujian, Westerners had yet to be expelled. Obliged to bribe local policemen a few precious rupees not to throw them in jail as illegal immigrants, they soon had to cable Rangoon for more money, and were lucky when Thakin Hla Pe (Let Ya) managed to send some by wire. Meanwhile, on the political front, nothing was happening. There were no communists in Amoy; or, if there were, they were not prepared to risk exposure by revealing themselves to two Burmese strays. Nor could any Guomingdang agents be found.

It seemed the mission was doomed to abject failure, in which case Aung San and Hla Myaing would have to return to Rangoon to face who knew what fate. Or perhaps, breaking out of Amoy, they would just 'disappear', the way people sometimes did in pre-war China. In that case Aung San would have gone down as little more than a footnote in Burmese history. But then a miracle happened. Aung San and Hla Myaing were approached by a Japanese agent – one Major Kanda, of the Japanese *Kempeitai*, military police. He listened attentively to their story and told them they could have all that they wanted. Within days they were on their way to Tokyo, in an aeroplane that landed at Haneda airport on 12th November 1940.

Even if, before setting out, they had not done their homework thoroughly, the Japanese had.

X

BO TEZA: RELUCTANT COLLABORATOR

*I also visualised the possibility of a Japanese invasion of Burma but here
I had no clear vision (all of us at the time had no clear view in this respect
though some might now try to show themselves, after all the events, to
have been wiser than others; in fact you might remember it was a time
when I might say leftist forces outside China and the USSR were in
confusion almost everywhere).*

Aung San, speaking at the City Hall, Rangoon, 29th August 1945

A short while before Aung San boarded the *Hai Lee* for Amoy, a senior
Japanese intelligence officer arrived in Rangoon from the Staff
Headquarters of the Imperial Army. Posing as a well-heeled journalist
accredited to the *Yomiuri Shimbun*, Colonel Keiji Suzuki assumed the
name Masuyo Minami, and as such had himself appointed secretary of
the Japan-Burma Society, recently formed for the furtherance of 'cultural'
ties. His mission was to find out more about the Burma Road and
Western supplies to Chiang Kai-shek's army at Chongqing, and to develop
channels to dissident Burmese that had already been opened by staff
(including the air and naval attachés) at Japan's consulate in the capital.

By encouraging, and even arming, seditious elements inside Burma,
the Japanese hoped to create problems for the British, as well as give
their 'Co-Prosperity' programme a positive spin. Beyond that, imperial
strategy was still being decided. The actual invasion and occupation of
Burma was a strong possibility, but as yet no more than that.

The two politicians who interested Japanese intelligence services the
most were U Saw and Ba Maw. U Saw's pro-Japanese sympathies were
well known. A visit to Japan as early as 1935 had convinced him that

only Japan held the key to ridding the East of its European overlords while at the same time ensuring material progress. He had a mercurial, shifty, unscrupulous character. Among members of the corrupt legislature, he was known for taking bigger backhanders than most. Once challenged by the Governor for charging 10,000 rupees for an appointment, he first denied the accusation, then boasted that the real figure was 15,000 rupees. But these very qualities made him pliable, and so he was assiduously groomed. To Suzuki's delight, when U Pu's government fell in December 1940, U Saw became the next to cobble together a coalition cabinet, and Burma's third Prime Minister.

Ba Maw was a tougher nut to crack, but, as president of the Freedom Bloc, promised to deliver rather more. Unlike U Saw, he was in league with the up-and-coming leadership generation: the *thakins* and their ilk. Ba Maw was not, however, noticeably ideological. He was, rather, an old-fashioned patriot with a lot of personal ambition. But, like other well-off Burmese, he used a Japanese doctor (another Suzuki), and it was through this physician, acting as an intermediary for the consulate, that Ba Maw was first approached.

Others of interest to Japanese intelligence included Aung San himself. There had been at least one clandestine meeting between Aung San and Japanese consular officials in July 1940, arranged by Ba Maw, but nothing had come of it. Aung San – knowing some at least of what the Japanese had got up to in China, and suspicious of Japan's real intentions – was a reluctant bridesmaid. For their part, the Japanese considered him a communist, and so unsuited to their purposes.

A couple of months in the squalor of back-street Amoy, and with yet more of his fellow *thakins* being put under lock and key by the British, changed Aung San's perspective. With no hope of either Chinese communist or Guomindang help, the Japan card was all that was left. Ba Maw meanwhile, knowing about Aung San's mission to Amoy, had worked on Colonel Suzuki to convince him that, as with himself, Burmese independence was what mattered most to the former student leader. Two other *thakins*, Hla Pe (Let Ya) and Dr Thein Maung, supported the idea that the Japanese should try Aung San again. Thein Maung helpfully provided Suzuki with photographs of both Aung San and Hla Myaing, while Hla Pe, wiring the much-needed additional funds to Amoy, advised his friend from Rangoon University days what to expect.

The photographs were passed on to a Major Kanda of the *Kempeitai* in Japanese-occupied Formosa (Taiwan), and Major Kanda then travelled to Amoy to 'collect' Aung San and his companion. At Haneda airport they were met, on 12th November, by Colonel Suzuki himself, who had flown from Rangoon to be there. Suzuki, in his own way a visionary whose attachment to the Burmese and their struggle for independence later caused him to be recalled to Tokyo, outlined his plans. He wanted Aung San to recruit a select band of fellow Burmans, who would be given intensive military training. Once this was done, they would be sent back to Burma to raise and officer an army that would fight the British and create the conditions for a general uprising. Japan would supply the necessary funds and materiel, and Aung San would be in charge of the operation on the Burmese side.

Ostensibly, this was all that (even more than) Aung San could have wished for. His boyhood dreams of becoming a great Burmese hero might still be realised. Once his army had achieved its objective of toppling the British, it could be used to defend the motherland against any other enemy – the Japanese included, should they (as Aung San's better judgement feared) have ulterior motives.

For several weeks there was an atmosphere of mutual suspicion. Suzuki and his colleagues probed away at Aung San, still uncertain where his real sympathies lay. It was not beyond the realms of possibility that he was part of an international communist network, and this needed to be meticulously checked out. And Aung San had to lay aside a distaste not only for right-wing militarism, but also for what he regarded as some immoral customs.

Aung San Suu Kyi's father was never much given to talking about himself. Whether, had he lived longer, this would have changed is a matter of conjecture. After his death two draft chapters of an autobiography were found. Otherwise his terse 'Self Portrait', penned in the final months of his life for the sake of providing his followers with basic information, is a small monument to reticence. In it he refers to his first trip to Japan in a bare sentence: 'I stayed in Tokyo for about three months and returned to Burma early in 1941 to convey the plans given by the Japanese to my friends.' Yet his relationship with the Japan of Emperor Hirohito and the likes of army supremo General Hideki Tojo, exposing him to the charge of rank opportunism, clearly troubled him to the end. In a speech made to the East and West Association at Rangoon's City Hall on 28th August 1945, entitled 'The Resistance Movement', he went out of his way to clarify his Japanese experiences:

My first impression was not so bad, even though misgivings still didn't leave me. The Japanese I met were very nice and courteous and easy, quite like our race. Everything about them was spick and span. They were very industrious and patriotic. There was nothing objectionable in these things. When we arrived in Tokyo [. . .] Japan was having a grand celebration of the 2600th anniversary of the Japanese empire. The next day after our arrival, we were taken before the Imperial Palace and bowed in its direction just as several Japanese men, women and children did. Well, we did not think much about this. This just showed the respect in which the Emperor was held by the Japanese people, though I did not believe like the Japanese in the divinity of the Emperor and I do not like a monarchy, whatever its form may be. When I bowed to the Imperial Palace, I did so only out of courtesy and with no intention of becoming his subject.

Colonel Suzuki, still in his civilian guise of plain press-man Mr Minami and secretary of the Japan-Burma Society, conveyed Aung San and Hla Myaing to a 'country hotel', to rest for a while after the privations of Amoy. Almost immediately he asked them whether they 'would like a woman'.

Speaking for his companion as well as himself, Aung San answered with a firm No.

'There is no shame,' Suzuki countered. 'It is like taking a bath. There is a women's quarter here.'

At the time Aung San thought this was an attempt to compromise or 'demoralise' him. But soon enough, at another country hotel, the offer was repeated. Again Aung San tetchily declined, and there were no more country hotels with women's quarters. But worse was to follow. As Suzuki slowly let his mask drop, he revealed that as a young man he had served in the war against Russia and had personally killed all the inhabitants of a peasant cottage outside Vladivostok, young and old, male and female alike.

'Similarly,' he continued, 'you must kill all British, including women and children.'

At this Aung San protested roundly. Anti-British as he was, he would never stoop to such 'barbarity'. He also refused, despite persistent questioning, to condone the manufactured incidents that had given the Japanese a pretext for their 1932 annexation of Manchuria and their subsequent invasion of China proper. Suzuki was gentleman enough (or wily enough) not to let such differences stand in the way of a partnership that promised each side great rewards. In his City Hall speech, Aung San even admitted that Suzuki 'acknowledged' his 'delicacy' on such matters, and modified his approach accordingly.

The greater criticism he reserved for himself. 'That was how,' he told his 1945 audience, with tangible bitterness in his voice, 'we invited the Japanese invasion of Burma, not by any pro-fascist leanings but by our own blunders and petty-bourgeois timidity.'

With or without the collusion of Aung San and the Freedom Bloc, or any other Burmese faction, Japan would still have annexed Burma: severing the Burma Road was strategically important. Nor, as Aung San was half-led to expect, was the Japanese incursion into Burma limited to a campaign through the Shan hills towards the Chinese border from Thailand (as Siam had become in 1932). Rather, Japan decided to take the whole of Burma, as part of its quest for empire. It would make life easier if this was accomplished with the aid of a carefully nurtured patriotic Burmese force.

Japan signalled its real intentions with its assault on Pearl Harbor, Hawaiian home to the USA's Pacific Fleet, on the morning of 7th December 1941. Bombers launched from six Japanese aircraft carriers unleashed a devastating strike that sunk or crippled eighteen American warships (eight battleships included), destroyed scores of aircraft on the ground before they could scramble to safety, and left nearly 2,500 US servicemen dead. Even though America was already involved in a proxy war against Japan in China, supplying and training Chiang Kai-shek's army, the Japanese action was greeted as a monstrous act of unprovoked aggression – 'a date which will live in infamy', as President Franklin D. Roosevelt famously put it, addressing Congress the following day.

Pearl Harbor conflated two separate wars, one being fought in the East, the other in the West, making it perhaps the true starting point for the Second World War. Japan, declaring war on the United States even as its warplanes took off from aircraft carriers in the middle of an ocean, shortly afterwards declared war on Britain and its empire. As significant as the bombing of Pearl Harbor was the creation of the Axis more than a year earlier, on 27th September 1940: a ten-year military and economic alliance between Japan, Germany and Italy, between Hitler, Mussolini and Hirohito, half-emperor, half-god.

A few months earlier, in July 1940, Britain had, at Tokyo's request, closed the Burma Road. Now supplies to Chiang Kai-shek resumed. But even before Allied trucks rolled back into Chongqing, Japan had begun its occupation of French Indochina (Vietnam, Laos and Cambodia), as early as 28th September 1940. With France under German control since

June, the puppet Vichy government 'authorised' Japanese forces to administer 'Indochine' on its behalf.

The seizure of Indochina was just one part of a military expansion across the entire Far East, the speed of which would have excited admiration in the breast of Genghis Khan himself. The day after Pearl Harbor the first Japanese battalions landed in British Malaya. A grave setback for the British was the sinking of two battle cruisers, the *Prince of Wales* and the *Repulse*, symbolising the Royal Navy's expulsion from Eastern waters. Simultaneously Japan attacked the Philippines, in effect an American protectorate, and then, in January 1942, the Dutch East Indies.

The capture of Malaya was followed by the fall of Singapore, on 15th February 1942. British guns pointed out towards the sea from their fixed emplacements, but the Japanese came at their rear, easily crossing the narrow Strait of Singapore from Johor Bahru. As a result they controlled the all-important Malacca Strait, the principal sea corridor between the Indian and Pacific Oceans. Beforehand, Hong Kong had been taken on Christmas Day 1941, and smaller Japanese detachments had started pushing deep across the Pacific, grabbing every island of strategic importance in their way and reaching the Solomon Islands – another British colony, as well as the 'gateway to Australia' – in March.

By then 'lower' Burma had also been overrun. The key to Japan's success there was the capitulation of Thailand, on 8th December 1941. The Thai prime minister, Phibul Songkram, mindful of what had already happened in neighbouring Indochina, decided it would be less painful to admit Japanese forces into his territory than attempt resistance.

Although Japan's military did not enjoy true air superiority over South-East Asia until the surrender of Singapore, in Siam it went immediately to business, launching the first air raids against Rangoon on 23rd December. Such aeroplanes as the British had in Burma were of little avail: those that were not destroyed on the ground were finished off in the sky.

The land campaign began in January 1942, with Japanese troops marching across two mountain passes out of Thailand into Tenasserim, Burma's southern tail. For a while the British and their largely Indian soldiery kicked like mules against the advancing tide, but each action of defiance heralded only another defeat in what became an ignominious rout. On the last day of January the Japanese stormed Moulmein, Burma's third city, and by March they were poised to take Rangoon.

There was no orderly retreat. Both Prime Minister Churchill and Field Marshal Lord Wavell, commander-in-chief of the Empire's eastern forces, believed Burma would hold. In the capital, a state of anarchy already prevailed. As the air raids increased in intensity, tens of thousands abandoned their homes, taking to the roads that headed north. Such police as remained at their posts were powerless to prevent the looting that followed. Criminals and the insane were either freed or escaped from detention. Large parts of Rangoon became no-go areas by day as well as by night.

Soon arsonists were at work, setting fire to ransacked stores and warehouses. Then, once the decision to abandon Rangoon had been taken, the British themselves began dynamiting everything of military value – most spectacularly the oil refineries across the river at Syriam, creating a dense, sticky pall that descended on Rangoon and blackened such buildings as had not already been burned out. Sir Reginald Dorman-Smith, who had taken over as Governor of Burma, quit Rangoon on 1st March, flying upcountry to the temporary safety of Maymyo (Pyin-Oo-Lwin), a hill station east of Mandalay. Sir Paw Tun (who had replaced the pro-Japanese U Saw as Prime Minister) and several of his cabinet colleagues followed hotfoot in his wake, pausing only to draw their parliamentary salaries. For a while the city belonged to no one.

The latest plan was to create a line of defence across central Burma that would protect the vital oilfields at Magwe, Chauk and Yenangyaung. In this venture the British, deprived by the war in Europe of any meaningful reinforcements from home, found support to the north. The Americans had persuaded Chiang Kai-shek to appoint one of their own generals, Joseph Warren Stilwell, as his effective Chief of Staff. 'Vinegar Joe', as Stilwell was known for his acerbic turn of phrase, wasted no time sending two Chinese divisions south to protect the Burma Road.

British forces also gained succour from intermittent air cover provided by the American Volunteer Group, Major-General Claire Chennault's legendary 'Flying Tigers'. But in the chaos of war there were misunderstandings and disagreements about who was responsible for what, and the Japanese with their superior weaponry and manpower again took advantage. Still attacking from the south, they outflanked the British to the east and, swinging round through the Shan states, entered Lashio on 29th April.

The Burma Road was cut. Henceforward Chiang Kai-shek could only be supplied from India over the 'hump', a lethal cross-mountain air corridor that was to cost scores of Chennault's fearless pilots their lives.

Three days before the capture of Lashio, Wavell had finally ordered the evacuation of Burma. The oilfields were set ablaze, bridges destroyed, roads mined. Thousands of bedraggled, battle-scarred soldiers, and hundreds of thousands of mainly Indian refugees, having made it across the Chindwin, now dragged themselves through the jungles of north-western Burma towards Assam and the relative sanctuary of Imphal. Some died of starvation. Many more died of disease – malaria, cholera and dengue fever. The old, as well as the sick and sometimes the newborn, were abandoned by the roadside and on the jungle paths, to perish in whatever way fate decided. Those who survived left behind them a country that in less than four months had been ripped apart by the scourges of modern warfare, and was now once more falling prey to the ethnic divisions that had so long haunted it.

After another, indiscriminate aerial bombardment, which reduced much of the city to rubble, the Japanese entered what remained of Mandalay on 2nd May 1942. They did so not as liberators, as they had promised Aung San, but as new imperialists whose harsh rule was such that many Burmese began longing for the old colonial set-up.

At the beginning of 1941, once Aung San and Colonel Suzuki had accommodated each other's idiosyncrasies, a trust between the two men ripened. Suzuki, regarded by his colleagues as something of a maverick, had to fight his corner against the Japanese high command, which was not uniformly convinced of the feasibility or desirability of bankrolling a Burmese resistance force. But on 1st February the top-secret Minami Kikan (Minami Organisation), taking its name from the alibi used by Suzuki in Burma, was formally approved, and two weeks later Aung San was on his way back to Rangoon, bringing with him a written undertaking of Japanese assistance.

In line with his original discussions with Suzuki, Aung San's task was to recruit a group of patriots who, after joining the Minami Kikan and undergoing military training, would form the nucleus of what would become the BIA: Burmese Independence Army.

This plan had been worked out in detail in January. Getting it accepted in Tokyo, however, had involved some deception. Suzuki himself drafted the proposal, but then asked Aung San to translate it into English, so that it could be presented as the Burman's (not Suzuki's) idea. Had it been rejected, Suzuki himself would not have lost 'face'.

His hair now cropped short, Aung San was kitted out with a set of

disfiguring false teeth to help him avoid capture by the British.
Accompanied by a Japanese minder, one Mitsuru Sugii, and provided
with false travel documents devised by the Japanese communications
ministry, he boarded the *Shunten-maru* (a cargo boat belonging to the
Daitoa Shipping Company) as an assistant purser, and landed at Bassein
on 1st March. Once in Rangoon, Aung San made immediate contact
with the Burmese Revolutionary Party and with such other *thakins* as
were still free. He wanted to enlist patriots of all shades, but convincing
everyone of the wisdom of Suzuki's scheme was fraught with difficulties.
A meeting was hastily convened at a secret location in Thingangyun
township, and as the night advanced, discussion became heated. The
more cautious *thakins* quizzed Aung San about the possibility and scale
of a Japanese invasion, and whether he wasn't being used. Aung San's
riposte was that should Japan attempt an invasion, it was probable it
would become locked into a border war with the British, giving the BIA
the opportunity to deliver a body-blow to the colonial power behind
their lines.

The communists Than Tun, Ba Hein and Thein Pe remained flatly
opposed to any kind of collaboration with the Japanese; but others were
won over by Aung San's arguments, including members of both wings
of the *Do-bama Asi-ayone*. Barely a week later Aung San reboarded
the *Shunten-maru* along with the first four of his recruits, who included
his stalwart friend Hla Pe (Let Ya), and set sail for Japan on its return
voyage.

Hla Myaing, who had accompanied Aung San to Amoy the previous
August, had also returned to Burma, on a different ship but with a
similar mission. Between them they enlisted twenty-eight others, so that
by July the Burmese component of the Minami Kikan numbered thirty
individuals, a group of 'heroes' who would go down in Burmese history
as the legendary Thirty Comrades.

An isolated camp for these men, masquerading as the Sanya Farmers'
Training Depot, was created on the southern Chinese island of Hainan,
since 1939 under the control of the Japanese navy. There the Thirty
Comrades were subjected to the most rigorous discipline, enforced by
the camp commandant, a martinet called Captain Tekenobu Kawashima.
Up at dawn, the Burmans had to exercise and drill until late in the
night. Sometimes they went on special manoeuvres in the surrounding
jungle, scrubland and crocodile-infested swamps. Every day there were
lectures on weapons maintenance, tactics and battalion management.

Food was basic – soup, rice, fish, pickled vegetables and the occasional ration of meat or poultry – and living conditions rough. But the regimen had the desired effect: it turned a bunch of politicals into potentially effective soldiers.

Physically the least robust of the group, Aung San sometimes collapsed with exhaustion, but would always get to his feet again, impressing the Japanese as well as his fellow countrymen with his sheer will-power. The same quality confirmed his role as the Comrades' natural leader.

In October 1941, their training well on the way to completion, the Comrades were transferred to another camp in Formosa (Taiwan). By then some fractiousness had developed, as cliques within the group hardened. In particular the old split within the *Do-bama Asi-ayone*, between the majority followers of Kodaw Hmaing and the minority followers of the Ba Sein-Tun Oke faction, resurfaced. For the sake of national unity, Aung San had wanted members from both wings to be represented, but now, as the Comrades became restless and increasingly suspicious of Japanese intentions, he had to use all his powers of conciliation to maintain cohesion.

More alarmingly still, returning from a visit to Tokyo, he discovered that nearly the whole group was on the point of mutiny against the Japanese, plotting to seize whatever weapons they could and stage an 'uprising' against their hosts. Only in the nick of time did Aung San convince them that such an action would be suicidal.

But Formosa did not last long. Now that the Comrades had been prepared, the next phase was to create the promised army in Thailand. Aung San's team was airlifted to a new camp on the outskirts of Bangkok.

The Burmese Independence Army was formally inaugurated on 26th December 1941. Those who had been trained by the Japanese now became trainers, as the first battalions were raised, mainly from Burmans living on the Siamese side of the border. Within days the Comrades had more than 200 raw recruits on their hands. Yet despite this sudden acceleration of preparations, sustaining morale was difficult, as it was still unclear what role the BIA was to play, or how much operational autonomy it would enjoy once fighting commenced. Further, Aung San himself, though without question the leader of the Comrades, had yet to be given any military rank or title.

In these circumstances he had what was later regarded as a stroke of genius. The Comrades should give themselves titles – and the more grandiloquent the better. Meeting with Hla Pe and two other *thakins* on 27th December, Aung San proposed that each give himself a new name and henceforward call himself 'Bo' ('commander').

One purpose of these *noms de guerre* was to prevent any recriminations against their families, should they be captured by the British. But just as important was the afflatus that went with them. Aung San adopted the name 'Bo Teza' ('Fire', or 'Powerful General'). Hla Pe became Bo Let Ya ('Right Hand'). By the end of the year twenty-eight of the Thirty Comrades had been rechristened – including the hapless Than Tin, who had already died of malaria in Hainan. Now instead of Thakin Aung Than there was a Bo Setkya ('Flying Weapons'); instead of Thakin Hlaing San (the oldest of the comrades) there was Bo Aung ('Victory'); instead of Ko Shwe there was Bo Kyaw Zaw ('Famous'); and instead of the humble Shu Maung there was Bo Ne Win ('Brilliant like the Sun'). While the other twenty-nine Comrades retained their *noms de guerre* after the war, Aung San did not.

As Bo Let Ya later put it, the Comrades all 'felt a few inches taller wearing the new names'. Nor did the bonding that had begun in the training camps in Hainan and Formosa end there. At another meeting on 27th December several of the Comrades met at Aung San's quarters in Bangkok. A silver goblet filled with water was produced and all those present performed a *thwe-thauk*, or ritual pledge. Blood taken from each man's finger was mixed in with the water, together with some fortifying alcohol. Then everyone took it in turns to drink from the goblet, swearing to die in the cause of independence if need be, and swearing allegiance to each other.

This ritual ceremony was repeated soon afterwards with the participation of other Comrades. On the last day of the year, an Order of Battle for the BIA was issued. Colonel Suzuki, who, to show solidarity with the Comrades, had taken the name Bo Mogyo ('Thunderbolt'), was listed as Commander-in-Chief, and another Japanese officer (Takeshi Noda) as Chief-of-Staff. Aung San was given the position of Senior Staff Officer, with the rank of Brigadier. Bo Let Ya, made Colonel, was appointed the senior Burmese officer in the 'Tavoy' battalion, while Bo Ne Win, now a Lieutenant-Colonel, was put in charge of 'sabotage' (guerrilla) operations.

At once, after a Japanese-style 'departing for the front' ceremony (*shutsu jin shiki*), the BIA marched out of Bangkok towards the border.

By the middle of January 1942 it had crossed into Burma. As the patriotic army advanced into its homeland – generally behind Japanese lines, but engaging with the British in a series of skirmishes – its ranks swelled with fresh recruits, so that the original hundreds rapidly became thousands. Bo Ne Win meanwhile had gone on ahead. Dressed as civilians, he and a handful of followers managed to reach Rangoon before the British abandoned it. There, amidst the gross disorder that had befallen the city, he set up base at the deserted English Methodist High School on Signal Road. His purpose was to prepare the ground for the 'victorious' entry of the BIA into the capital.

In the event, the BIA trailed in some two weeks behind the Japanese 15th Army. By the time Aung San arrived at the head of three columns of Burman infantry, comprising 2,300 men, on 18th March, the Japanese had occupied all the main government buildings.

In the eighteen months since his low point in Amoy, Aung San had come a long way. He now had an army at his back, and the satisfaction of witnessing the British retreat. But in his heart he knew that Burma was still no nearer independence, while about his own, newly exalted position there was a sickening ambivalence. The 'fourth and final Anglo-Burmese war', as some Comrades optimistically described it, was nothing of the sort.

XI

SNAKES, LADDERS AND A WIFE

I went to Japan to save my people who were struggling like bullocks under the British. But now we are treated like dogs. We are far from our hope of reaching the human stage, and even to get back to the bullock stage we need to struggle more.

Aung San, at Maymyo, June 1942

FOR the next three years Aung San was forced to play an invidious game of cat and mouse with his fellow-Asian sponsors, while striving as best he could, under near-impossible circumstances, to maintain some sort of unity within the patriotic movement. Month by month, week by week, day by day it became increasingly obvious that he and the other Comrades had been sold a pass. And Colonel Suzuki was not entirely to blame. Often the orders he gave were countermanded by his superiors in the Japanese military. He too had envisaged something different. One of his boasts was that an ancestor had been a Burman king: a lie, but one he half-believed. Yet just because he was a soldier, and loyal to the emperor, there sometimes came a point when he had no option but to toe the imperial, authoritarian line; and though he never admitted it, his recall in July 1942 was probably as much a cause of relief as of heartache.

In the first flush of their occupation the Japanese were not unwelcome among all the Burmese. Their propaganda machine had worked overtime, air-dropping and distributing leaflets that promised all of the joys, and none of the horrors, of the Greater East-Asian Co-Prosperity Sphere. A Burmese woman, Daw Thi, married to a

Japanese dentist, issued soothing messages in daily radio broadcasts – in the manner of a Tokyo Rose or a Hanoi Hannah. When Japanese warplanes passed overhead, villagers stopped whatever they were doing to cheer them, for all that their bombs might be destined to fall on their city cousins. But it was all a gross deception. Convinced of their racial and cultural superiority, Japanese soldiers and administrators began treating those Burmese they controlled with the contempt they thought they deserved. After all, what sort of people allowed themselves to be colonised in the first place?

One relatively innocuous expression of their arrogance, but peculiarly insulting to Burmans (who, as Theravada Buddhists, regarded a person's head as sacrosanct), was the slap across the face. This could be delivered on the slightest pretext – a scowl, a reluctance to obey orders, some task clumsily done – and as often as not was administered in public, adding to the humiliation.

There was no comeback, because Japanese officers always carried pistols, or had soldiers armed with rifles beside them. The slap across the face, though, was as a tickle compared to other punishments meted out. Burma's British-built prisons, having emptied as the British withdrew, soon filled up again, and inside them torture became routine. Needles under the fingernails, fingernails pulled out, cigarette butt burns, electric shocks, that sort of thing. Or the Japanese version of the water torture: the victim hoisted upside down, and boiling water poured onto his genitals and into his nostrils.

The Japanese also expected Burmese women to gratify their physical cravings. Soon the system of 'comfort women', which had already been instituted in Korea and China, spread to Burma's towns and cities. For just a few rupees, Burmese women had to surrender their bodies to whomever. They had no choice. And when comfort women were not available, the likeliest recourse was rape.

In addition, the Japanese quickly devised schemes of forced labour. Whenever a road needed repairs, a bridge rebuilding or supplies shifting, it was the locals who had to do it, unpaid. Some soldiers took to helping themselves to whatever caught their fancy in shops and markets. For who would complain? And to whom? Especially dreaded were the ubiquitous *Kempeitai* or military police. Find yourself in their bad books, and not just you, but your entire family, were liable to suffer.

Not all Japanese in Burma (as elsewhere in their lightning-fast empire) indulged in such cruelties, but enough did, and it remains one of the conundrums of the twentieth century how a people ordinarily so addicted to courtesy and thoughtfulness towards others could have behaved so atypically.

Tensions between the officers of Aung San's BIA and their Japanese superior counterparts were present from the outset. Even before he entered Rangoon, there had been a spat in Moulmein, not long after the BIA had come out of Siam. Why should Burmans take orders from the Japanese, when the Japanese said they supported Burmese independence? Yet that's how it was, and that's how it had to be. The Japanese 15th Army had decided that it should assume responsibility for the administration of Burma, and the 15th Army was not to be trifled with.

A problem for the Japanese was that the BIA was growing at an inordinate rate. In March 1942 it had 10,000 enlisted in its ranks, and by May more than 25,000. Nor was any quality control exercised over its intake. It attracted, as well as patriots, those recently freed from British imprisonment and other criminal elements. And sometimes it got out of hand. There were incidents of looting and depravity. In the Shan states unpleasant episodes occurred at Hsipaw and elsewhere, when BIA soldiers indulged their own racial supremacism, wounding and killing numbers of Shan people.

The Japanese wanted and expected the BIA to be of assistance in policing and controlling Burmese communities – to be their running dogs. But that was not why Aung San had joined the Minami Kikan. As early as the end of March 1941 he and others of the Thirty Comrades wrote a letter to Suzuki expressing their misgivings, and asking for the BIA to be removed from Japanese command. Suzuki responded by inviting Aung San and his colleagues to his residence in Rangoon. Arriving after nightfall, the first thing Aung San, Let Ya and their colleagues noticed was that the entire compound was packed with armed soldiers. Inside the house they were made to wait until Suzuki appeared. At first he was civil, asking them to remain seated; then, suddenly, he produced the letter that had been written, flung it down on the table and unsheathed his sword.

'You are all my own sons,' he bellowed. 'If you have anything to say you must come to me and say it to my face. Don't write letters to me!'

Probably the letter had been read by Suzuki's superiors, for Suzuki himself was now under surveillance, and he was just passing the buck.

But one rush of Burman blood and the situation might easily have got out of hand. Involuntarily Aung San's own hand had reached for the handle of his sword, a finely crafted Japanese instrument that Suzuki had earlier given him.

Even so Aung San and the Comrades had to be treated with kid gloves. The Japanese were not yet confident that they had Burma under their thumbs, and so a little window-dressing was called for. In April Suzuki was able to tell Aung San that a parallel Burmese administration was to be set up, headed by the older, less radical *thakin* Tun Oke. In addition, the BIA itself was to be reorganised into two divisions. Aung San was to be Commander-in-Chief, Let Ya his Chief-of-Staff, with the divisional commands going to Bo Zeya and Bo Ne Win. These arrangements did not, however, disguise the fact that the BIA was to continue doing what the 15th Army wanted it to do; and shortly afterwards it was sent upcountry, away from Rangoon.

Aung San was not taken in by any of this, but knew he must bide his time. The important thing was to maintain and improve a Burmese fighting force, so compliance with Japanese wishes must, in the long run, be his preferred course. But he did register protest in his own, inimitable way. Although he now sported a shaven head, in the Japanese military manner, throughout the Japanese occupation he eschewed wearing the full officer uniform to which he was entitled, except on ceremonial occasions when he had no option. Instead he habitually donned the simplest clothing a soldier knows: khaki shorts or an old *longyi*, sandals and unmended shirts.

Maung Maung, a main apologist of the dictator-to-be Ne Win, but also a historian of the Burmese independence movement, would later record how Aung San's vest 'grimaced with many holes' whenever he removed his jacket on a hot day. The two uniforms he did have were 'worn threadbare'. 'He could not,' Maung Maung wrote, 'look like a conquering general if he tried, and he did not. He was curt in speech, blunt in manners.'

Similarly Aung San disregarded the privileges that went with his rank. Rather than be driven around in a jeep or staff car, he relied on an ancient Ford saloon that he had acquired in Rangoon; and when that broke down he took to marching on foot beside his soldiers. Such eccentricities did not go unnoticed, and soon songs were written about him, celebrating Aung San as the people's soldier. But he was not winning any war that mattered, and he came in for sharp criticism from

Soe, Than Tun, Ba Hein, Thein Pe and other communists who rem.
opposed to any kind of collaboration.

Matters nearly came to a head at the end of May 1942, when Aung
San was summoned to Maymyo, the hill station east of Mandalay, where
the 15th Army had established a headquarters. He was now told that
the BIA was to be disbanded. It had become too large, too unruly, and
(though the Japanese did not say so to his face) the use of the word
'Independence' was objectionable. Instead there was to be a new,
sized-down Burmese force called the Burma Defence Army (BDA). As
the name implied, this was to be deployed for maintaining domestic
security. Its numbers were to be limited to 3,000, and it was to be based
at Pyinmana, on the Sittang river. Aung San would remain its senior
Burmese officer, but he was now effectively demoted, to the rank of
Lieutenant-Colonel. As a sop, Tun Oke was to be replaced by Ba Maw
as the chief of a newly reconfigured 'Provisional Burmese Executive
Administration', ahead of 'actual' independence.

In the confusion of war Ba Maw had escaped from the jail at Mogok,
where the British had detained him following his Mandalay trial. He
had travelled incognito back to Mandalay, and there resumed contact
with the Japanese. With U Saw now held by the British in, of all places,
Uganda, Ba Maw became Japan's preferred candidate for the role of
puppet leader.

These were humiliating terms, but again Aung San had no choice but
to comply. He had contemplated an armed uprising against the Japanese,
but knew the situation was unpropitious. The communists, particularly
the quixotic Thakin Soe, had gone on the offensive, distributing
anti-Japanese propaganda and indulging in the occasional act of sabotage,
but the impact of these was negligible.

So Aung San went along with the Japanese. Before long it was
agreed that the BDA could be expanded beyond its planned 3,000
enlistment. As well as at Pyinmana, a Burmese officer-training school
was opened at Mingaladon, on the outskirts of Rangoon, with the
most promising candidates being forwarded to the Imperial Training
Academy in Tokyo.

There was something to be said for managing a more professional,
compact army than the old BIA. Both loyalty to its leaders and secrecy
– so important for Aung San's hidden agenda – would be easier to
maintain. The Japanese snake might yet turn out to be a ladder. But
there was another angle to the dissolution of the BIA that resonated

with the enduring intractability of ruling Burma. The Japanese were by no means able to stamp their authority on the whole land, even for a week. The hill peoples – the Chins, Kachins, Karennis and Karens – wanted nothing to do with them. The ousting of the British by a power in league with the Burman resistance was not at all to their liking, and many remained loyal to the defeated colonialists. Large swathes of Burma's uplands became no-go areas for Japanese soldiers, even before the Allies launched their counter-attack.

Tellingly, at the outbreak of hostilities, while the colonial Burma Army maintained by the British mainly for peace-keeping purposes did by then contain almost 2,000 Burmans, these were far outnumbered by 5,000-odd 'tribals' – the Karens representing the largest ethnic group with almost 3,000 men at arms, more even than Britain's imported Indian soldiery at the time.

Some units of the Burma Army made it to Imphal; others disintegrated. The tribals either returned to their homelands, carrying their weapons with them, or, under pressure from the Japanese, agreed to surrender their guns on condition they were not made prisoners of war. The Karens especially created a problem, partly because they were not confined to their traditional mountain homeland, partly because of the bad blood that had existed for centuries between them and the majority Burmans. Within living memory, tensions had been exacerbated by the use of Karen soldiers and police to crush the nationalist Saya San rebellion of 1930–2.

Marching into Burma from Thailand through Karen territory, the BIA, which was very much a Burman force, treated such Karens as got in their way harshly. In Papun there were ugly episodes. Karen fighters taken prisoner were machine-gunned or bayoneted by over-zealous BIA troops. Then in March, BIA detachments were sent into the Irrawaddy delta, to maintain order in the Karen townships and districts there. Again, whether returning fighters or ordinary civilians, the Karens were treated brutally. By April 1941 there was widespread communal violence, with Burmans and Karens attacking each other.

At first the Japanese were not overly concerned, but matters took a different course when a senior officer, and a friend of Suzuki – Lieutenant-Colonel Ijima – was cut down during a Karen guerrilla raid. Through Suzuki, the BIA was ordered to take reprisals. Two Karen villages in Myaungmya district, south-east of Bassein, deemed to be the epicentre of Karen insurgency, were to be razed, with all their occupants eliminated as a warning to other Karens. A bloody massacre ensued. In the mixed Burman-Karen town of Myaungmya itself, a former Karen member of parliament and cabinet minister, Saw Pa Tha, was hacked down together with his English wife and children and 150 other Karens on 26th May 1942.

Compared to these events, whatever had gone on in the Shan states was inconsequential, and it was in Japan's interests to rein in the BIA, or get rid of it altogether. The 'Myaungmya Incident', as it became known, also deeply concerned Aung San, who was upcountry when the massacre occurred. Although he had sometimes spoken of the need to bring all the peoples of Burma within a common understanding, henceforward 'national unity' became a main item on his agenda.

As long as the Japanese occupation continued, Aung San conducted clandestine meetings with fellow patriots, at great personal risk. Once Suzuki had returned home, had the Japanese discovered what Aung San was up to, they would have had no hesitation in executing him. But now he also began covert discussions with Karen and other minority leaders, outlining his vision of an independent Burma in which all of its 'nationalities' would enjoy the same rights.

It was an uphill struggle, but sometimes progress of sorts could be made. Significantly, in November 1943, Aung San held talks in Rangoon with Saw San Po Thin, an acknowledged leader of the Karen people who was in touch with British-backed Karen fighters in the mountains of Tenasserim. Aung San made an unreserved apology for the actions of the BIA the previous year, and the two men, entering into each other's confidence, established a good rapport that augured well for the future.

By then the unlikeliest thing had happened. Aung San, on record as saying that it was better that true patriots be castrated 'like oxen' than risk romantic distraction, had found himself a sweetheart and married her. Quite coincidentally, Ma (later Daw) Khin Kyi, three years older than Aung San, was a native of Myaungmya.

Love happened because he fell ill. Shortly after the end-of-May conference at Maymyo, Aung San developed a fever and had to spend time in Rangoon General Hospital. The gruelling last two years had finally caught up with him. The war, soldiering, jungle-bashing, malaria, an uncertain diet and the burden of leadership – each took its toll. He needed respite, but he also needed companionship and an intimacy of a kind his patriotic comrades were finally unable to provide. He needed someone he could trust absolutely, and who would trust him absolutely. A person if not of the same prominence as himself, then of the same convictions, truthfulness and dependability. And he needed what most men want, a woman – however much he might pretend to himself that he did not.

The hospital in Rangoon had been through the mill. Many of its staff had fled before the Japanese occupation, and earlier in March it had all but closed. In June 1942 it was still getting back up on its feet, under the supervision of one Dr Ba Than. But the doctors under him generally lacked experience, and most of the nurses were trainees. In Ma Khin Kyi, his senior staff nurse, he had a decided asset. Although still young for the position, she had a cool, organising head and a fierce commitment to her job.

Nursing was not her original choice of profession. The eighth of ten children, and known in her family as 'Baby', she had started out as a teacher. As a child she had attended primary school in Myaungmya, then gone as a boarder to the Kemmendine Girls' School in the capital. Failing to gain admission to Rangoon University, Khin Kyi attended the Morton Lane Teacher Training College in Moulmein instead. Once qualified, she returned to Myaungmya, where for a year or so she taught at the township's government school. But neither her position there, nor being stuck in a provincial backwater, exercised sufficient appeal to make her want to stay. Two of her elder sisters had already become nurses. Khin Kyi decided to follow suit, despite her mother Daw Phwa Su's vigorous protests. Amongst Burmans, nursing was not highly regarded. Mainly it was a job for Karen, Shan and Kachin girls. If Burmans wanted to enter the medical profession, they should do so as doctors. Teaching, on the other hand, was an esteemed calling.

Khin Kyi refused to be deterred. She was not a rebel, but she had an independent streak, which the years she had spent away from home had served to strengthen. Having made up her mind, she returned to Rangoon. As a probationary nurse at the General Hospital, she fast began to shine – hard-working, thorough and conscientious – and soon she was working in the operating theatre.

Simultaneously Khin Kyi joined the Women's Freedom League, a body set up in the late 1930s to promote patriotism and women's rights. Perhaps because of her concern for women's interests, she transferred to the Dufferin Maternity Hospital, also in Rangoon, and gained an extra qualification in midwifery. But, pressed by Dr Ba Than, who had greatly valued her assistance as a theatre nurse, she returned to Rangoon General Hospital when war broke out in December 1941.

Inevitably a large number of the patients under her care were of Indian origin. As people lost heart that the city could be defended, Rangoon's large Indian population began leaving in droves. There was an obvious problem with those too sick to travel. A 'hospital' ship was arranged, and Khin Kyi was one of very few nurses who volunteered to accompany the Indian patients to Calcutta. Having seen them to safety, she took what turned out to be the last boat back to Rangoon, at the end of February 1942, before the Japanese closed Burmese shipping lanes to Allied vessels.

Now Rangoon Hospital was virtually deserted, but Khin Kyi stayed on to help Ba Than maintain a skeleton service. Every day there were fresh cases – people injured by Japanese bombs, or by each other in the fights that had spread from one district to the next. By June, medical supplies were still scarce, but, with law and order restored in Rangoon, some of the staff who had escaped to the countryside were returning. There was also a healthy intake of young women volunteering to work in the wards. Patients could once again be cared for adequately. But with Aung San there were particular problems. As his daughter would one day write: 'his stern looks and impenetrable moods ... together with his growing reputation as a hero, made him an object of awe to the junior nurses, who hardly dared approach him.' He had scant regard for the feelings of those detailed to care for him. Almost wilfully he vented his frustrations on anyone who entered his room. As a result, his condition was slow to improve.

Dr Ba Than's solution was to put his senior staff nurse in charge of his most illustrious patient. Again in Aung San Suu Kyi's words, Khin Kyi 'handled Aung San with firmness, tenderness and good humour'. She was no beauty, and was on the short side, but even at thirty Khin Kyi exhibited the grace and charm enduringly associated with younger Burmese women – Rudyard Kipling had once written that Burma was a country full of 'bad cigars and very pretty girls'. Unlike Aung San, she was always punctilious about her appearance. Every day she applied *thanaka* (a yellow cosmetic paste made from sandalwood) to her face, and often wore a carefully chosen flower in her hair.

Within days Aung San decided he must marry her, and told her so. Khin Kyi was slower to make up her mind. Would he still feel the same when he recovered? Should any man who gave way to amorous passion so quickly be trusted? Her tenderness and good humour persisted, but so did her firmness.

This only enflamed Aung San. That she was such a sensible woman was much to his liking. He knew that once he left hospital he would have to return to his military duties and the independence struggle. What he wanted was a wife who would understand all that. When she brushed aside his advances, he resorted to a trick he had used as a child. He refused to take any food unless Khin Kyi personally fed it to him. Aung San too could be persistent; indeed, persistence was the essence of his character.

Little by little he won her round. When he was discharged from hospital he would, whenever the demands on his time permitted, take her boating on Lake Victoria (Inya Lake), and it was there, alone together on the water, that he finally persuaded her of his sincerity. They agreed that they should marry on 6th September the same year.

The courtship, misleadingly described by Nu and other *thakins* as a 'whirlwind romance', lasted less than four months. However, it caused a commotion in the ranks of Aung San's friends and colleagues. They were used to him 'growling' about their own weddings and marriages, accusing them of going 'soft' on the revolution. Now it seemed the Bogyoke himself was losing his resolve. Some of the Comrades feared they might be losing their leader.

That such fears were groundless became apparent once Khin Kyi was introduced to Aung San's circle. The Comrades and others on the inside understood that Aung San had chosen her because she would not distract him, though that did not prevent songs about the General and his beloved being sung by the soldiers of the BDA. The wedding, however, very nearly did not take place. A group of Japanese officers, delighted that the abstemious Aung San seemed human after all, decided to give him a stag night. At the time Aung San was quartered, along with other senior Burmese officers, in a fine colonial villa that had once belonged to the owner of the Irrawaddy Flotilla Company, and would one day become the residence of the British ambassador. When the Bogyoke finally arrived home in an army car, he was half-unconscious with drink. He was also being supported, on each arm, by a young kimono-clad beauty.

Khin Kyi was waiting for him on the porch. First she gave the Japanese officer a piece of her mind, and then, once he and the girls had been sent packing, she told Aung San that the marriage was off.

Hearing this, Aung San vomited. Next he apologised, assuring the teetotal Khin Kyi that he had never got drunk before, and never would again.

Khin Kyi forgave him, and the wedding went ahead next day as planned. While special guest Dr Ba Than sang beautifully, those Japanese officers present looked appropriately and agreeably sheepish.

XII

OLD ENEMIES, NEW FRIENDS

Don't think that you are going to have a good time when the British arrive. Don't think that you will get your promotions and live swanky and happy ever after. Get rid of your conceit and complacency. Hard struggle lies ahead.

Major-General Aung San, addressing Burmese officers and
troops at Prome, 24 March 1945

HIS marriage to Ma Khin Kyi accomplished, Aung San resumed his double life, nurturing the independence movement while playing along with the Japanese. In January 1943 Prime Minister Tojo announced in the Imperial Diet that the government of Burma would be handed over to its own people 'within a year'. In March, Dr Ba Maw, Aung San (at the time still a Lieutenant-Colonel) and two others (Thein Maung and Bo Mya) were invited to Tokyo. There, on the 18th, they were given an audience with Emperor Hirohito, who bestowed upon them the Order of the Rising Sun, third-class. Burma's independence – along with 'equal partner' status in the Greater East-Asia Co-Prosperity Sphere – would take effect on 1st August, it was now proclaimed.

There was a farce when Ba Maw, travelling back via the Philippines, arrived in Rangoon without an all-important document conferring independence. It had been left in his hotel room in Manila. Before it turned up safe and sound, his Japanese minder had seriously to consider hara-kiri – ritual self-disembowelment.

Aung San was co-opted onto an Independence Preparatory Commission. In order that he could retain at least nominal control of

the BDA – now renamed the Burma National Army (BNA) – it was
decided he should become Defence Minister, with the rank of
Major-General. Predictably, the top position went to Ba Maw, who, as
well as becoming Prime Minister, was to be known as the *Naingandaw
Adipati* (Great National Leader). But this was a hollow title. Off stage,
Ba Maw took his orders from the Japanese military, although that did
not stop him wallowing in what he took to be an actual assumption of
power. When, on 1st August 1943, 'independence' was celebrated with
a surfeit of carefully choreographed parades in Rangoon, he pranced
around like a middle-aged popinjay. Brandishing the slogan 'One Blood,
One Voice, One Command' (*Ta-thwe, Ta-than, Ta-meint*), Ba Maw for
a moment looked like a Mussolini or a Franco. Even quarter of a century
later, publishing his memoirs (*Breakthrough in Burma*, 1968) Ba Maw,
then in his late seventies, clung to the conviction that he, and not Aung
San, was the true architect of Burma's liberation. By then he had been
imprisoned twice by his fellow Burmans, as well as being reimprisoned
by the British. The exaggerated sense of his own importance, which the
Japanese had so cleverly manipulated, consumed the once, brilliant young
lawyer who had defended Saya San, until at last he died in 1977,
unmourned and unloved.

The Declaration of Burma's Independence was accompanied, on the
same day, by a declaration of war against Britain and the United States,
as had been agreed by Ba Maw and Tojo in a further meeting in Singapore
in July. No mechanism to elicit the views, let alone approval, of the
Burmese people at large in this important matter was put in place.
'Self-government', it seemed, was not to be graced with even a British-style
simulacrum of democracy. Soldiers of the Burmese National Army had
to give the fascist salute, particularly to Japanese officers. Although the
Japanese Military Administration was formally dissolved, the 15th
Army and its commander, General Iida, remained the nation's undisputed
rulers.

To pre-empt trouble, the Japanese dispersed the BNA around the country
in small units, with little communication between them. Aung San, who
should have been the one giving orders, obligingly lent his compliance,
just as a few months later he acceded to Japanese demands that the BNA
be gathered together again in just a handful of bases, the better to keep
an eye on them. His strategy was, wherever possible, to avoid arousing
Japanese suspicions, even though, on the first anniversary of independence,
during a speech given in front of Japanese commanders at Rangoon's

Jubilee Hall, he pointedly said that 'if freedom is only for a select group of people it is not freedom'. Simultaneously he published a piece in the Burmese-language paper *Bama Khit* ('Burma Era') in which, apropos independence, he admonished: 'We should not claim that our mission has succeeded.' Such utterances caused some consternation in Tokyo, but the view was taken that although the titular Minister of Defence might not be entirely happy with present arrangements, it was better to have him on side than make a martyr of him.

As before, Aung San was constantly surrounded by Japanese military advisers, telling him, after consultation with their own superiors, what he could and could not do. But whenever their backs were turned, Aung San was busy plotting rebellion while preventing a premature misfire. A constant worry was that sections of the BNA might act unilaterally, and thus place the whole body in jeopardy. As early as October 1942, a group of young Burmese officers, led by (amongst others) Aung Gyi, had begun planning an uprising, but it was not until the following August that Aung San, tipped off by Bo Ne Win, got wind of their preparations.

There were also the communists to contend with – among those who resisted the Japanese the most militant and best organised. While Than Tun had mercifully agreed to cooperate with Aung San, even becoming Minister of Agriculture in Ba Maw's puppet government, and two other prominent communist leaders, Thakin Thein Pe and Thakin Tin Shwe, had escaped to India, Thakin Soe remained at large – a firebrand just as willing to direct his invective against 'collaborationists' as against the occupying Japanese. The danger was that if Soe or anyone else attracted sufficient numbers to their cause, Aung San and the BNA might be obliged by the Japanese to root them out, thus creating civil war.

Not until August 1944, following a secret head-to-head between the two men at Pegu, was Aung San able to persuade Soe – of all his rivals for the hearts and minds of the Burmese people the ablest – to join him in a new united front. This took shape from September onwards as the Anti-Fascist Organisation, soon to become the Anti-Fascist People's Freedom League (AFPFL) – by far the most important party in Burmese politics until its dismemberment by Ne Win in 1962.

While Aung San reserved for himself the position of Commander-in-Chief of resistance forces, Soe was appointed the league's first chairman, and Than Tun its general secretary. Also on board were a group of socialists, representing the BRP (Burma Revolutionary Party), and spokesmen for the Karens. Not on board was the *Adipati*. While Aung

San continued to work alongside Ba Maw, so enamoured had the latter become of the trappings of fascist dictatorship that the Bogyoke no longer thought it wise to keep him in his confidence.

Far more important was the Karen connection, which encouraged the British in a belief that, as and when the Japanese were driven out of Burma, Aung San was the Burmese leader to do business with.

One of the romantic heroes of the war in Burma was Major Hugh Seagrim. He had stayed on in Burma in 1942 to organise an anti-Japanese resistance force among the Karens in the mountains on either side of the Salween river. Utterly devoted to his Karen fighters, he willingly shared their guerrilla lifestyle – makeshift jungle-huts, poor rations, endless mosquitoes – and became known amongst them as 'Grandfather Longlegs'. His small force, supplied by risky night-time air drops from far-away Imphal, was sufficiently irritating for the Japanese to make his capture a priority. Until that was done, Karen villages in the area he controlled were singled out for bloody reprisals.

Eventually, rather than see any more of his beloved Karens suffer, Seagrim gave himself up. For this act of selflessness, which even the Japanese admired, he was first imprisoned at Insein, then shot, in September 1944, along with several of his Karen 'co-conspirators'. A year earlier, however, in November 1943, Seagrim had radioed a message to the British in India that 'a certain Aung San' was contemplating revolt against the Japanese.

The British high command already knew about Aung San. To some he was simply a vile traitor, a former colonial subject who had turned coat and joined the enemy. That he might 'change sides' again was, at the least, 'interesting'. Seagrim's report was echoed by intelligence coming out of the Irrawadddy delta, where Aung San had direct contact with Karen leaders who wanted nothing so much as an Allied victory and where indeed, towards the end of 1944, Aung San visited, specifically to enlist Karen support for what he had in mind.

Above all, Aung San's plans depended on reading the war at large. His anti-fascist league might succeed in uniting most (if not all) of Burma's 'patriotic' factions in an anti-Japanese uprising, but if it struck too soon or too late, disaster would strike back. Either it would be crushed by the Japanese or brushed aside by the victorious Allies.

That Japan was heading for defeat was becoming more certain by the week. For the British, the first consideration had been to protect

India, where anti-colonial sentiment ran higher than it ever had in Burma. As well as the Congress Party – under Mahatma Gandhi's leadership absolutely, but non-violently, committed to Indian independence – there were the likes of Chandra Bose, for whom armed rebellion was the chosen option. If India had gone, then the whole game would have been up. Astonishingly perhaps, in their hour of triumph the Japanese, having taken Burma with relative ease, failed to press home their advantage. The 15th Army might well have advanced into India's northern plains. Similarly Ceylon (Sri Lanka), where the British Far Eastern high command had regrouped at Kandy, and where the Royal Navy struggled to maintain some sort of presence, was a sitting duck.

In May 1942 the folly of attacking Pearl Harbor began to tell. The United States launched a counter-attack in the Pacific, halting a Japanese fleet in the Coral Sea. Then, in June, it inflicted a crippling defeat on the same fleet at Midway. But as well as its Pacific campaign, the USA gave support to Britain on the Asian mainland. Allied strategy was coordinated through SEAC (South-East Asia Command). Their confidence renewed, as early as December 1942 the British mounted a relatively small-scale incursion down the seaboard of Arakan from Chittagong and Cox's Bazaar in Bengal. Even if the outcome was inconclusive, it sent a clear message to the Japanese.

The greater action centred on Imphal, in Assam, where the British had retreated in 1942, and from where the Americans kept Chiang Kai-shek's Guomindang supplied over the 'hump'. Not until January 1944 did the Japanese attempt to take Imphal, by which time more or less adequate defences had been prepared. The battle, spread over a broad area of land surrounding the Allied base, lasted until July, when the 15th Army was decisively crushed at Kohima, fifty miles to the north, in Nagaland.

Ultimately the Japanese were repulsed by the determination and endurance of Britain's loyal Indian troops. At Kohima the fighting was of the utmost severity. Combatants' hair could turn white between dawn and dusk. Kohima also hosted perhaps the most poignant of all memorials inscribed during the Second World War:

> *When you go home*
> *Tell them of us, and say,*
> *For your tomorrow*
> *We gave our today.*

In essence, however, the battle fought was one between a moribund imperial power (Britain) propped up by an emergent super-power (America) against another disciplined, but hopelessly overstretched would-be new imperial power (Japan), which did not have the luxury of an established colonial force (the Indian Army) to draw upon.

Nonetheless, Kohima was the hinge of the war in South-East Asia. Thereafter the British XIVth Army, moulded and commanded by arguably Britain's ablest Second World War soldier, Bill (subsequently Viscount) Slim, could realistically anticipate driving the Japanese out of Burma. In the Allied victories that ensued, a multiplicity of elements were involved, not least the tenacity of Chiang Kai-shek's Guomindang divisions, which in northern Burma tied up a disproportionate number of Japanese troops. But there was also a new kind of audacity on show, and with it a new kind of military activity that was to influence the post-Second World War world profoundly. Backed by Churchill as well as Slim, Orde Wingate developed and applied the concept of 'deep penetration warfare' – guerrilla operations conducted behind enemy lines supported by modern communications (the radio) and modern air power (dropping men as well as supplies, bagpipes included). Or, in Wingate's own words, 'bring in the goods like Father Christmas down the chimney'.

Wingate's rigorously trained commandos were misleadingly called the 'Chindits' – a corruption of the Burmese *chinthe*, the statuary lion often found standing guard outside a pagoda or temple. In action, they were anything but sedentary. During two operations led by Wingate, in February 1943 and January 1944, the Chindits demonstrated that a combination of stealth and speed could disrupt the Japanese military where it least expected an attack. As Wingate graphically put it, 'We have inflicted complete surprise on the enemy. All our columns are inserted in the enemy's guts.'

Such operations were not enough to win a war, but were of use in softening up the Japanese ahead of the main offensive. When Wingate was killed in an air crash returning to Imphal on 3rd March 1943, his place was taken by Brigadier-General Frank Merrill, an American commander who created his own Chindit-like force, known as Merrill's Marauders. In May 1944, Merrill's men – officially known as the US Army's 5307th Composite Unit (Provisional) – played a major role in the capture of Myitkyina, in Burma's northern Kachin territory. Although the Burma Road remained closed (the Americans were busy building an alternative, the Ledo Road), the use of Myitkyina's landing strip made flying the 'hump' appreciably less hazardous. It also provided a forward base for the Allies' campaign to recapture Burma itself.

Slim's XIVth Army began its advance in December 1944. By the second week of March 1945 the British were dug in around Mandalay. But the more significant victory was the capture of Meitkila, on 4th March – for it was at Meitkila, south of Mandalay, that the Japanese had concentrated their forces in 'upper' Burma.

Aung San and the BNA had taken part in none of these actions. Aware of how unpopular their occupation had become for a majority of Burmese, the Japanese dared not use the indigenous army against their principal enemies. Instead Burman soldiers were deployed on domestic policing duties – an arrangement that played into Aung San's hands. On 3rd March he had convened a secret meeting of his anti-fascist leaguers at his residence in Rangoon. At last he had decided the time was ripe to create a revolt. Even so, the date set – 3rd April – had quickly to be revised, such was the stampede of unfolding events. The last thing he wanted was for the reconquering British to think he was a simple opportunist and nothing else. The new date was 27th March. But even this was partially pre-empted. In Mandalay, on 8th March, before the British regained the city, the BNA commander Bo Ba Htu unilaterally went on the offensive against the Japanese. There was also a spontaneous uprising in the western province of Arakan.

Meeting his Japanese counterparts in Rangoon, Aung San expressed the view that it was time for the 'loyal' BNA to go to the front and help their Asian 'allies' against the Western imperialists. The Japanese, perhaps surprised by Aung San's continuing cooperation, immediately agreed, and on 17th March a great 'setting off for war' parade was arranged at the army barracks on U Wisaru Road. Ba Maw was present, as was the Japanese Commander-in-Chief, General Sakurai. Aung San himself delivered the keynote address. 'Our army will fight for the benefit of the country,' he said. 'We will fight the enemy with all the strength in our possession.' Unnoticed by the Japanese, he avoided specifying the enemy's identity. Ba Maw applauded vigorously. Within a fortnight he would accuse Aung San of being the ultimate traitor.

The parade finished, such units of the BNA as were in Rangoon began marching out of the city, towards eight designated areas of 'resistance' against Slim's encroaching army. On 23rd March Aung San himself left the capital for Prome, to help prepare for the 27th. For two days the Japanese had no idea where he was, and suddenly their suspicions were aroused. But on the 25th he was back in Rangoon. Then he left again. On the night of the 26th he travelled in a bullock cart to Thayetchaung, a village in Thayet township district. There he set up his 'revolutionary' headquarters.

The following morning the Japanese discovered that every unit of the BNA had turned against them. As Slim rolled down the Irrawaddy towards Rangoon from Mandalay and Meitkila, the BNA went to work. Hundreds (but not the 20,000 later claimed by Burman propagandists) of Japanese, beating a hasty retreat towards the safety of 'neutral' Thailand, were picked off in Burma's eastern hills and jungles.

It was the biggest gamble of Aung San's life. Before making his move he had had no direct contact with the British. Unbeknown to him however, Slim and his superior, Admiral Lord Louis Mountbatten – Supreme Commander of SEAC, as well as a great-grandson of Queen Victoria – had already made up their minds. If Aung San and the BNA deserted the Japanese, then they should, *pro tem* at least, be accommodated.

But now a channel of communication was opened, through 'Force 136', a British SOE (Special Operations Executive) unit at work in the Karen hills. Slim, Aung San was advised, would very much like to meet him. Until 15th May Aung San prevaricated. His own intelligence network told him that many British officers wanted him strung up as a traitor. But Slim promised safe conduct, as well as the use of an aeroplane, and on that understanding Aung San presented himself at Slim's temporary headquarters at Meiktila on 16th May.

Slim began by telling Aung San that, welcome though it was, the BNA's cooperation was scarcely indispensable to getting rid of the Japanese. Further, the only civilian government that Slim was mandated to recognise was the exiled colonial government of Sir Reginald Dorman-Smith. Aung San riposted by demanding that he be treated as an Allied commander. Had he not in effect joined forces with Britain and the USA by rising up against Japan?

All well and good, Slim replied, so long as Aung San placed himself under his own command.

Then he tested Aung San more closely. 'I have been urged to place you on trial,' he told him. 'You have nothing in writing. Don't you think you are taking considerable risks in coming here and adopting this attitude?'

'No,' Aung San replied without hesitation.

And why was that?

'Because you are a British officer.'

Slim smiled, then laughed. The ice was broken. But still he could not resist taunting Aung San a little further.

'Go on, Aung San,' he said, 'you only came to us because you see we are winning!'

'It wouldn't be much good coming to you if you weren't, would it?' Aung San snapped back.

And so they got down to the hard bargaining.

'He was not the unscrupulous guerrilla leader I had expected,' Slim wrote in his memoirs: 'I judged him to be a genuine patriot and well-balanced realist.'*

'I could do business with Aung San,' Slim added, anticipating by forty-odd years what Margaret Thatcher would one day say about Mikhail Gorbachev. Had Field Marshal Slim's judgement swung the other way, Aung San would have been dead and buried.

* Field Marshall Sir William Slim, *Defeat Into Victory* (1956)

XIII

GETTING THERE

He is not a gangster as are some of the men in similar positions in the colonies. He lives a simple life and believes in what he advocates. Therefore we must take notice of Aung San not as a person but as a symbol. He is part of the restless, turbulent changing life in the East.
Lt.-Col. Rees Williams, MP, speaking in the House of Commons,
7th April 1946

FIGHTING continued until (and, in one or two isolated places, beyond) 14th August 1945, when Emperor Hirohito surrendered to General Douglas MacArthur in Tokyo. Had the USA not dropped atomic bombs on Hiroshima (6th August) and Nagasaki (9th August), it is probable that some at least of the forces that Britain had in Burma, which by then included Gurkha and West African as well as Indian regiments, would have been deployed elsewhere in East Asia, in order to tighten the noose around Japan's neck. In that case any semblance of order inside Burma might well have collapsed.

Again, Aung San rode his luck. Winston Churchill, Britain's wartime leader, had wanted to retain the Empire, most especially the British Raj in India. But even before the war ended, his coalition government left office. In its place came a Labour administration under a new Prime Minister, Clement Attlee, who favoured a Commonwealth of free and independent nations bound together by a general loyalty to the British Crown. India was to have her independence. And what applied to India applied also to Burma. Britain's final gift to Burma, therefore, following the expulsion of the Japanese, was to be the resurrection of order – at least superficially. Only then would the reins of power be handed over to whatever indigenous political group Whitehall deemed most appropriate.

Aung San and the AFPFL were in poll position. But victory was by no means assured. Although Dr Ba Maw, having escaped to Japan, found himself in Sugamo prison by the end of August, there was no shortage of other rivals. The communists had come under the umbrella of Aung San's anti-fascist league, but they might strike out on their own at any time. Several older *thakins*, too, began reckoning their chances, notably Tun Oke, and from 1946 U Saw, whose *Myochit* party had survived his wartime detention in Uganda. Aung San knew that the longer independence was delayed, the more likelihood there was that his anti-fascist league would fall apart. But there was also a dark skeleton in his cupboard, which might derail him at any time.

Back in March 1942, whilst recruiting for the Burmese Independence Army in Thaton district, south of Moulmein, he had personally shot dead in cold blood a Karen headman who was being held in detention locally. And not just that. It was said that he had ordered the body to be removed in a pig cart, knowing that the headman was a Muslim.

For those British who wanted to see him hanged as a traitor, the Thaton episode was heaven-sent. Aung San's best hope was to build on the understanding achieved with Slim during their meeting on 16th May, and on the rapport he developed soon afterwards with the Briton who carried most clout: the Supreme Allied Commander Lord Mountbatten.

As soon as he learned that the BNA had swapped horses, Mountbatten made it his policy to promote cooperation between Slim's forces and Aung San's army, with a view to incorporating it eventually within a reconstituted Burma Army. He sensed, accurately enough, that otherwise there was a real possibility that the BNA would begin fighting the British once the Japanese had been cleared out. To a degree, though, Mountbatten's hands were tied. He could influence, but not dictate, political decisions – they were the purlieu of the cabinet and Burma Office in London; and he knew that many of his subordinates disagreed with him, especially with regard to Aung San. Even Major-General C.F.B. Pearce, whom Mountbatten had put in charge of a temporary military administration of Burma until the country was returned to civilian rule, requested, as early as 9th May, that the Burmese leader be put on trial for his past misdemeanours.

Mountbatten at once replaced Pearce with another Major-General, the eminently pragmatic Sir Hubert Rance. A week later the British government produced a White Paper outlining its intentions for Burma – a document based on the recommendations of Sir Reginald Dorman-Smith, who was waiting at Simla to return to Burma as its Governor, and for whom Aung San had been a thorn in the flesh. Although the White Paper conceded that an eventual handover of power to the Burmese was to be desired, it proposed delaying the start of the independence process for a full three years. During that interval Burma was to return to its pre-war condition, with the Governor presiding over an Executive and (in due course) a Legislative Council.

This disappointed Mountbatten, and infuriated Aung San and his anti-fascist leaguers. Why should they have to wait so long? And what if the British government reneged and decided to keep Burma as a colony? The White Paper was, after all, only a policy document, not a binding pledge.

A ticklish moment arrived on 15th June. British soldiers, quickly followed by the BNA, had re-entered Rangoon in the first week of May, soon after an RAF pilot flying over Insein prison had reported seeing the words 'JAPS GONE EXTRACT DIGIT' daubed in large letters on the jailhouse roof. Now there was to be a grand victory parade. Should Aung San march at the head of his troops? Or would that be giving the 'traitor' too much headspace?

A compromise was reached. Aung San attended the parade, but only as an 'official' spectator. The following day Mountbatten had a first meeting with him, accompanied by the communist Than Tun (now married to Daw Khin Kyi's sister, Khin Gyi) amongst others from the League. Like Slim, Mountbatten was impressed by Aung San's coolness and integrity, and soon reached the conclusion that keeping him in the frame was paramount.

Over the next three months important details concerning what to do with the BNA (renamed the Patriotic Burma Forces, or PBF), which numbered in excess of 10,000 men at arms, were thrashed out. Mountbatten finally agreed, during a meeting at Kandy in early September 1945, that some 200 officers and 5,200 men should be absorbed into the Burma Army in four distinct battalions (called the Burma Rifles, or 'Burrifs'), keeping them regimentally separate from their Karen, Kachin and Chin counterparts.

The bulk of those BNA/PBF soldiers who did not join the Burma Army were to be disbanded. To take care of them, Aung San set up the People's Volunteer Organisation, or PVO. Officially this body, inaugurated in December 1945, was a welfare organisation supposed to assist in post-war national reconstruction. In reality it was a paramilitary organisation that became Aung San's militia, and his principal source of leverage whenever the British were slow to give him what he wanted.

In Burma, there was a history of such private armies, called *tats* (literally 'armies'). Both before and after the war anyone who was rich and ambitious enough would support a band of young men who met regularly for training sessions and who developed a strong group loyalty. Ba Maw had had a *tat*, as had U Saw. But the PVO, both in its size and geographical spread, was of a different order entirely. In nearly every major Burmese conurbation it had an office and a parade ground. Further, many PVO men were still armed, even though demobbed BNA soldiers were supposed to hand in their weapons.

Before the PVO was founded, Mountbatten offered Aung San on 7th September, whilst he was still in Kandy, one of the two highest military positions in the Burma Army that he was empowered to give to a Burmese national: the job of a Deputy Inspector-General, with the rank of Brigadier-General. The other Deputy Inspector-Generalship was to go to a Karen, partly as a reward for the fierce loyalty that Karen soldiers had displayed during the Japanese occupation, and partly as a means of achieving 'balance' within the reconstituted colonial army. It took Aung San the best part of three weeks to make up his mind. In the end, in a letter written to Mountbatten dated 25th September 1945 and beginning 'My dear Lord Louis', he declined. 'I have put your proposition regarding my appointment in the Burma Army before my colleagues in the AFPFL as well as in the PBF,' Aung San wrote. 'I regret very much that I shall not be able to serve further in the Army; but this has been the democratic decision of my colleagues and I will have to submit to them.' He added, 'Personally, a military profession is one which I would have preferred to choose of all others if only it is [a] purely personal question of selecting a permanent calling for myself.'

In the same letter Aung San proposed that the Deputy Inspector-Generalship be offered instead to Bo Let Ya; and requested that Mountbatten 'keep forever my present of the Japanese Samurai dagger' as a 'souvenir' of their friendship. What he did not explain to Mountbatten – perhaps because Mountbatten already knew it – was that the real stumbling block was the White Paper, which both individually and collectively the anti-fascist league had decided to oppose. Only by returning to civilian life (or half-returning, since he would become the 'commander' of the PVO) could Aung San pursue his political objectives. As a serving officer of the Crown, it would have been unprofessional and unethical to go against government policy.

With Dorman-Smith slated to resume office on 10th October, Burma was already reverting to civilian rule. All the more reason therefore for the decks to be cleared, so that Aung San could mount a challenge without having his hands tied.

If it is true that Aung San bowed before his colleagues in the League – the communists certainly would have preferred him to stay on in the military, so that they could have the political floor to themselves – he can hardly have taken much persuasion. But it is just as likely he was glossing over the difficulty of saying No to someone he in turn admired, and who had already done him several favours.

Sir Reginald Dorman-Smith sailed into Rangoon, aboard HMS *Cleopatra*, on 17th October, only ten days late. In so far as he still had any steady opinions – three years away from Government House had done nothing to sharpen his mind – he was suspicious of Aung San, but also recognised that it would be better to have him indoors rather than out. Unhappily for Dorman-Smith, it was his brief to implement the White Paper, while it was Aung San's and the AFPFL's most earnest wish to see it binned as soon as possible. He offered the League four places (out of eleven) on a new Executive Council, but, as the conditions imposed by Aung San would have meant turning over to the Burmese every function of government other than the sensitive matter of defence, Dorman-Smith had no option but to look elsewhere.

The AFPFL at once went on the offensive, Aung San telling its Executive Council that 'we will not be soft soaped' on 29th October. He also began dropping hints that the use of force should not be ruled out, though he was careful not to incite outright rebellion. Beginning in November, the AFPFL launched a nationwide propaganda campaign condemning the White Paper. At a rally in Chauk on the 11th, Aung San told a gathering of labourers and farmers that the British sought only to re-establish the pre-war system, and as such were no better than the Japanese. A week later, at a mass meeting in Rangoon, he called for an immediate nationwide election, to elect a Constituent Assembly that would prepare a constitution, which would then be referred back to the people for their approval. Between 17th and 23rd January 1946, the AFPFL organised an 'All Burma Congress' at the Shwedagon pagoda,

attended by more than 1,300 delegates, including representatives of the
'national minorities'. On the 20th Aung San himself delivered a speech
that lasted three and a half hours. At points he had to hand his
seventy-five-page text over to a colleague to read out for him. But it
was perhaps the most important speech of his life, certainly the most
important to date. Patiently he expounded his vision not only of an
independent Burma – a Burma that would be modelled along socialist
lines, with state ownership of key industries – but also his view of recent
world history. The British, he said, practised nothing but 'economic
fascism'. He had a few kind words for the USA, rather more for the
Soviet Union, and many kind words for Buddhism. Yet he warned
specifically against making Buddhism, or any other faith, a state religion.
All religions should be tolerated and respected in the coming Burmese
state, just as all its ethnically diverse peoples should be accorded tolerance
and respect. 'Politics,' he declared, 'is frankly a secular science.'

As his daughter Aung San Suui Kyi was to repeat in the same place
forty-two years later, Aung San made a particular appeal for national
unity. 'I must tell you quite frankly,' he said, 'that I cannot dangle any
promise of speedy results or sudden windfall of millennium before you.
No man, however great, can alone set the wheels of history in motion,
unless he has the active support and cooperation of the whole people.
No doubt individuals played brilliant roles in history, but then it is
evident that history is not made up of individuals only.'

Finally, he reiterated the AFPFL's demands for elections and a
constituent assembly.

As Aung San spoke, and an unseasonal drizzle fell, his audience
moved around and sometimes helped themselves to food. It was not the
speech of a firebrand: rather it was a measured appeal by a new Aung
San – Aung San the educator, Aung San the people's father.

In the wake of his Shwedagon address Aung San's popularity scaled
fresh heights – the reason why perhaps, shortly afterwards, he had a
major falling-out with the communist Thakin Soe, who then left the
AFPFL to set up an underground communist group known as the 'Red
Flags'. But Than Tun, leader of the larger and more moderate 'White
Flag' communist group, as well as Daw Khin Kyi's brother-in-law,
remained inside the AFPFL, at least for the time being, and so the League
continued to be politically ecumenical.

All of which was greatly disturbing to Governor Dorman-Smith and
the Executive Council he had managed to cobble together from

non-AFPFL elements. Its number included, as well as the pre-war Prime Minister Sir Paw Tun and three members of U Saw's *Myochit* party, Thakin Tun Oke, the elder of the *Do-bama Asi-ayone* movement who had been a leader of the minority faction opposed to Kodaw Hmaing. Possibly egged on by Dorman-Smith, Tun Oke decided he had had enough of young Aung San. When, at the end of February 1946, the pre-war Legislative Council was reconvened, he raised the matter of the 'murder' committed by Aung San back in 1942, which he claimed to have witnessed at first hand – even though Tun Oke himself was wanted for several wartime atrocities by General MacArthur in Tokyo. Aung San should be tried in a criminal court, Tun Oke insisted. Quickly his call was taken up by anyone with a grudge against the Bogyoke, including a tranche of British officers and administrators.

It was not an issue that London could duck – by coincidence or otherwise it was the very moment when, in Tokyo, the Japanese war trials commenced. But there was a neat calculation to be made. Arrest Aung San, and there was a palpable danger of setting off a nationwide conflagration. Fail to arrest him, and justice would fly out of the window.

The crux of the matter was whether the British had sufficient forces inside Burma to quell a revolt. The answer was probably not. Already most of Slim's Indian and West African regiments had been withdrawn. To his credit, Aung San made no attempt to conceal what he had done. Instead, speaking to the press, he explained what, from his perspective, had happened. The headman was one of several who had been 'arrested' by his own villagers. Since his crimes were particularly reprehensible, after a hasty court martial Aung San decided that he merited the death penalty. It being the middle of a war, he had taken out his pistol and shot him there and then. It was 'rough and ready justice', Aung San conceded, but under the circumstances had to be done.

The Governor's response was to prevaricate – on this, and almost every other matter. One day he cabled the Burma Office in Whitehall saying it was his opinion that Aung San should be arraigned, and the next he cabled saying he shouldn't. Then the headman's widow wrote to Dorman-Smith, and of course – Aung San must be charged.

By April cooler heads, backed by Mountbatten, prevailed. Aung San was under no circumstance to be put on trial. In London he had acquired a growing following, particularly on the back benches of the ruling Labour government. Tom Driberg, more independent-minded than most

Composite of Aung San Suu Kyi and her father General Aung San,
the architect of Burmese independence

The Shwedagon pagoda, seen at dusk from Rangoon's Kandawgyi (Royal) Park

A view of Pagan, Burma's magnificent medieval Buddhist capital

The *Adipati* Ba Maw, Burma's puppet dictator during the Japanese occupation of World War Two

Iconic images of Bogyoke Aung San as they appeared on Burmese banknotes in the early 1980s

The house in Tower Lane where Aung San Suu Kyi was born, today preserved as the Bogyoke Aung San Museum

The pond in the garden at Tower Lane, where the younger of Suu Kyi's two brothers, Aung San Lin, drowned in January 1953

Suu Kyi's mother Daw Khin Kyi in retirement, *circa* 1986

Sir Paul (later Lord) Gore-Booth with his wife Patricia bidding Indira Gandhi and India farewell at Palam Airport, New Delhi, March 1965. Back home in London, the Gore-Booths became Aung San Suu Kyi's informal guardians whilst she studied at Oxford

St Hugh's College, Oxford, where Suu Kyi studied for a degree in Politics, Philosophy and Economics

Aung San Suu Kyi assays the difficult art of punting while at Oxford

The Aris twins, Anthony (left) and Michael (right), with their father John Aris

In the 1930s Ma Than – Suu Kyi's mentor and friend in New York – was a well-known Burmese beauty, captured here by the portraitist Sir Gerald Kelly RA

Christmas at Oxford, *circa* 1983: Suu Kyi, Michael Aris (by the fireplace), her two sons and friends at 15 Park Town

Suu Kyi in Kyoto, 1985, with her Japanese language teacher and companion, Michiko Terai

The room used by Suu Kyi at CSEAS (Centre for South-East Asian Studies, Kyoto University) during her time as a research fellow there

Suu Kyi and Michael Aris at Simla in 1986, with a mutual friend U Kyaw Win

54 University Avenue, Rangoon, where Daw Khin Kyi and her children moved in 1953, and where Aung San Suu Kyi is presently under house arrest

MPs, went so far as to liken Aung San to Marshal Tito of Yugoslavia, who was still regarded as an absolute hero of the Second World War. Then, in a Commons debate on 7th April, Driberg launched a withering attack on Dorman-Smith.

The Governor was also in two minds about the AFPFL, and whether or not to secure the League's representation on the Executive Council. Also, there was the matter of the PVO, Aung San's paramilitaries, who had been parading in uniforms and drilling with dummy weapons made of wood. As, in further speeches, Aung San upped the ante by directly evoking the spectre of armed resistance, Dorman-Smith issued orders that the PVO (as well as other *tats*) was not to drill or wear uniforms. On 18th May several PVO officers were arrested at Tantabin by over-zealous policemen for failing to comply with Dorman-Smith's dictates. Two days later other police opened fire on protestors demonstrating against the arrests in Rangoon, killing three.

Both in Rangoon and in Whitehall the alarm bells rang. When Dorman-Smith refused to discipline the policemen concerned, Aung San called openly for 'mass civil disobedience combined with non-payment of taxes and strikes'. Cleverly, the Bogyoke had dropped any call to arms just at the moment when it might have been justified. Instead, imitating Gandhi, he was able to project himself as the man of reason and moderation. Dorman-Smith, sensing that he had been comprehensively outmanoeuvred, and stricken with (amongst other ailments) amoebic dysentery, recommended in June that all the AFPFL leaders be reined in. For Prime Minister Attlee, who had taken a close interest in Burmese affairs, this was the last straw. Who wanted another colonial war? Dorman-Smith had lost the plot. He was recalled to England, leaving Rangoon on 14th June.

Although the infamous White Paper remained on the table, the removal of Dorman-Smith represented a significant victory for the AFPFL, and for its president, Aung San. Even before he left Rangoon, Dorman-Smith was replaced at Government House by Sir Henry Knight, a common-sensical senior official in the Indian Civil Service appointed Acting Governor until a more prestigious replacement could be found. Following instructions issued by Whitehall, almost his first act was to issue an order banning prosecution of wrongdoings committed during the Japanese occupation, except where the Governor's express authorisation was given. This effectively let Aung San off the hook vis-à-vis the Thaton incident. Behind-the-scenes talks to work out a way of bringing the League into the Executive Council began in earnest. It was not until Knight himself was replaced, however, that meaningful progress could be made. Sir Hubert Rance had already headed up the military administration of Burma in the immediate post-war period in 1945. In July it was announced that he would take over as the civilian Governor of Burma, once he had resigned his army commission.

This was as clear an indication as any that the British government was prepared to compromise. Mountbatten's trusted confidant, Rance would, over the course of his fifteen-month tenure, play much the same role as Mountbatten did in India, securing and smoothing the path towards early independence. He arrived back in Rangoon at the beginning of September 1946. That he needed to negotiate with the AFPFL was apparent the moment he stepped off the plane from Calcutta. On 5th September the Rangoon police had begun a strike, for better wages and conditions. The strike was spreading quickly and had turned political. Teachers, rail- and post-office workers and students came out in sympathy, and a crippling general strike threatened.

Although the AFPFL commandeered the strike for its own purposes, both Red Flag and White Flag communists were also making hay out of it. In addition, Thakin Soe's Red Flag guerrillas were starting to have a serious impact on upcountry government facilities, with a series of bombings and arson attacks. On 18th September Rance held the first of several secret meetings with Aung San, during which the essentials of a deal were thrashed out.

The first step was to dissolve the existing Executive Council, which Rance forced through on 26th September. Although U Paw Tun and U Saw would retain their places on a new council, their influence was sharply curtailed by the AFPFL being given a majority of seats. Just as significantly, Aung San persuaded Rance that not only should he become 'Deputy Chairman', second only to Rance himself, but that he was to get the key portfolios of defence and foreign affairs – matters that the British had previously insisted on reserving to themselves.

Given that Rance's inclination was, as far as possible, to take a back seat, these arrangements effectively meant that Aung San had become Burma's Prime Minister. But they also created a split inside the AFPFL.

Following a personal appeal by Aung San, the strikes were called off on 2nd October. But for Than Tun and Thein Pe, the two White Flag communist leaders still in the AFPFL, there was a sense of a lost opportunity. They had wanted the strikes to escalate into an all-out Marxist revolution. When this did not happen, they attacked both the League and its president. The showdown came at the end of October. Amid acrimonious exchanges at emergency meetings of the AFPFL's Supreme Council, Thein Pe denounced Aung San as an 'imperialist stooge'. Aung San retaliated by castigating the communists for their treachery and betrayal. They were, he said, 'very dirty people' who had 'sowed confusion amongst the masses' and should be dealt with accordingly.

It was an important moment in Burma's history. Aung San's long flirtation with communism was finally over. With Than Tun and Thein Pe expelled from the League, the secretary-generalship of the AFPFL was given to a socialist, and leader of the BRP (Burmese Revolutionary Party), Kyaw Nyein. The air had been cleared. Although Aung San never wavered in his commitment to anti-imperialist and anti-capitalist values, during the last months of his life he was free to adumbrate a suddenly mature vision of democratic socialism that he believed best suited for Burma's future. Yet although power on his own terms was now firmly within his grasp, two great challenges remained: the advancement of independence, and the inclusion of his country's minority peoples within a comprehensive settlement that would define the coming 'Union of Burma'.

Unless these issues were resolved, Aung San knew that only trouble lay ahead. Ongoing negotiations with Rance and the British were conducted in tandem with a punishing programme of visits to Burma's 'frontier areas', to enlist the support of the country's minority leaders. Although he personally trusted Rance, Aung San kept alive the prospect of a PVO revolt led by the AFPFL, even when he headed up a delegation, mainly comprising members of the Executive Council, to London in January 1947.

By then Whitehall knew exactly what he wanted: an early, elected constitutent assembly to draw up a national constitution, and full independence outside the Commonwealth within a year. The breakthrough came on 20th December, when Prime Minister Attlee, guided by a top-secret memorandum submitted by the senior British soldier then in Burma, Major-General Harold Briggs, announced to the Commons that the White Paper needed to be 'reconsidered'. This was political code for saying that it was a dead letter, and that Burmese independence should be fast-tracked.

Aung San and other senior Burmese politicians left Rangoon on 2nd January. On his way to England he stopped over first in Delhi, where Pandit Nehru provided him with a much-needed new suit of clothes, and then in Karachi, where he met al-Jinnah, president of India's Muslim League, and soon to become president of an independent Pakistan. He arrived in London on 9th January and talks got under way at Downing Street on the 13th. By the 16th Aung San and Attlee had resolved any differences. The following day, 17th January, an agreement was signed, with only two members of the Burmese delegation – U Saw and Ba Sein – declining to add their signatures.

The Aung San-Attlee Agreement gave Aung San very nearly everything he wanted. There would be a nationwide election to a Constituent Assembly in April; the Burma Army was to be placed under the control of the AFPFL-dominated Executive Council; and there was also an £8 million loan forthcoming to help with national reconstruction. Both sides agreed to work towards the inclusion of the minorities within the forthcoming independent state, though the British stipulated that such inclusion should only be effected with the 'free assent' of each of the ethnic nationalities concerned.

The minorities question was the biggest issue of all, and Aung San, returning to Rangoon on 2nd February 1947, this time via Cairo and Karachi, wasted no time addressing it. Even before he persuaded the AFPFL to adopt the 'Attlee agreement' unanimously, on 16th February, he travelled upcountry on the 7th to the village of Panglong in the Shan states, to consult with Shan, Chin and Kachin leaders and persuade them to join the Union.

The Shan, Chin and Kachin leaders had already prepared some of the ground for him, having formed a 'Supreme Council of United Hill Peoples' that had also previously met at Panglong. But it was in Panglong that Aung San finally came face-to-face with the enduring problems of Burma. Some of the minority representatives were with him, while others were not. Among individual minorities there was suspicion and disagreement. No other Burman leader had ever proposed that Burma's principal minority peoples should be allowed even a modicum of autonomy within their own lands, or be given equal rights with the Burman majority. In the Burmese context, such proposals were revolutionary. Aung San worked overtime – talking late into the night with individual leaders in their huts – to secure compliance. But the problems confronting him were legion. Quite apart from the fact that the Karennis, who believed they already had an independent state and wanted nothing to do with any 'Union', stayed away, each of the other main minorities had its own idiosyncratic profile. Also other important minorities were not represented – notably the Muslim Rohingyas of Arakan, the Wa and the Pa-O.

Nonetheless Aung San, for once relying on his own charisma (which was the charisma of intelligence and understanding, not of a military commander), was able to construct the 'Panglong Agreement', signed on 12th February (ever after known as 'Union Day'). This at least went some way to realising his desires. The Shans, Chins and Kachins agreed in principle to join a union of Burmese peoples provided they retained a degree of autonomy.

Most worrying for Aung San was his failure to co-opt the recently formed KNU – Karen National Union, a body that claimed to represent all the Karen people (though it did not). Although later on the KNU centred its power-base along the mountainous border with Thailand, in 1947 it drew its strength from Karen townships in the Irrawaddy delta. In January the KNU had called for a separate Karen state. Aung San could only hope that in time the Karens would be brought into the fold.

As Aung San returned to Rangoon to prepare for the April elections, his standing in Burma was higher than ever. With the Attlee and Panglong Agreements in his pocket, he had pulled not one but two rabbits out of the hat. For once, it seemed, there was a Burman leader whom nearly all Burmese could trust. Even the KNU, though unwilling to participate directly, indicated that it might after all be prepared to attend the Constituent Assembly as 'observers'.

But there were still some adversaries: not only the communists, busy hell-raising in the sticks, but also the three senior Burmese politicians: Dr Ba Maw (now back in Burma), U Saw and Thakin Ba Sein. These leaders, who had so often quarrelled amongst themselves, in desperation created a coalition, known as the Saw-Sein-Maw opposition group. Yet so lacking in confidence were they that they could make any impact on the 9th April poll that they decided, like the Red Flag communists, to boycott the election altogether. The result – which may or may not have been determined by the presence of PVO men at many of the polling stations – was an overwhelming victory for the socialist AFPFL, winning 172 out of 255 seats. Of the remainder, White Flag communists won seven, independents three, while four seats were reserved for Anglo-Burmans. Sixty-nine seats were allotted to the minorities, of which twenty-four went to Karen constituencies.

Given that many of the successful 'minority' candidates were AFPFL supporters, the margin of the League's victory was even greater than it appeared on paper. Aung San now had not just a mandate, but virtual *carte blanche* to forge a new Burma. A 'pre-convention' was held at the Jubilee Hall on the Shwedagon Road between 18th and 23rd May. Then on 10th June came the first plenary meeting of the Constituent Assembly, convened at the governmental Secretariat building. Above what had hitherto been a bastion of British colonialism fluttered the flag of the Burmese resistance – a lone white star on a red ground.

To begin with Aung San presided, but from mid-June onwards he persuaded his old Rangoon University and *Do-bama Asi-ayone* comrade U Nu to assume the role of President. In a series of speeches, Aung San outlined how he thought the constitution should be framed. In accordance with his vision of a socialist federal democracy, drawn from a variety of existing models, he urged that state ownership of Burma's major industries, guarantees for the rights of every minority and an end to 'landlordism' all be written into the constitution.

By mid-June the Assembly was ready to begin work on the small print of the forthcoming constitution. It would take many weeks for its several committees, advised by Cambridge-trained lawyers, to arrive at a definitive text, but that was a matter Aung San could safely leave in the hands of others. In other respects, progress was rapid and encouraging. Well trained by the British, the Burma Rifles or Burrifs were making headway against communist insurgents, while in nearly all the 'frontier areas' peace prevailed. Britain had further scaled down its own military presence, and was preparing to hand over yet more responsibilities to the Burmese.

In Rangoon, Mandalay, Moulmein, Bassein and other towns, life was gradually returning to 'normal'. The economy was slowly picking up. Roads that had been cratered by Japanese and Allied bombs, rail tracks that had been twisted out of recognition, bridges that had been blown were being restored, and all without resort to forced labour. Cinemas and theatres were reopening. More and more people were celebrating their traditional *pwe*, or festivals, and learning how to laugh again. After the horrible privations of the war, there was just about enough to eat.

Lord Wavell, that paladin of the British empire and its military, had written to Under-Secretary Lord Pethick-Lawrence in Whitehall shortly after lunching with Aung San in Delhi on 4th January, during the latter's outward-bound journey to London, that the Burmese leader 'struck me as a suspicious, ignorant but determined little tough'. But at thirty-two, Aung San was the master of Burma, and was going about his still-difficult mission with a maturity and sure-footedness that belied his years.

He, as much as anyone, understood that the Union, when finally it came about, would of necessity be a frail organism and would require years more fattening and care if it were to survive. But Aung San and the League, and a majority of the Burmese people, were getting there, however slowly and painfully.

Until, on the morning of Saturday 19th July 1947, in the blink of an eye, it all went grotesquely wrong.

PART TWO

THE DAUGHTER

XIV

19TH JULY

How long do national heroes last? Not long in this country; they have too many enemies. Three years is the most they can hope to survive. I do not give myself more than another eighteen months of life.
Aung San, confiding to Sir Reginald Dorman-Smith, February 1946

IN a better world they would have grown old together, watching their children come of age and pursuing their individual life paths. But for Daw Khin Kyi and Aung San fate, or human malevolence, or the national dialectic – call it what you will – determined otherwise.

About the Bogyoke's chosen partner there was something unexplained. Various myths surround her. She was Karen, half-Karen, a Christian, a Baptist, even a Seventh Day Adventist. And all because she came from Myaungmya. The truth, as ever, was more simple, and more complex. Khin Kyi was born into a Burman, Buddhist household that was wealthy enough to employ mainly Muslim Indian servants. Her father, U Pho Hnyin, was an individualist who liked to go hunting and shooting. And the best hunters and shooters in his vicinity happened to be Karen Baptists. In the jungle scrub, around the evening camp fire, Pho Hnyin was regaled with stories of God and Jesus, of Redemption and the Life Everlasting. As the hot night air filled with the screeches and flutterings of Burma's endlessly varied wildlife, his Karen Baptist friends would read him passages from the Bible, so that in due course he converted to their religion and joined their Baptist Congregation.

This did not go down well with his devoutly Buddhist wife, Daw Phwa Su, or with other members of the family, including a nephew who was a *pongyi*. For many weeks there were heated arguments and smouldering stand-offs, but eventually both sides accommodated each other. Khin Kyi's childhood home became a two-religion household. Her parents decided that their children should be free to follow their own inclinations in the matter of faith. Khin Kyi therefore grew up worshipping in church and pagoda alike – not quite so strange a state of affairs as it may appear, since many Burmese are adept at belonging to communities or organisations that in the West seem exclusive of, even antithetical towards, one another. Indeed, Burmese Buddhism itself is laced with rites and beliefs that derive not from the teachings of the Gautama, but from a 'native' animism, particularly the worship of *nats*, Burma's home-grown spirits. Even so, Khin Kyi was unusual in that she was perfectly au fait with the two religions, which gave her a tolerance and understanding of different creeds, just as, with her memories of the family's Indian servants and her father's Karen hunting friends, she was understanding towards people of different ethnic backgrounds.

How much her attitudes rubbed off on Aung San is an imponderable, though it is clear that from the time they were married he became a more rounded, open, mellow individual. This might have happened anyway, as he moved from his late twenties into his early thirties; or it might have been a consequence of being happily married. Conversely, Khin Kyi was more inclined towards Christianity than Buddhism when they first met, but became, under Aung San's influence, overtly Buddhist. Later on in life, when religion mattered more and more to her, she developed close relationships with a number of Buddhist monks, and came to prize *metta* – in Buddhism, the equivalent of loving-kindness – above every other human quality.

Her knowledge of Christianity, however, must have been valuable to Aung San in his dealings with some Karen, Karenni and Kachin leaders. Both before and after the Japanese occupation, when he went 'upcountry', Khin Kyi very often accompanied him. She was also deft at putting visitors at their ease at their home in Rangoon – something Aung San, with his well-documented ability to come straight to the point and plainly speak his mind, had never adequately mastered.

Until the end of 1945, 'home' meant a succession of dwellings in and around Rangoon. They then acquired a picturesque colonial villa in a dusty road just north of the Royal (Kandawgyi) Park and Park Road (later renamed Natmauk Road in honour of the Bogyoke's birthplace) that ran around its upper perimeter. No. 25 Tower Lane had been built in the 1920s, for either an Indian or Chinese businessman. Downstairs was a generous veranda, kitchen, eating area and large reception room. There, Aung San would entertain important visitors, often late into the night, while his two sons and daughter slept upstairs, side-by-side in wooden cots in one of two bedrooms.

It was scarcely palatial – indeed, its interior was almost spartanly simple – but its high ceilings and electric fans represented a real advance on what they had had before. It was not an altogether unfitting residence for a Burmese General who had taken unprecedentedly early retirement. As well as being set in a good-sized garden full of tropical trees and plants with an ornamental pond, it had a turret at one of its corners.

The turret's narrow spiral staircase was accessed through a door off the master bedroom, where Aung San kept his modest but distinctly political library. At its top was a tiny 'meditation' room, with a window that looked out towards the Shwedagon, a mile or so to the west. With no space for anything other than a chair and small table for writing on, this was where the General sought the solitude essential for his evolving thoughts.

The children – each a token of their parents' deepening love for each other – had been born in quick succession: Aung San Oo, the older boy, little more than nine months after the September 1942 wedding; Aung San Lin, the younger boy, in 1944; and Aung San Suu Kyi (her name means 'Strange Collection of Bright Victories') in 1945, on 19th June. The incorporation of their father's name was unusual, though not unique, particularly among the offspring of the illustrious. There had been a fourth child, Aung San Chit, a second girl, born in September 1946; but to her parents' grief, Chit (meaning 'love') died a few days after coming into the world.

The most difficult pregnancy had been the third, Suu Kyi's: not because of any unusual medical problem, but because of what happened during its last few months.

During the Japanese occupation Aung San and Khin Kyi had sometimes sheltered Burmese on the run from the dreaded *Kempeitai*. Whatever the danger to themselves, they could not turn away such fugitives. A much greater danger, however, threatened the young family in March 1945, when, under Aung San's direction, the Burmese National Army defected to the Allies. To take Khin Kyi and the two boys with him to his battle headquarters at Thayetchaung carried too many risks. But leaving them in Rangoon was even riskier. If they fell into Japanese hands once the BNA turned coat, the punitive revenge that might be exacted was unthinkable. The solution – overseen by the ever-reliable Bo Let Ya – was to secrete them in the depths of the Irrawaddy delta until such time as the danger had passed.

They left Rangoon on the night of the 18th, arriving at Pyapon three days later on the 21st, accompanied by five BNA soldiers dressed as poor civilians and by one of Khin Kyi's sisters. The Japanese were told they were off to make a short visit to relatives in Myaungmya.

To get to Pyapon they travelled by river boat and sampan. Alarmingly, at one point on the Twante waterway, a huddle of sampans close to them was strafed by an overflying Japanese aircraft. More alarmingly still, they found Pyapon crawling with Japanese military. So they pressed on, to Kyetphamwezaung, a minuscule fishing village that could only be reached by rowing across the sea. But even in Kyetphamwezaung there was a nervous moment when they ran into a Japanese soldier standing on the village's narrow wooden wharf. Khin Kyi explained to him that they lived nearby and had come to Kyetphamwezaung to buy fresh fish. Mercifully the Japanese soldier laughed. He said that was why he was there too.

Within a day or two dreadful rumours circulated that the BNA rebellion had collapsed, and that Aung San had been killed. But after two weeks a note written unmistakably in Aung San's own hand arrived, telling Khin Kyi to bring the boys back to Rangoon. The capital had been abandoned by the Japanese.

This was the most desperate passage in their marriage: enforced separation with no guarantee of reunion. But they lived through it, as well as other crises. Now, five years on, they were beginning to enjoy something that approximated to a normal existence. Against the odds perhaps, Aung San showed every sign of becoming a well-adjusted, loving father, as well as an attentive husband. His temper was becoming more moderate by the day. Around the house he was known as Phay Phay. There were nursemaids to look after the children when the parents were absent on political work, and a cook, since by her own admission Khin Kyi was 'useless' in the kitchen. But on the rare evening they were alone together, she would darn or embroider whilst he sat quietly reading. They even managed to snatch a brief first holiday together, immediately after the elections to the Constituent Assembly in April 1947. They went up to Maymyo, the hill station outside Mandalay. For some time Aung San had been saying that after independence he would retire from politics and devote his time to writing. Now he talked about starting a market garden, up there in Maymyo, as well.

Probably it was just a pipe dream. Running Burma would keep him more than busy for the foreseeable future. Yet at least, as deputy chairman of the Executive Committee and Burma's effective Prime Minister, Aung San had begun settling into a routine existence. He left 'for the office' each morning after breakfast. Whenever he could, he came back at midday for lunch with his wife and children, before returning to the Secretariat for further meetings. Because he liked to read important documents on his way to work, he allowed himself the luxury of an official car and driver. But those were the limits of the trappings of high office that he found permissible.

Saturday 19th July 1947 was just another day, though with the added excitement that, later on, he was to see Colonel Suzuki. Having been apprehended in Japan, Suzuki had been brought back to Rangoon while possible war crimes were investigated, and was presently incarcerated at Insein. That meeting Aung San was looking forward to immensely. Suzuki might have been a servant of Japan in its fascist incarnation, but he could not forget the help given to him by Suzuki during the most critical days of his life.

Wearing traditional Burmese clothes – collarless shirt, silk jacket and gold-coloured *longyi* – at 10 a.m. he lightly kissed Khin Kyi's cheek and hugged Aung San Oo, Aung San Lin and little Suu Kyi, all of them the apples of their papa's watery eye. Then he set off for the city centre, to chair a provisional government cabinet meeting.

It was the last time they would see him alive.

His assassins came from a little further out, from another colonial villa – no. 4 Ady Road – set on a promontory jutting out into the waters of Rangoon's Lake Victoria (Inya Lake). U Saw's murderous crew, gathered at his residence, had been up since daybreak, checking their weapons in anticipation of the deed ahead.

U Saw himself was confident and phlegmatic. In his late forties, and exuding all the charm of a cornered bullfrog, he had several scores to settle with the upstart Aung San. Had not he, U Saw, been Prime Minister once, before the British transported him to Uganda and put him in detention because he would not bend to their demands in the war against the Japanese? Had not he, U Saw, also gone to London in 1941, five years before Aung San, to tell the British that the price of his cooperation was a guarantee of full independence once the war was over? The British had spurned his offer. Now they had given Aung San precisely the terms that he, U Saw, had asked for.

Aung San! So close to the Governor, so close to the British: could he really be trusted? And still close to some of the communists, whom U Saw despised. At least there were none of them in Aung San's cabinet any more. But then nor was he, or Dr Ba Maw. Burma's two most experienced politicians had been frozen out by that wily snake from Natmauk.

As if that were not enough, on 21st September 1946 there had been an attempt on U Saw's own life. As he drove home from Government House along the Prome Road, a jeep had drawn level and a man dressed in the uniform of the PVO, Aung San's militia, fired a shot at him. The bullet missed, but U Saw was badly cut by flying glass from the shattered window.

At least, that is what U Saw had told everybody: for there was a suspicion that the bungled assassination had been contrived. U Saw's own private militia, assembled before the war, had been called the Galon Tat, after Saya San's Galon Army – lest anyone forget the part U Saw had played during Saya San's trial. And that perhaps was what rankled with him most: he, not Aung San, was the original, founding patriot.

Though the Galon Tat had been disbanded, there were still men whose loyalty was to him and him alone. At 8.30 a.m. on 19th July a Fordson truck left U Saw's compound. Inside were his wife's nephew, Khin Maung Yin, and three others. None was armed. Rather they were being sent ahead to reconnoitre the two-storeyed Secretariat building: to ascertain that a cabinet meeting was still slated for 10.30, and to confirm that security was as lax as ever.

The advance party had no difficulty in entering the Secretariat. It even used one of its telephones to report back to Ady Road. Given the all-clear, five more men, dressed in pre-war jungle fatigues and led by the oldest, Maung Soe, left the compound in a jeep at the same time as Aung San was leaving Tower Lane. Three of them were in the back of the vehicle, concealed under a tarpaulin with their weapons: four Tommy guns and one sten gun.

They arrived at the Secretariat just as, upstairs, Aung San's meeting commenced. As they drove through the central archway, no one tried to stop them. With well-rehearsed precision they stormed up a staircase and burst into the long room used by Aung San for discussions with his ministers. The Bogyoke himself was seated at the far end, at the head of a square horseshoe of tables. On either side of him sat his colleagues.

'Don't run away!' Maung Soe bellowed. 'Don't get up!'

Before Aung San could rise to his feet the assassins opened fire, hitting him first with thirteen bullets, then most of the others. In the space of thirty seconds, four other ministers were killed immediately: Thakin Mya (Councillor for Finance); U Abdul Razak (a Muslim, and Councillor for Education and National Planning); Mahn Ba Khaing (a delta Karen, and Councillor for Industry and Labour); and Aung San's eldest brother, U Ba Win (Councillor for Commerce and Supplies), who had looked after Aung San so well in Yenangyaung twenty years before. Two other ministers – U Ba Choe (Councillor for Information) and Sao Sam Htun (a Shan *sawbwa* and Councillor for the Frontier Areas) – died within hours of being taken to Rangoon General Hospital.

Of the Executive Council members killed, Aung San was the youngest, by a full eight years. The average age of his colleagues was forty-six – proof, if proof were needed, of the Bogyoke's leadership qualities.

The flower of Burma's administrative talent had been taken out in one fell swoop. Also killed that morning were U Ohn Maung, deputy secretary of the Department of Transport and Communications, who had come to deliver a report; and Ko Htwe, Razak's eighteen-year-old personal bodyguard.

The assassins hastened out of the room, raced downstairs again, climbed into the jeep and headed back to Ady Road. There U Saw was waiting for them. Although they had failed to locate and eliminate Thakin Nu, who had also been on the hit-list, U Saw was well pleased with what had been done and served celebratory drinks. It was only a matter of hours, he surmised, before Governor Sir Hubert Rance summoned him to form a new government. Instead, at three o'clock in the afternoon, a large body of police flooded into the compound. Although security at the Secretariat had been non-existent – despite a forewarning passed on to Aung San three days before that a conspiracy was afoot – the jeep's number plate had been taken down by an alert newspaper reporter as the men made their getaway. The comings and goings at 4 Ady Road had also been observed by curious neighbours.

A desperate attempt was made to throw the guns used at the Secretariat into the lake. Other than that, U Saw did not attempt to obstruct what the police had come to do. A glass of whisky in his hand, he still believed he would emerge triumphant. After all, *thoke-thin-ye* – getting rid of one's rivals – was the Burmese way of achieving power. But it was not the British way, which preferred the rule of law. U Saw spent that night and every other night of what remained of his life at Insein prison. To his unspeakable chagrin, it was U Nu, not himself, whom Rance requested to form a new cabinet.

In the immediate aftermath of the multiple assassination, 800-odd possible suspects, including Dr Ba Maw and Ba Sein, were rounded up and detained, since the authorities had no idea how widely U Saw's conspiracy extended. But except for U Saw himself and those directly involved in the attack on the Secretariat, all were released once initial investigations had been concluded.

However, there was one embarrassing complication that became caviar for conspiracy theorists. A few days after 19th July a cache of weapons carefully stored in watertight drums was found in Lake Victoria, just a few feet from the bottom of U Saw's garden. These, it transpired, had been supplied (for a price) by one Captain David Vivian and two other British officers, having previously been pilfered from a police arms depot. In due course Vivian too found himself a guest at Insein. But this has never discouraged those wishing to believe that Aung San's assassination was planned by mandarins in Whitehall – for all that, by the summer of 1947, the British government wanted nothing so much as to wash its hands of Burma as swiftly and cleanly as possible.

Just as far-fetched is the notion that U Saw was in league with Bo Ne Win, Burma's eventual dictator. If he was, no compelling evidence has ever been produced. On 20th September 1947 a special tribunal ordered by Rance to try U Saw, the assassins and their accomplices began its work. On 30th December, six days ahead of Independence, it delivered its judgment. All those accused were found guilty. U Saw appealed against the verdict, but failed in his action. On 8th May 1948 he and five others were hanged. Their unarmed accomplices were given lengthy prison sentences.

The Bogyoke's body was taken first to the house in Tower Lane and then to Rangoon General Hospital, where Daw Khin Kyi herself, drawing on her wartime experience as a nurse, cleaned her husband's wounds. This done, his corpse, like those of the other murdered ministers, was placed in a casket and taken to Jubilee Hall, on the Shwedagon Road. Eventually, in April 1948, their remains were interred beneath the Martyrs'

Monument at a site just north of the Shwedagon pagoda. Tens of thousands turned out for the belated funeral cortège, and 19th July, the day of the killings, was designated Martyrs' Day in the Burmese calendar.

Had Aung San not been assassinated, but continued at the helm through and after independence, which came on 4th January 1948, it is probable that Burma's history might have taken a different course. If there was one man capable of knocking sense into antagonistic, warring heads, it was Aung San. But it is equally probable that even he would have struggled to contain and manage the problems that beset Burma from independence onwards.

One unknown is how Aung San himself might have changed. Power might well have corrupted him, as it corrupted other single-minded revolutionary leaders in Asia: Mao Zedong and Bung Sukarno, though not Ho Chi Minh.

Although his final months are astonishing for the accelerating maturity of his political thought, expressed in a dozen or so speeches at a variety of forums, Aung San had not yet fully conquered his latent impatience. In one angry outburst during a speech made on 6th February 1947, he rounded on the press. 'Some newspapers, knowing everything, go on writing what they like,' he said. 'To be frank they are like goats' testicles.' This did not augur well for freedom of expression, any more than Aung San's reliance on the PVO during the critical immediate post-war period suggested much other than a means-justifies-the-ends mentality. Amongst the ends cherished by Aung San was the union of Burma, which for him was non-negotiable. However diligently he worked to persuade Burma's minorities that there was a future for them within the coming state, any notion of an independent Kachinland, for example, or 'Karenistan' (a word much bandied about in 1947) was anathema to him.

One well-regarded English historian of Burma, Hugh Tinker, in his book *The Union of Burma* (1961), wrote about Aung San that 'His whole life (except, perhaps, his last six months), was devoted to bitter and often unscrupulous opposition to Britain; his methods were often violent and sometimes cruel; he acted treacherously, first to the British, and then to the Japanese; his concept of independence was narrowly nationalistic; and he failed to grasp the potentialities of the new multi-racial [British] Commonwealth.' Tinker had the sense to add: 'But all this is, of course, completely irrelevant to the great mass of Burmans, whose admiration for Aung San is akin to worship.'

Aung San Suu Kyi, being a Burman herself, reflected a commonly held view when, in the outline portrait of Aung San that she published in 1984, she wrote: 'He would not tolerate self-seekers, irresponsible actions, or dereliction of duty which threatened the independence cause. He believed in the principles of justice and democracy, and there were times he deferred to his colleagues when he might better have trusted his own judgement . . . He was not infallible, as he freely acknowledged, but he had the kind of mind that did not cease expanding, a capacity for continuous development.' Further, in his daughter's view:

Aung San's appeal was not so much to extremists as to the great majority of citizens who wished to pursue their own lives in peace and prosperity under a leader they could trust and respect. In him they saw that leader, a man who put the interests of the country before his own needs, who remained poor and unassuming at the height of his power, who accepted the responsibilities of leadership without hankering after the privileges, and who, for all his political acumen and powers of statecraft, retained at the core of his being a deep simplicity.

This, the notion of St Aung San, may have been over-egging the cake. Yet the truth remains that, not unlike his daughter, Aung San became (and remains) an iconic figure in Burma, and one whom both sides – the military regime as much as the democratic opposition movement – seek to claim as their own.

To have had him even as an unremembered father was a privileged distinction. But it was a poisoned chalice too. However small or great the gap between the real Aung San and the popular conception of him, it was the latter that set a near-unattainable standard for his daughter to emulate.

XV

THE GOLDEN RAIN IS BROWN

In Burma there is no prejudice against girl babies. In fact, there is a general belief that daughters are more dutiful and loving than sons and many Burmese parents welcome the birth of a daughter as an assurance that they will have somebody to take care of them in their old age.

Aung San Suu Kyi, *Letters from Burma* (1997)

As a grown-up Suu Kyi was unsure how much, if anything, she could remember about her father. In a conversation with Alan Clements, an American rights activist and writer with a special interest in Buddhist psychology, she said in 1996 that she had 'a memory of him picking me up every time he came home from work'.* But she also wondered how real this memory was, and whether it was not 'reinforced by people repeating it to me all the time'.

He might be dead, but the house in Tower Lane continued to be filled with Aung San's presence for as long as the family lived there. A constant stream of visitors included, as well as Prime Minister Nu, many of the Thirty Comrades who had formed the nucleus of the Burma Independence Army in 1942, and other officers who had fought alongside Aung San. Dangling the Bogyoke's tiny daughter on their knees, and telling her how great a man her father had been, was intended not only as a comfort to the child, but as a way of maintaining a bond, however vicarious, with their vastly respected leader.

Daw Khin Kyi too regularly evoked her husband's memory, both for

---

*Aung San Suu Kyi, *The Voice of Hope* (1997)

sentimental reasons and as a moral example for her children to follow. She was punctilious in inviting Buddhist monks to her home, not just on each succeeding anniversary of the assassination, but on the 19th of every month. But 19th July was always a special occasion, when no fewer than thirty-five *pongyis* would be welcomed at no. 25: one for each year of Aung San's life, with a further three to symbolise the three bedrocks of his faith, the Buddha, the Dharma and the Sangha – the Teacher, the Path and the Monkhood; or, in another register, the Messiah, Message and Church.

The example Khin Kyi herself set was forceful, and may be said to have moulded Suu Kyi's character. Because Aung San had laid aside his General's uniform, there was no question of an automatic army pension. The colonial government made a discretionary award of 100,000 Indian rupees to each of the murdered ministers' widows, but, handy though this was, it was never going to be enough to keep the household going and give the Bogyoke's children an upbringing commensurate with the status achieved by their father. Following independence, the Burmese government could have been prevailed upon to care for Aung San's family, however stretched public finances were. But for Daw Khin Kyi that was wrong. She might be widowed, but she still wanted to pull her weight in society. Not long after Aung San was finally interred at the Martyrs' Mausoleum, she began putting out feelers. She had given up her job at Rangoon General Hospital immediately after marrying – to help her husband in his political work and have his children – but now she approached the medical authorities to see if she could resume her nursing career. Hearing this, U Nu himself intervened. It was unthinkable that the widow of the country's founding statesman should find herself back on the wards. What she needed was a dignified position that would enable her to put her administrative talents to use. She was offered, and accepted, the post of director of the National Women and Children's Welfare Board.

This marked the beginning of a twenty-year career in public service. In 1953 she was appointed chairman of the Social Planning Commission, and continued in that capacity until 1958, when she left to organise the women's wing of U Nu's Union Party. In 1960 she became, at the age of forty-eight, the first woman to be appointed an ambassador by the Burmese government. Her posting, to India, was at once a diplomatic plum and hugely demanding. She acquitted herself with distinction. But in 1967 she took retirement, having decided that she could no longer represent a state ruled by the despotic dictator General Ne Win, with whom she had never got along and about whom Aung San himself had grave reservations.

Along the way Khin Kyi briefly represented her husband's constituency (Lanmadaw) as its MP, was a member of Burma's film censorship board and led Burmese delegations to WHO (World Health Organisation) conferences in Geneva. In 1950 she was accorded the title 'Mother of Burma' by the US government, and in 1955 received the Yugoslav Star as well as Thailand's Noble Order of the Crown. Yet when it became clear that Ne Win had no intention of restoring Burma's democracy, and now worn out, she decided to have nothing more to do with his regime, preferring instead to spend her later years tending her garden and lending support to such women's organisations as Ne Win permitted.

After Aung San's death, Khin Kyi lost her Burmese bloom. She stopped putting flowers in her hair and steadily put on weight. But she did not turn her back on society. First in Tower Lane, then at 54 University Avenue, she kept an open house, always willing to serve Burmese food to those friends and admirers who, in the Burmese way, dropped by unannounced. There were also many foreign and Western guests – among them diplomats and distinguished visitors to Burma – who had to be catered for less informally.

With so many public and social duties to perform, Khin Kyi was not what would today be called a 24/7 hands-on parent. She cherished her children, but there was an objectivity about her affection for them. With no husband to share the responsibilities of parenting, Khin Kyi knew that it was down to her to enforce discipline and instil the values of integrity and truth-telling that she and Aung San prized. Again in her conversations with Alan Clements, Suu Kyi would recall that, naturally warm-hearted though she was, 'She was very strict at times.'

As a youngster, Suu Kyi felt this to be a 'disadvantage'. Only later, after she herself had become a mother and begun Buddhist meditation, did she understand that Daw Khin Kyi had, in her characteristically selfless way, chosen the harder, better option. Unlike her father, Suu Kyi was never over-indulged during her early childhood. Her most treasured possession was a doll that Bogyoke Aung San had brought back for her from London in January 1947, following his talks with Clement Attlee. But the doll was not a plaything so much as a trophy. It remained in pristine condition throughout and beyond Suu Kyi's childhood.

Like all children of above-average intelligence, Suu Kyi was prone to asking questions. Her mother did not encourage her in this, but nor did she discourage her. When she came back from her office in the late afternoons, Khin Kyi would often lie down on her bed for a while, especially if she had guests or some other engagement in the evenings. Suu Kyi, eagerly awaiting her return, would run into the bedroom, then walk round and round her bed. Each time she reached its foot, she would pop another question. Some of them, such as. 'Why is water called water?', were impossible riddles. If Khin Kyi knew the answer, she would give it; if she did not, she would say so. But what she would not do was pretend that she knew what she did not, or close the door, or tell Suu Kyi to run away and play.

In an important way, Khin Kyi was always there for her daughter. On and off there were other grown-ups in the household: a maternal great-aunt who lovingly recounted the *jatakas* – Buddha stories; and U Pho Hynin, Suu Kyi's adored and adoring Christian grandfather. When she was old enough, and he had become blind, she would read him passages from a Burmese translation of the Bible. But mainly it was Khin Kyi who held everything together.

Despite the loss of her husband, her demanding schedules and the uncertainties that plagued Burma once the first of an interminable series of civil wars broke out in 1948, Khin Kyi provided the material and emotional security every child needs. In so doing she furnished Suu Kyi with a model of selflessness – indeed, to label someone 'selfish' was the ultimate mark of Daw Khin Kyi's disapproval – that would one day replicate itself in dramatic circumstances.

For herself, there was never any question of a second marriage. As she constantly imparted to her children, Aung San was irreplaceable in every way. It was not just a devoted husband she had lost, but an entire people's figurehead. How could there be any other? It would have been a betrayal of the basest kind. A sacrilege.

When she became an adult, Suu Kyi would tell women friends how her mother never let her leave the house or come downstairs to be presented to guests in the evenings, unless she was perfectly turned out. This meant no dirty or creased clothes, and above all meticulously combed hair – not just because, in Burmese culture, the female is expected to look her best, but because it was part of the discipline of self-management. In former head nurse Daw Khin Kyi's view, a person's outside was a reliable guide to their inside. Self-respect and the respect of others were intimately entwined, and between them could produce respect for others, which was all-important. And if this meant training Suu Kyi to spend a part of the day combing her hair, then so be it.

The adult Suu Kyi had other memories. She was, she was sure, during her earliest years at least, a 'normal, naughty child', who much preferred going out to play to sitting indoors with her schoolwork: otherwise what was the point of having such a large garden? She knew what she should and should not do, because her mother told her, but even so often took delight in wilful disobedience – what child psychologists call testing the limits of permitted behaviour. Not until she was ten or eleven did she begin channelling her precocious talents into something definably serious, but once that happened she became, by her own estimation, 'a bookworm'. As a very young child, Suu Kyi read Burmese and Western fairy tales, and sometimes comics, but her first ambition, fired by the lingering aura of Aung San, was to become a soldier. 'Everyone referred to my father as *Bogyoke,* which means General,' she told Clements in 1996, 'so I wanted to be a general too because I thought this was the best way to serve one's country, just like my father had done.' But dreams of military prowess gave way to another ambition that she shared with Aung San, to become a writer. This stayed with her. By her own admission, the critical moment came when a cousin introduced her to Sherlock Holmes, Arthur Conan Doyle's idiosyncratic, violin-playing sleuth, and staple reading in the English-speaking world of the 1950s. 'How could Bugs Bunny's adventures compare with those of a man who could, from a careful examination of a battered old hat, gauge the physical and mental attributes, the financial situation and the matrimonial difficulties of its erstwhile owner?' Aung San Suu Kyi enthused. 'I decided that detectives were much more interesting and entertaining than anthropomorphised animals.'

So began an abiding, and discriminating, addiction to crime fiction. Georges Simenon's Maigret would become preferable to Agatha Christie's Hercule Poirot, not least because he had a more credible taste in food. 'The small restaurants he discovers in the midst of his investigations seem to specialise in robust, full-flavoured provincial dishes reminiscent of Elizabeth David's French cooking.' 'Does George Smiley ever eat?' she would ask, taking a bite out of John Le Carré's spymaster. Her chosen thriller writers were Dorothy L. Sayers, Josephine Tey, P.D. James and (later on) Ruth Rendell, all of whom she noted for their 'excellence'. But, as one thing leads to another, so detective stories opened up the whole field of literature. Suu Kyi discovered that she greatly loved 'real books'. By the time she was thirteen she was into the classics. Wherever she went the teenager took something serious or sensible to read. 'For example,' she told Clements, 'when I went shopping with my mother I would bring a book along.' Unfortunately, reading while the car was moving made her feel sick; but whenever the car stopped, say at a traffic light, her head dived back down into the printed page.

The diminutive, impeccably turned-out word-guzzler did well at school. Like her brothers, Aung San Oo and Aung San Lin, Aung San Suu Kyi began at St Francis Convent, a small private establishment that admitted both boys and girls into its kindergarten and primary divisions, and was located conveniently near Tower Lane. There Suu Kyi began learning English – considered an essential attainment by Burma's upper classes as much after independence as before. There too she might have stayed, to complete her secondary education. But in 1956, aged eleven and already showing academic promise, Suu Kyi transferred to the more prestigious Methodist English High School in Signal Road.

Along with the Anglican St John's Diocesan Boys' School and the Roman Catholic St Paul's High School, the Methodist English High School was rated among the best in Burma – if not *the* best. That it was nominally 'Christian' was neither here nor there. Most pupils came from non-Christian backgrounds, whether Burmese Buddhist, Chinese Daoist, Indian Hindu or Muslim. Any effort to inculcate Christian values was by the back door. The Methodist English High School thrived because it offered Rangoon's elite an education palpably superior to anything the struggling state could provide in its public-sector schools. It was not a charity, but a fee-paying, self-sufficient enterprise, and had the advantage of being close to Daw Khin Kyi's office.

It also had a curious history. Before the war, on the same site the Methodist English Girls' School had existed, but this had been all but destroyed by the Japanese. The adjoining English Methodist church was spared bombardment because, for a while, it had been used by the staff of Chandra Bose's Indian National Army (which, like the BIA, was bankrolled by Japan). When the British returned, three individuals combined to get the school up and running again, on a mixed-sex basis: Dr Frank Munton, an English Methodist minister who became the chairman of its Board; the Scotsman George Logie, a director of the Valvoline Oil Company, who provided financial guidance; and his wife, Doreen A. Logie, who became the school's formidable headmistress.

The initial pupil enrolment, housed in the vestry of the Methodist church in 1946, was a bare sixty-four. By 1963 this number had swollen to 4,300, and went on rising even after General Ne Win nationalised the school as State High School Number One Dagon the following year. Betwixt and between it had benefited from $1,000,000, raised and donated by Methodists in the United States – at the time a colossal sum of money.

Doreen A. Logie was a no-nonsense principal who, in the best traditions of Miss Jean Brodie, liked to keep her female charges under particularly close scrutiny. According to Ma Thanegi – a slightly younger pupil than Suu Kyi who would one day become her political assistant and suffer imprisonment – Daw Logie was 'She Who Must Be Obeyed, First Class'.* She waged war against whatever latest fashion threatened to pervert the hearts and souls of her girls – be it provocative stiffened underwear or 'beehive' hair-dos. Even though the headmistress herself wore high heels, she could creep up on you 'silent as an Apache', and it was only due to her 'advance guard', a yapping Dachshund, that the awesome Daw Logie could most times be evaded.

The school was bilingual (English and Burmese), just as it was bi-curricular (both the national matriculation, opening the way for admission to Rangoon University, and England's GCE, General Certificate of Education). But there were heavy fines for any pupil speaking the Burmese language in English classes. Partly as a result of such rules, Suu Kyi became the fluent English speaker her mother wanted her to be.

Yet the Methodist English High School was not altogether draconian. Many of its staff were eccentric, as happens in any school, state-run or private. Some had the true teacher's vocation, to impart the excitement of knowledge as well as knowledge itself. Among these was Daw Khin Bu Swe, whose artful lessons in Burmese literature inspired all who sat at their desks in front of her, Suu Kyi included.

Suu Kyi responded well to her, and to other 'arts' subject teachers. She did less well, at first, at maths and science. But by steely application by the age of fifteen she was regularly coming first in her class in every subject.

For the *Bogyoke*'s daughter, the Methodist English High School was a clever choice, however much it cost. Just because Aung San was her

* See the MEHS alumni website: www.inwa.com.

father, nowhere in Burma could Suu Kyi hope to enjoy quotidian anonymity for long. But the school's exacting ethos, and its multi-ethnic intake, meant that her parental profile was reduced to manageable proportions – the more so since the children of many other leading Burmese figures also attended MEHS. These included all six sons and daughters of General Ne Win, even though, at the time Suu Kyi left, Ne Win was already contemplating imposing a root-and-branch 'socialist' regime on Burma.

Daw Khin Kyi neither asked, nor expected, that her daughter be accorded special treatment. If Suu Kyi stood out, she did so on her own merits, and because of the diligence she had acquired at home. Yet her education at the Methodist school was abruptly cut off when she was in Tenth Grade, two years before she was due to sit her matriculation examinations, by her mother's appointment as Burma's ambassador to India in 1960. Daw Khin Kyi wanted to keep Suu Kyi – in whom she invested many of her own womanly aspirations – at her side, at least for the time being. And so, aged fifteen, Aung San Suu Kyi embarked for Delhi – the prelude to a twenty-eight-year sojourn outside the land of her birth.

Neither at 25 Tower Lane, nor later at 54 University Avenue, were luxury goods conspicuous. During the war Khin Kyi had sold such jewels as she had to help the Burmese Independence Army. She made no attempt to replace them, other than accepting the occasional gift of a well-wisher or close friend. The furniture in both residences was simple: well-made, practical wooden chairs, tables, beds and cupboards, but nothing exceptional. There were no elaborate dinner services, no collections of expensive Buddhist antiques, no fancy electric gadgets, just homely items fit for everyday use. Once purchased, a clock or radio was intended to last, however often it needed to be repaired. The American concept of consumer disposables, which was creeping into post-War Burma through an influx of Japanese manufactures, was firmly resisted.

Daw Khin Kyi dressed herself and her children neatly and presentably, but never at too great cost. She preferred traditional Burmese garments, which could be bought in Rangoon's markets, to the Western styles on offer at Rowe's and other downtown department stores. This aspect of her upbringing aside, Suu Kyi's childhood was one of privilege and expectation. The education she received was the best in Rangoon that money could buy, and was supplemented by what she would one day call the 'important people' who came to pay their respects to her mother. From a very young age she learned how to comport herself in front of men and women whose achievements were not inconsiderable, and to absorb some at least of what they talked about.

That Khin Kyi's friends and acquaintances were a cosmopolitan crowd, and that she entertained (whether in person or in the abstract) members of Burma's increasingly threatened minorities, added to the broadening of Suu Kyi's developing outlook. Even before she left for India, she had begun to acquire that sophistication about the peoples of the world that, thirty years later, would irritate her lesser-educated antagonists in the military. But when she left Burma she took with her other, more ordinary memories – memories of classrooms and playgrounds, of the busy, bustling streets of Rangoon and the excitements of the Burmese calendar, with its battery of *pwe*, Buddhist and other traditional festivals.

Best of all was *Thingyan*, the water festival, held in April to usher in the Burmese New Year. The whole country ran amok, with everybody drenching each other by whatever means was to hand, or had been devised in the days leading up to *Thingyan*. But it was not just indigenous festivals that gave the people a ready excuse to take yet another day off work. Even though they were not Hindu, many celebrated *Divali*, while the Chinese New Year earlier in February was, with its dragon parades and heart-stopping firecrackers, a must for all. Christmas was also celebrated by some. Santa Claus was as good a way as any to bring delight to children's faces. Usually Santa Claus could be found presiding over a Lucky Dip at a charity fair.

Suu Kyi would long recall winning a bottle of whisky, then 'a rare and expensive object' in Burma.* At once she was surrounded by a gaggle of men, eager to congratulate her. This she could not understand – a bag of sweets would have been much nicer. Swiftly she complied with her mother's command that she give the beastly thing away as quickly as possible. 'The whole incident,' the latent governess in her reflected, 'somewhat diminished my faith both in lucky dips and in adult taste.'

But it was not all fun and games, or riddles to be solved. 'As a child,' she later wrote, 'I would stand on the veranda of the house where I was born and watch the sky darken and listen to the grown-ups wax

* See Aung San Suu Kyi, *Letters from Burma* (1997)

sentimental over smoky banks of massed rain clouds.' During the monsoon months, May through to September, the rain fell 'in rods of glinting crystal'. Sharing the spectacle with her, a 'musically minded cousin' would call out, 'Oh, the golden rain is brown' – words from a popular Burmese ballad.

Suu Kyi was not sure whether this was an apt description, whether indeed the line was intended to be 'poetic or comic'. But even as a six-year-old the phenomenon of a tropical downpour, lasting hours at a stretch, stirred within her 'undefined yearnings for times past'. Perhaps there just was, among the adults who gathered in Tower Lane and the atmosphere they generated, a feeling of something better, gone before – hardly surprising, since everything that independence had seemed to promise was turning sour.

Too soon, Suu Kyi had a reason of her own to look back with regretful dismay. Of her two brothers, it was Aung San Lin with whom the little girl got along best. Aung San Oo, the eldest, could be moody and aloof, and was usually unwilling to play games that he felt were beneath his age or dignity. But Lin was something else. He was rowdy, boisterous and always fun to be around. There was about him something of the 'little tough' that Lord Wavell had identified in his father, but no less lovable for that.

Suu Kyi adored him. But on the morning of 16th January 1953 Aung San Lin was taken from her. In the middle of the dry season they had been playing in the garden at Tower Lane. Suu Kyi went inside for a while, and Lin went down to the ornamental pond in a hollow beside the driveway leading up to the front of the house. A toy gun fell in the water. In retrieving it, he got one of his sandals stuck in the mud just below the water's surface. Aung San Lin rushed to find his sister, handed her the gun and told her to look after it while he went back for the sandal. The next thing anybody knew, Lin's body was drifting face-down across the middle of the pond. Thirty-eight years afterwards, on 15th October 1991, the *New York Times* reported (probably erroneously) that Daw Khin Kyi, told of this ghastly accident, stayed at her desk in her office until the normal time to leave. For Aung San's widow, the reporter moralised, public duty always preceded personal suffering. Or perhaps Daw Khin Kyi was too used to having someone dear to her taken away not to realise there was nothing that could usefully be done, except leave Tower Lane.

Suu Kyi was too young to comprehend fully the meaning of death.

She could not understand why her mother wanted to move house. But she was affected nonetheless. Not just her favourite brother, but her best playmate and closest friend had somehow vanished, with no forewarning. She did not grieve so much as find herself filled with a profound sorrow, which would sometimes return to haunt her when she watched falling rain, whether in Burma or later in Delhi and Oxford.

Sorrow was new to the seven-year-old girl, and contrasted sharply with such other emotions as sculpted the first few years of her life. It also contrasted with the orderly, protective environment that her ceaselessly responsible mother had built around her. Humanity was not, after all, as robust as she had been led to suppose.

XVI

AN INDIAN IDYLL: THE 'UGLY ONE'
TAKES WING

In courtesy I'd have her chiefly learned; ...
W.B. Yeats, 'A Prayer for My Daughter' (1921)

THE move to no. 54 University Avenue that followed Aung San Lin's death was facilitated by U Nu's government. The compound by Inya Lake was gifted by the government to Daw Khin Kyi and her family. In return the house in Tower Lane was made over to the state, to be preserved as the Bogyoke Aung San Museum.

Burma's military rulers being perennially desirous to claim Aung San as their own, the museum has remained open to the public, though its opening hours are restricted. When, posing as a tourist with an interest in the history of the Second World War, I visited the Tower Lane villa in April 2005, I was surprised to find photographs of Aung San Suu Kyi together with other members of her family adorning the walls upstairs and downstairs. There were no individual pictures of her, but no attempt had been made to erase her image from family composites.

I was less surprised to be trailed from room to room by an army type more interested in finding out whatever he could about a lone middle-aged British male than he was in divulging any information about himself. I pointed my finger at each of the children, beginning with Aung San Oo, asking, 'And that is?' When it came to Suu Kyi, the army type replied: 'That is the ugly one.' I took care not to ask him what he meant, but instead enthused about the Bogyoke. It was so good, I purred, to see for myself his collection of books, and his modest wardrobe – including a military topcoat given to him by Jawaharlal Nehru – stacked neatly in a glass-fronted cabinet.

Having gained the man's confidence, I was allowed as a favour to climb the turret (normally roped off) and behold for myself the view of the Shwedagon pagoda that Aung San must have gazed at so often sixty years before. When I returned downstairs to the master bedroom I looked again at a group of family shots. The army type must have sensed what was on my mind. 'She came here a few years ago,' he said, 'to pay respects to her father on the anniversary of his death. That is our custom in Myanmar. To honour our parents all our lives.'

'You mean the ugly one?' I teased.

'Yes. Her. And she looked so beautiful.'

I turned as casually as I could, to see if this was intended as a bait, but I don't think it was. His forbidden confession seemed sincere enough, for he was looking intently at Aung San Suu Kyi's childhood incarnation. And in Burma it happens like that. At the oddest moments, the most unlikely individual will let slip a hasty homage to the woman the generals love to disparage, not least because of her cosmopolitan upbringing, which in every case is in stark contrast to their own.

Setting off for Delhi with her mother towards the end of 1960, Suu Kyi, her long hair now plaited, was joining the vanguard of post-war East Asian urban youth: eager to encounter new countries, new cultures, while taking advantage of a broader, better education than could be had at home. Yet for as long as she remained in India, Suu Kyi continued under Daw Khin Kyi's close supervision. Whether Khin Kyi simply wanted to ensure that her daughter turned out well, or, having already lost two children, inclined towards the overly custodial, she maintained a watchful eye – the more so since her surviving son, Aung San Oo, had already been sent to boarding school in England and came to Delhi only for the holidays.

Then as now, India was the world's largest democracy, under President Nehru striving to forge a distinctive post-colonial identity, but also bedevilled by potentially calamitous problems. Top of the list was an ongoing communal stand-off between majority Hindus and minority Muslims, which periodically erupted into violence and bloodshed. Indian communists too threatened the still-fragile political order, while famine, accompanied by food riots, was a regular occurrence in some of India's poorer provinces.

Relations with Muslim Pakistan (which at the time included East Pakistan, before it separated as the independent state of Bangladesh in 1971) were at best uneasy. There were also mounting tensions with China, brought about, in the first instance, by India's decision to give sanctuary to the Fourteenth Dalai Lama, following the People's Republic's invasion of Tibet in 1959. Three years later, the two countries went to war.

It was the time when the Cold War, between the Soviet Union and its satellites on the one hand and an American-led West on the other, was at its peak. But Nehru's enlightened solution was, as far as possible, to remain neutral or 'non-aligned', without becoming (as Ne Win's Burma increasingly became) definably isolationist. In practice this meant receiving billions of dollars in economic aid from Washington, while agreeing to buy arms (including MiG fighter jets) from Moscow.

With so much on his plate, Nehru might have been forgiven for overlooking the arrival in Delhi of Aung San's widow and her family. Instead the Pandit saw to it that Daw Khin Kyi was accorded special status. For the duration of her embassy she was given a particularly fine residence in New Delhi. Temporarily renamed 'Burma House', 24 Akbar Road formed part of the complex of government buildings designed and built by Sir Edwin Lutyens between 1911 and 1925, and widely regarded as not only the acme of British colonial architecture, but a masterpiece of early Modernism.

Post-Indian independence, 24 Akbar Road – quietly imposing on the outside and wondrously cool inside, with its large, elegant rooms and cleverly crafted layout – was reserved for the use of the most senior civil servants. At Nehru's insistence, the residence and its complement of domestics and gardeners were placed at Daw Khin Kyi's disposal, for the duration of her office. For the first time Suu Kyi experienced luxury, even if her mother did her best to replicate the frugality that had characterised their life in Rangoon.

To complete her secondary education, Suu Kyi spent her first eighteen months in New Delhi at the Convent of Jesus and Mary School – a much-admired Catholic establishment close to the Cathedral of St Joseph. The teachers were mainly nuns (Sisters of Jesus) who maintained an even stricter regimen than Suu Kyi had experienced at the Methodist English High School. She then enrolled at Lady Shri Ram College, to study (at her mother's insistence) political science.

Affiliated to Delhi University and with 2,000 students, Lady Shri Ram College, occupying a large, leafy campus at Lajpat Nagar IV in the south of the city, is today regarded as India's finest institute of higher education for women. In 1962 it was in its infancy, just six years old. It had 300 or so students, and still occupied its first, modest premises, at Daryaganj in central Delhi. The purpose of the college was to produce a new kind of female graduate who could take her place alongside any male – confident, skilled and dedicated to the public good. Its eponymous founder, Sir Lala Shri Ram, was a friend of Nehru, and a leading industrialist and philanthropist who also created the Shriram Institute of Industrial Research.

'This time,' Sir Lala was fond of saying, 'like all times is a very good time, if we but know what to do with it.' While the college itself was intended as a memorial to his late wife, its accent was on meeting the needs of the future, moderated by an understanding of women's particular social and spiritual needs, of their whole selves.

Although Suu Kyi spent only two years at Lady Shri Ram and did not finish her course there, and despite her non-Indian nationality, on the college website she is placed first on the list of distinguished Old Girls – such is the prestige of the Nobel Peace Prize won by her thirty years later. 'Her grounding in the complexities of political thought via classroom teaching,' the citation reads, 'coupled with her recognition of the vital living quality of the modern democracy – a system characterised by its multivoicedness – contributed greatly toward crafting Suu Kyi into the politicised entity she is today.'

A tad self-congratulatory perhaps, but at Lady Shri Ram Suu Kyi was introduced in a formal, pedagogic way to the politics and philosophy of Mahatma Gandhi, the guiding spirit of India's independence movement, whose advocacy of non-violence, passive resistance, civil disobedience and *satyagraha* ('force born out of truth') provided a radically original model for opposing authoritarian government, which became embedded in Suu Kyi's slowly evolving mindset.

Among Suu Kyi's contemporaries was Malvika Karlekar, who would later play a leading role in setting up the Centre for Women's Development Studies (also in Delhi), as well as following Suu Kyi to Oxford. In 2005 she recalled her impressions of the Bogyoke's daughter when first she met her: 'She would always sit bolt upright, and never spoke out of turn.' She dressed in Burmese clothes, and sometimes came into college with *thanaka* daubed on her face.

Getting to know her better, Malvika Karlekar was surprised to discover how 'creative' Suu Kyi was – remembering in particular a 'spoof' on Shakespeare's *Antony and Cleopatra* that she wrote for her fellow students to perform. She could be witty and sometimes irreverent, though never in a malicious way. Yet Malvika doubted whether, at this juncture of her life, Suu Kyi had a consuming interest in politics. Rather politics was something she studied from a sense of duty instilled in her by Daw Khin Kyi.

Outside college, others remember Suu Kyi in Delhi as being somewhat demure, particularly in the presence of her mother, whose manner had become one of poised reserve, as befitted her ambassadorial station. U Thet Tun, trained in Japan during the war under a civil-assistance programme, and later Burma's ambassador to France and director of UNESCO, recalled visiting 24 Akbar Road in 1961. 'It was the first time I saw Suu Kyi,' he said. 'She was just a teenager then, and rather shy. If her mother sat on a sofa, she would sit on its arm, but I don't remember her saying very much.'

Suu Kyi was kept constantly busy. Ambassador Khin Kyi, determined that her daughter should become the finished article, arranged lessons in horse riding and flower arrangement for her. She was also taught to play the piano – an instrument she took to with enthusiasm as well as aptitude. Significantly, her penchant was for the nuanced subtleties of Bach's elaborate mathematics, and the delicacies of Mozart, rather than the *cris de coeur* of later Romantic composers.

For her riding lessons, she was taken to the exercise grounds of the Presidential Bodyguard. There she was introduced to Nehru's two grandsons, Sanjay and Rajiv, amongst others.

Sanjay and Rajiv were Suu Kyi's contemporaries, born one year either side of her. They were also the sons of Indira Priyadarshani, Nehru's daughter, who had married, and then separated from, Feroze Gandhi, a Parsi who was no relation of the Mahatma. It is unlikely, though, that Suu Kyi or Daw Khin Kyi took any great shine to Mrs Gandhi, as she became known, or either of her boys. The mother, already president of the Congress Party, was an astute but unscrupulous politician bent on turning her family into a ruling dynasty. About Sanjay there was something palpably uncouth, while the vainglorious Rajiv was lacking in intelligence.

All three – the mother and her two boys – would come to untimely ends, but theirs was a circle that Daw Khin Kyi and Suu Kyi had perforce to mix with graciously, if their benefactor, President Nehru, were not to be insulted. If there were 'comments' to be made, they kept them to themselves in the best traditions of Burmese womanhood.

*   *   *

Ever faithful to her own culture, Daw Khin Kyi strove to uphold the Buddhist connection in what had become a Hindu-Muslim land. Among several extra-diplomatic projects, she encouraged the renewal of the Ashoka Vihara, a decayed Buddhist shrine in Delhi that, with her supportive fundraising, was placed under the care of a Cambodian Theravada abbot. Equally she gave generously to the lamas of the Tibetan Ladakhi monastery. Although, at her table, she hosted religious figures of all faiths and denominations – among them the papal nuncio James Knox – Khin Kyi was especially welcoming towards U Rewata Dhamma, a Burman monk whom the family had known in Rangoon, and who would become one of Suu Kyi's Buddhist mentors.

Born in 1929 in Hanthada (Henzada), U Rewata Dhamma was well on his way to becoming a highly venerated Buddhist teacher and an acknowledged authority on *nirvana*. He had come to India in 1956, to pursue Sanskrit and Hindi studies at the Varanasi University, as well as learn more about Mahayana Buddhism – the 'Great Wheel' school that sets particular store on compassion. In his own understanding of the Buddhist heritage, U Rewata Dhamma emphasised the centrality of *arahanta* – 'to be worthy of deserving'. The good Buddhist, while striving for *nirvana* as the only sure release from the cycle of suffering, death and rebirth that characterises the imperfect world of humanity, should at all times demonstrate consideration towards others, if the attainment of *nirvana* is to become a realistic possibility.

Contrary to popular Western perceptions, in essence Buddhism does not unambiguously extol the 'path of selflessness'. Amid a spectacular welter of contending doctrines and philosophies that flourished in Vedic India in the early fifth century BC, the Buddha's message was revolutionary precisely because it took the self as its starting point – but the self redefined as something endlessly vulnerable to suffering, contamination and distortion. The Buddha did not deny the existence of India's rich pantheon of gods and goddesses, but neither did he incorporate them into his system. Similarly he eschewed the elaborate, superstitious rituals of the temple. Only by fully realising (to the exclusion of all else) its own innate but beleaguered purity – through a punishing discipline of 'right' conduct, but also with the powerful aids of meditation and contemplation – can the self hope to progress towards ultimate serenity; though paradoxically at the point of attainment (*nirvana*), the self itself vanishes (hence the imputation of selflessness), as its final residue enters a permanent state of blissfulness that is neither individual nor collective, but of a different order entirely, unimaginable to those who have not approached it.

By highlighting *arahanta*, Rewata Dhamma promoted the social responsibility that has long underpinned the Buddhist faith, and that may be overlooked by outsiders going to Buddhism for personal enlightenment. A key element of the Buddha's own life is that, having attained enlightenment, he returned to the 'ordinary' world for the benefit of all others. Implicitly, therefore, the Buddhist quest for self-purification (or at least self-improvement) has the general good as one of its objectives.

Philosophically, Buddhism, like every other system and faith, is subject to all kinds of scrutiny and refutation. For instance, part of the Buddha's teaching was to characterise the world and everything in it as an illusion (as well as the natural habitat of suffering). But if that is so, what guarantee can there be that the Buddha's teaching itself is not illusional? As with the three great monotheistic religions, Buddhism requires an act of faith, a belief in something that is not necessarily self-evident, though it does so with greater tolerance. Denial of Buddhist precepts, unlike the denial of God or Allah, has rarely attracted persecution or ostracism.

Culturally, however, Buddhism as a way of life and as a mindset is irrefutable. It is the sea that tens of millions in East and Central Asia are spawned in, and grow up in.

For Suu Kyi, there was a risk that by leaving Burma and living in non-Buddhist countries for more than a quarter of a century, she would lose some of her Buddhist identity, as perhaps happened to a degree. But happily, in 1975, Rewata Dhamma moved from India to Britain, where he founded the Birmingham Buddhist Vihara, as well as the Dhammakalaka Peace Pagoda; and contact between the two resumed.

Later still, in 1994, after Suu Kyi had returned to Burma and been placed under house arrest, U Rewata Dhamma finding himself in Rangoon, agreed to act as an intermediary between the junta and its most celebrated detainee.

In time, Suu Kyi would have other Buddhist gurus – notably Hsayadaw U Pandita. While she did not, on her own admission, adopt meditation as a daily practice until coming under house arrest in her mid-forties, there is a sense in which her engagement with Buddhism has been ongoing and accumulative. 'Contemplation' gradually became an integral component of Suu Kyi's formidable mental armoury, in part explaining her startling ability to remain apparently unperturbed by the severest setbacks.

In India, though, Suu Kyi was still a teenager, and very much under her mother's directing thumb – a cipher of experience, far more than its accomplished assessor (as she would become). Among those faces already familiar to her from Rangoon, it was Sir Paul and Lady Gore-Booth who were to have the biggest hand in shaping her immediate future.

For Aung San Suu Kyi, the Gore-Booths became 'dearly-loved friends who taught me much about kindness and caring'.* Paul Gore-Booth had been British ambassador to Burma between 1953 and 1956. It was in that capacity that he and his wife Patricia first met Daw Khin Khi and her children: for Rangoon in those days still had an open society in which the great, the good and the interesting mixed freely. Now, in the early 1960s, he was Britain's High Commissioner in Delhi, his last overseas posting before he became Permanent Under-Secretary at London's Foreign Office, the highest pinnacle that a career diplomat may ordinarily hope to achieve.

In *With Great Truth and Respect*, his memoirs published in 1974, Lord Gore-Booth (as he had then become) referred to Khin Kyi as a 'special friend', a 'quiet lady of few words but of great depth and strength of character' – an encomium all the more meaningful because of the distinction of its writer. Born in 1909, Gore-Booth came from a prominent Anglo-Irish family whose ancestry could be traced back to the 1580s. Its members included the Earls of Arran. Two aunts, Eva and Constance, daughters of Paul's grandfather Sir Henry Gore-Booth, were much admired by the poet W.B. Yeats:

> *Two girls in silk kimonos, both*
> *Beautiful, one a gazelle . . .*†

Eva was also a poet, Constance Markiewicz a stridently effective supporter of the Irish republican movement.

After Eton and Oxford Gore-Booth joined the British foreign service. At the end of 1941 he found himself in Tokyo, where, along with other Allied diplomats, he was interned before being evacuated the following

---

* Aung San Suu Kyi, 'Towards a True Refuge', lecture delivered by Michael Aris at Oxford, 19th May 1993
† 'In Memory of Eva Gore-Booth and Con Markiewicz', 1933

year. There he met his Australian wife, Patricia Ellerton, his assistant
at the embassy and a dozen years his junior. Transferred to Washington,
he played an active role in the UK delegation to the United Nations
Preparatory Committee, before being put in charge of the British
Information Service in the United States. By the time he went as
Ambassador to Rangoon, Gore-Booth was already marked as a high-flyer,
and his superiors were not disappointed. A good six foot tall with
wonderously craggy, Hibernian eyebrows, Gore-Booth went all the way.
Yet although he embodied patrician decency with its serious-mindedness
and commitment to public service at its best – qualities shared by his
wife – there was another, lighter side to him. When a cable arrived from
a remote and fractious corner of Central Asia on his Under-Secretary's
desk, reporting 'RULER HAS DIED SUDDENLY. PLEASE ADVISE', Gore-Booth
at once wired back: 'HESITATE TO DOGMATISE, BUT SUGGEST BURIAL'.

The only, marginal blot on a long and distinguished career came in
April 1968, when the Gore-Booths were seen boarding a plane for
Switzerland dressed as Sherlock Holmes and Irene Adler. For all that
Gore-Booth was president of the Sherlock Holmes Society and was off
to participate in a re-enactment of Holmes's fight with Moriarty at the
Reichenbach Falls, and had in any case been given permission by Foreign
Secretary Michael Stewart to travel in costume (on condition he did not
follow Holmes's example and disappear to Tibet for two years afterwards),
the then Lord-President of the Council, Richard Crossman, wrote
angrily to Prime Minister Harold Wilson about what he regarded as
'an extremely vulgar publicity stunt' that did 'no credit' to the Foreign
Office or 'the British government in general'.

Crossman was one of only a very few not to be won over by
Gore-Booth's pedigree and wit. The Gore-Booth's circle was both
eclectic and distinguished. Friends included Lord Mountbatten, the
American economist Kenneth Galbraith, the philosopher Sir Isaiah
Berlin and the orchestral conductor Sir Malcolm Sargent. Just as Suu
Kyi had been exposed to Rangoon's leading lights at her mother's house
as a child, so as a young woman she had opportunities to meet the
famous in London.

All of which made the Gore-Booths the perfect (albeit informal)
'British' guardians for Suu Kyi when, in 1964, she won a place at St
Hugh's College, Oxford, to study Politics, Philosophy and Economics
(PPE). Daw Khin Kyi was loath to let her daughter go. But she also
wanted the best for her. In the 1960s that still meant an Oxbridge

education. The Gore-Booths, packing their bags in readiness to return to Britain, volunteered to provide Suu Kyi with a 'home' while she was in England, at least during her vacations – home being a discreet but spacious townhouse in the heart of London's fashionable Chelsea.

Such an offer was not to be refused. If Daw Khin Kyi could entrust Suu Kyi to anyone, it was Sir Paul and Lady Patricia – though if she had known that this would eventually entail her daughter's marriage to an Englishman, she would probably have changed her mind.

XVII

THE DAUGHTER OF SOME OR OTHER
BURMESE GENERAL

*I hate admitting reading [PPE]. I would much prefer to have read English,
Japanese or forestry, but I did it because economics seemed to be of most
use to a developing country.*
        Aung San Suu Kyi, in the *Financial Times*, 24th October 1988

OXFORD in the mid-1960s was a place of contrasts and surprises, as
well as everlasting tradition. The centre of the city belonged, as ever,
to its university, which dated back to the Middle Ages. But on its streets
were signs of a new kind of student. During the 1950s, as Britain 'got
back to work' after war, the Oxford undergraduate was, more often
than not, a serious-minded, unassuming individual who spent (and was
expected to spend) more time in libraries and lecture halls than anywhere
else. But as Beatlemania, the Rolling Stones and the Kinks seized the
country's imagination, there were more daring, prancing souls about.
Some of the male students wore their hair long, and some of the female
students mini-skirts. Kaftans, velvet jackets, platform shoes and floral
ties, imported from London's Carnaby Street, appeared in the city's
narrow, winding lanes. Sometimes the scent of hashish drifted through
the ancient stone cloisters.

'Are you on the pill?' was the question of the time. And: 'What about
It?' Virginity became an obsession, one way or the other. With the
flowering of the first openly gay contingent since the 1920s, the university
arrived at its own characteristically pedantic classification. One was a
'virgin to one', a 'virgin to neither' or a 'virgin to both'. Explicitly or

implicitly heterosexual male students classified female students, whom they then outnumbered by four to one, as tarts, nuns or in-betweens. For the female student there were difficult choices to be made. Whether of upper-, middle- or lower-class upbringing – and Britain then was still class-conscious to a suffocating degree – she knew that winning a place at one of Oxford's five women's colleges was a rare opportunity. Therefore was there not one's integrity to maintain? One's purity, of body as well as mind? But if the lately invented birth-control pill averted unwanted pregnancies and unlooked-for marriages, it liberated attitudes as well as behaviour. At last the female of the species, soon to be assailed by rivalrous versions of a radical feminism emanating chiefly from America, was free to explore and engage the predations of her male counterpart, without being castigated as an eccentric, fallen individualist.

When the sun did shine upon marshy Oxford, there was a beguiling air of decadence about the place. In the summer months, college lawns were bedecked with champagne-and-strawberry parties, paid for by richer undergraduates. But there was also much seriousness afoot. At the King's Arms, a mid-town hostelry, the world-famous logical positivist and atheist philosopher Sir Frederick (Freddie) Ayer and other luminaries held mid-morning court, urging (amongst other concerns) opposition to the USA's growing involvement in Vietnam. Oxford might be known as the home of lost causes, but, like other universities, its political temperature was rising, spurred on by the polemics of the avowedly Marxist historian Christopher Hill.

In October 1964, a month after Suu Kyi arrived in England, the Labour Party scraped to victory in a general election. Harold Wilson, once an Oxford economics tutor, became Prime Minister. The following year, Hill was appointed Master of Balliol, one of the university's oldest and best-regarded colleges. For the left, weaned on the reformist triumphs of Clement Attlee's post-war government, it was a time of hope and anticipation. For conservatives, it was a time of despondency, the more so as Wilson's administration soon showed itself vulnerable to pressure from Britain's militant trade unions, some of them allegedly in Moscow's pay.

Despite the surface glitter of the Swinging Sixties, Britain was entering troubled waters, not helped by Wilson's inability to repair a flagging economy. Yet for a while to come, the tenor of life at Oxford remained steady. The odd visiting cabinet minister might be pelted with rotten eggs or bad tomatoes, usually because of Labour's retention of nuclear weapons.

But not until 1968 – the year of ravening student unrest throughout western Europe – did Oxford's undergraduates organise protests in meaningful numbers. Even then, there was a distinct flavour of *sans-culottes manqués*. As well as an anti-American, anti-capitalist political agenda, demonstrating students in Paris, Madrid and Milan had real grievances about their living conditions. But their Oxford counterparts had nothing much to complain about. In college, not only were their sometimes spacious rooms cleaned, but even their beds were made up, by college 'scouts'. In fact, the Oxford undergraduate, only sometimes attired in gown and mortar-board, led a privileged, pampered life.

As at Cambridge, the 'tutorial system' ensured close scholastic supervision, often on a one-to-one basis. Tutor and student could get to know each other, to the advantage of the student's individual development. Nor was attending lectures compulsory. Some ignored that side of university life altogether. Conversely, the Oxford student was at liberty to attend lectures outside his or her own field, and indeed was encouraged to do so, as a means of 'broadening the mind'.

Oxford remained set in its ways. Tutors continued to offer their charges an occasional glass of sherry, and addressed male undergraduates respectfully as 'Mr'. Not until the 1980s did men's colleges open their doors to women and Oxford's five women's colleges open their doors to men. Until then, there were prohibitions against entertaining friends of the opposite sex late at night in a college room, and students were required to be back in college well before midnight. University proctors patrolled the city's streets to catch miscreants. But there were always ways around unwelcome restrictions, especially for those who lived out of college in digs. For most who went there, 'Oxford' was still a curiously civilised, and sometimes civilising, experience.

As one of only a handful of girls from the Far East studying there, Aung San Suu Kyi was immediately noticeable, quite apart from her striking looks. 'Who's that?' one might ask, if she happened to ride by on her bicycle on the Banbury or Woodstock Road. To which the informed response was: 'The daughter of some or other Burmese general, or so I'm told.' But if she had novelty value, she never sought to exploit it, never spread herself about. In the line-up of nuns, tarts and in-betweens, she belonged unerringly with the nuns.

Partly this was on account of the modesty inculcated by her mother; partly a more general cultural conditioning (the better sort of Burmese girl simply did not disport herself); and partly a matter of resolute personal conviction. She told her female friends that she would only ever sleep with one man in her life, and that would be her husband – whom she fully expected would be Burmese. Even if the political positions for which she has become so celebrated were still at the seedling stage, on issues of personal morality her mind was already made up. To any corrupting influence she was sublimely impervious.

Among those prone to judge others on first impressions, or who wanted more from her than was on offer, this earned the young Suu Kyi a reputation for being sanctimonious – a word used by more than one of her Oxford contemporaries. Diminutive and austere, there was something of the elfin prude about her in her late teens and early twenties. She could come across as being unusually reserved, remote and judgemental. There was no quick way into her emotional world, which in any case had been formed in a very different culture. Yet those who did get to know Suu Kyi at Oxford discovered a warmer, more debonair personality than her exterior manner portended.

An English contemporary, asking Suu Kyi what her name meant in Burmese, misheard her reply. Instead of 'Strange Collection of Bright Victories', he thought she said 'Strange Collection of Bright Fig Trees'. But, with its puritanical connotation of fig leaves, this seemed appropriate enough, so – much to her amusement – he gave her the nickname Fig Tree.

Ann Pasternak Slater, a grand-niece of the author of *Doctor Zhivago*, who would one day teach literature at Oxford and marry the celebrated 'Martian' poet Craig Raine, was Suu Kyi's fellow 'fresher' at St Hugh's. Together they became student members of the college in the Michaelmas term of 1964. Twenty-seven years later she would write a short but unusually intimate memoir of 'Suu Burmese' (as she had always called her, to distinguish her from other friends called Sue).* She records how she was immediately drawn towards Suu Kyi by her beauty and exoticism, and by her 'inherited social grace'. Like others, she was struck by the excessive tidiness of Suu Kyi's appearance, by her Burmese *longyi*, which she nearly always wore in college, and by the small flowers (plucked from the college's well-stocked rock gardens) with which she adorned her hair. But like others, she too was quickly apprised of Suu Kyi's 'firm moral convictions'.

*Pasternak Slater's memoir is contained in Aung San Suu Kyi, *Freedom from Fear* (1991)

Suu Kyi was, Pasternak Slater wrote, 'instinctively straight-laced', at once 'laughably naïve, and genuinely innocent'. Habitually, her 'eyebrows furrowed under a heavy fringe' as she expressed 'shocked incredulity and disapproval' at some or other transgression of her rooted moral code. But none of this deterred a friendship that lasted twenty years and more. As she got to know Suu Burmese better, she came to appreciate her 'determination' and 'fierce purity', as well as her ever-vigilant curiosity.

Once every so often Suu Kyi allowed her curiosity, and perhaps her *amour propre*, to get the better of her. In the parlance of the day she realised it was just too 'square' always to follow rules slavishly. During her second summer at Oxford she decided that at least once during her student career she must climb the college wall after curfew (which at St Hugh's was set at 10 p.m.). A dependable Indian student (male) was detailed to take her out for a late dinner and then escort her back to St Hugh's, to be 'lifted over' back to sanctuary. 'No infringement of university regulations could have been perpetrated with greater propriety,' Pasternak Slater wryly commented.

On another occasion Suu Kyi decided to taste alcohol. Again, an act of high deviance was carried out with the ruthlessness of a scientific experiment. The laboratory chosen was the ladies' lavatory of the famous Bodleian Library, and the instrument of investigation was a miniature bottle of some intoxicating liquid. 'There, among the sinks and the cubicles, in a setting deliberately chosen to mirror the distastefulness of the experience', and with two more Indians (this time female) in attendance to protect and observe her, 'she tried and rejected alcohol for ever'.

Pasternak Slater tells us too how, eager to participate in all the permissible traditions of Oxford, Suu Kyi taught herself to punt along the city's narrow rivers and to ride a bicycle. In return, she taught Pasternak Slater and other contemporaries at St Hugh's how to eat rice with their fingers and sit on the floor Burmese-style, with the legs artfully tucked under an erect torso so that, dressed in a *longyi*, there was no showing of an ankle.

Similar impressions of Suu Kyi stuck in the minds of other contemporaries. Forty years on Dr Margaret Stearn, also of St Hugh's, would recall how 'Suu had the knack of putting one on one's best behaviour – not in a restrictive sense, but in the sense of bringing out the best in you. In her company I always felt a better person.' She too was impressed by Suu Kyi's boundless curiosity. 'In conversation she seemed to be on a permanent fact-finding mission.'

Then there was Shankar Acharya, a fellow PPE student from Keble College, destined to become chief economic adviser to the Indian government. They met in their second term, and for a while Shankar was somewhat smitten. Because of her time in Delhi, they found they had much in common. Suu, he discovered, was genuinely absorbed by the ideals of Mahatma Gandhi and Pandit Nehru, though she seldom kept her father out of their conversations for long. 'Even then, she thought she must one day do something for her people.' But what delighted him most was the 'sudden stiffening of her spine and pursing of her lips' whenever something untoward cropped up. 'She was not the staircase party type, but nor was she a prig. Her responses were not put on for show, but were a manifestation of an unusual purity of mind and heart.'

St Hugh's was an apposite 'Oxford home' for Suu Kyi. Located between the Banbury and Woodstock Roads in north Oxford, it was some way out of town and was considered the most secluded of the women's colleges. It had been founded, in 1886, by Elizabeth Wordsworth, not only a great-niece of the poet William Wordsworth, but also the daughter of a Bishop of Lincoln. Its original premises were a simple house in nearby Norham Gardens, and its mission was to offer underprivileged girls especially a chance to benefit from an Oxford education, while promoting the principles of the Anglican faith. Inevitably, many of its early alumnae became headmistresses of Christian girls' schools, although later old girls included the novelist Mary Renault, and the pugnacious Labour Party politician (and member of Harold Wilson's cabinet) Dame Barbara Castle.

Initially St Hugh's intake consisted of just four women students. Today its total enrolment is close on 600, postgraduates as well as undergraduates, males as well as females. Astute financial management enabled the college to acquire its present multi-acre site in 1912, and four years later it was 'incorporated', taking it out of private into public hands. Architecturally it is nothing special, its Art Deco library apart: a cluster of presentable institutional buildings from different periods of the twentieth century, with somewhat spartan interiors. However, its gardens are generous, adding to St Hugh's oasis reputation. Without any actual cloisters St Hugh's provided Daw Khin Kyi's daughter with a cloistered environment of which her mother could only have approved.

For the three years of her bachelor's degree course, Suu Kyi stayed in college, spurning any opportunity to live in digs. Likewise, all her tutors were college Fellows. Most are now deceased, but an exception is Julie Jack, an intellectually combative American philosopher who specialised in Logic, and who taught Suu Kyi for one eight-week, eight-tutorial term. Although by 2005 Ms Jack had been retired for many years, she was still, and most splendidly, committed to the passions of pure reason. Suu Kyi, she insisted, had been one of her better (even outstanding) students.

She too had been drawn by Suu Kyi's poise and grace, and remembered her as a self-contained, but 'tough-minded' student, who, when she took a position, would stick to it doggedly. During one tutorial on the English philosopher John Locke's theory of transmigration (of the memory), Suu Kyi insisted that transmigration in a broader sense, and with it rebirth, was not just a philosophically 'allowable' concept, but an actual and indisputable phenomenon.

'My lasting impression of her is of a wholly composed, self-aware young woman: not in a calculated way, but in the manner of an instinctive thoroughbred. She was neither shy nor timid, as many others were during tutorials, but used herself sparingly. She dressed beautifully, sat beautifully, and walked beautifully.'

But Suu Kyi did not take a beautiful degree, when she sat her finals in the early summer of 1967. When I met Ms Jack in 2005, she kindly showed me around St Hugh's after lunch at high table. The Junior Common Room had been renamed in Suu Kyi's honour: as with Lady Shri Ram, she is the college's most celebrated alumna by a mile. Coming to the library, I asked whether I might see Aung San Suu Kyi's college record. A helpful librarian said she would dig it out, but it would take a few minutes since it had 'gone upstairs', following Suu Kyi's election to an Honorary Fellowship in June 1990.

We repaired to the Senior Common Room, to meet some of St Hugh's Fellows. Soon the librarian appeared with photocopies of the two relevant pages. When I saw that Suu Kyi had got a third class degree, I let out an involuntary chuckle. Something strangely similar had happened ten years before, when, researching the life of the Welsh poet and nationalist R.S. Thomas, I had been given access to his college record at Bangor University. He too had been placed in the third class division.

'Is there something funny?' asked the most senior Fellow present.

I explained.

'But you won't put that in your book, will you?'

I could understand his nervousness. Aung San Suu Kyi had become the college mascot. Her photograph adorned the main college corridor. Hers was the shining example to be followed by the present and all subsequent generations of St Hughsites, even more than the eponymous St Hugh of Avalon himself (another Bishop of Lincoln). Yet on the hard evidence before me, she had messed up academically.

'If I do,' I said, 'it will be out of respect for Aung San Suu Kyi's insistence on never concealing the truth. And I'm sure she'd prefer the warts-and-all approach.'

Someone behind me in an armchair muttered tersely, 'Aung San Suu Kyi doesn't have any warts.'

Instead of prolonging the debate I shrugged, and placed the photocopies in my briefcase. It seemed silly. Some eminent individuals have got third class degrees at Oxford. J.R.R. Tolkein even contrived to scrape a fourth. At its worst, Oxford can be intolerably sniffy. Added to which, I felt that Suu Kyi herself, an inveterate foe of humbug, would have giggled.

Exactly how or why she did so poorly in her degree examination is a matter of more than academic curiosity. Sir Robin Christopher, a contemporary who also read PPE, and whom Suu Kyi could count among her most dependable Anglo-Saxon friends, confided that she had been expected to do much better, perhaps even gain a first. That she did not was the cause of some surprised dismay. But he could think of no adequate explanation. 'She taught me almost everything I know about economics,' he said, 'besides introducing me to the novels of Jane Austen – and me an Englishman!'

One clue may have been just that: literature – poetry as well as fiction, French as well as English – meant much to Suu Kyi, and she has frequently said that she would prefer to have enrolled on a literature course. Did she spend too much time reading Jane Austen, and too little boning up on British constitutional law, or the *laissez-faire* economic theory of Adam Smith? Certainly it cannot have been because of a surfeit of extracurricular activities. She no more joined clubs than she was a staircase-party type. Nor does anyone who knew Suu Kyi at university recall her being remotely politicised, though certainly she was avowedly patriotic, in the way people transplanted from a poorer to a richer nation often are. Years later, the military regime in Rangoon, in one of its routine efforts to besmirch her name, would, quite laughably, put it about that at Oxford Aung San Suu Kyi had been a regular participant in debates at the Oxford Union – as though that were some kind of crime. But the truth was quite otherwise. Suu Kyi did not stand up to speak, any more than she ever appeared in the gossip column of *Cherwell*, the university magazine.

Another clue may be in the John Locke tutorial she had with Julie Jack. The Oxford way especially (not unlike the old Chinese mandarinate way) has always been to focus on skill in argument. It is better to argue a bad cause well than a good cause badly. But the moralist in Suu Kyi tended (and has always tended) towards assertion of what she instinctively knew (or knows) to be true, without too much need for exposition. That became her strength as a champion of liberty. But scholastically it was a liability.

XVIII

THINGS FALL APART

Ne Win has repulsed many abler men than I who want to write his biography, saying that his story must be read in his deeds.
Maung Maung, *Burma and General Ne Win* (1969)

SHORTLY before Suu Kyi finished her degree course at St Hugh's her mother, Daw Khin Kyi, decided to relinquish her ambassadorial posting in India. Although, after six years in Delhi, she had perhaps served long enough, her actual reason for returning to Rangoon, and taking relatively early retirement, was that she no longer felt inclined to represent the military regime headed by General Ne Win. She had never liked the man, but had wanted to serve her country in whatever capacity she could. But as Ne Win's junta bedded down, the gulf between them grew too great. The man who had emerged as Burma's dictator was busy wrecking what remained of Aung San's legacy. On balance, she preferred that she should go home.

Aung San himself had been wary of Bo Ne Win, for all that he was one of the Thirty Comrades. A well-authenticated story tells how, in 1941, when the Bogyoke was preparing to move the first units of the Burma Independence Army out of Bangkok, progress was delayed by Ne Win's unexplained absences. Aung San learned that, instead of preparing his recruits, Ne Win was pleasuring himself in one of the Thai capital's many brothels. Incensed, Aung San told one of his most junior colleagues, Bo Ta Yar, to go and shoot Ne Win 'on the spot'.

With no great difficulty, Ta Yar tracked Ne Win down, but lacked the bottle to carry out his leader's orders. Instead, he advised Ne Win to return hastily to barracks for his own safety, then told Aung San that Ne Win was in fact 'on duty'. Realising he had been made a fool of, and that perhaps he should never have given such an order in the first place, Aung San, wearing his army boots, angrily landed a heavy kick on Ta Yar's foot. Forty-seven years later, in the midst of the 1988 'uprising', Ta Yar proudly showed the scar to Moe Thee Zun, a prominent student leader, and others at his apartment in Rangoon. 'If I had followed Bogyoke Aung San's orders,' he said, 'we would not have so much trouble now.'

When he seized power in 1962, however, Ne Win was not perceived as the cause of Burma's woes, so much as their hoped-for resolution. The United States, enlisting the support of whatever allies it could during the Cold War with the Soviet Union, tacitly approved of his coup, as it approved of the coups of other dictators in the Third World throughout the 1960s and beyond. In Britain the Foreign Office helpfully detailed juniors (at least one of whom would become an ambassador, though not to Burma) to caddy for him on the links, whenever Ne Win visited England to play golf (which was fairly often).

Burma had been an unhappy, tortured land ever since independence in 1948. From the outset, U Nu's fragile coalition government encountered the gravest difficulties. In some measure this was because Nu lacked the finesse to hold the country and its squabbling factions together. A well-intentioned, well-mannered man, he had neither the political nous nor the personal authority, as Aung San had, to forge unity. That, during the war, he had stayed at home instead of going to Japan counted against him and made him overly dependent on the Tatmadaw, Burmese Army. But in other respects the challenges presented would have been beyond the wits of even the most astute politician, Aung San perhaps included.

Even as, in the early hours of the morning of 4th January 1948, the Union Jack came down, the flag of the Union of Burma was hoisted aloft and HMS *Birmingham*, at anchor in the Rangoon river, fired a twenty-gun salute to mark the end of British rule, Thakin Soe's minority Red Flag communists were at war against the government. Within three months (and much more threateningly) the more numerous White Flag communists, led by Thakins Than Tun and Ba Thein, had joined them in rebellion.

U Nu tried to bring the mainstream communists back on board, but failed. They gave as their excuse their opposition to the 'Let Ya-Freeman

Defence Agreement', negotiated by Bo Let Ya, whereby Britain would continue to provide Burma with military assistance after independence, and which was appended to a final agreement for the handover of power that Nu had negotiated with British Prime Minister Attlee in October 1947. Since this allowed for the continuation of some British bases inside Burma for 'training purposes', the communists (Red as well as White) argued that it represented an infringement of Burma's new-found sovereignty. It was an instrument for the former colonial power to re-establish itself in Burma when and as it pleased. In reality Than Tun and Ba Thein sensed that, with Aung San out of the way, there was a clear opportunity for the communists to reassert themselves, even to seize power.

In February and March 1948 the White Flag CPB (Communist Party of Burma) orchestrated a series of strikes that threatened to bring Rangoon to a halt. On 18th March Than Tun addressed a massed rally in Pyinmana, and was pleasantly surprised by the turn-out – more than 70,000 mainly rural workers. A week later, U Nu ordered his arrest, but, evading capture, Than Tun launched an insurrection that would last forty years.

The first shots between the CPB and the Tatmadaw were exchanged at Paukkyongi, a village near Pegu, on 2nd April. Within weeks, communist-inspired sedition had spread to central and upper Burma. Army units were attacked, police stations burned down, bridges blown and bombs detonated in towns and cities. Quickly the communists learned the arts of guerrilla warfare, in time building mountain bases both in the Pegu Yoma (mountain range) and in the Shan states.

U Nu's ruling AFPFL (Anti-Fascist People's Freedom League) coalition also faced difficulties in Arakan, where a group of Rohingyas formed themselves into a band of *mujahin*, Muslim holy fighters. These wanted to have nothing to do with the Union. There was also in Arakan a small but virile separatist movement among the Buddhist Rakhines. And from July onwards elements of the paramilitary PVO (People's Volunteer Organisation), which Aung San had used to gain political leverage in 1946 and 1947, went on the rampage.

But these setbacks were just the beginning of Burma's prolonged internecine strife. U Nu was no more successful at persuading militant Karens to join the Union than the Bogyoke had been. A full-scale Karen insurrection at the beginning of 1949 gave heart to others among Burma's ethnic minorities who keenly resented the reimposition of Burman rule in their ancestral homelands.

*   *   *

Many Karens, under the forlorn impression that the British had promised them a state of their own, felt particularly aggrieved. The fierce exchanges between Karens and the BIA (Burmese Independence Army) during the early stages of the Japanese occupation could not easily be forgotten – let alone a history of mutual antagonism stretching back hundreds of years. Even before independence, in October 1947, the mainly Christian KNU (Karen National Union) had convened a congress at Moulmein, attended by 600 delegates. Adopting the slogan 'Righteousness Exalteth a Nation', and led by Saw Ba U Gyi, the KNU demanded complete separation and a body of land commensurate in size to that occupied by the whole Karen population. If not, then the KNDO (Karen National Defence Organisation, later called the KNLA, Karen National Liberation Army) would go on the offensive.

Saw Ba U Gyi enunciated four principles that, in modified form, have survived to this day, and for which countless thousands have died, both on and off the battlefield: 1) There shall be no surrender; 2) recognition of the Karen state must be secured; 3) the Karens shall always retain their own arms; 4) the Karens must decide their own political destiny.

In retrospect, the KNU's 1947/8 position may seem unrealistic. Neither did the KNU command the support of all Karens – far from it – nor (it has been argued) was a separate Karen state ever a viable proposition. Relatively ill-resourced, it would quickly have fallen prey to its larger, more powerful neighbours, Thailand as well as Burma. Yet at the time the KNU, as well as feeling that God and natural justice were on its side, had at least some military advantages. The KNDO's men were well trained, mainly by the British before and during the war, and comparatively well armed. With Burma already sliding into disarray, thanks to the antics of the communists and others, there was a reasonable expectation of success.

Negotiations between U Nu's government and the KNU dragged on intermittently throughout 1948, with both sides refusing to make any significant concessions. For Nu, even more than for Aung San before him, the Union was non-negotiable, while for the KNU distrust of the Burman was just too great to contemplate risking incorporation within the Union as a quasi-autonomous territory.

Later, both sides blamed the other for initiating hostilities. Some Karen separatists were already engaged in insurrectionary activities as early as August 1948, while in December of the same year a horrible massacre occurred at Palaw in Tenasserim. Around eighty Karen villagers were slaughtered by government troops as they celebrated Christmas. It was a civil war waiting to happen, and anything could have triggered it. On 1st January 1949 the KNDO launched a surprise attack against Twante, near Rangoon, and held the township for a few days. At the end of the month Karen forces first occupied parts of Bassein, then dug in at Insein, the important township to the immediate north of the capital, famous for its prison. There the KNDO succeeded in fending off everything the government could throw at it for 112 days, before a ceasefire was brokered.

A major headache for U Nu and his ministers was the bald fact that many of the government's own troops were 'ethnics' – Kachins and Chins as well as Karens. Soon enough many of them either deserted or defected. In a bid to promote unity, a Karen – General Smith-Dun – had been appointed army Chief-of-Staff. He now 'resigned', to be replaced by Lieutenant-General Ne Win, who in April was also appointed Deputy Prime Minister, as well as Supreme Commander of Burma's armed forces. More worryingly still, the Karen and communist rebels sometimes joined forces, notably in March 1949, when they occupied Mandalay. By the middle of the year the situation in Burma was not unlike the situation in South Vietnam twenty years later, when the South Vietnamese government managed to cling on to the capital Saigon (just about), but very little else. Few towns and cities remained unambiguously under government control, and at one point the KNU alone could count on the loyalty of 10,000 soldiers, against the government's 3,000.

To make matters even more tenuous, on 1st October 1949 Mao Zedong, addressing a mass rally in Beijing's Tiananmen Square, proudly proclaimed the People's Republic of China. Henceforward Burma's largest and most powerful neighbour was a hardline communist state.

Although Mao had driven Chiang Kai-shek from the Chinese mainland, to set up a new nationalist Chinese state on the island of Formosa (Taiwan), some of Chiang's Guomindang forces remained behind, to be hunted down by the People's Liberation Army. At the beginning of 1950, 2,000 Guomindang troops sought sanctuary across the Burmese border in the Shan states, to be followed later by several thousand more. Politically, and militarily, this created a precarious situation, made all the more hazardous when the Guomindang inside Burma began receiving covert aid from the United States as well as Taipei – for a while so covert that even the US ambassador in Rangoon knew nothing about it.

All the while a horrendous war raged in Korea, where Chinese-backed

North Korea slogged it out with South Korea, backed by the West. The last thing Burma wanted was for China, or any other power, to find a pretext for a main invasion. Yet, in the critical early years of independence, U Nu's government badly needed the military aid given it by the Americans as well as British. Without such aid, the fight against Burma's indigenous communists and rebellious ethnics would have been so much the more uncertain.

At any moment Burma could have been sucked into a greater conflagration, as Vietnam and Korea were. U Nu deserves credit at least for avoiding that extremity. Both the Americans and the Chinese held back from becoming overly (or at any rate overtly) involved in Burma's affairs. Yet the essential ingredients of Burma's tragic nightmare were already in place. Not only was there conflict between the government and a growing number of internal enemies, but sometimes different rebel groups fought each other, when not forging unholy pacts and alliances.

The Karens, for example, at first sided with the communists, then with Guomindang elements. The KNU would also, in time, undergo a tortuous identity crisis: whether it was primarily Christian or primarily sympathetic to communism. Local warlords, whether dressed in civilian clothes or wearing a uniform, quickly learned to manipulate the fluid situation around them. Outside help too was assiduously courted by every warring party. Increasingly it became apparent that Beijing was secretly funding some of Burma's insurgents – the communists most obviously, but sometimes the communists' temporary minority allies, too. Like the USA, the People's Republic became adept at fighting proxy wars.

Funding was also available from another source: opium, either raw or refined into heroin. Although the opium poppy had long been cultivated in northern and north-eastern Burma, production had been small-scale, limited to domestic consumption. Now, with the arrival of the Guomindang, it became a main export crop, and Burma itself a focal supply point of a growing worldwide narcotics network. Minority leaders, and local warlords, routinely denied involvement in the opium trade, but directly or indirectly nearly all were party to it, to the overwhelming advantage of the adjacent Thai economy, where profiteering from the narcotics trade played a major role in creating the most vibrant economy in South-East Asia.

Step by step, though, U Nu's government, aided by local *tats* (private armies) as well as by British and American military assistance, was able to re-establish control over Burma's flatlands and reoccupy lost towns and cities. Rangoon too recovered its balance. For a few years, from the mid-1950s onwards, it regained a reputation as one of the Far East's premier watering holes. But the uplands remained an enduring problem, especially when first the Karennis and then some Shans took up arms against the Union, sometimes citing as their pretext a 'ten-year right to secession' clause built into the 1947 Constitution, which had enticed the Karennis into the Union.

Although General Ne Win subsequently took the lion's share of the credit for having 'saved' the Union from complete collapse during the first decade of its existence, his strong-arm methods as often as not incited further insurrection. Least of all did he endeavour to reduce traditional ill-feeling between Burmans and non-Burmans. It was also the case that Ne Win himself spent less and less time at the 'front', wherever that was, relying on more able field commanders (notably General Kyaw Zaw) to do the actual fighting. He preferred to stay at home in Rangoon, where he could attend the races, play golf, enjoy the nightlife and keep one eye at least on the evolving political scenario, and on U Nu in particular.

U Nu survived more than ten years as Burma's first Prime Minster by default as much as by ability. Not until 1956 was there a concerted attempt to remove him. An affable individual, he could charm diplomats and visiting dignitaries, but depended too much on the support of Ne Win's Tatmadaw to give Burma's newborn democracy, and the 1947 constitution, the bone it needed. As time passed he became increasingly religious and, among Burmese colleagues, somewhat autocratic: a combination that was in keeping with the deeper currents of Burmese history, but which was inappropriate to the rapidly changing world order of the 1950s.

In 1952, in the first general election to be held in Burma since independence, the AFPFL won 60 per cent of the vote, and U Nu continued in office. Four years later, in a second election, the League's share of the vote slipped to 55 per cent. In June of the same year U Nu was forced to resign following a vote of no confidence in the lower house of the Burmese parliament. Ba Swe, at the head of the Socialist Party – easily the largest faction within the AFPFL – and supported by Ne Win, took over as Prime Minister, but lasted just nine months, whereupon U Nu was reinstated, in March 1957.

During his second administration, Nu had signed up to the

Non-Aligned Movement, a pact among Third World countries launched in Indonesia at the Bandung Conference in April 1955. The brainchild of Indonesian President Bung Sukarno, India's Prime Minister Jawaharlal Nehru and China's Foreign Minister Zhou Enlai, the pact was designed to help the world's poorer countries stand together and resist becoming client states of one or other of the two 'super-powers', America and the Soviet Union. Nu had always favoured an even-handed approach to outside powers, but without the absolute support of a 'big brother', and without a clear-cut policy of national reconciliation, his administrations struggled to contain the problems caused by Burma's many insurgent groups. Nor, despite a temporary rapprochement with Ba Swe's socialists, was Nu able to stop the AFPFL falling apart.

The decisive split came in the early summer of 1958, when the League divided into a 'Clean' party, led by U Nu himself, and a 'Stable' party, led by Ba Swe. Neither could command a parliamentary majority. As a result, on 26th September Nu turned, in some desperation, to General Ne Win, whom he asked to form an emergency government for a period of limited duration.

Ne Win did not need to be asked twice. Yet his 'caretaker' administration, though it witnessed the introduction of several army officers into senior government positions, did not abuse the trust placed in it. Substantial progress was made towards resolving outstanding differences with China, including the final demarcation of the Sino-Burmese border; corruption amongst middle-ranking civil servants and other government employees was significantly reduced; Rangoon was given a facelift; and when, after sixteen months, the time came for Ne Win to step down, the General duly obliged.

Another general election was held in April 1960. U Nu's Cleans, now called the Union Party, did not win a landslide, but 52 per cent of the vote enabled Nu again to become Prime Minister. Burma returned to civilian rule. However, U Nu now seemed bent on a new path. Even before handing over power to Ne Win in 1958, he had talked about making Buddhism Burma's 'state religion'. His first act was to pass a law to that effect.

In practice little changed. Christianity, Islam and other religions, such as the animism practised by some of Burma's smaller, more remote minorities, were not outlawed, but the Kachins especially took fright, and one consequence was the creation of the KIA (Kachin Independence Army), which now joined other insurgencies against the government.

The old spectre of a Buddhist theocracy revived, especially when U Nu began urging the populace to build sixty thousand sand pagodas, to 'help resolve the country's sixteen thousand problems'. Even such a long-time friend and political associate as Edward Law Yone would later write: 'U Nu started as a Fabian Socialist and ended up being *Bawashin Mintaraggyi* ("Lord Almighty").'*

Nu's religiosity was not at all to Ne Win's liking. The General suspected Nu of wanting to revive the monarchy. Neither was Nu's apparent willingness to take seriously the concerns of some minority leaders, particularly the Shan princes, welcome. Although the 1947 constitution gave the Shan states the right to secede from the Union after an interval of ten years, the princes had collectively decided to remain incorporated – largely because, left entirely to their own devices, they would have had a hard time combating communist and Guomindang incursions, not to mention some unprincely Shan insurgents. Already they had agreed to surrender most of their traditional feudal powers. But in return they expected a greater degree of autonomy for a new, unitary Shan state than either the constitution or actual practice since independence indicated.

Prime Minister U Nu started talking to the Shan princes, convening a seminar early in 1962 specifically to discuss 'federalism'. For Ne Win, this was unacceptable. In his view all the minorities – Buddhist, Christian, Muslim and animist alike – should be brought, and firmly held, under centralist sway.

Later, Ne Win would claim that no sooner had Nu become Prime Minister again than the economy took a nose-dive. In fact the economy was the one aspect of Burma that was doing relatively well: throughout the 1950s GNP (gross national product) had grown by an average 6 per cent per annum, albeit from a rock-bottom base. There is no good evidence that in 1962 this was tailing off. But perhaps uppermost in Ne Win's mind was the brief taste of absolute power that he had already enjoyed: not something easily relinquished by anyone.

At the personal level, Ne Win had little time for U Nu, who was altogether too bookish. On 1st March 1962 the General and some of his military colleagues attended a performance by a visiting troupe of Chinese ballet dancers in the capital. The show continued late into the evening. At the end, all smiles, Ne Win offered the dancers his

* Edward M. Law Yone, 'One Who Waited Upon the King', date unknown

congratulations. Still smiling, he left the theatre with his entourage and drove off towards his home. At midnight, the tanks rolled out. Tatmadaw soldiers – as well-drilled as any of the Chinese dancers whom their supreme commander had earlier been watching – moved swiftly into key positions around the city, seizing government buildings and installations. U Nu and several cabinet ministers were apprehended and taken into custody.

At 8.50 on the morning of 2nd March Ne Win made a radio broadcast to the nation, announcing that the army had assumed power. The same day Burma's parliament was dissolved and the 1947 constitution suspended.

The *coup d'état* took the nation by surprise. There had been no hint beforehand that the army, or those units closest to the General, had been preparing any such action. Equally, there was little reason to anticipate the draconian regime that followed.

Ne Win was the archetypal Burmese 'big man', even though (or perhaps because) he was of mixed Chinese-Burman descent. Born in either 1910 or 1911* in Paungdale, central Burma, Ne Win grew up tall and good-looking. Intellectually, though, he was never the sharpest knife in the drawer. Coming from an affluent family, he managed to enter Rangoon University in 1929, to study biology, with a view to becoming a doctor, but left after two years having failed his exams. Wanting a public role for himself, and fired by the emergent nationalist politics, he joined the *Do-bama Asi-ayone* ('We Burmese Association'), but rather than follow the Kodaw Hmaing faction, as Aung San soon afterwards did, he attached himself to Ba Sein and Tun Oke. Notwithstanding, in 1941 he was recruited as one of the Thirty Comrades selected to undergo military training by the Japanese. When the Burmese Independence Army transferred to Burma, he was detailed to build up resistance forces behind British lines, and perpetrate acts of sabotage and other guerrilla operations.

There is no reason to suppose that, as a young commander, Ne Win was anything but effective in the field. He was popular with his troops, who admired him for his womanising and liked a leader prepared to

---

* Different sources give different birth dates for Shu Maung Ne Win, 'Apple of the Eye': 24th May 1911 was the date most usually given, but since his death in 2002, when his family said he was ninety-two, 10th July 1910 has been preferred

drink with his men. Less attractive was his quick temper. Even as a young man Ne Win was given to volcanic outbursts, sometimes for no obvious reason, but this too doubtless promoted respect amongst both officers and the ranks. He was not a man to be trifled with, but could be counted upon to repay loyalty twice over.

After independence, Ne Win established himself as the army's leader. Aung San had always preferred the more bureaucratic, cleverer Bo Let Ya, but with Aung San no longer alive, Let Ya was sidelined. Kyaw Zaw also threatened Ne Win's position, by virtue of being the better soldier, but in due course he too was seen off, when, in a murky episode, documents were produced suggesting that he was colluding with the state's enemies. Meanwhile Ne Win directed the government's military campaigns against the minority insurgents with relentless purpose from his headquarters in Rangoon. He was not, in the late 1940s and 1950s, interested in pursuing any policy of conciliation. The more fighting there was, the more the Tatmadaw grew in stature.

It is unclear when Ne Win began thinking in terms of imposing himself on Burma as the country's formal ruler. All along he had steadily expanded the army's remit, turning it into his personal power base. He regularly advanced the careers of those who had served under him in the Fourth Burma Rifles, whether or not their skills and attainment levels merited promotion. At the same time he took care to weed out officers whose political opinions deviated from his own. Similarly he paid special attention to the Military Intelligence Service (MIS, more usually just MI), set up by him in the early 1950s, which even before the coup of 1962 had begun taking an unusually close interest in civilian affairs, to the extent that it rivalled and outperformed other state security agencies.

U Nu's government was too pusillanimous to check these developments. At a time when post-war national reconstruction was still far from complete, those officers favoured by Ne Win received educational advantages: they were sent overseas for training by, amongst others, the British, American, Australian and even Israeli militaries. Simultaneously, the Burmese army's manpower was steadily increased, year in, year out.

In retrospect it is tempting to think that for close on fifteen years Ne Win groomed himself as Burma's strong-man elect. Perhaps it is more remarkable that he did not strike sooner. But when he did, the effect was deadly. Ne Win called his policies 'The Burmese Way to Socialism'. Superficially at least, the regime he created bore some resemblance to the hardline communist states of Eastern Europe and elsewhere. But he left nobody in any doubt that the kingpin of his new order was the Tatmadaw. There were no political commissars as such. The Burmese Way to Socialism entailed markedly fascist elements, learned (and never really forgotten by Ne Win) from the Japanese.

Either way, the outcome was totalitarian. Having dispensed on day one with the constitution, Ne Win instituted a Revolutionary Council, composed of loyal army officers with himself at its head. The two civilian exceptions were Dr Maung Maung, the regime's literary apologist, and Ba Nyein, an orthodox Marxist charged with running the economy. But even that was not enough. Ne Win assumed the powers of a dictator when it was announced that his personal decrees, as well as the decrees of the Revolutionary Council, would have the force of law.

And the decrees came thick and fast. Within the space of two years Burma's social landscape was transformed beyond recognition. Political parties were outlawed. In their place Ne Win created the monolithic BSPP (Burma Socialist Programme Party), although to begin with membership was restricted to members of the Revolutionary Council. Buddhist monks had to register with the government, or disrobe. Nearly all Burma's industries and businesses (including the banks) were nationalised. Foreign companies such as Burmah Oil were offered minimal compensation – payment of which was in any case delayed. The state was empowered to buy rice and other agricultural products at its own (not a market) price. Shops were replaced by increasingly expensive, and increasingly empty, army-run stores. Private schools were placed under state control, and all privately owned newspapers were closed down. Rigorous censorship was applied to all other kinds of publication. Reuters was expelled, and other foreign news agencies (the BBC, for example, and Associated Press) were obliged to employ 'local' staff only. Foreign journalists were discouraged from entering the country. Indeed, except under special circumstances, foreigners could only get a one-day entry visa.

The consequences of such root-and-branch, isolationist measures were dire. Burma – once the rice granary of South-East Asia – became a desperately impoverished land. The only growth area was a thriving black market, opening up opportunities for corruption, inside as well as outside the army, that simply had not existed before. Many of Burma's better-educated citizens fled abroad, if they could. There was an exodus of tens of thousands of Indians and Chinese – precisely those whose business and entrepreneurial acumen the country had depended upon. When harvests failed, malnutrition, and sometimes famine, followed. Educational and healthcare standards collapsed.

There was, inevitably, an escalation in levels of insurgency, as communists and the minorities alike became less and less enamoured of Ne Win and his junta. Correspondingly, campaigns against insurgents were pursued with fresh impetus, as the country was now divided into three sorts of territory – white, brown and black – according to the level of security achieved. Amongst the techniques devised by the Tatmadaw was the infamous 'Four Cuts' (*pyat lei pyat*) programme, in part modelled on the 'strategic hamlets' initiative instigated by the USA in South Vietnam, which in turn derived from counter-insurgency methods used by the British against Chinese communist rebels in Malaya in the 1950s.

The four cuts aimed to deprive insurgents of food, funds, intelligence and recruits. The army burned what it could not take from fields and orchards farmed by ordinary minority peasants in areas where there was fighting. The villagers themselves might be moved to special camps ringed with barbed wire. The Shan princes especially were dealt with harshly during the first weeks of the regime, even though they had refrained from raising the standard of revolt. Lured to Rangoon for 'talks', some were put in prison, while others – including Sao Kya Seng, the Prince of Hsipaw, married to an Austrian woman, Inge Sargent – were murdered.

But it was not just the minorities and captured communists who suffered. Within five months of his coup, Ne Win turned ferociously on his own kind, in the heart of Rangoon. In July 1962, amid severe rice shortages, students at Rangoon University began protesting. On the 7th there was a big rally at the main campus, by Inya Lake. Ne Win ordered troops armed with German-made G-3 assault rifles to University Avenue. When evening fell, under the immediate command of Sein Lwin – one of the General's bloodiest henchmen – the troops moved into the grounds of the university and opened fire. A hundred were killed, many hundreds more wounded. The following dawn, 8th July, Rangoon awoke to the sound of mighty explosions. Overnight the Student Union Building had been laced with dynamite. Now it was blown up. In the 1930s, under the guidance of Aung San, U Nu and others, the same building had incubated the Burmese revolution. Ne Win had decided it would never again incubate anything.

Many students were detained in prison. The university itself was closed down until such time as 'order was restored' – a pattern that became familiar over the next twenty-five years, to the detriment of higher education in Burma.

Another affront offered to his own people by Ne Win was his first assay in demonetarisation. Without warning, on 17th May 1964 the Revolutionary Council decreed that henceforward 50-and 100-*kyat* notes were of no value. Overnight, tens of thousands of Burmese had lost the best part of their savings, though special arrangements were made to compensate foreign diplomats. For the sake of appearances, Burma's criminal and civil courts were kept going, but the former especially were used to rubber-stamp decisions already taken by a clique of army officers bunched around Ne Win. The application of extreme authoritarianism spelled the end of the rule of law in any meaningful sense.

For Daw Khin Kyi, it was galling to watch Ne Win subvert her husband's legacy while claiming that he was Aung San's natural successor. Nor was the man himself anything but despicable. Instigating an inward-looking totalitarian regime, Ne Win affected a puritanical style, much to the chagrin of ordinary Burmese people. Beauty pageants were banned, and Rangoon's principal race track was converted into a military parade ground. But Ne Win himself was not bound by such regulations. On his frequent trips to England, where one of his overseas residences included a large house in suburban Wimbledon, he continued to attend the races at Ascot, and he continued to womanise – all at the expense of his own impoverished people.

Just as disturbing were his visits to Switzerland and Austria. In Zurich he had a private bank account, as all Third World dictators did. But in Vienna he attended the clinic of a well-known Freudian pyschoanalyst, Hans Hoff. Somewhere along the line he had acquired an undisclosed personality disorder.

Khin Kyi held on in Delhi for as long as she thought fit, hoping that, once past the first flush of power, the Burmese Way to Socialism would settle down into something more positive. But when it showed no signs of amelioration, she resigned. Soon after she had returned to Rangoon, she was served with a tax bill for 40,000 *kyat*. Because their meagre salaries and adverse exchange rates set them at a disadvantage, Burmese diplomats were exempt from having to pay income tax while working abroad, but Ne Win decided to make an exception of the Bogyoke's widow. This was his revenge, personal and autocratic, for her decision to sever all links with his regime.

Unable to pay out of her own pocket, Daw Khin Kyi had of necessity to rely on the generosity of friends. Much as she disliked having to accept the charity of others, it was preferable to pleading her cause at the feet of Asia's newest despot.

Khin Kyi's daughter likewise was not enamoured of the dictator. Aware of how her mother had been treated, when Ne Win summoned Suu Kyi to his Wimbledon lair in the spring of 1967, she flatly refused to go. She was, she coldly told his secretary, too busy preparing for her final examinations at Oxford.

But now that her course there was finished, the question of what to do next arose. Her entire upbringing had been geared towards acquiring skills and knowledge that could be put to use for her country's benefit. But with Ne Win at the helm, there was little point in her returning to Rangoon. Yet there was another, equally compelling reason for Suu Kyi to remain abroad. Even before she left St Hugh's, in June 1967, she had met the man she would marry.

XIX

BETWEEN THREE CONTINENTS

What say you? Can you love the gentleman?
William Shakespeare,
Romeo and Juliet Act I, scene iii

IT was as well that Suu Kyi got on famously with her London 'guardians', the Gore-Booths. In a moment of extraordinary prescience, Lord Gore-Booth (as he had become) wrote of her in his 1974 memoirs that she was an 'exceptional' young person whom he fully hoped would 'do some service' for her country – for all that her country had done 'so little' for her. Thirty years later his widow, Lady Gore-Booth, spoke of Suu Kyi as a 'perfect guest, another daughter' even, to add to the two she already had. 'She never made any noise, but I always knew when she had come into the room. If she passed in front of her elders, she would gently incline her head, the way only an exquisite oriental girl can.'

Their Chelsea townhouse, at 29 The Vale, had indeed become Suu Kyi's London home, as the Gore-Booths had promised Daw Khin Kyi it would. A stone's throw from the King's Road, it was a little set back from a tree-studded pavement, lending it an air of dignified reserve. On the ground floor was an elegant drawing room opening onto a walled garden at the rear of the building. On the topmost floor, under the roof, was a self-contained flat, which the Gore-Booths made over to Suu for her personal use, both during her Oxford vacations and after she had left St Hugh's.

To earn her keep, or at least some pocket money, Suu Kyi hired herself out as a private tutor. She also worked part-time as a research assistant to Professor Hugh Tinker at the School of Oriental and African Studies (SOAS), London University.

Before becoming an academic, Tinker had served first in the Indian Army, then as an administrator in the subcontinent. In the mid-1950s he spent a year teaching at Rangoon University – an experience that focused his attention on recent Burmese history. In time he would compile and edit *Burma: The Struggle for Independence* (1983–4), a landmark publication in Burmese studies. However, his was a broad mind, not overly given to specialisation. Among the many posts he either held or would come to hold were Director of the Institute of Race Relations and vice-president of the Ex-Services Campaign for Nuclear Disarmament. He was, too, an active member of the Liberal Party, standing for Parliament in three general elections. A 'big-picture' man, he was a friend of the Gore-Booths. Under his tutelage, Suu Kyi had once again landed on her feet.

But there was the other reason why the Gore-Booth household drew Suu Kyi to London. As well as two daughters, the Gore-Booths had twin sons, David and Christopher. While David, destined to follow in his father's footsteps into a distinguished Foreign Office career, had enrolled at Christ Church, Oxford, his brother read Modern History at Durham University, in England's north-east. There, among the friends he made, were two more identical twins, Michael and Anthony Aris.

Chris Gore-Booth's friendship with the Arises flourished. Soon Michael Aris, also studying Modern History, was being invited to Chelsea, which meant that he too met the supernumerary member of the Gore-Booth family. That Suu Kyi was almost a year older, and busy preparing for her Oxford finals, as he was preparing for his at Durham, did not prevent Aris becoming immediately infatuated. She was just the person to answer his youthful, but also curiously filtered, dreams. Nor, as those around them observed, was Suu Kyi herself unmoved. She was not yet prepared to surrender her puritanical virginity; nor would she until she married. But in the presence of young Michael Aris she lit up as she had seldom done before. Her avowals that she would only ever marry a Burmese began to melt.

Perhaps what appealed to her most was that, tall and good-looking though he was, if somewhat gangly and tousle-haired, Michael was neither an obvious Lothario, nor someone who banked on any inherited credentials. Though young – when they first met he was just turned twenty – he was already a centred individual, in a way that suggested to Suu Kyi a relationship of cultural equals and cultural opportunity. For Aris was something of an oddball, the way that many of life's achievers are. Already he had mapped out for himself his principal area of interest: Tibet, and the equally Buddhist Himalayan kingdoms of Bhutan and Nepal. Not Burma quite, but close enough to make him attractive.

His family was also intriguing. A grandfather, John Arundel, had been an explorer of the Pacific islands, as well as a friend of Rudyard Kipling and a pioneer of the industrial use of guano – dried seagull droppings. Though long since dead, his adventurer's legend in the Aris household encouraged Michael, and his twin brother Anthony and older sister Lucinda, in their taste for the exotic. Their father, John, was a British Council administrator, whose postings included pre-Castro Cuba, where Michael and Anthony were born in Havana on 27th March, 1946. There was, too, a background of diplomatic service on his mother's side. Josette Vaillaincourt was the daughter of a French-Canadian envoy who had encouraged his daughter's artistic talents. Josette attended the *École des Beaux Arts* in Montreal, turning herself into a more than competent painter somewhat in the manner of the Parisian Symbolist-Impressionist Édouard Vuillard.

After moving from Cuba to Peru, the Aris children grew up in rural Sussex, where both Michael and Anthony attended Worth School, a small 'public' (that is, private) school near Gatwick airport, attached to Worth Abbey and its complement of Benedictine monks. The twins habitually played games with their cassocked teachers, the one pretending to be the other. Both learned to play the violin well, sitting at the same desk in the school orchestra. But they also imbibed the special ethos of Worth, much as Suu Kyi had imbibed the ethos of Lady Shri Ram and St Hugh's colleges. The Benedictines provided a classroom education in line with the National Curriculum, but they also emphasised the importance of the spiritual side of life. They aimed, through their 'holistic' approach, to produce more rounded, caring individuals than more run-of-the mill examination factories.

For this educational approach, at once Catholic and catholic, Michael Aris was well suited. When he was twelve, his father John, returning from a visit to India, brought with him a prayer-wheel purchased from a Tibetan fleeing the Chinese occupation of his country: one of those drum-like upright cylinders, which the supplicant spins as one of a thousand ways of earning Buddhist 'merit'. Michael's natural curiosity was drawn by the peculiar letters inscribed on the prayer-wheel. By chance, one of his teachers at Worth, Andrew Bertie (later to become Grand Master of the Knights of Malta) had studied the Tibetan language and helped Michael decipher what was written. Thrilled by the mystery uncovered, young Aris resolved one day to learn Tibetan for himself. Although at Durham University he took the Modern History course, his spare time was spent studying such accounts of Tibetan history and culture as he could lay his hands on. Tibet and its southerly neighbours, he realised, was where his future lay. But there was a fly in the ointment. Tibet itself – that vast, desiccated plateau ringed by some of the world's highest mountains – was, by 1967, closed to outsiders. The communist Chinese had staged two invasions, the first in 1951 to enforce Chinese suzerainty, and the second in 1959 to quell an uprising.

But it was not entirely hopeless. While the Fourteenth Dalai Lama fled to northern India, where he has remained in exile ever since, many other lamas escaped to neighbouring Bhutan, the Himalayan 'hermit' kingdom that could be regarded as a 'Little Tibet', such were the centuries-old ties between the two countries. Among the classic accounts of Tibet that Aris had read was *Peaks and Lamas* (1939) by Marco Pallis, the last British Resident to Lhasa, the Tibetan capital. Though in his seventies, Pallis still had good connections in the Himalayan world. Impressed by the young student from Durham, he secured for him a dream assignment: Aris was to be engaged as a tutor and English-language instructor by the Bhutanese royal family.

Such an adventure resonated with previous English tutors appointed to far-away and hidden courts – Anna Leonowens and King Mongkut of Siam in the 1860s, or Reginald Johnston and the 'Last Emperor' Puyi in China at the turn of the century. For Aris, it would present a unique opportunity to capture the heights of Himalayan scholarship. Given access to the royal and monastic libraries (and in Bhutan there was little distinction between the two), with permission he microfilmed their contents. But it was no quick excursion. Aris was to spend six years away from home. Would the special feeling that he and Suu Kyi had for one another survive such time and distance? Or would the impracticalities crush his hopes?

For a Burmese girl to consort with a foreigner, particularly a Briton, was, in the circles in which Suu Kyi grew up, taboo. If she were to defy convention, she needed to know for sure that she was making the right choice. Feelings on both sides had to be tested before she could commit herself. Yet the circumstances were nothing if not utterly romantic. Though in the late 1960s the postal service to Bhutan was slow and unreliable, except through diplomatic channels, there began between them an intimate correspondence, long since placed under lock and key in Oxford's Bodleian Library, in which their affection for, and understanding of, one another deepened and developed.

But that still left open the question of Suu Kyi's own career. She needed to be kept busy. However stimulating her life in Chelsea, she was aware that it could, or should, be no more than a happy interlude. The solution lay the other side of the Atlantic, in New York.

Despite her poor showing in her Oxford finals, Suu Kyi was welcomed into New York University on a postgraduate programme. Her mentor there was Frank N. Trager, the Professor of International Studies. Like Hugh Tinker, Trager had worked in Rangoon in the 1950s, where he had come to know Daw Khin Kyi, and was busy writing his own book about Burma: *Burma: From Kingdom to Republic*, published in 1976. Also like Tinker, he was no narrow specialist. With a background in economics and philosophy, as well as politics, he had intermittently advised the US government on South-East Asian affairs. Although in *Marxism in S.E. Asia: A Study of Four Countries* (1960) and *Why Vietnam?* (1966) he had advanced arguments supportive of American military involvement in Indochina, Trager's work on the relations between national security and economic interests was of more lasting benefit to his country. Academically Suu Kyi was again in good hands.

New York furnished another family friend of even greater importance in her life. In her youth Ma Than É had been a famous Burmese beauty. Born into a Baptist Christian family in 1908, she gained a place at Rangoon University. Then, like Khin Kyi, she enrolled at a teacher training college, before winning a scholarship to pursue her studies in England. Back home before the Japanese war, she became celebrated as a singer of Burmese love songs. During their courtship Khin Kyi and General Aung San often listened to her recordings, though it was not until January 1946 that she came face-to-face with the Bogyoke. When the Japanese invaded Burma, Ma Than É escaped to India, where she worked for All India Radio's Burmese service, and then to San Francisco, where she performed similar duties for the broadcasting division of the US Office of War Information – what was to become VOA (Voice of America). The end of the war found her in London again. When Aung San's delegation arrived for its momentous negotiations with Prime Minister Attlee, Ma Than É was sometimes invited to dine with them in the spacious, but ill-heated suite at the Dorchester Hotel that the British government was paying for. She would sing her songs for the Bogyoke and his guests, and undertake shopping expeditions on his behalf, buying presents for Khin Kyi and their three tiny children.

Soon afterwards Ma Than É joined the permanent staff of the newly created United Nations. Although her job, and marriage to an Austrian film-maker, kept her away from Burma, she visited Aung San's widow whenever circumstances permitted. To the young Suu Kyi, she became known as 'Auntie Dora' – the Christian name Ma Than É had been given at missionary school when she herself was a child. Later Suu Kyi would also sometimes refer to her as 'my emergency aunt'.

While Suu Kyi was at St Hugh's, Ma Than É was posted to Algeria, whither Suu Kyi went for one of her summer vacations, in 1965. Arriving days after the socialist regime of Ben Bella had been ousted by the more moderate government of Houari Boumédienne, Suu Kyi expressed the wish to meet as many 'ordinary' Algerians as she could. She spent most of the ensuing weeks living and working with a group of international volunteers who ran a social reconstruction project. But if Ma Than É saw less of her charge than she had anticipated, she was not displeased. She admired Suu Kyi's youthful idealism, sparing her the tedium of endless UN and diplomatic cocktail parties.

The year of 1969 found Ma Than É working in the UN headquarters building in New York, and renting an apartment nearby in fashionable Beckman Place, off 49th Street on First Avenue. Although the apartment was scarcely spacious, she insisted that Suu Kyi stay with her. For the next three years, despite an age difference of almost forty years, the two women lived as housemates, sharing domestic chores and preparing, whenever they could find the right ingredients, Burmese food together. But Ma Than É was also supremely helpful in another way. The long journey across Manhattan to the New York University faculty building in Washington Square was not just tiring for Suu Kyi. The bus rides made her giddy. Much as she was exhilarated by the cosmopolitan bustle of New York, she found the attitude of some of its streetwise denizens threatening, so that when, after a few weeks, Ma Than É suggested she take a job at the UN instead, Suu Kyi readily agreed. Her postgraduate studies could wait a while.

She had to be screened and vetted, and there were the inevitable delays with her application – thanks to the workings of an organisation that had already established its reputation as a bureaucratic monster, but soon enough she was 'in'.* It helped that at the time the UN Secretary-General was none other than U Thant, the most capable Burman alive. After initial training, Suu Kyi joined the permanent staff of the Advisory Committee on Administrative and Budgetary Questions, tasked with reviewing the management and financial operations of such frontline UN agencies as the UNDP (United Nations Development Programme) and WHO.

Although the Advisory Committee was distanced from both the Security Council and General Assembly, and therefore from the political decision-making process, being employed by the United Nations gave Suu Kyi insights into both the rationale and workings of the world's largest human-rights organisation – insights that would later feed into her own political outlook. Under Ma Than É's guidance she performed her relatively low-level duties with diligence and thoroughness, and was regarded as someone with considerable potential. She also spent some of her spare time doing voluntary work, at the Bellevue Center, an adjunct of New York's City Hospital that offered care and respite for destitutes of all races and ages. Mostly this involved just listening and talking, sometimes reading to them, but it was another formative part of Suu Kyi's education. Whereas in Algeria she had witnessed a society on the mend after a prolonged and bloody civil war, at the Bellevue she came face-to-face with an urban underclass whose needs were ignored by the city's surrounding and assertive affluence: not the wretched of the earth so much as the wretched of the gutter. For someone who had lived a sheltered, privileged life, such contact was shocking. Wasn't America supposed to be the modern Golden Land? Suu Kyi began taking an informed interest in Martin Luther King, Jr, the doyen of civil-rights activists who had been assassinated in Memphis, Tennessee, the year before she arrived in Manhattan.

But Suu Kyi's New York was not all hard work and applied humanitarian commitment. By a stroke of good fortune Robin Christopher, her exact contemporary at Oxford whom she had met and befriended in her first

*Ma Than É, 'A Flowering of the Spirit', in Aung San Suu Kyi, *Freedom from Fear* (1991), supplemented by an author interview conducted in 2006

week there, was in America for much of the time, first as a student at the Fletcher School of International Law and Diplomacy in Boston, then at the UN itself, on his first overseas posting for the British foreign service. Michael Aris excepted, of all her English male friends Christopher was the one she liked and trusted most. As and when they could, they met and kept each other entertained.

On one memorable occasion, Christmas 1970, Christopher and two fellow Foreign Office 'juniors', Robert Cooper and Richard Dalton, accompanied Suu Kyi on a carol-singing expedition. Their audience was to be Secretary-General U Thant, the venue his cabinet room at the UN headquarters.

'We were, the three of us, a little daunted by the prospect of giving a private performance in such august company,' Christopher recalled, 'though Suu as always seemed to take things in her stride. Not only U Thant, but some of his senior colleagues were there as well, and it was not as if we were an experienced, professional choir. In any event, we decided we should have a rehearsal on the way there, and that meant, to the amusement of other passengers, singing "Good King Wenceslas" on a public bus bowling along an ice-bound Third Avenue with Suu dressed in her finest Burmese costume. Fortunately, the Secretary-General was similarly amused.' When the story was recounted to Lady Gore-Booth, Christopher, Cooper and Dalton immediately became Suu Kyi's 'Three Musketeers'.

U Thant had very much taken Suu Kyi under his wing, making her regularly welcome at his 'Sunday lunches' – long, lazy affairs at his Riverdale residence overlooking the Hudson river, which upheld the informal traditions of Burmese hospitality at their best. Immensely quick-witted, U Thant possessed, in the words of Norman Lewis, who had encountered him twenty-five years earlier in Rangoon as Permanent Secretary at the Ministry of Information, 'more than even the normal measure of Burmese charm'.* Although he was more closely associated with U Nu before being unanimously elected the third UN Secretary-General in succession to Dag Hammarskjöld (killed in an air-crash in 1961), U Thant had known Aung San and had kept up with Daw Khin Kyi. It was only natural therefore that he should become one of their daughter's 'uncles'.

*Norman Lewis, *Golden Earth* (1952)

Because of the immense gravity of the issues he had daily to grapple with – the Cold War, Vietnam, and endless troubles in the Middle East – U Thant made it a rule that his Sunday guests refrain from political debate. Sunday was his day off too, if he could manage it. But U Thant had also to juggle two very different Burmese communities resident in the United States. On the one hand were the 'sheep': Burmese embassy officials, as well as members of the permanent Burmese delegation to the United Nations; they were ostensibly pro-regime. On the other were the 'goats': fiercely anti-regime Burmese émigrés. While U Thant himself nursed an abiding distaste for General Ne Win, the UN Secretary-General could not afford to be seen to be partisan. He was, after all, the world's premier peace-keeper. At his table therefore Suu Kyi and Ma Than É sometimes found themselves rubbing shoulders with those they would not normally have given the time of day to. Yet because of U Thant's avuncular presence, swords were seldom crossed.

The same did not apply one autumn when hospitality was offered by the head of the permanent Burmese UN delegation, U Soe Tin. On his own or at U Thant's, Soe Tin was affable enough, and sometimes ambiguous about his support for Burma's military dictatorship. Even so, Suu Kyi and Ma Than É were surprised to receive an invitation to his house during the busiest period of the UN calendar. The General Assembly was in full session, and so not just members of the permanent Burmese delegation to the UN were in town, but many other Burmese diplomats and officials.

When they arrived at Soe Tin's residence (also in Riverdale), Ma Than É immediately suspected something was afoot. 'The large rectangular living room was filled with plants and flowers and an excess of black-and-gold Burmese lacquer had been rearranged so that sofas and chairs were placed against the wall with large coffee tables in front of them. And on those sofas and chairs was ranged a whole battery of Burmese ambassadors attending the General Assembly.' But not just ambassadors. There were also men from Rangoon who had nothing to do with the diplomatic corps, among them one Colonel Lwin, to whom the rest deferred. Even U Soe Tin looked unusually sheepish.

Suu Kyi was led to an empty chair at the end of the room, and Ma Than É was seated near but not beside her. For a few moments polite banalities were exchanged. Then Colonel Lwin launched his assault. Why, he wanted to know, had Aung San Suu Kyi not surrendered her diplomatic passport, given to her when her mother was still ambassador in India? Did she not know that its retention was unlawful? And what in any case was she doing working for the UN as a non-delegation staff member?

To Ma Than É it was obvious that Colonel Lwin was acting under orders from Rangoon. Ne Win, already exhibiting the symptoms of paranoia that sooner or later affect all tyrants, clearly wanted Aung San's daughter reined in. But Suu Kyi held her ground. She had, she replied, applied for a new, regular passport in London, but had heard nothing from the Burmese embassy there. She was quite happy to surrender her existing passport, but not until the new one was ready. A passport was her right, and so was working for the United Nations if she wanted to. What possible objection could Colonel Lwin have?

As chance would have it, Burma's ambassador to London was also present. With Suu Kyi's eyes trained upon him, he blusteringly confirmed that she had indeed applied for a replacement, but that he was still awaiting instructions from Rangoon. At once the company began to relax. 'All of us in that room knew, of course, of the bureaucratic confusion and incompetence in Burma which had created similar delays,' Ma Than É recorded. 'The ambassadors now joined in to agree that Suu had no other choice of action.' Colonel Lwin alone was nonplussed. He had been sent on a mission without being given the full background.

What Suu Kyi had demonstrated was that, in Ma Than É's words, 'being the daughter of General Aung San and Daw Khin Kyi she could not be taken down'. Ma Than É herself had once cocked a snook at Ne Win. When she was asked to attend a dinner given by him, he had suggested that she 'sing for her supper' for the benefit of his other guests. Ma Than É at once riposted, 'I'll sing for my supper after I've had it' and sat down to eat. But she did not sing afterwards. Suu Kyi had dealt with Colonel Lwin, and through him with the General himself, with equal firmness.

A few years later, visiting her mother in Rangoon in 1974, she was informally interviewed by regime officials to sound out her long-term intentions. They wanted to know if she would engage in 'anti-government activities'. She gave an unequivocal assurance that she would never involve herself in Burmese affairs so long as she remained outside the country. Ne Win must have been well satisfied. At the time it seemed unlikely Aung San Suu Kyi would ever go back to Rangoon for more than a holiday.

*　　*　　*

She and Michael Aris became engaged to be married in 1970, when Aris stopped by New York on his way home to England for a well-earned vacation. It was almost three years since they had seen each other, but, through their letters, their growing love had put down its essential tap root. At the same time, Suu Kyi promised Michael that she would visit him in Bhutan during her annual leave the following year.

Aris had made wondrous progress. The huge adventure he had embarked upon in 1967 had turned up trumps. As Suu Kyi herself would later write, Bhutan, the 'Land of the Thunder Dragon', was 'a tiny and remote kingdom barely known to foreigners – a country of lovely, peaceful Himalayan valleys, huge medieval fortresses and handsome people clad in traditional, hand-woven robes'.* For centuries nothing much had changed, except that in 1908 a complex web of theocratic fiefdoms governed by high lamas had been unified under a common, temporal crown. Outside the diminutive mountain-bound capital of Thimphu, there were no roads or vehicles and very little electricity. Tourists were excluded, and the only place to obtain a visa was either in Delhi or Kathmandu. But Aris had been made to feel most welcome and appreciated by King Jigme Dorje and his family. Moves were afoot to modernise, but the cautious Bhutanese were adamant this should be done in such a way as to preserve their culture. Aris, with his scholarly interest in Bhutan's past, his Buddhist leanings, and his aptitude for learning the official language, Dhzongkha, was the acceptable face of the outside, Western world.

Soon the dowager queen, Jigme Dorje's mother, put at his disposal a handsome traditional Bhutanese dwelling at Uchu, just outside Thimphu, for when he wanted to be alone to study. Much of his time was spent at the Wangdicholing Palace, tutoring the king's children and other princes and princesses. Sometimes his young charges ran him ragged. During one early lesson, they told him the classroom was about to be inspected by a royal minister. Aris asked how such a great dignitary should be greeted. The children replied 'O lyonpo shang bom dag la.' Too late he discovered these words translated as 'Oh Minister, your nose is enormous.' But the minister took no offence, and the children adored Aris all the more for falling into the trap they had set.†

* Aung San Suu Kyi, Let's Visit Bhutan (1985)
† Karma Phuntsho, in the European Bulletin of Himalayan Research, no. 17 (1999)

Sometimes there were less-welcome chores. Once he had mastered Dzongkha, Aris was often required to translate government documents, for forward dispatch to Delhi and beyond. But already he was wise enough to understand the game of give and take. Not least among the boons on offer was the accessibility of Bhutan's most venerated lamas, both indigenous and Tibetan. Among the latter was the figure of Dilgo Khyentse, a 'realised being' who had an unrivalled knowledge of Tibetan scriptures. He had also been one of the Fourteenth Dalai Lama's teachers in Lhasa. Aris sat at his feet and imbibed his wisdom. When Suu Kyi arrived, he made a point of introducing her to him, and Dilgo Khyentse became their first shared Buddhist master.

Suu Kyi could see that Michael was in his element in Bhutan, and wanted to join him there. In the little time available to them they decided to marry on Michael's next trip home, at Christmas 1971. She would resign her position at the United Nations, then return with him to Thimphu.

The ceremonies took place on 1st January 1972. Following a perfunctory appearance at the Registry Office at Chelsea Town Hall in the King's Road, Buddhist rites were performed in the Gore-Booths' Chelsea drawing room. Friends were invited to wind the white string of connection to the Buddha around their two bodies, seated on the Gore-Booth's floor. Afterwards a reception was given at the Hyde Park Hotel in Knightsbridge, with the Gore-Booths again acting as hosts, together with the groom's father and stepmother, John and Evelyn Aris, dressed in Bhutanese costume.

From the outset there were shadows in the background. That the Burmese ambassador declined to attend their wedding was only to be expected – probably he would have got the sack had he done so. But also absent were Suu Kyi's surviving brother, Aung San Oo, and, more woundingly still, Daw Khin Kyi. Her mother was disappointed that Suu Kyi had not after all married a Burmese, but an Englishman. Had her husband not sacrificed himself fighting British colonial rule? As for Aung San Oo, who was already permanently domiciled in the USA, the two siblings had never got on. Now the gulf between them was wider than ever.

Within a year Daw Khin Kyi was won round by Aris, and bestowed upon him the affection due to a right-minded son-in-law. An old family friend, U Myint Thein, a former Chief Justice who had been imprisoned by Ne Win and was known to Suu Kyi as 'Uncle Monty', played peace-maker. But some other Burmese, particularly those dependent on Ne Win's largesse, were not so forgiving. For them, Aung San's daughter's union with an 'imperialist dog' was an act of ultimate apostasy.

Even that was scarcely the be-all and end-all. Suu Kyi herself had laboured hard to reconcile her birthright with the pure romance that had enveloped her. During the eight months between her visit to Bhutan and their London wedding she wrote Aris no fewer than 187 letters. A principal theme was her feeling that she must one day return to Burma, to help 'her people'. 'I only ask one thing,' she wrote, 'that should my people need me, you would help me to do my duty by them.' It was not inevitable, but 'the possibility was there'. And again, 'Sometimes I am beset by fears that circumstances and national considerations might tear us apart just when we are so happy in each other that separation would be a torment.' Such fears, she conceded, were 'futile and inconsequential', and she was sure 'love and compassion will triumph in the end'.*

It was no more specific than that. Just how Suu Kyi might one day be called upon to assist her compatriots was utterly obscure. What she sought from Michael Aris was an understanding only – a 'favour', not a cast-iron pledge. But he, being a 'gentleman' in the classic English mode, acceded to the imprecision of her wish. The future was not theirs to see. If 'duty' called her from his side, then so be it. He would not stand in her way. Rather, he would stand by her.

And so they were married. On the one hand there was Suu Kyi the modern, independent woman, come of age and free to love as she chose. Just as Daw Khin Kyi had once 'rebelled' against her family by choosing nursing over a teaching career, so her daughter staked out her individual preference. On the other hand there was the simple, indomitable fact of who Suu Kyi's father was, or had been, his ghost calling her back to redress the archaic and anarchic world of Burmese politics.

* Aung San Suu Kyi, *Freedom from Fear* (1991, p. xvii)

XX

THIMPHU, KYOTO, SIMLA

*I have been blessed with the good karma that took me into the closed
territory of my childhood dreams and with a family that constantly
encouraged my interests.*

Michael Aris, in his preface to
Bhutan: The Early History of a Himalayan Kingdom (1979)

NEVER one to do anything by half-measures, Suu Kyi sought to turn
herself into an exemplary wife, and then an exemplary mother, while
continuing to think about Burma and not ruling out a career for herself.
But for the first ten years and beyond, it was Aris's career that determined
where and how they lived. He was the breadwinner, and his Suu seemed
content enough to keep house for him. To the dismay of her more
radical women friends, she uncomplainingly ironed his shirts, his socks
and his underwear, and cooked his meals and cleaned their house. She
became adept at making clothes and running up curtains. As a young
academic, Michael's earning power was limited, and at the start especially
money was tight. But, having been raised to hold luxury in disdain, Suu
Kyi gritted her teeth and persevered. Committed to a family life, she
went about her housewifely duties almost with a vengeance.

Following their wedding, they returned to Bhutan and lived together
in Thimphu. Even compared to her native Burma, living standards outside
the capital were low, and Suu Kyi was sometimes miffed by local custom.
Their favoured pastime was hiking through Bhutan's hauntingly barren
landscapes, either on foot or on pony-back, taking with them Puppy, a
Himalayan terrier that had attached itself to the strange English tutor.

Since, as Aris later told friends in England, Bhutan's geography was 'quite simple really, just three enormously lengthy mountain valleys arranged in parallel north to south', it was difficult to get lost – 'so long as you knew which valley you were in'. It was hard work, and after a day or two Suu Kyi would long for a shower or a bath. But she learned not to ask for such a thing when they stayed overnight in villages. On the first long hike they took she was led to a hollowed-out tree trunk lying on the ground, full of water heated by hot stones. To her horror, she realised she was expected to perform her ablutions in full view of the whole village. She had her bath, but only after Michael persuaded the headman to organise grass screens to be placed around her. As a further protection of her modesty, Suu Kyi declined to remove her undergarments, to the puzzlement and dismay of youngsters poking spy-holes through the dried foliage.

Another time they had what may have been Bhutan's first motor accident. With road-building proceeding apace, Aris acquired a Mini Moke, making him, for a while, the only non-royal to own an automobile. It ended up in a ditch one afternoon, when the road ran out. Going for help to pull the vehicle out, they found that all their belongings, including a stash of money, were gone when they got back. Although the thief was quickly caught, and the money returned, it was an experience that took some of the shine off Shangri-La.

Nor was everything quite as Suu Kyi would have wished in Thimphu. In the royal family, and among courtiers, there was resentment that the tall white tutor had chosen not to marry some Bhutanese beauty. While Suu Kyi accepted that she should kowtow before the king and other senior royals, it irritated her that she had to kowtow before young princesses especially. Had one of them been eyeing Michael for herself in the royal classroom? It was hard to tell, for there was so much protocol involved, but . . .

Yet she was able to leave Bhutan feeling she had done the country at least some good. Whilst she was in New York, the Himalayan kingdom had joined the United Nations. Suu Kyi willingly offered her services to the Bhutanese foreign ministry. She became adviser to the government on UN relations. But it was never likely she and Michael would remain there indefinitely. After six years, Aris had assembled sufficient material to write a university thesis that would set him on his way to the academic career he wanted. And, to their mutual joy, in August 1972 Suu Kyi discovered she was pregnant.

They returned to London in time for Christmas. With help from Michael's family, they bought a very small flat in Ifield Road, close to Brompton Cemetery. Visitors remember it as white and spotlessly clean, and sparsely furnished. Aris needed to be in the capital because, guided by Hugh Richardson, an acknowledged expert in Tibetan studies, he wanted to take his doctorate at SOAS, London University. On 12th April 1973, at the Princess Beatrix Hospital in Brompton, Suu Kyi gave birth to a boy, Alexander Myint San Aung Aris. But within a few weeks the fledgling family was on the move again. Aris had been asked to assume the responsibilities of leader of an expedition to Kutang and Nubri in Nepal, sponsored by the University of California. Suu Kyi and baby Alexander went with him. As they would be away for the best part of a year, Ifield Road had to be let out. But going to Nepal also meant going to Burma. Meeting Michael for the first time and being introduced to her grandson, Daw Khin Kyi laid aside the misgivings she had had about her daughter marrying an Englishman.

When they returned to England for a second time, towards the end of 1974, they briefly resumed residence in Brompton. But, with a very young child on the premises, Ifield Road was altogether too cramped. Instead they went up to Grantown-on-Spey in Scotland, where Michael's father and stepmother, John and Evelyn Aris, had bought a more spacious house for their retirement. There they stayed for the best part of a year, well into 1975, as Michael began organising the notes he had made in Bhutan.

Suu Kyi got on especially well with Evelyn Aris, just as she got on well with Michael's mother Josette. A close and enduring bond formed between them. For whatever reason, it seems that Suu Kyi needed the presence of an older woman in her life, a substitute for her own far-away mother perhaps. For several years Patricia Gore-Booth had filled that role; now, Lord Gore-Booth having himself retired, Suu's 'guardians' were more often than not away somewhere on travels of their own. In Grantown-on-Spey – a small town deep within the Scottish highlands, twenty-five miles east of Inverness – Suu Kyi also established a close friendship with a near-neighbour, Nessa Mackenzie. Together they attended dress-making classes. Suu Kyi impressed her fellow classmates with her skills, and with her personality. In Grantown-on-Spey she would be remembered for her 'cheerful serenity'.

In due course Michael Aris submitted to SOAS a synopsis of the thesis he wanted to write. It was at once clear to his assessors that not only had his time in Bhutan been spent profitably, but he had the intellectual equipment to turn his materials into something of lasting value. His PhD topic was 'A Study on the Historical Foundations of Bhutan with a Critical Edition and Translation of Certain Bhutanese Texts in Tibetan'. In 1979 this was turned into a book with the more convenient title *Bhutan: The Early History of a Himalayan Kingdom*. It immediately secured his reputation as the coming star of Himalayan studies. But it took him four years to complete. Just as crucial to his progress was the offer of a Junior Research Fellowship at St John's College, Oxford, in 1976, followed by a full Research Fellowship at Wolfson College in 1980. Most agreeably to his wife, Oxford became their home, with an almost acceptable salary to accompany it.

It took time, however, to sort out their accommodation. They lived for a while in Sunninghall House, some distance outside Oxford. But while Suu Kyi had never been a city girl, neither was she a country lass. The house was cold, damp, isolated and, with another child on the way, impractical. When St John's offered them a college flat in Oxford itself, they moved once again, in 1977. It had a large, high-ceilinged drawing room, but only one bedroom and the smallest of kitchens. However, there was also a boxroom that Suu Kyi turned into a nursery, and it was better than shivering to death every night.

A second son, Kim – after the eponymous boy-hero of Kipling's novel, full name Kim Htein Lin Aris – was born on 24th September 1977. In the intimate memoir of 'Suu Burmese' written by her in 1991, Ann Pasternak Slater recalls Suu's disappointment at being unable to breastfeed her second child, though not for want of trying. To compensate, she showed her love for Kim by laying him out on a towel and massaging him. Although she always presented a brave face to the world, Suu Kyi was suffering. 'Hidden away among the kitchen's stacked pots and pans,' Pasternak Slater wrote, 'was anxiety, cramp and strain.'

Only later, once the flat in Ifield Road was sold, did they acquire a more substantial property of their own. This was 15 Park Town, a narrow five-storey dwelling in what was then a shabby-genteel crescent in leafy north Oxford, near St Hugh's. That this house was divided in two was also a help financially. The upper floors made up a separate maisonette, and were rented for much-needed extra income. Downstairs offered more space than they had had before. There Suu was able to properly institute the family regimen that, among her women friends, became something of a talking point. With her children she was caring and loving, but also strict. Noticing that Alexander had an aptitude for mathematics, she saw to it that he attended his homework diligently. When she gave birthday parties for them – and it was de rigueur that children have birthday parties – they were closely supervised affairs. Any child (whether someone else's or her own) caught cheating at a game was immediately disqualified. Similarly her husband, who liked cigarettes, was banned from smoking indoors – or at all, if she had anything to do with it.

That governessy side of Suu Kyi's character, honed by a passion for the novels of Jane Austen and noted by her Oxford contemporaries, had survived London, New York and Bhutan intact. Taking after her mother, she instinctively organised everything and everyone around her, sometimes to comical effect. A great boon in her life was the immediacy of the affection extended to her by all of Michael's close relatives: his father, his mother Josette, his stepmother Evelyn, his twin brother Anthony and his sister Lucinda. It was her sister-in-law however, that Suu Kyi would see most of. Married to Adrian Phillips, Lucinda lived in a splendidly capacious period house in the historic Wiltshire village of Warminster. With Adrian, and Anthony, she had started a publishing company – Aris & Phillips – that, amongst other orientalia, produced Michael's history of early Bhutan. Regular invitations at Easter, Christmas and other festivals lightened Suu Kyi's domestic load. But she found it hard to receive hospitality without giving something in return. Her efforts to prepare Peking duck in the Warminster kitchen became a family legend. To give the fowl its required wind-dried, glazed finish, the entire household was drafted to apply a hair-dryer in relays, as Suū Kyi busied herself preparing plum sauce and pancakes, chopped cucumber and sliced spring onions.

Away from Warminster, she could be as reproving as ever, characterising what others might consider foibles as moral defects. Yet as Pasternak Slater records, Suu Kyi was endlessly self-sacrificing. When Ma Than É or any other Burmese friend visited London, she would insist they come and stay in Oxford, for however long. She was also mindful of the needs of one or two local 'down-and-outs', including a solitary and irascible elderly German artist, 'Miss Plachte', whom Suu Kyi kept company during her final senility, when she was not sewing, washing or mending her children's clothes, or getting them to school on time, or preparing endless meals from inexpensive ingredients.

* * *

It was a familiar pattern – the female graduate taking the strain of raising a family while the husband ploughed forward with his earnestly important career. In Suu Kyi's case, however, there was little question of allowing her mind to atrophy. Encouraged by Dr Aris, as he became in 1978, she had more time for her other interests once the boys were out of their nappies, through kindergarten and lodged at the Dragon, a celebrated preparatory school, also in north Oxford. Significantly, when in 1980 Michael edited a volume of essays dedicated to his cherished academic mentor – *Tibetan Studies in Honour of Hugh Richardson*, again published by Aris & Phillips – Suu Kyi was credited as 'Co-Editor'.

Shortly afterwards she took on a part-time position at the university's world-class Bodleian Library, helping to catalogue and build up its Burmese collection. This was not lightly undertaken. During her annual trips back to Burma to see her mother, Suu Kyi sounded out U Tin Moe, Professor of Burmese Literature at Rangoon University, for his advice. Then in his early fifties, U Tin Moe willingly obliged. A fervent admirer of Daw Khin Kyi, he recognised in Aung San Suu Kyi a potential counterweight to General Ne Win and his accomplices, whom he loathed. 'You must help our country,' he would tell Suu Kyi, though when she answered, 'Of course, Uncle, but how?' he was less certain of the answer. He helped her locate copies of Burmese classics, ready for shipment back to England, at the same time treating her to a considered overview of Burmese literature and arts. Later he would be imprisoned and tortured by the regime, driving him into eventual exile in Thailand.

U Tin Moe helped Suu Kyi refocus on Burmese affairs. Briefly she flirted with the idea of re-enrolling at St Hugh's, to take a second BA degree in English Literature, but was stopped short in her tracks by the college's rejection of her application. Her 'poor' showing with her first degree counted against her. There was a feeling that to sit two first degrees smacked of dilettanteism. Instead, Suu Kyi opted to concentrate her intellectual energies on Burma and its history, beginning with her short, idealised biography of her father, first published as *Aung San* by the University of Queensland Press in its 'Leaders of Asia' series in 1984, then as *Aung San of Burma* by the Scottish firm Kiscadale Publications in 1991.

Suu Kyi had always wanted to be a writer. With the authorial bit between her teeth, she signed up to contribute three titles to another series of introductory guides published by the Burke Publishing Company in London, and co-published by Mainline Books in the USA: *Let's Visit Burma*, *Let's Visit Bhutan* and *Let's Visit Nepal*. All three appeared in 1985, and were subject to a demanding, even censorious, format devised for a 'juvenile' (that is, secondary-education level) readership. Their attraction lay in a profusion of exotic illustrations, mainly photographic, supported by a 'quiet' text. When writing about Bhutan, whatever interesting experiences she had there were suppressed by Suu Kyi. 'Archery is practised in Bhutan the whole year round, but it is in the cold weather after the harvests that contests take place between villages' pretty much encapsulates the bland tone. Was the 'official' Bhutanese language, Dzongkha, predicated on the word *dzong*, meaning fortress, rendering 'fortress-speak'? No answers to this sort of question can be found in *Let's Visit Bhutan*. Aung San Suu Kyi's sole political comment about contemporary Bhutan is reserved for her concluding sentence, and even this is soft-punched: 'The intelligent caution with which it has started out on the road to modernisation promises well for the future of the country and its people.'

Ditto her treatment of Nepal, and very nearly ditto her treatment of her native Burma. In *Let's Visit Burma*, a touristy title that later caused her some embarrassment, Suu Kyi – still the patriot first and the liberationist second – soft-pedals any condemnation of Ne Win and his regime. 'Burma under army rule became a socialist republic, guided by the Burma Socialist Party Programme,' she writes. 'No other political party is permitted. This and other measures limiting the political liberties of the people are aimed at creating a stable government and a united country.' No word about imprisonments, the use of torture or the perpetual, infernal wars against minority insurgents. *Let's Visit Burma* presents Burma's ethnic minorities as curious, and therefore charming, instances of lingering tribal custom, meet to be protected and preserved, but with little indication of the searing conflicts that, by 1985, had plagued Burma's uplands for thirty years and more.

It was all tame stuff, written with good intentions, but with a limited understanding of the actualities of Burma's troubled condition. In a rare instance of self-deception, Suu Kyi would refer to her three undistinguished *Let's Visit* books as 'potboilers', produced to help pay her sons' school fees. While she welcomed her mother's friends as guests in Oxford, no one who knew her then has any recollection of her consorting with the handful of Burmese dissidents resident in London and other English cities. She preserved herself as her father's daughter, somehow above the petty, factional squabbling of her Burmese contemporaries. Yet the more her father's ghost, or what she took to be her father's ghost, whispered in her ear, the more uncomfortable she felt. A fearsome reckoning lay ahead.

Someone else who knew both Aung San Suu Kyi and Michael Aris well at Oxford during the 1980s was Dr Peter Carey, a Fellow of Trinity College and tutor in Modern History there. Born in Rangoon, he sometimes wrote about Burma, but more usually about Indonesia and the independence struggle in East Timor. He first encountered Dr Aris through the Asian Studies Centre at St Antony's College, in 1979. The two men became close colleagues and good friends, each holding the other's work in high regard. Suu Kyi, however, sometimes left Dr Carey puzzled. Some days she was witty and engaging, others she could be distanced and aloof. As he came to know her better, he realised that a part of her was unresolved and unfulfilled. She was 'destiny's child, but with no very clear idea of where her destiny lay'. Her father, he thought, was increasingly on her mind, and there could be flashes of temper. She did not, for instance, take it kindly when Professor Robert Taylor, a Burma specialist, jokingly compared Aung San to Elvis Presley: both had made 'a good career move by dying young'. She would talk about one day establishing a new library in Rangoon, or setting up a scholarship programme for Burmese students to study overseas; but as yet, for all her interest in Burmese history, there was no hint of Suu Kyi becoming directly involved in her country's politics.

There were, it struck Dr Carey, three distinct aspects to her character. As a mother and family-maker she was conspicuously conscientious. 'Pukka may seem an old-fashioned, colonial word to use, but that's how she often came across. One noticed how, every year, she was the first to get her Christmas cards out.' Then there was her determination to 'remain Burmese', making regular trips home, continuing to wear Burmese dress and meeting Rewata Dhamma and other monks as and when she could. Whether Suu Kyi was especially 'religious', Carey doubted. Aris, he recalled, once told him 'That's not Suu's thing at all.' Rather, Buddhism was there for her as part of her cultural baggage. If, on a family trip to Rangoon, Alexander and Kim underwent novitiate rituals, that was because their mother wanted them to think of themselves as Burmese as much as English. Thirdly, there were her writing and academic ambitions. But in this respect she was 'rather on the fringe of things'.

In her late thirties she had yet to launch herself properly as something other than an academic's loyal, hard-working wife.

In due course Suu Kyi chose to follow Michael's path and apply to SOAS, to write a doctoral thesis on Burmese political history. She wanted to write a full-scale, scholarly biography of her father, to augment the sketch she had already published. To her chagrin, her application was rejected. Her assessors, among them Professor Taylor, doubted that her poor undergraduate degree in PPE had given her sufficient grasp of political theory to become a college teacher – the endgame for most doctoral candidates.

Some while later she found herself at a dinner party where Taylor was present. Such was Suu Kyi's anger with him that she left the table and sat smouldering in a corner, leaving it to Dr Aris to continue the conversation as best he could. But all was not lost. It was suggested that she reapply to SOAS to research a PhD on Burmese literature. This time she was accepted. Asked to sit a written as well as an oral examination, she came through with flying colours. To the surprise of her new assessors, her Burmese language skills were impeccable – not always the case with émigrés who spoke English as well as she. Her research would mean irregular journeys up to London, but that was a small price to pay. Better still, at SOAS she learned of an exchange programme with CSEAS, the Centre for Southeast Asian Studies at Kyoto University in Japan. With a little arm-twisting, she secured an eight-month research scholarship at CSEAS specifically to investigate Burma's independence movement, beginning on 1st October 1985 – a few months after her fortieth birthday. Dr Aris meanwhile had won a two-year fellowship at the Indian Institute of Advanced Studies in Simla. After finishing at Kyoto, Suu Kyi would join him there.

By now Alexander was ready for boarding school. The difficulty was Kim. Just eight years old, he was too young to be left behind. Suu Kyi decided to take him with her. Kyoto University provided self-contained apartments for visiting scholars and their families, so accommodation would not be a problem. Kim could also attend the Shu-gakuin, a city primary school. This, she hoped, would enable him to learn Japanese fast – a task Suu Kyi herself was experiencing some problems with. Having elected to teach herself Japanese before she left, she had turned the bathroom at 15 Park Town into a 'language laboratory', with Japanese *kanji* taped to the walls ready for her to memorise at any time of the day or night. But they were not sticking in her memory. While she was in Kyoto she had to rely on her language teacher, Michiko Terai, to double as an interpreter.

With its hauntingly beautiful Imperial Park and Palace, its plethora of Buddhist and Shinto temples and other old wooden buildings, and its ring of surrounding mountains, Kyoto remains Japan's most attractive city, quite unlike the unappetising urban sprawls of Tokyo, Osaka or Kōbe. The university too, amongst Japan's most prestigious, had its own district. Its feel was not wholly unlike Oxford. On weekdays Suu Kyi took Kim to school, then cycled to the Centre, where she either studied in its library or worked in a room provided for her. At the weekends, taking Kim with her, she went to interview old Japanese soldiers who had fought in Burma or had known her father in Japan. Three or four times they took the *Shinkansen* (bullet train) to Tokyo, so that she could access files relating to her father held by the Foreign Ministry and the National Diet (parliament).

But Japan was not a hugely happy experience. Suu Kyi had always liked the delicacy and healthy balance of Japanese food, and relished the way the Japanese took care of their plants and flowers. But there the joys of Nippon stopped. Just as Aung San had been shocked by the offer of 'comfort women', so Suu Kyi ran up against the inveterate chauvinism of the average Japanese male. Away from the Centre, she was made to feel inferior as a woman, and as a Burmese. Asked what she was doing in Kyoto, she would tell people about her father, and what a great man he was. But why then was she going around on a second-hand bicycle, watching how much she spent and sending her son to an ordinary Japanese school? To her face the Japanese were infinitely polite, but behind her back she wondered whether some were not laughing at her. To make matters worse, Kim had a rough time at the Shu-gakuin. That he could not speak a word of Japanese did not arouse the sympathy of his classmates – only their bullying arrogance. Soon he got bored with sitting in silence during lessons that were a complete fog to him and began to misbehave. The principal wrote to Suu Kyi asking her to discipline her son. Uncharacteristically, this reduced her to tears. Of her two boys, Kim was the wild one, though no less lovable for that. He reminded her perhaps of her beloved lost brother, Aung San Lin. Her tears may not have been for Kim alone.

Years later, after she'd become world-famous, the Centre would turn the room where she worked into a 'museum' to commemorate her stay.

Yet the room continued to be used by other visiting scholars, and little effort was made to assemble anything like the available literature on Aung San Suu Kyi and contemporary Burmese politics. In a sense she was an embarrassment. The Japanese wanted to forget about the war. Their interest in Burma was overwhelmingly commercial. Like others, Japanese businessmen eyed Burma's natural resources. A CSEAS newsletter of November 1991 spoke warmly about Aung San Suu Kyi. 'She was loved by all,' it said. 'People here still talk of her dignity and her sense of presence.' But that was by no means the whole story; and in a way she made difficulties for herself.

Professor Yoneo Ishii, the then director of CSEAS and himself a noted humanitarian, recalled how, as well as Suu Kyi, there were two other Burmese postgraduates in Kyoto during 1985/6: Michael Aung Thwin, a traditionally minded Burman, and Aye Chan, a more radical Rakhine. In Ishii's presence, the three of them would discuss the problems of Burma's multi-ethnicity. 'In Burma there are Shans,' he recalled Suu Kyi saying. 'There are also Karens. And there are Kachins and Chins and Arakanese. They all make up Burma. Burma doesn't belong just to the Burmans.' Ishii remembered 'the flush on Suu Kyi's beautiful face and the resonance of her flowing Queen's English as, a little hotly, she spoke these words'. Michael Aung Thwin could be less circumspect. Suu Kyi had sided with Aye Chan against him. She was, in his opinion, a divisive figure, forever harping on about her dad.

The only close Japanese friend she made in Kyoto was her *sensei* (teacher), Michiko Terai, ten years older than herself. The two women would take walks together, along with Michiko's dog Yuki ('Snowy'). Visits by Ma Than É, and by Michael and Alexander at the end of 1985, must have come as a welcome relief. It must also have been a relief when, the following summer, Suu Kyi left Japan and was able to spend a full three months with her mother in Rangoon, again taking Kim with her, before travelling on to Simla.

At Simla, Dr Aris had persuaded the Institute to give Suu Kyi a one-year visiting fellowship. Simla itself, nestling in the Himalayan foothills in Himachal Pradesh 200 miles north of Delhi, was a place full of history. Built by the British Raj as a recuperative hill station, it had served as India's capital during the hot summer months, when the Gangetic plains became unbearable for white people. It was also where the British had withdrawn its Burmese administration during the Japanese occupation

of the Second World War. Aung San himself had visited there. Reunited
with her husband and able to share reminiscences of Bhutan with him
just by looking at the snow-capped mountains to the north, Suu Kyi
found herself able to think and write in the way she wanted, while at
the same time aligning herself more closely with what she was supposed
to be researching at SOAS.

Soon she had two essays cooking: 'Literature and Nationalism in
Burma', first published in 1987, and the more substantial 'Intellectual
Life in Burma under Colonialism', published in 1990 by the Simla
Institute.* While the first is a somewhat perfunctory review of 'nationalist'
Burmese writers in the first half of the twentieth century, the second is
genuinely wide-ranging. asking important questions about a perceived
inferiority of Burmese compared to Indian literature produced under
British domination. Though it is probable Dr Aris was closely involved,
by way of proffering seasoned editorial and supervisory advice, Suu Kyi
pursues a line of her own. 'Swami Vivekananda, Sir Aurobindo, Tagore,
Gandhi, Radhakrishnan, Nehru – these men were able to use the English
language to make their views known to the world,' she wrote. 'Because
they handle the western intellectual idiom so masterfully, the world
regarded their views as worthy of serious consideration.' But Burma
had not been so blessed. While it had a vigorous vernacular literary
tradition of its own, her country remained inward-looking. Not a cultural
mistake, but, given its present political situation, a strategic error.

Through her own intellectual endeavours, was it too much to ask or
expect that Suu Kyi herself might redress the imbalance? If so, she could
resolve the tensions between her academic-authorial aspirations and her
residual patriotism. She could serve the Burmese people, while at the
same time belatedly allowing her intellect to flower.

One can see it now. The kids grown up, her doctoral thesis completed
and accepted, Aung San Suu Kyi slowly becomes not just an authority,
but *the* authority on all matters Burmese, perhaps at Oxford, perhaps
at SOAS, perhaps at some other university, side-by-side with Dr Aris
the prince of Tibetologists. An honourable and fulfilling mission, even
if it were tinged by the enduring melancholy of an essentially émigré
existence.

It could have been, but was not. Suu Kyi never did complete her
PhD.

---

*Both essays can be found in Aung San Suu Kyi, *Freedom from Fear* (1991)

Dr Aris and Suu Kyi returned to Oxford in the summer of 1987. He resumed his tutorial duties at Wolfson College, and she her trips to London. The family was decently together again, the husband, wife and two boys safely ensconced at 15 Park Town. But then the thunderbolt. In Michael Aris's own oft-quoted words, 'It was a quiet evening in Oxford like many others, the last day of March 1988. Our sons were already in bed and we were reading when the telephone rang. Suu picked up the phone to learn that her mother had suffered a severe stroke. She put the phone down and at once started to pack. I had a premonition that our lives would change for ever.'

Dr Aris's premonition proved chillingly accurate. Bogyoke Aung San's ghost had to be appeased. In retrospect, it was the troubles of Kyoto, not the bliss of Simla, 'Queen of the Hills', that defined the coming months and years.

PART THREE

SIXTEEN MONTHS

XXI

NUMBER ONE AND NUMBER NINE

The Government have certainly proved that power comes out of the barrel of the gun and it is possible that they will now gradually revert to their previous policies of autarkic Socialism, isolation from the rest of the world and severely authoritarian rule at home.

British ambassador T.J. O'Brien, annual report to the Foreign and Commonwealth Office, 1st January 1975

BY March 1988, when Suu Kyi returned to Burma to tend her ailing mother, Ne Win had been in power for twenty-six years. In his mid-seventies, he was well past his sell-by date; yet, in the manner of all despots, he was nothing if not tenacious. He had turned Burma into his personal fiefdom, and wanted to keep it that way. Anyone who mounted a challenge to his authority knew that failure must carry a heavy penalty. Even amongst senior army officers, those who questioned any aspect of his rule were liable to find themselves in prison. Both Daw Khin Kyi and her daughter had nothing but contempt for him, however guarded each might be in what she said. Ne Win had systematically undone everything that Aung San had achieved and stood for, and his character was the antithesis of the great, beloved Bogyoke's.

Not least among the dictator's ill accomplishments was how he had isolated Burma, wrecking its economy in the process. Although it continued to occupy a seat at the UN General Assembly, in 1979 Burma withdrew from the Non-Aligned Movement, and baulked at joining ASEAN (Association of South-East Asian Nations), the regional trading bloc created in 1967 that had already done much to improve living standards in Thailand, Malaysia and other member nations. Fearing assassination, Ne Win had also isolated himself – at least when he was not overseas gambling, womanising or seeking medical treatment. His large residence, at the end of Ady Road on a promontory jutting out into Rangoon's Inya Lake, had become a veritable fortress, guarded day and night by heavily armed soldiers. Inside, as an added security measure, the dictator employed a food taster of Muslim Bengali descent.

When Ne Win did venture out, for a game of golf on Rangoon's links, the course was sealed off. Soldiers invested the surrounding gardens, or hunkered down on the fairways, their guns trained on every building in sight. If he had to cross Rangoon for any reason, there was no telling which of several black-windowed limousines escorted by a convoy of jeeps and other military vehicles was his. If he travelled outside the capital, he did so in a flight of helicopters, his staff having made sure that all stray dogs in the vicinity he was visiting had been rounded up and slaughtered. For Ne Win was fearful of stray dogs – especially those with crooked tails, which his personal soothsayers had told him to avoid – just as he was fearful about pretty much everything else, himself included.

According to one story, whispered by downtrodden Burmese to such foreigners as were allowed inside the country, whenever his soothsayers warned him of an impending assassination attempt, Ne Win would perform an arcane ritual in his bedroom. Trampling either on the entrails of a dog or in a bowl of pig's blood, he would raise his revolver, which at all times he kept ready to hand, and shoot himself in the mirror. By so doing he propitiated, or fooled, whatever *nat* or spirit had it in for him.

But not every story told about Ne Win belonged to the realm of the fantastical. Some were all too real, attested to not only by reliable Burmese sources close to the 'throne', but also by the foreign diplomatic corps, whose job it was to keep an objective eye on Burma's *de jure* ruler.

Many believe that Ne Win became unhinged after his third wife, Daw Khin May Than, died in 1974. In all (and aside from an unquantified number of mistresses), the despot had between six and eight wives – exactly how many remains a matter of conjecture. There is little doubt, though, that Khin May Than – better known by her assumed Anglo-Saxon name, Kitty – was his favourite, for all that (or maybe because) their relationship was stormy.

Kitty began her climb to fame as a nurse at Rangoon's General Hospital, which is where she first met Ne Win, much as Daw Khin Kyi had met Aung San. However, she was quite unlike Suu Kyi's mother. In her spare time she was an amateur cabaret artist, and she relished being Burma's first lady. Her avarice was insatiable. A sensual woman, she saw being married to Ne Win as a means of self-enrichment.

About personal wealth Ne Win was disjunctive. He had several residences overseas, as well as a Swiss bank account. But at home he liked to promote a spartan image in tune with his 'Burmese Way to Socialism' – for all that his Rangoon villa was filled with every comfort. But such was Kitty's brazen flaunting of her position, and of the jewels she persuaded her husband to buy for her, that more than once Ne Win ejected her from Ady Road. Yet within a few days his fury would abate and Kitty would return. That she had a hold over Ne Win, comparable to Supayalat's hold over King Thibaw a century before, few doubted. Once, when the dictator thought a subordinate was flirting with her during an Ady Road cocktail party, he punched the man unconscious. But Kitty alone could control his rages. When Ne Win ranted, she would sit at a piano, sometimes accompanying herself with a song she knew he loved. She may not have been Burma's sweetest nightingale, but for her unmusical husband the dulcet warbles worked.

Kitty was of use to Ne Win socially. She could charm, as increasingly he could not, almost anybody. This was of particular benefit when dealing with the diplomatic fraternity. But it was not just social. Indirectly as well as directly, she pandered to his prolific sexual appetite.

Despite his reluctance to appear in public, in the 1960s Ne Win still liked to entertain carefully vetted guests, and play tennis with them on his private tennis court. Few diplomats could, or dared, refuse an invitation. Martin Morland, who first served at the British embassy in Rangoon from 1957 to 1961, and who returned in 1986 as Ambassador, recounts how, when Kitty was still alive, members of the embassy were asked to attend a weekend party and stay overnight. 'One secretary, a pretty girl, was approached by Kitty after supper and asked if she would mind leaving the bedroom door open, since the General planned to pay her a little visit.' After reflecting on how far she was prepared to go for queen and country, the secretary locked her door and was not invited a second time.

No other woman understood the dictator's needs as well as Daw Khin May Than. But she had her own foibles, including an extreme

squeamishness about the sight of blood. Suffering a kidney disorder –
sometimes severe, but not life-threatening – and well into her fifties, in
1974 she travelled to London to undergo a routine operation.
Unfortunately, the anaesthetist misjudged the level of anaesthetic needed.
Kitty felt the surgeon's knife go in, opened her eyes, rolled over and
had a fatal heart attack when she saw the small pool of her own blood
on the sheet covering the operating bench.

So at least the story goes. The following year occurred the most
widely reported of Ne Win's recorded tantrums. Towards the end of
1975 there were glimmers that the General's ruthless regime was softening.
As it turned out, such glimmers were illusory, but they were sufficient
for Rangoon's foreign community to stage a grand Christmas Eve party
at the Soviet-built Inya Lake Hotel, at the time the capital's only halfway
decent hotel, the Strand having long since fallen into rat-infested disrepair.
Anyone who was anybody was invited, Burmese as well as foreign.
Ticket-paying guests ate and danced on the lakeside lawn to the sound
of a band. But around 11 p.m., as the party was getting into full swing,
soldiers arrived.

Harriet O'Brien, the daughter of the British ambassador in Rangoon
at the time, recorded what happened next: 'A murmur of "The President"
became audible and I naïvely thought that Ne Win himself had come
to join the party, bringing along a few soldiers for good measure. The
band continued playing for a while, but people on the dance floor
rapidly melted away as more men in khaki with guns and heavy boots
swarmed in. Ne Win leapt up on to the bandstand and the music stopped
abruptly.' A 'deafening' silence ensued, before the General, seizing the
drummer's drumsticks, thrust them through the skin of his drum. 'The
noise was picked up on the band's microphones. It made a hideous
sound.'*

Some guests protested that they had not finished their beers. When
pistols were cocked, they too joined the exodus. Ne Win himself
half-ripped off the low-cut dress of a European woman who stood up
to challenge him. As he pushed her back into her seat, his uniformed
bodyguards assaulted her husband.

Afterwards it was put about that the reason for the dictator's uncouth
intrusion had to do with Sanda Win, the favourite of his three daughters.
She was supposed to have taken up with an English dental technician,

* Harriet O'Brien, *Forgotten Land: A Rediscovery of Burma* (1991)

working in Rangoon at the time. Hearing this, and learning of the Inya
Lake Hotel party, Ne Win ordered Sanda to remain at Ady Road that
night. When he discovered that she was not at home, and hearing
raucous Western music across the lake, Ne Win assumed his daughter
was dancing the night away with her filthy *kala* friend, became enraged
and called out his guard.

With Kitty gone, Ne Win took as his next wife a distant cousin and
academic historian at Rangoon University, Daw Ni Ni Myint, a much
less ostentatious woman who sometimes had the temerity to query the
General's policies. Either because of that, or because Ne Win had already
met wife number five (or six), the marriage was dissolved.

June Rose Bellamy, aka Yadana Natmai, was a well-known expatriate
beauty of mixed Burman-Caucasian blood whom Ne Win had admired
for many years. Her mother, Princess Ma Lat, was descended from one
of King Mindon's brothers, and had married an Australian who ran a
race track at Maymyo. June Rose herself had spent much of her life in
Europe and the United States, and her past was punctuated with romantic
attachments to men of various nationalities. Along the way she had
married an Italian doctor and somehow acquired a British passport.

No sooner was Ne Win divorced from Ni Ni Myint than June Rose
Bellamy flew into Rangoon, prompting speculation that what interested
him most about her was her royal lineage. Was he planning to restore the
Burmese monarchy? If so, his hopes were quickly grounded. The rows
began when Ne Win demanded that she surrender her British passport;
his marriage to her became even stormier than his marriage to Kitty.

One night the General became so livid with June Rose that he hurled
an ashtray at her, hitting her on the throat. The following day she left
Burma for good, flying straight to London, where she presented herself
to a Wimpole Street consultant. His written report (a copy of which
somehow found its way to the British embassy in Rangoon) confirmed
that a week after sustaining her injury she was still unable to speak
properly. A later, unconfirmed rumour suggested that Ne Win, fearing
potential bad publicity, made over a substantial sum of money to dissuade
June Rose from writing her memoirs. Or the money may have been her
divorce settlement. By 1978 Ne Win was remarried to Ni Ni Myint,
the longest-serving of his wives, though subsequently he took as another
wife a woman not half, but one-third his age.

*   *   *

Ne Win's credentials as a Grand Guignol tyrant matched those of Idi Amin of Uganda or Nicolae Ceausescu of Romania. By 1988 the Burmese people had long since stopped referring to him by name, instead calling him 'Number One', or sometimes 'The Old Man'. Of the stories told about him, by no means all concerned his private life. Some shed light on otherwise inexplicable state policies.

Ne Win having, in a fit of anti-colonial zeal, banned the teaching of English soon after assuming power in 1962, English was reinstated as a mainstream subject when Sanda Win failed an English examination in a bid to obtain the medical qualification that had eluded her father. Similarly, in the 1970s, Burmese drivers were ordered (at considerable expense to the state) to drive on the right-hand side of the road, not the left-hand side. The reason? It might have been that left-hand driving was another hangover from Burma's colonial past fit to be expunged. Or (more probably) it might have been that Ne Win's soothsayers had warned that danger would 'come from the right'. Again, when the owner of a private language school outbid Ne Win's youngest daughter, Kye Mon, in the purchase of a house near her father's on Ady Road, it became state law that owners of tutorial establishments must not earn more than a general.

Entertaining as such shenanigans were, they did not distract serious Burma-watchers from monitoring a progressive meltdown of Burma's civic institutions. By 1967 – the year Suu Kyi took her Oxford degree – it was clear that military government had come to stay, and that its benefits were non-existent. Routinely, the regime offered as its raison d'être the continuing threat of insurgency, which, it claimed, only a military government could contain. Yet the longer Ne Win remained in power, the more insurgents there were.

It was not just an increase in insurgency levels that was noted. Under Ne Win, Burma became a major producer and exporter of opium. By the mid-1970s virtually the whole of the mountain apron around the Burman plains was infested with communist fighters, ethnic armies and warlord militias. Among those engaged in armed rebellion were, as well as the CPB (Communist Party of Burma) and the KNU (Karen National Union), remnants of the Guomindang, Kachins, Karennis, Nagas, Mons, Rakhines and Rohingyas, as well as such smaller minorities as the Lahu, the Pa-O, the Padaung and the Wa. Those that could, part or wholly funded their armies by entering the narcotics trade.

Shan state, with its Chinese, Thai and Laotian borders, its multi-ethnic population and its rich poppy fields, was particularly troublesome. The regime's response was to pursue a policy of divide and rule. One warring group would be bought off with privileges and promises of amnesty, if it agreed to fight against another – a recipe for every kind of double-dealing and chicanery.

The legendary Khun Sa – as much a symptom as an agent of the problems faced by Burma under Ne Win's rule – was only one of several drugs barons, but his gift for self-publicity ensured worldwide fame. As his real name, Zhang Qifu, intimates, he was of mixed Shan (possibly Padaung) and Chinese descent. Born in 1933, by the early 1960s he was working for Guomindang elements organising opium convoys into Thailand. But from 1967 he openly challenged his Chinese paymasters and rapidly built up a private army. His great rival was Luo Xinghan (Lo Hsing-han), who it is thought had a hand in Khun Sa's arrest by the Tatmadaw in 1969. For five years he languished in Mandalay prison, but was then released after his followers traded two captured Soviet doctors for their leader's liberty. Shortly afterwards, it was Luo Xinghan's turn to experience Burmese prison life.

Now posing as a Shan nationalist opposed to Burman rule, Khun Sa rebuilt his jungle force, known to begin with as the Shan United Army, and later as the Mong Tai ('T'ai Country') Army or MTA. Reasserting his authority over the Golden Triangle (that corner of South-East Asia where Burma, Laos and Thailand converge), he seldom admitted to involvement in the drugs trade. Yet he persistently hinted that opium production would fall if the USA chose to back his army and Shan separatism.

At first Khun Sa operated from the safety of a base across the Thai border. Soon, however, he was placed on the 'most wanted list' of several US agencies – including the CIA and DEA (Drug Enforcement Administration) – and the Thai government was pressured into hunting him down. Given advance warning, Khun Sa (who later boasted he had survived forty-four assassination attempts) slipped back into Shan State, creating a new base – Ho Mong, or 'Tiger Camp' – across the border from Mae Hong Son.

By 1985 Ho Mong had become a town, with running water, shops, hostels for visitors, casinos and a pagoda. Khun Sa's army was 10,000 strong, while Khun Sa himself had a private bodyguard of 500. It was also claimed that he had a harem of a hundred Shan, Thai and Chinese women. Western journalists were sometimes welcomed, though none of them was shown the state-of-the-art laboratories for refining opium into heroin or the dozens of qualified chemists who ran them. Even by South-East Asian standards, for a local warlord Khun Sa, nicknamed 'The Prince of Death', had done well. So well in fact that few doubted he must be protected by the regime itself. For, despite its every effort, the US government singularly failed to persuade Ne Win to go after Khun Sa with a big stick.

'Protection' was not necessarily direct. Although Shan state was an unstable patchwork of wars and warlords, it was a posting that most aspiring Tatmadaw officers wanted. It offered almost endless opportunities for turning a blind eye: to drugs trafficking, and illegal gem and timber smuggling. Backhanders, from Khun Sa's representatives and from other warlords, were plentiful and generous. Some of the proceeds the officers kept for themselves, others they handed to their superiors – a system of reverse patronage that, as well as ensuring promotion and other favours, systematically corrupted the Tatmadaw. One reason why officers were rotated around the country was to give all concerned, commanders included, a chance to share the Shanland spoils.

Year in, year out, the regime fought against insurgents without pacifying any one problem area for very long. The main thrust was against the communists, whose ambitions by definition extended beyond securing any one traditional homeland against the Tatmadaw's predations. The most signal 'victories' came when a communist leader was killed in battle, as happened to Bo Zeya, one of the Thirty Comrades, in 1968; or was assassinated by regime agents, as happened to Thakin Than Tun – Daw Khin Kyi's brother-in-law – in the same year. Another scalp was taken in November 1970. Thakin Soe, leader of the Red Flag communists, surrendered in Arakan, effectively putting an end to the Red Flag rebellion. But elsewhere the CPB, funded by the People's Republic of China (as was, amongst other insurgency groups, the Kachin Independence Army), regularly caused disruption, keeping whole regiments of the Tatmadaw tied up.

The ruthless but corrupt authoritarianism of Ne Win and the Tatmadaw – so much at odds with what Aung San had envisioned – seemed only to ensure the prolongation of Burma's bitter civil wars. Without political change in Rangoon the best hope of seeing off the communist threat (and one that would eventually bear fruit) was political change in China.

Mao Zedong's death in 1976 paved the way for the emergence of Deng Xiaoping and his rapprochement with capitalism. The Chinese government gradually became more interested in promoting trade with Burma in place of bankrolling armed struggle. Before then, however, Mao Zedong's Cultural Revolution had caused further unrest. In both the Pegu mountains and the north-east, Burmese communists had conducted self-purges, executing some of their leaders as well as 'rotten cadres' – an ideological zealotry that made joining the communists unattractive to some would-be adherents. But from 1966 the impact of the Cultural Revolution was felt in Rangoon and Mandalay. Students avidly absorbed Mao's *Little Red Book*.

Sensing that his 'Burmese Way to Socialism' was being undermined, in 1967 Ne Win ordered a crackdown against Rangoon's budding Maoists. The regime orchestrated a series of anti-Chinese riots, during which possibly hundreds of ethnic Chinese citizens were killed, giving the Revolutionary Council a pretext for declaring martial law. As Sino-Burmese relations plummeted, Rangoon University and other schools and colleges were closed down.

Two years later, educational facilities were again closed following student riots in Mandalay. While the Tatmadaw might be fighting a dangerous and glorious struggle against Burma's communists and ethnic trouble-makers, the government was failing to bind even the core Burman population together. The classic Machiavellian formula – to unite a people, wage war against others – seemed not to be working.

This was brought home by the emergence of another group of insurgents. Released from prison, in August 1969 former Prime Minister U Nu set off for India, ostensibly to make a pilgrimage to historic Buddhist sites. But he journeyed on to London, where he announced the formation of the PDP (Parliamentary Democracy Party), which had as its specific mission the overthrow of Ne Win. A few months later, with the help of Aung San's old stalwart Bo Let Ya and other senior dissidents, he began assembling an army known as the PLA (Patriotic Liberation Army) close to Myawaddy on the Thai border.

Partly to appease international opinion, and therefore encourage much-needed international aid, and partly to discourage U Nu, Ne Win began dropping hints that he was contemplating limited democratisation. The problem was that in his heart he could countenance no such thing. In 1971 a commission was set up to draft a new constitution. Together with twenty other senior army officers, Ne Win resigned his military commission, in order for his regime to pose as a civilian government. But few were fooled. The Tatmadaw remained Ne Win's creature, and the main instrument of his power.

The new constitution was put to a 'nationwide' referendum in December 1973. But the referendum was rigged. Those voters who turned out were told to put their 'yes' votes into white boxes and their 'no' votes into black boxes, whilst heavily armed soldiers watched inside the polling booths. To no one's surprise, the constitution was 'approved' by a shade more than 90 per cent of the votes cast.

The constitution came into effect at the beginning of 1974, but changed nothing. It merely confirmed the BSPP (Burma Socialist Programme Party) as the ruling party in a one-party state. Since Ne Win was chairman of the BSPP, his influence was undiminished. There were no provisions for multi-party elections, and the ethnic minorities were especially hard done by. The Chins, Mons and Rakhines were granted their own 'states' within the Union of Burma, but no meaningful autonomy to go with them. The response of the minorities was made clear when each of the ethnic independence armies rejected a proposed amnesty. The Socialist Union, as redefined by Ne Win, was of no interest to them.

As chance would have it, 1974 was marked by particularly severe food shortages, and therefore price hikes. In April and May there was widespread labour unrest, followed by illegal strikes. In June, soldiers moved in, killing up to a hundred protestors. Greater disturbances rocked the capital at the end of the year. Ne Win had never liked U Thant. The erstwhile Secretary-General of the United Nations, who had been so hospitable to Suu Kyi, was the nation's best-loved living individual. When, on 25th November, he died in New York, arrangements were made to bring him home for a burial without any ceremony. This decision enraged Rangoon's students, who seized U Thant's body soon after it landed at Mingaladon. Vast demonstrations ensued, with columns of students marching through the capital's streets. Significantly, for the first time in almost ten years, Buddhist monks participated in the protests. Predictably, the Tatmadaw moved in. Scores of students were slaughtered in a night-time assault on Rangoon University; many more were locked up in prison.

Ne Win had hoped 1974 would be the year in which his reconditioned regime would turn a corner, but his schemes misfired. The British ambassador, T.J. O'Brien, filing his confidential annual diplomatic report on 1st January 1975, described how 'New Year's Eve was spent under martial law and a curfew, while tanks rumbled around the streets of Rangoon and between 6000 and 8000 of Rangoon's citizens languished in jail awaiting summary trial (and few of their relations even knew whether they were alive or dead).'*

'Burma is slowly closing down,' O'Brien commented tersely. Over the decade that followed his diagnosis were grimly borne out. The regime kept open some of Burma's doors, but not many. The country received a limited amount of development and military aid, chiefly from Japan and West Germany (as then was), but foreign relations were kept to a minimum – even though in 1978 Ne Win became the first head of state to pay an official visit to the Cambodian capital, Phnom Penh, after it had fallen to Pol Pot's murderous Khmer Rouge.

Five years later Ne Win attempted to enlist the support of South Korea. His efforts were sabotaged when a bomb exploded at the Martyrs' Mausoleum in Rangoon on 9th October 1983, just as a high-ranking South Korean delegation was paying its respects to the tomb of Aung San. Among a reported twenty-two killed were four South Korean cabinet ministers. The incident was blamed on North Korean agents, and indeed two North Koreans were apprehended and executed. But the bombing did little to enhance Burma's reputation as a country to do business with.

Meanwhile ever larger quantities of opium and heroin were leaking out of Burma's borders. In New York, San Francisco and other American cities, heroin sourced from Burma gained a reputation for being amongst the world's purest, sold under such brand names as US Air and Sweet Lucy's Tit. The US government, not realising that the Tatmadaw was itself involved in the narcotics trade, embarked on an ill-informed drugs-eradication programme with its Burmese counterpart. Funds and reconnaissance aircraft were channelled to Rangoon, yet production continued to grow. The aircraft, however, were useful to the regime's surveillance of Burma's troublesome insurgents.

It was not just narcotics that found their way into the outside world. As the 1980s unfolded, the number of refugees seeking sanctuary from Ne Win's oppressive regime rose steadily, creating major headaches for both Thailand and Bangladesh. Most refugees came from the ethnic minorities – Karens, Karennis and Mons opposite the Thai border, and

*The National Archives; declassified in April 2006

Muslim Rohingyas opposite the Bangladeshi border. As early as 1978 up to 200,000 Rohingyas fled from Arakan, taking with them alarming accounts of how their villages and food stocks had been destroyed by the Tatmadaw. But if this temporarily alerted world attention to the horrors being suffered by some at least of Burma's minorities, UN intervention and the largely involuntary repatriation of most of those Rohingyas involved gave out a false impression that the regime was mending its ways.

Despite every effort by the regime to confound accurate reporting of what went on inside Burma, tales of all manner of gruesome goings-on circulated in South-East Asia. These were picked up by the authoritative Hong Kong-based *Far Eastern Economic Review*, as well as by the *Bangkok Post* and other regional English-language newspapers. Increasing numbers of political dissidents were being given lengthy jail sentences, often on minor charges. Torture was routine in Burma's many prisons. Tatmadaw soldiers used rape as a 'weapon of war' against ethnic-minority women, and were going unpunished. Both the Tatmadaw itself and some of the insurgent armies were recruiting boy soldiers, some as young as twelve or thirteen.

The regime's rapacity was noted in other ways. Although even a brigadier's salary amounted to just a few hundred dollars a year, somehow Burma's officer class contrived to live well beyond its declared means. One clue as to how this could be emerged at the end of 1975. On 8th June that year a major earthquake had struck Pagan and its innumerable ancient pagodas. Stupas cracked open, revealing vast quantities of religious relics and other treasures hidden away for centuries. At once Pagan was cordoned off by the army and its inhabitants relocated. A few months later Burmese antiquities began flooding the antique markets of Bangkok, Singapore, even far-away London and New York.

By 1987 the situation had become dire. In January a group of US-based Burmese exiles set up the CRDP (Committee for the Restoration of Democracy in Burma). Although U Nu's armed rebellion had collapsed in 1978 with the death of Bo Let Ya, allegedly killed by Karen rebels, the government was no closer to resolving the country's multiple-insurgency problems than it had been in 1962. Inflation was spinning out of control. Rice production had dropped to such low levels that food shortages were becoming endemic. There were also shortages of petrol and essential medicines. Burma's meagre foreign reserves were all but exhausted, whilst its external debt had swollen to US $4,000 million.

Even Ne Win recognised that calamity lay just around the corner. But, never one to accept responsibility when things went wrong, his response was to distance himself from the ruinous economic policies of his own creation, and from the monolithic BSPP. Despite the rigorous censorship operated by his regime, on 21st July 1987 an 'open letter' to Ne Win, written by former Brigadier-General Aung Gyi, was published and widely disseminated.

Aung Gyi had helped orchestrate the 'premature' uprising against the Japanese in Mandalay in 1945. Thereafter, as an officer of the 4th Burrifs, his military career had advanced swiftly. A member of the post-coup Revolutionary Council in 1962, he had been widely regarded as Ne Win's eventual successor. Yet within a year he had fallen from grace, being dismissed from the Revolutionary Council in February 1963. Aung Gyi's sin was to criticise BSPP economic policies whilst they were still in their infancy. Strangely, however, he had neither been stripped of his rank nor imprisoned. Now, a quarter of a century later, earning his living as a shopkeeper, he reiterated his charges. Burma was in a mess, and the BSPP was to blame. Addressing his letter to 'my leader', he wrote that Ne Win had been misled by incompetent sycophants. New financial policies, and some political liberalisation, were what a crisis situation called for.

No attempt was made to reprimand Aung Gyi, prompting many to suppose that he was in collusion with his former commander. Coincidentally or otherwise, on 10th August Ne Win himself made a rare radio broadcast, hinting that he too was aware of 'flaws' in the BSPP's economic programming. Yet nothing concrete was done until, on 5th September 1987, the Burmese people awoke to find that, not for the first time, the regime had robbed them blind. The three highest-denomination banknotes – for 75, 35 and 25 *kyat* – were no longer legal tender.

There had been two previous demonetarisations: one soon after Ne Win's 1962 coup, the other two years before, in 1985. But neither was as sweeping as this one. The last time round, compensation had been offered up to the value of 5,000 *kyat*. This time no compensation whatsoever was offered, except to diplomats and some other foreigners. The reason? In 1986 too many rich Burmese had simply sent relays of their poorer relatives and servants to launder 5,000 *kyat* apiece.

The effect was devastating. Many Burmese, distrusting the state-owned banks, kept their savings in cash at home. At a stroke such savings were rendered largely valueless. Indeed, it has been estimated that up to 75 per cent of banknotes in circulation were affected.

As a counter-inflationary measure, demonetarisation made no sense. All it did was further destabilise the country's frail economy. But soon it emerged that economic planning had little or nothing to do with it. When new-denomination banknotes were issued, they were for multiples of nine: 45 *kyat* and 90 *kyat*. The government gave out that demonetarisation was aimed at hobbling Burma's ethnic insurgents and a thriving black market. But since both insurgents and the black market tended to rely on the US dollar and the Thai *baht*, such claims were wholly spurious. Rather, Ne Win and his soothsayers had finally excelled themselves. Nine was either the dictator's lucky number or one that required expiation. On the whim of a superstitious geriatric, Burma was about to be plunged into yet another maelstrom. Aung San Suu Kyi arrived in time to witness the consequences.

XXII

WHITE BRIDGE, RED BRIDGE

'Would you like to know what my uncle was sent to prison for?' asked Yi Yi Win.
'Of course!' I said.
'So would he.'

Karel Van Loon, *The Invisible Ones* (2006)

To be with her ailing mother, Suu Kyi flew from London to Bangkok, then boarded a connecting flight to Rangoon – a journey that took the best part of twenty hours. Arriving on 2nd April 1988, she wasted no time making her way to Rangoon General Hospital, where Daw Khin Kyi had been put in a room of her own. The doctors had fought hard to save her life, but still the prognosis was uncertain. A stroke had badly affected her mobility, but less so her mental faculties.

To help nurse Daw Khin Kyi, and prepare her food, Suu Kyi virtually took up residence at the hospital. In Burma and other East Asian countries this was normal practice. Especially for the very sick, a round-the-clock presence of close relatives is considered conducive to the patient's recovery. And who could be closer to Daw Khin Kyi than her only daughter? Some nights Suu Kyi slept in her mother's room, only returning to the family home at no.54 University Avenue for a change of clothes or to pick up any mail that had come. But Daw Khin Kyi was scarcely the only patient at RGH. Alarmingly, the wards were disproportionately full of young people: students recovering from battered limbs and gunshot wounds.

These patients were the aftermath of a carnage that had gripped

Rangoon in the third week of March. The demonetarisation of September the preceding year had created a climate of grave unrest across Burma, but nowhere more so than in those towns and cities that sported universities and colleges. September was a time when students were expected to pay their tuition fees and other costs for the academic year ahead. Many had arrived back on campus only to find that the money in their pockets was not worth the paper it was printed on. Nor had demonetarisation put the brakes on runaway inflation. The price of rice was rocketing by 20 or 30 per cent each month.

The same day that demonetarisation was announced, several hundred students at the Rangoon Institute of Technology, affiliated to Rangoon University, swarmed out of their campus in Gyogon township, in the north of the capital. In violent mood they threw missiles at government buildings, trashed government vehicles and wrecked several sets of traffic lights along Insein Road. The regime, anticipating trouble, sent in troops and police, who had been prepared in advance. Order was restored, but to prevent further disturbances all of Burma's universities and colleges were shut down. The regime even laid on buses to take back home those students who lived in the sticks.

The closures lasted six weeks. When the universities and colleges reopened at the end of October, trouble at once flared again. This time it was students at Sittwe in Arakan who went on the rampage, followed by serious rioting at the Ye Zin Agricultural College in Pyinmana.

These protests the regime had relatively little difficulty containing. A display of force was enough to send the students packing. More worrying for Ne Win and his cronies was a spate of seemingly random acts of sabotage. Small bombs were detonated in Mandalay and Moulmein. In Rangoon a cinema was targeted, and then, mystifyingly, the embassy of the Republic of Czechoslovakia. Portraits of the General were burned or slashed and some public monuments desecrated. Military Intelligence worked overtime in a vain attempt to finger the perpetrators of what the regime called 'terrorist activities'. What was clear to everyone, however, was that a group or groups opposed to the government and the BSPP were beginning to organise themselves effectively.

In desperation, and under pressure from Japan, Burma's biggest loan-giver at the time, in December 1987 the regime applied for, and was granted, 'Least Developed Country' status from the UN – putting Burma on a par with Ethiopia, Chad and other basket-cases. Henceforward the country was designated one of the ten poorest in the world.

Although this move brought with it some economic benefits – applications for aid and assistance from the World Bank, the IMF (International Monetary Fund) and the ADB (Asian Development Bank) could be fast-tracked – it was perceived by many Burmese as an affront to the nation's dignity, as well as incontestable evidence that Ne Win's regime was manifestly incompetent. Nor did it help that ordinary Burmese only learned about their Least Developed Country status by tuning in to the BBC World and Burma Services and to VOA. To listen to these and other foreign radio stations was an imprisonable offence. Nonetheless people routinely fine-tuned the dials on their often antiquated radio sets to find out what was really going on in Burma. The media – newspapers, radio stations and a laughably rudimentary television channel – were all state-controlled, their content propaganda at its crudest. State newscasters delivered the gospel according to St Ne Win in flat, deadpan voices, as though they were either terrified of injecting a wrong note or did not believe a word they were reading. Characteristically, the end of a sentence spoken in the Burman language is marked by a cadence, a tailing away of volume and emphasis. But in the hands of Burma's regime-approved broadcasters, even this feature became another form of deadening foreclosure.

The military and police crackdown continued well into the New Year. Unusual numbers of uniformed men patrolled Burma's streets, particularly those near colleges and universities. But just as the regime began thinking that it had everything under tight control, all hell broke loose. And it started in a tea-shop.

In Burma, the tea-shop enjoys an almost hallowed status, equivalent to the London pub or Manhattan bar. It is where people can meet, talk, relax, listen to music or (more recently) watch a video – most Burmese being too poor to own a video-player. Tea is served, with small cakes and other snacks, but rarely anything more than that. The average tea-shop does not serve alcohol. It is also an unpretentious place: concrete walls, bare floors, a tattered calendar, perhaps a fan or two on the ceiling. Customers sit at small tables, usually on stools, sometimes for hours on end and at no great cost. A visit will ordinarily set you back less than twenty cents.

Under the rule of Ne Win's BSPP, tea-shops, with their slender profit margins, were one of the few businesses permitted to remain in the private sector. Nor were tea-shops discouraged, since they were as good as anywhere for MI types and other government spies to pick up information. By the same token, ordinary Burmese became wary. If a stranger sat at the next table, conversation might stop altogether. And some tea-shops enjoyed better reputations than others.

On 12th March 1988 three students from the RIT (Rangoon Institute of Technology) in Gyogon decided to take tea in an establishment close to the campus on Insein Road. Two of them shared the same name, Win Myint, while the third was called Kyaw San Win. They brought with them some cassette tapes of a popular singer, Sai Hti Hseng, whose songs were the closest thing to Bob Dylan that any Burmese musician dared record. By a curious coincidence, the name of the tea-shop was Sanda Win, though it had nothing to do with Ne Win's daughter. The students politely asked the owner to put one of their Sai Hti Hseng tapes on his tape-deck. At once a group of older men sitting noisily at a nearby table objected. They did not want to listen to Sai Hti Hseng. His songs were crap, they shouted. Why not play something decent: Kaizar, for instance. Kaizar sang proper Burman love songs, none of this newfangled stuff.

The older men were clearly intoxicated, and the students disregarded them. But when they repeated their request to the owner, one of the drunks stood up and threw his chair towards them. Within seconds a brawl developed. Other students and non-students joined in, and mayhem ensued. In due course a police squad arrived and the drunkards, as well as some students, were carted off to the police station. Next day, however, the drunkards were released without charge, while the students were kept in detention.

It emerged that the man who had started the fight by throwing his chair was the son of the chairman of the local People's Council. Enraged, thirty-odd RIT students went to the People's Council office to lodge a complaint. When the chairman refused to come out, they began hurling stones at the office, smashing its windows. Soon other men appeared, friends of the drunkards, and another fight erupted. One of the two Win Myints was wounded with a knife.

The students, realising they were outnumbered, returned to the Institute to round up more support. Now 200–300 poured onto the Insein Road, heading for the Sanda Win tea-shop. There, however, they were confronted by 500 *Lon Htein*, armed riot police (literally 'security control'). Undeterred, the students threw more stones. The *Lon Htein* responded first with water cannon, then with a baton charge, wielding their *lathi* (wooden sticks) with brutal effect.

The students, seeing that the dreaded *Lon Htein* meant business, started to disperse. But the *Lon Htein* were not finished yet. Gunshots rang out. The riot police were firing at will on the unarmed, fleeing crowd. Several students were hit, one of them, Maung Phone Maw, fatally, though he only died back in his hostel a few hours later.

Maung Phone Maw was twenty-three years old, and popular with most of his fellow students. Ironically, he belonged to the Lanzin Youth, the youth wing of the BSPP. It was perhaps for this reason that he refused to be taken to hospital. A dozen or so other students who had received bullet wounds had no such qualms and ended up at Rangoon General Hospital. There, despite their condition, they were chained to their beds. The surgeons were ordered not to operate, and two more students died. Others were removed by the police and not heard of again.

The Sanda Win tea-shop incident was not, overtly, a political matter. Scraps between students and non-students in Gyogon were not uncommon. It was town-versus-gown stuff. But the heavy-handed response of the *Lon Htein* turned it into a tipping point. When, the following morning, the state-run media failed to report what had happened, unrest spread among Rangoon's student population. On the afternoon of 15th March there were further clashes. The *Lon Htein* stormed the Institute of Technology. Again many students were severely beaten attempting to run away. Emptying the entire campus, the paramilitaries removed several hundred in a convoy of army trucks.

Now the media did take notice, putting all the blame for the Gyogon disturbances squarely on the students themselves. On Wednesday 16th March the *Working People's Daily* reported that Maung Phone Maw had not been shot by the *Lon Htein*, but had been stabbed by an unidentified 'local'. This fuelled further unrest. Several thousand student protestors gathered at Rangoon University's main campus at Inya Lake. 'Down with Ne Win!' they chanted, and 'We want democracy!' Mid-afternoon the swarming students decided to march to the Institute of Technology, six or so miles away, as an expression of solidarity with their oppressed comrades. At their head one student swung a large banner emblazoned with a peacock against a red background – the old symbol of Burmese independence. Behind him others cheerfully sang marching songs. But they did not get very far. Ne Win's close associate and lethal henchman, Lieutenant-General Sein Lwin, was waiting for them.

Advancing north-westwards along the bank of Inya Lake, the students came to 'White Bridge', a narrow defile flanked by buildings on its left and the lake on its right. Ahead of them, barring their way, they saw around fifty armed soldiers, in combat formation. A coil of barbed wire had also been strewn across their path. Beyond were more troops, as well as *Lon Htein* and police. And beyond those were trucks and armoured vehicles.

The marchers halted. Three student leaders stepped forward and politely requested of the soldiers that the march be allowed to proceed. Among them was Min Ko Naing ('Conqueror of Kings'), a third year geology student whose real name was Paw U Tun, but whose assumed name helped establish him as the best known student leader of his generation. The conversation lasted for several minutes, with no sign that the soldiers were about to relent. Then, from behind, came anguished shouts and screams of pain. A detachment of *Lon Htein* had caught up with the demonstration's rear. The students had been trapped in a lethal vice. The ensuing massacre lasted twenty to thirty minutes. While some students – mainly those at the front, since the soldiers forbore to open fire – managed to escape by swimming across the lake or climbing into surrounding buildings, many did not. The *Lon Htein* mounted charge after charge, ferociously clubbing all those they could catch.

Exactly how many were killed remains disputed, for the dead were quickly piled into lorries and driven away. The usual figure given is at least a hundred, and possibly twice that number. Others sustained ghastly injuries. Nor were girl students exempt from the *Lon Htein's* brutal methods. Some were dragged to the water and drowned by hand. Others, it was reported, were gang-raped on their way to prison. It was also claimed that *Lon Htein* thugs pillaged the dead and dying students of watches and other valuables.

The morning afterwards the whole area was hosed down by the authorities, to remove the blood-stains and other telltale evidence. Notwithstanding, White Bridge now became known as the Red Bridge. What went through the minds of the *Lon Htein* as they carried out Sein Lwin's orders is scarcely to be contemplated. Yet one man has tried. An English Christian political activist, James Mawdsley, won fame and honour for himself ten years after the White Bridge / Red Bridge incident by deliberately provoking the Burmese government into arresting him. For fifteen months he endured incarceration Burmese-style for distributing anti-regime pamphlets. When he was finally released and deported, he wrote up his experiences. Among several memorable passages to be found in *The Heart Must Break* (2001) is one that looks back to that hot Rangoon afternoon in March 1988. Mawdsley writes:

I nearly cry every time I think about it. What horrifies me every time is trying to imagine a man who is fit, strong, well-armed and surrounded by colleagues, who is backed up as well by one of the world's largest armies, charging after hapless young girls and clubbing them to death. What is he thinking as he smashes his baton into her face? When she screams in the water and goes under does he reach down to pull her up by the hair so he can break her skull? She will not die with one or two blows. He must hit her on the arms and back and chest before getting a few good shots in at her face. They are floundering in the water and he cannot get a good clear swing. But blows to the face will not kill her either. They just mash her into a pulp. At last he gets one on the back of her skull and suddenly she is still and her face sinks below the water. He has got one. And now look! There is another one. She is trying to escape but she cannot swim so she is stuck. Her wet clothes are sticking to her body so she cannot move her arms freely to defend herself, and crack! crack! crack! the blows start falling and her cries of terror change to cries of pain.

The Inya Lake massacre was not the end of the matter. Ne Win's security services sensed that brute force alone no longer sufficed to hold a desperate people at bay. But the concessions that the regime offered were risibly disproportionate to the events that prompted them. Hospital doctors were permitted to treat the wounds of those who had survived the White Bridge massacre, and first thing on 17th March a 'judicial' commission was announced to investigate the circumstances of Maung Phone Maw's death. But as regards White Bridge itself, the government took the line that there had been very few deaths and that the *Lon Htein* had been provoked.

Up to 2,000 students gathered in front of Rangoon University's Convention Hall and demanded the creation of a new, independent Students' Union. All morning Min Ko Naing and other student leaders stood up and spoke out against the regime, condemning its actions and demanding a return to parliamentary government. But an equal number of *Lon Htein* and other security types surrounded the campus. In the early afternoon the paramilitaries flooded through the university gates and began tear-gassing the crowd of youngsters. Although some managed to flee to their dormitories, hundreds were seized and crammed into the usual convoy of waiting trucks. But the trucks did not drive off immediately. In one of them forty-two students, suffering the after-effects of the gas and extreme midday heat, suffocated to death.

The following day, 18th March, pandemonium erupted across the city, as gangs of students staged lightning attacks against government-owned targets: offices, vehicles, traffic lights, even the state-run People's Department Store on the Shwedagon Road. But the main event was a mass gathering at the Sule pagoda in the centre of the city, attracting a crowd of more than 18,000, including hundreds of non-students who joined the demonstrations to air their own grievances against Ne Win.

Yet again the *Lon Htein* moved in, as did army units brought in from outlying barracks. Troops took up defensive positions in front of important government buildings, and foreign embassies were also ringed – not so much for their protection as to prevent anyone seeking sanctuary inside. For hours the uniformed authorities fought running battles with protestors. There were not so many gunshots as before, but those caught were badly beaten, then taken away to Insein jail, and, since Insein became full to bursting, to Ye Kyi Aing, a detention centre run by MI near Mingaladon airport.

In these latest disturbances dozens more were killed. But by nightfall Rangoon's streets had been cleared. Eerily, the only sound to be heard came from loudspeakers mounted on Tatmadaw trucks and jeeps, advising citizens to remain indoors, otherwise they would be shot on sight. For the moment, Brigadier Sein Lwin appeared to have achieved all that Ne Win had asked of him, and more. The students and their sympathisers had been cowed into submission. As dawn broke on 19th March, the city was quiet. But in the process Sein Lwin had acquired a new name for himself. Henceforward he was known as the Butcher of Rangoon, and his actions could neither be forgiven nor forgotten.

It may have been pure happenstance, with her mother being so ill, but in April 1988 Rangoon General Hospital was the place to be for anyone with a serious interest in Burma; it was where the nation's pulse beat the hardest – the more so since the government had again shut down the country's higher-education establishments. In a sense, RGH was the university that remained open. In its wards, corridors and courtyards, canteens and recreation areas, visitors and patients talked earnestly about the recent atrocities – once they were confident no intelligence-type was within earshot.

Suu Kyi listened intently to everything that was told her, but kept her counsel to herself. Students and medics, astonished that Aung San's daughter was in their midst, spoke to her about what had happened, not just in March, but for as far back as they could remember. She nodded appreciatively and asked some searching questions, but did not yet commit herself to any specific course of action. In England the woes of her homeland had been just hearsay, while her frequent but brief return visits to see relatives and friends had not thoroughly exposed her to the misery that constituted the lives of most ordinary Burmese. But here, at RGH, the evidence lay all around.

Soon, students who had been arrested in March, but (if they were lucky) were now being released from detention, began dropping by to visit their wounded friends, bringing with them gruesome accounts of how, at Insein and Ye Kyi Aing, they had been subjected to cruel beatings and sometimes tortured – usually by electric-shock treatment. And they had the scars to prove it. Typically, a group of arrested students would be held in a single room. Then, one by one, they were led away for interrogation. MI would pick the weakest-looking first. As he screamed with pain, the others had to listen. Then it was the next student's turn.

For Suu Kyi, long conditioned to the gentility of Oxford and other academic centres, as well as to Britain's sometimes rambunctious but characteristically democratic politics, such accounts were more than shocking. They were the ugliest assault she had yet experienced on her core sensibility, her addiction to the tenets of basic, universal decency and humanity. Those she encountered at the hospital made a deep impression on her. The plans and ideas she had previously entertained for assisting her country – creating a library, fostering an overseas student-exchange scheme – now seemed woefully inadequate. What was needed was a fundamental, root-and-branch reform of Burma's political structures. But for Suu Kyi, as for many others, the abiding conundrum was: how could such a thing be brought about without recourse to further violence and bloodshed?

She bided her time. Nothing was clear yet, least of all what her own role might be. But Suu Kyi made an immediate impact upon those who approached her, even though, at this early stage, she said little. What impressed students, visitors, nurses and doctors alike was her mental composure: her grace and her attentiveness, as well as her willingness to be of use in small, practical ways. To the amusement of some, she refused to use the hospital elevators, as she 'didn't want to waste the nation's precious resources'. But overwhelmingly those who met Suu Kyi for the first time in the middle months of 1988 remarked how like her father she was – in manner as well as looks. To a degree this may have been wish-fulfilment in an hour of need, but few doubted that she was an individual of intrinsic strength.

XXIII

8.8.88

---

*When I first decided to take part in the movement for democracy, it was
out of a sense of duty rather than anything else. On the other hand, my
sense of duty was very closely linked to my love for my father. I could
not separate it from the love for my country, and therefore, from the
sense of responsibility toward my people.*

Aung San Suu Kyi, in *The Voice of Hope* (1997)

FOR two months the political temperature in Rangoon flattened out.
But when schools and colleges were permitted to reopen at the end of
May 1988, the temperature rose again. Soon there would be turmoil
everywhere.

Sensing which way the wind was blowing, on 8th June retired
Brigadier-General Aung Gyi issued another open letter addressed to Ne
Win. In it, he went much further in his criticisms of the regime than in
his first letter of 1987. Whereas previously he had targeted the BSPP's
mismanagement of the economy, now he addressed human-rights abuses
perpetrated by the regime. This echoed a wide-ranging report published
by Amnesty International in May, taking the regime to task for its
callous maltreatment of civilians in insurgency areas. Although Aung
Gyi still did not challenge Ne Win himself, he lambasted Sein Lwin for
persuading army Chief-of-Staff General Saw Maung to bring an
unnecessary number of troops into the capital from their barracks at
Prome. If resentment against the regime had reached a new intensity,
then senior members of that regime had only themselves to blame.

Aung Gyi also put a precise figure on the number killed in the White

Bridge/Red Bridge incident: 282. It is unlikely that this time around he had Ne Win's tacit approval for going public with his concerns. His letter was too openly hostile, and was circulated largely by students.

Dissident students had learned important lessons from the March upheavals. Spontaneous reactions to the regime's heavy-handedness led nowhere except greater repression. The will to resist was widespread, just as it had been fifty years before against the British. But it needed better organisation and coordination: more secret planning sessions, more consciousness-raising, more pamphlets and posters and painted slogans, and more properly thought-out tactics.

All the same, violence re-erupted, and for ten days, beginning on 14th June, the streets of Rangoon were again given over to demonstrations, disorder and reprisals by the *Lon Htein*. Most protests were organised by agitators at Rangoon University, but worryingly for the regime, textile workers as well as monks joined in. On 20th June Rangoon University's four campuses were again closed. This did not prevent an ugly confrontation between students and the *Lon Htein* at the Institute of Medicine, adjoining Rangoon General Hospital, on 21st June. Armed with bricks and *jinglees* – a sort of dart made from the spokes of bicycle wheels, sometimes tipped with poison – protesting students fought back against the authorities. Soldiers of the Tatmadaw were also present and opened fire. Ten *Lon Htein*, it was claimed, were killed, but many more students died.

Later the same day the bodies of the dead protestors were driven around Rangoon by students for everyone to see. The intention was to stimulate a general strike. Not for the first time the authorities moved swiftly to pre-empt collective action. On 22nd June a strict curfew was imposed on the capital, lasting from six in the evening until six in the morning, and there was a ban on all public gatherings. Anyone disobeying these orders was to be shot. That the regime meant what it said became apparent when an elderly noodle-seller and his daughter were gunned down as they wheeled their noodle-trolley back home after dark.

There were incidents elsewhere, notably at Moulmein, Mandalay, Prome and Paungdale, the small township a few miles east of the Irrawaddy midway between Rangoon and Mandalay, which had the unenviable distinction of being Ne Win's birthplace. On 23rd June an anti-government demonstration in Pegu (Bago) was met with main force. Some seventy demonstrators, few of them students, were wantonly slaughtered as they headed for the steel bridge that carries the main Rangoon–Mandalay highway across the Pegu river.

The regime tried other tactics, too. In a bid to deflect attention from its own misconduct, it first accused the communists of fomenting sedition, then started a scare campaign, expressed in a flood of 'anonymous' leaflets, that pinned Burma's troubles on its minority Muslim population. Most gave these leaflets no credence, but in Taungyyi – the principal city of Shan state – anti-Muslim riots resulted in yet more deaths.

By July an atmosphere of unease, unprecedented in its scale, hung over the whole country. The economy continued to sicken. The state-run media, always ready to accuse others, castigated traders for profiteering. But a more credible explanation of escalating prices was shortages of foodstuffs and consumables, reinforced by rumours that yet another demonetarisation was in the offing. Panic buying may have played into traders' hands, but it was not the traders who had created the panic.

The unease spread to within the BSPP and Ne Win's council of ministers. If Burma was to be put back on anything like an even keel, something drastic had to be done. Yet only those closest to the throne had any inkling of Ne Win's next shock manoeuvre.

Towards the end of June it had become clear to the doctors at Rangoon General Hospital that Daw Khin Kyi would not recover; indeed, that she was dying. Under these circumstances, on 8th July Suu Kyi decided that her mother should be brought home to University Avenue, so that she might spend her last days in peace and dignity. For several weeks, from the middle of the same month, Khin Kyi would also benefit from the company of her son-in-law and two grandchildren. As Suu Kyi was so tied up looking after her, it made sense for Dr Aris to bring the teenage boys to Burma during their respective summer vacations. Whatever reservations Khin Kyi had had about her daughter's marriage to an English academic had long since evaporated, and she was moved by love for Alexander and Kim.

There was certainly no shortage of space for Khin Kyi's extended family at no. 54. The compound comprised several smaller buildings – servants' quarters, a laundry hut, storage and a garage – in addition to the main house. These were mostly set back from the road, to the right and left of a driveway that pointed towards Inya Lake. At its top end, however, the driveway forked. In one direction was Daw Khin Kyi's residence; in the other a smaller dwelling, where her sister Daw Khin Gyi had come to live after her husband Than Tun's death.

Ever a woman of extreme practicality, Suu Kyi readied one of the

downstairs rooms in the larger residence to receive Khin Kyi. It wanted
nothing that her room in the hospital had had. There was the added
advantage that it overlooked part of the garden that Daw Khin Kyi had
nurtured for so many years. Similarly, no. 54's small staff – a cook and
a couple of maids – were rostered to provide round-the-clock care, with
Suu Kyi herself assuming the responsibilities of chief nurse.

Dr Aris would later recall that during the summer of 1988 the
compound was 'an island of peace and order under Suu's firm, loving
control. The study downstairs had been transformed into a hospital
ward and the old lady's spirits rallied when she knew her grandsons
had arrived.' But the family was not left alone. Doctors were not the
only visitors from Rangoon General Hospital. Many of those whom
Suu Kyi had got to know there came to see her, and there was a steady
stream of Daw Khin Kyi's contemporaries: men and women who had
known Bogyoke Aung San as well, and who came to pay their respects.
Alexander Aris, fifteen at the time, would some years afterwards
remember how the hallway of Daw Khin Kyi's house was taken over
'by an odd assortment of people, from students to octogenarians . . . a
bunch of odds and sods'. Although he himself could not speak Burmese,
he had the impression that all they wanted was 'to sit around and chat,
basically, nothing constructive'.* He also remembered how, during curfew,
which was strictly maintained, gunfire could sometimes be heard in the
streets outside.

The young Alexander, however, misconstrued the throng of visitors
to his grandmother's and mother's Rangoon home. His scholarly father,
who had a working knowledge of the Burman language, had a better
idea of what was going on. 'Suu's house,' he wrote, 'quickly became
the main centre of political activity in the country and the scene of
continuous comings and goings as the curfew allowed. Every conceivable
type of activist from all walks of life and all generations poured in. Suu
talked to them all about human rights, an expression which had little
currency in Burma till then.'† Visitors included lawyers, writers, artists
and others drawn from the ranks of Rangoon's embattled intelligentsia.
But significantly Suu Kyi also began to be courted by a handful of
retired senior army officers – men who had served the nation during

* *Warminster Journal*, 6th December 1991.
† Michael Aris, in his Introduction to Aung San Suu Kyi, *Freedom from Fear* (1991)

the period of U Nu's democracy, but who one by one had fallen foul of Ne Win.

The best-known was U Tin Oo (U Tin U), a former general. Born in 1927, he joined the Burmese Independence Army in 1943, aged just sixteen, and quickly proved his aptitude for soldiering. During the 1950s he was put in command of operations against the Guomindang in the Shan states, and was later rewarded with a seat on Ne Win's Revolutionary Council. In 1974 he rose to the dizzying heights of Minister of Defence and Chief of Defence Services. Like Aung Gyi, he was considered by some a possible successor to Ne Win himself. But his undoing was his popularity. Not unlike Zhou Enlai in Mao Zedong's China, Major-General Tin Oo was viewed by the people with some warmth. He represented such little humanity as there was within the Tatmadaw and the BSPP. By 1976 Ne Win had decided it was time for him to go. Tin Oo was dismissed from his various posts, then put in prison for four years on a manufactured charge of sedition.

U Kyi Maung was another high-flyer whose career had been derailed by the Old Man. Older than U Tin Oo, he had participated in anti-British activities in the late 1930s while studying at Rangoon University. When the war came, he eagerly joined the BIA, and was amongst a small band selected to receive advanced training at the Rikugun Shikan Gakko, Japan's elite military college. By 1962 Kyi Maung was a regional commander, with a special responsibility for maintaining security in Arakan, and a reasonable expectation of rising even further. But he was critical of Ne Win's *coup d'état*, and let it be known that he thought the army should keep out of politics. Ne Win forced him to retire the following year, then stuck him in prison.

U Aung Shwe had been a brigadier in the 1950s, but in 1962 was retired from the army and sent safely overseas on diplomatic duties. U Lwin had also attended the Rikugun Shikan Gakko in Tokyo, and had served briefly as a deputy prime minister under Ne Win before 'resigning' in 1980.

All four soldiers held the memory of Aung San in the highest esteem, and all four were dismayed by the way Burma was being run into the ground by Ne Win and those who remained loyal to him. Equally, each was impressed by the Bogyoke's daughter, and urged her to become involved in her country's affairs. If Aung San's standard was to be resurrected, she was the fittest (perhaps only) person to do so – given that her surviving brother, Aung San Oo, seemed determined to have as little as possible to do with Burma's plight.

Critics of Aung San Suu Kyi have sometimes insinuated that if her return to Burma during a time of national upheaval was adventitious, then her assumption of a leadership role was opportunist. In reality, almost from the moment she set foot in Burma in April 1988, Suu Kyi came under mounting – even unrelenting – pressure to take a public position. She responded to such pressure slowly and cautiously. That she wanted, and had always wanted, to do something for her fellow countrymen was not in question; but as the magnitude of the role she was being urged to adopt sank in, only a measured response seemed appropriate.

Both the number of visitors to 54 University Avenue and the urgency of the conversations held there accelerated dramatically from 23rd July onwards. On that day General Ne Win delivered his bombshell, announcing his own 'retirement', no less. According to Dr Aris, he and Suu Kyi first heard the news via an evening state radio broadcast, which they listened to in each other's (and nobody else's) company. Suu Kyi 'like the whole country was electrified'.

An 'extraordinary' meeting of the BSPP, convened by Ne Win, had begun the morning of the same day at the Saya San Hall – close to the old British race-track in Kyaikkasan township, one of Rangoon's many suburbs. Flanked by Colonel Khin Nyunt, his head of Military Intelligence (more correctly, Director of the Directorate of Defence Services Intelligence), the Old Man gave a long, prepared speech that left most listeners dumbfounded. Public discontent with government policies, he said, could no longer be ignored. For the first time in his life he expressed a willingness to shoulder at least a smidgeon of the blame. 'As I consider that I am not totally free from responsibility, even if not directly, for the sad events in March and June,' he went on, 'and because I am advancing in age, I would like to request party members to allow me to relinquish the duty of party chairman and as party member.'

He further announced that he was standing down as Commander-in-Chief of Burma's armed forces, and that U San Yu – Burma's titular, stuffed-shirt President since 1981 – would also be vacating his office. A tranche of other ministers were also pressured into resigning.

News of Ne Win's retirement was greeted with widespread disbelief. Was the dictator really on his way out? And was his resignation really voluntary? It was altogether too good to be true.

Soon enough the country's mood shifted from muted euphoria to outrage. The BSPP conference continued for three days, at the end of which Ne Win was 'persuaded' not to surrender his party membership. Although the reforms he had advocated in his 'valedictory address' included economic liberalisation – the private sector, after twenty-six years' strangulation, was to be revitalised – it was not until 29th July that Ne Win's effective successor was announced: Brigadier-General Sein Lwin, the Butcher of Rangoon.

Sein Lwin was detested even more than Ne Win, if that were possible. His role in March's Red Bridge massacre was just the latest in a long list of bloody deeds. As a young commander he had directed the Tatmadaw in its assault on Rangoon University in 1962. At the end of the same decade he had devised ruthless methods aimed at rooting out insurgency in Shan state, liquidating the families of those suspected of being involved in anti-regime activities. Between 1970 and 1972 he used the same techniques to crush political opposition in Mandalay Division, making a point of targeting concerned young monks and their relatives.

There was nothing remotely attractive about the man. He was simply a thug. Born near Moulmein, his education had never advanced beyond primary school. He was a typical army type – or typical of what the army had become. But he had served under Ne Win in the 4th Burma Rifles and so, as long as he implemented his master's policies, his promotion had been assured. By 1981 he was back in Rangoon as a member of the Revolutionary Council, and in 1983 was elevated to joint-secretary of the BSPP. His other brief was the *Lon Htein*, over whom he exercised full operational control.

While General Saw Maung – another Ne Win loyalist – became Commander-in-Chief of the Tatmadaw, Sein Lwin was nominated President. Khin Nyunt, promoted to Brigadier-General, continued to head Military Intelligence. That the people had been comprehensively duped became immediately apparent when Aung Gyi, U Kyi Maung and eight other retired officers of the rank of colonel and above, who had voiced criticisms of the regime, were rounded up and imprisoned. It was obvious that Burma had been placed in the hands of three of Ne Win's deadliest henchmen and that Ne Win himself had probably not retired at all. Rather, the suspicion set in that, like China's Deng Xiaoping in 1987, he had surrendered the trappings, but not the actuality, of power. Khin Nyunt, in league with the dictator's daughter Sanda Win, was observed making daily visits to the 'palace' on Ady Road. And although Ne Win had suggested a referendum on whether the 'one-party' state should continue, the Tatmadaw remained out on the streets.

To anyone listening attentively to Ne Win's speech, or reading it in the *Working People's Daily*, none of this should have come as a surprise. In his closing remarks, the Old Man had divested himself of some chilling sentiments. 'In continuing to maintain control,' he warned, 'I want the entire nation, the people, to know that if in the future there are mob disturbances, if the army shoots, it hits. There will be no firing in the air to scare.' Foreign media organisations, paraphrasing Ne Win's address, put it even more bluntly: 'When the army shoots, it shoots to kill.'

Suu Kyi was as aghast as anyone at this latest turn of events. Those who knew her best concur that it was this episode more than any other that persuaded her to commit herself unambiguously to the cause of Burmese freedom, and to remain in Burma at least until that objective was secured.

A bare fortnight before Ne Win rose to his feet inside the Saya San Hall, Suu Kyi published a book review in the *Times Literary Supplement*. The book in question was *The State in Burma*, written by her old adversary Professor Robert Taylor – the man who had been instrumental in blocking her application to study for a PhD in politics at SOAS – and widely regarded as a regime-friendly account of Burmese politics in the modern period. Suu Kyi refrained from going for Taylor's jugular. Nor did she use the review as an opportunity to expatiate on the barbarities of Burma's government. Instead, in the best academic tradition, she damned Taylor with faint praise. His book, she wrote, was 'competent' and 'valuable', and contained 'much useful statistical data produced since 1962'. But, in her view, Taylor did not understand the relationship between Burmese culture and Burmese politics, while there was 'a touch of unreality' about his image of Burma's last monarchs (and by implication Ne Win's regime itself) striving for the 'legitimisation of the state'. Her sharpest criticisms were reserved for Taylor's transliteration of Burmese words. Here he committed too many errors, and these were 'scattered throughout'.*

Though cool understatement was, or became, a main item in her intellectual and polemical armoury, Suu Kyi would never again be so coy in either print or utterance. Yet she delayed entering the public

---

*Aung San Suu Kyi, 'A Difficult Relationship', *TLS*, 8–17th July 1988

arena for close on another month. By then thousands more of her fellow countrymen had been slaughtered by the military. Continuing to nurse her mother while receiving cohorts of visitors at 54 University Avenue, she (and with her Dr Aris) calculated that 'watch and wait' was still the more prudent course.

Others were less patient. Min Ko Naing, who had narrowly escaped death at the White Bridge, Moe Thee Zun and other student leaders sensed that even if Ne Win's resignation was a feint, a break-point against the junta had been reached. No sooner did Sein Lwin assume office than leaflets urging a general strike appeared first in Rangoon, then in other towns and cities. A particular, numerologically and astrologically auspicious date was set: 8th August, or 8.8.88. Even though the string of eights belonged to the Western (not Burmese Buddhist) calendar, it had a grand ring about it. It also marked the fiftieth anniversary of the beginning of the '1300' movement, back in 1938. Just as significantly, 8 preceded Ne Win's talismanic number 9.

An important part in the lead-up to what became a national uprising was played by a BBC World Service reporter. Posing as a tourist, Christopher Gunness had arrived in Rangoon on 22nd July to cover the extraordinary session of the BSPP. Given only the maximum one-week tourist visa, he left on the 29th. But he took with him incriminating taped interviews with some of those who had suffered at the hands of the regime, as well as evidence that morale in parts of the Tatmadaw was at an all-time low. Gunness's radio broadcasts, including a pitiable account by a young woman describing how she had been raped by the *Lon Htein*, were splashed into Burma and added to the swell of popular resentment. More significantly yet, Gunness reported the anticipation ahead of 8.8.88 itself. Subsequently the regime accused him, accurately enough, of colluding with its opponents by advertising their timetable.

VOA (Voice of America) picked up on Gunness's initiative, and began broadcasting its own coverage of the unfolding drama in much the same vein. In no time at all there was scarcely a corner of the country that was not aware of the impending uprising. But equally the regime's intelligence services also monitored the BBC and VOA broadcasts, so that Sein Lwin and his fellow generals were not unprepared.

From the beginning of August, students and monks began camping outside the Shwedagon, with the result that on 3rd August the pagoda was sealed off. At once up to 10,000 protestors, from various quarters of Rangoon, marched on the central Sule pagoda. Effigies of both Sein Lwin and Ne Win were burned in the streets. Some demonstrators went so far as to display their coffins. Both generals, the message was, deserved to die. The same night martial law was declared, and the crowd dispersed. But next day there were further protests. Markets, tea-shops and Rangoon's main railway station filled with noisy crowds, preparing themselves for what lay ahead. At the end of each day students leafleted workers as they left their factories and offices. For the moment the police, the *Lon Htein* and the Tatmadaw watched impassively, at least in the capital. In Pegu and Yenangyaung police opened fire on similar assemblies, killing some and wounding others.

From all over the delta, thousands made their way to Rangoon, camping out in the city's parks and other open spaces. There was nothing secretive afoot. Rather, the feeling was that if the whole country participated in 8.8.88, then the army would have to stand aside and allow civilian government to resume. But Sein Lwin had no intention of giving in so meekly. What followed was, even by Burmese standards, a ghastly bloodbath. At dawn on Monday the 8th, Rangoon was more crowded than ever before in its history. As the sun climbed in the eastern sky, struggling to break through the usual morning haze, huge numbers prepared a simple breakfast for themselves – tea, a little rice, some vegetables perhaps, or the leftovers of whatever they had eaten the night before. For a while there was an almost miraculous restraint. As popular uprisings go, this one was to be marked above all by peaceableness, if that were possible. The city was awake, but nothing much was happening, until, at 8.08 a.m. precisely, Rangoon's dock workers staged a walkout.

This was the signal for the beginning of a nationwide general strike, and of vast demonstrations. Now, from all over Rangoon, hundreds of thousands of protestors converged on City Hall, some waving banners or the fighting peacock flag, others bearing portraits of Bogyoke Aung San. All chanted anti-government slogans.

In Mandalay and Moulmein, in Prome and Bassein, in Taunggyi and Myitkyina, and in other centres there were similar scenes. And still the armed forces stood back. As the day wore on, apprehension about the regime's likely response began to give way to a kind of festive joy. Both before City Hall and other venues in central Rangoon, student leaders, monks and other worthies reiterated their message: when an entire people expresses its will, no government can withstand it.

The students had also worked out how to deal with onlooking units of the Tatmadaw and *Lon Htein*. They were not in any way to be attacked. Instead they were greeted as comrades and brothers and were offered flowers.

Not until early in the evening did the regime issue its first response. But that response was ominous. At 5.30 p.m. Brigadier-General Myo Nyunt, the military commander of Rangoon, came out of the main doorway of City Hall. Standing on the steps of its portico, he told the crowd spread out before him to go home. Otherwise they would be shot.

No one was in the mood to listen, and for another six hours nothing untoward happened. But some of those who had gathered in central Rangoon, especially around the Sule pagoda, began heading in the direction of the Shwedagon. At 11.30 p.m. the shooting started. Suddenly the rumble of army trucks and armoured vehicles was heard in all directions. Surrounded by soldiers, many demonstrators sang the national anthem. But that did not deter the Tatmadaw, which had been brought in from outside Rangoon and told that communists were trying to take over the country. Outside both the Sule and Shwedagon pagodas there was an indiscriminate slaughter of civilians: students, monks, workers, teachers and civil servants.

As the crowds, realising now that the junta would not give in, began breaking up and running for their lives, the shooting continued far into the night: not just rifles and pistols, but Bren guns and machine guns.

The same night there was another massacre, in Sagaing, north of Mandalay. But if Sein Lwin thought the army's stock reaction to civil unrest would work again, he was mistaken. The next day there were more protests and demonstrations, with much the same result. As Ne Win had warned, the army shot to kill. It also used bayonets, sometimes on young children caught up in the confusion. Bodies were hurriedly removed, sometimes just dumped in Rangoon river. There were, too, hundreds of arrests, with some of those taken away never seen or heard of again. But such measures only incensed the people further. Bravely they continued marching and demonstrating. Increasingly, too, the violence was reciprocated. Small detachments of the Tatmadaw or *Lon Htein*, or individual MI officers, were ambushed with sticks and rocks and *jinglees*. On the 10th four policemen unlucky enough to be isolated in North Okkalapa township were ceremoniously beheaded with an ancient sword.

The unrest and killings went on all week. The wards of Rangoon's hospitals filled with the critically wounded. On Thursday the 12th a group of nurses came out through the main entrance of Rangoon General Hospital bearing placards begging the army to lay aside its weapons. But the Tatmadaw opened fire on them as well. Four nurses were gunned down.

A handful of foreign journalists, who, following Christopher Gunness's lead, had entered Burma as tourists, succeeded in filing reports and the occasional brief video clip. NHK, Japan's state television company, gathered more comprehensive coverage. But because NHK had a contract to run Burma's own state television service, such footage was suppressed.

The foreign embassies were another matter. Diplomats from five continents relayed to their governments graphic descriptions of what went on around them. As early as the 10th the US Senate passed a resolution condemning the actions of Sein Lwin's government, offering support for what now became known as Burma's democracy movement. But whether the mounting chorus of international disapproval had any effect on the junta is unknown. It is likely that the refusal of some Tatmadaw soldiers to obey orders and fire upon their fellow Burmese evoked the spectre of a full-scale army mutiny. Often, demonstrators had walked right up to the armed forces and, unbuttoning their shirts, challenged them, 'Shoot me if you dare!' What is known is that Ne Win convened an urgent meeting at Ady Road on the morning of the 12th. That same afternoon Sein Lwin announced his resignation, less than three weeks after becoming Burma's President.

The army withdrew to barracks and martial law was lifted. The people, it seemed, had won out, through sheer persistence in the face of brute force. Sein Lwin was replaced (on 19th August) by Dr Maung Maung, Burma's Attorney-General and the only civilian to have achieved prominence within Ne Win's regime. That he was also Ne Win's hapless biographer was overlooked. At least Burma now had a President who knew how to read and write, people said.

There was hope after all, despite the fact that somewhere in the region of 3,000 civilians had been killed in the 'Battle of Rangoon', and despite the continuing visibility of Khin Nyunt's Military Intelligence. Except in Moulmein, where on 21st August a further fifty were mown down by the Tatmadaw, the state's violence against its own subjects appeared to have abated. Although many families were left to mourn their lost ones, or worry about those who were missing, the streets of Rangoon played host to joyful celebrations. Demonstrations and marches proliferated as leaders of the democracy movement urged the restoration of a fully civil, accountable government. When housewives were criticised for not participating in the demonstrations, they organised marches of their own. Throughout Burman Burma there were calls for the overthrow of the BSPP. Amid scenes reminiscent of the Paris Commune of 1871, local communities began taking matters into their own hands. Guided by students and monks, people's committees were established, to oversee essential services and preserve at least a semblance of law and order.

Yet although students had played a major role in securing a 'people's victory', the democracy movement still lacked a steady focus. Anarchy might follow at any moment. Now more visitors than ever flocked to 54 University Avenue, to urge Suu Kyi to show her hand. A declaration by the Bogyoke's daughter was desperately needed. Among the many delegations was a group of six teachers from the history faculty at Rangoon University. The group's spokesman, Nyo Ohn Myint, was a physically imposing twenty-six-year-old who had supported his students during their protests in March and June, at one point even distributing some of their leaflets. For this Nyo Ohn Myint had been reprimanded by his department head, and warned that he faced immediate dismissal unless he dissociated himself from student politics. Undeterred, Nyo Ohn Myint threw himself into 8.8.88. Although the course he taught concerned US–Soviet Cold War relations, he was equally steeped in the history of the 'Burmese revolution'. He distributed more pamphlets prior to the uprising, openly denounced the BSPP and urged other teachers to side with the student rebels.

He and his five colleagues made their way to University Avenue, to meet Suu Kyi, on 15th August. The meeting lasted two hours. It was the beginning of a close and vital relationship. Nyo Ohn Myint's first impression of the Bogyoke's daughter was that she was 'a people person', and he knew at once that if she asked, he would follow her. But would she ask? Never shy to speak his mind, Nyo Ohn Myint told her directly that the democracy movement needed a leader – that is, Aung San Suu Kyi herself – even though he shared the traditional Burman male's scepticism about allowing women into politics.

Suu Kyi gave Nyo Ohn Myint the same reply she gave others. Even though she had, that very morning, written to the State Council offering her services as a mediator between protestors and the regime, and recommending the creation of a 'people's consultative committee' to ease the transition to democracy, she had no personal desire to become a national leader. Yet within two days her attitude shifted, as news of fresh killings broke. When Nyo Ohn Myint returned to her compound on the morning of the 17th, Suu Kyi talked to him about taking a more pro-active role, as a 'temporary co-ordinator' of the movement. But to do that she needed all the back-up she could get, and some kind of steering committee, made up of a mixture of elders and younger people.

She told Nyo Ohn Myint that if he wanted her to pledge herself to the movement, then he must make the same pledge. Nyo Ohn Myint unhesitatingly agreed, and became one of a dozen or so 'helpers' who found themselves virtually living at 54 University Avenue. Sometimes his duties were strictly menial – going out to buy food, or tidying up her 'office'. At other times she took him fully into her confidence, discussing not just policy with him, but also testing her knowledge of Burmese history against his. Even as she was being propelled onto the national stage, her insatiable curiosity remained intact, just as, each evening, she and Dr Aris reserved to themselves at least an hour's 'reading time' – an aspect of their domestic life in Oxford that they had brought with them to Rangoon.

Those who had gravitated to 54 University Avenue were aware that, at the end of each day, Suu Kyi and Dr Aris held long discussions. Unwilling to leave her mother's side, Suu Kyi had not thus far directly participated in the August uprising. But the couple had followed events as best they could. They now agreed that for Suu Kyi not to make some public statement would be a betrayal of both her father's legacy and the Burmese people. Conversely, if she were to make a statement, every effort should be made to guarantee its efficacy.

Among the writers and intellectuals who had courted Suu Kyi was U Win Khet, formerly an editor of *The Working People's Daily*. In his younger days he had flirted with communism, but had declined joining the CPB not because he 'disliked the idea of communism', but because he 'didn't like communists'. By 1988 he thought of himself as first and foremost a 'patriot'. Recalling the role of the Rangoon University Students' Union in the 1930s, he had assiduously contacted RU's latest generation of student leader. Willingly too, he had participated in the mass rallies of 8th August and the days that followed.

It was now Win Khet's privilege to act as master of ceremonies at a further mass rally held inside the main courtyard of Rangoon General

Hospital – still a focal point of anti-government protest – on 24th August. By his own estimate, some 50,000 demonstrators collected in front of the heart clinic. As well as other writers, a sizeable tranche of artists, actors and film-makers came along to signal their solidarity. An emotional moment occurred when Win Khet, holding a microphone on an improvised rostrum, had to ask the crowd to make way for two nurses pushing towards the clinic on their way to work. Alluding to their four colleagues who had so recently been killed, Win Khet stormed through his mike, 'The People's Nurses are Our Nurses', and at once his words were taken up as a chant.

The nurses blushed and smiled, and cried and disappeared. But that was not the highlight. The highlight came when Aung San Suu Kyi appeared on the stage beside Whin Khet and gave her first public address.

She was brief and to the point. Thanking Whin Khet and his media colleagues for their support and help, she confirmed what the student network was already spreading around town. She would indeed be making a more important speech at the Shwedagon in two days' time.

Military Intelligence, which had plants at Rangoon General Hospital, did its best to thwart Suu Kyi. On the 26th Khin Nyunt's men tried telling people that Aung San Suu Kyi was not coming to the Shwedagon, but would give her speech in another part of town. Already, too, pamphlets defaming her character had been printed, accusing her of being the puppet of a foreign power and of being a 'Genocidal Prostitute'. Boxes of these were discovered in a pick-up in downtown Rangoon. In a chilling throwback to Hitlerian propaganda, one pamphlet even caricatured Dr Aris as a communist Jew working for Moscow. MI may also have been responsible for generating a rumour that if Suu Kyi made her way to the Shwedagon, she would be assassinated – another reason people should steer clear of her. Further attempts were made to break up the meeting through a series of bomb scares.

Suu Kyi's personal security was already a concern to those around her, though she herself was characteristically debonair about any threat to her well-being. Nyo Ohn Myint wanted her to wear a bullet-proof undergarment, but Suu Kyi refused even to contemplate such a notion. Her father had never worn one, so why should she? But she did allow Nyo Ohn Myint and others to take some precautions. Suu Kyi, Aris and the boys, and her swelling entourage, were to make their way across town in a single convoy comprising eight or nine vehicles. Inside each would be at least one female and one 'bodyguard' – a young man who, though he might be unarmed, was chosen for his physical strength. Setting out from University Avenue, the convoy was led by an old army jeep. Then came a pick-up truck with young men in the back, then the Toyota saloon carrying Suu Kyi herself. Aris, Alexander and Kim followed in another car.

While the boys' spirits were buoyed up by the drama and excitement of the occasion, Aris was unusually subdued, both on the way to the Shwedagon and afterwards on the way back to no. 54. Knowing the brutal methods of Burmese power-holders, he was apprehensive about his wife's and his sons' safety. But he was also struggling to figure out where the extraordinary step Suu Kyi was taking would lead.

The convoy had to stop well short of the Shwedagon, so huge was the crowd. But a large body of students waving tricolour flags in imitation of the French Revolution, as well as a sampling of monks, cleared a path to the rostrum. Shortly after 11 a.m. the diminutive figure of the Bogyoke's daughter, introduced by the well-known actor Htun Wai, stood up in front of the microphones and began speaking to the nation (see Chapter 1).

Seventeen years later, in voluntary exile in Thailand, U Win Khet's eyes still watered at the memory. 'What surprised me,' he said, 'what surprised us all, was how mature she was. She spoke elegantly but simply, so that everyone could understand exactly what she meant. It may be an old man's delusion, but for me she became Aung San in August 1988. Her actions, her commitment, most of all her manner, were exactly his.'

Others embraced the same perceptions. However well or little they knew Suu Kyi, or indeed had known Aung San, it became an article of faith for the democracy movement that father and daughter were cut from the same cloth. Henceforward Suu Kyi would be known to her people as Daw Aung San Suu Kyi. Later, when Burma's military rulers began punishing those who dared breathe her name, she was known more simply as 'The Lady'. Later still, inside and outside her country, some of her followers would offer prayers not just for her, but also to her, as though she were a *bodhisattva* – or an incarnation perhaps of the Goddess of Mercy.

XXIV

SHADOW OF THE HUNDRED FLOWERS

It is a strange and horrifying situation where the people are trying to preserve order and unity while a faction of the government does its utmost to promote anarchy.

Aung San Suu Kyi, 'In the Eye of the Revolution', September 1988

FOR a few, heady weeks from the middle of August until the third Sunday of September 1988 it seemed that the people's uprising must succeed and democracy be restored to Burma. On 15th August the country's highest lawyers' association, the Burmese Bar Council, issued a toughly worded statement condemning the regime's heavy-handed response to the demonstrations that had begun on 8.8.88 as being against both 'the constitution' and 'international human rights law'. The Bar Council had on occasion issued similar statements, but unusually, this time around, more than fifty of its members appended their signatures. People were no longer so afraid to speak out against the regime as individuals and be identified.

Next day the Burmese Medical Association followed suit, roundly castigating the security forces for their assault on Rangoon General Hospital. Specifically, the Minister for Health was denounced. The hapless Dr Maung Maung, catapulted into the hot seat of power by Ne Win on 19th August, quickly announced, as well as the lifting of martial law, the release of Aung Gyi and the other senior retired army officers who had earlier been taken into custody. Other political prisoners were also set free. Although many doubted that the sixty-three-year-old Maung Maung was in any way his own man, his proclamation of a special

BSPP congress to authorise a referendum to determine whether Burma should continue as a one-party state, slated for 13th September, was at least a step in the right direction, as well as an apparent sign of weakness on the regime's part.

Dr Maung Maung's conciliatory gestures, however, were insufficient to quell the unrest, which now gripped every town and city in the land. Rather they encouraged further protests, demonstrations and a fresh round of strikes. British ambassador Martin Morland, in a confidential dispatch sent to the Foreign Office in London a few months later,* noted how, during the week beginning 22nd August, 'a new phase' set in:

Permanent banners appeared stretched across the streets declaring the people's peaceful intentions and begging the army not to shoot. I spent the morning with my US colleague watching crowds march past hour after hour, with contingents in their working dress – nurses, lawyers with black jackets, Christian nuns, doctors with stethoscopes, all calling for Democracy. Throughout this period the joy and good discipline of the demonstrators, who numbered tens of thousands, was astonishing.

The only 'visual sign' of disrespect towards the regime, Morland noted, 'was to carry the national flag introduced by Ne Win in 1962 upside down'.

Every day one of Burma's best-loved comedians, Zagana, lampooned Ne Win and his cronies outside the General Hospital, drawing huge crowds. Previously Zagana had been a dentist, and allegedly instigated a famous anti-regime joke: to have their teeth fixed Burmese always travel abroad, not because Burma's dentists lack skill, but because at home no one dares open his mouth. At the same time a wicked cartoon went the rounds, depicting General Win relying on a helium-filled balloon marked BSPP to keep his flagging penis aloft, as he endeavoured to make love to his latest concubine.

As expectations soared, more and more government employees joined hands with the students and other dissidents, many tearing up their BSPP membership cards or ceremoniously incinerating them on street corners. Propitiously, although none of the ethnic insurgency forces ventured out of their mountain fastnesses, in Rangoon, Mandalay and elsewhere resident Chins, Kachins and other minorities swelled the ranks

* 9th November 1988; circulated to a dozen other embassies and missions

of the marchers, proudly donning their 'tribal' costumes. In Arakan, Buddhist Rakhines and Muslim Rohingyas made common cause. Equally, the students themselves were inspired with a new confidence. The old Students' Union at Rangoon University, which had been banned for twenty-six years, was revived, apparently with the tacit consent of the Maung Maung-led state council. On 28th August a new All Burma Federation of Student Unions (ABFSU) was formed, with Min Ko Naing its elected chairman.

Other unions proliferated, as every trade and profession scampered to seize the rights that the regime had so long denied them. On 2nd September the emboldened Bar Council declared the 1962 military coup 'illegal'. The following day, US Congressman Stephen J. Solarz flew in from Washington on a mission to broker a deal between Maung Maung's administration and such senior leaders of the democracy movement as had emerged. These included, as well as Aung San Suu Kyi, Aung Gyi, U Tin Oo and U Nu.

Like Suu Kyi, Aung Gyi and Tin Oo had addressed large rallies. All three now called for the immediate creation of an interim government, composed of men and women from across the political spectrum, to oversee an orderly reintroduction of democratic government through a properly managed general election. U Nu went one step further. Now in his eighties, more given to Buddhist mysticism than ever, and with some doubting his mental condition, the prime minister whom Ne Win had deposed in 1962 re-emerged from the shadows two days after Suu Kyi's Shwedagon speech. He was, he said, setting up a new political party, named the League for Democracy and Peace. On 9th September he declared that he was still Prime Minister and, with U Tin Oo, was setting up a provisional government.

But U Nu did not attract the mass support he anticipated, and his initiative fell flat. His 'cabinet' consisted of too many old cronies, too many relatives. People felt that he represented failure and compromise, an old order that had already been found wanting. Significantly, he was unable to persuade either Suu Kyi or Aung Gyi to join his bandwagon. U Tin Oo quickly withdrew his backing.

By then Solarz had returned to the USA. His informal, multilateral talks had not produced a breakthrough. At a news conference held in Bangkok on 5th September he sombrely warned that unless the Burmese military swiftly agreed to democratic reforms, then a 'devastating civil war' was likely to ensue.

Solarz's flying visit may have encouraged rumours that an American task force was assembling in the Bay of Bengal in readiness to intervene. More wildly still, the US Marines were alleged to be preparing an invasion with Suu Kyi's estranged brother Aung San Oo at its head. In reality, the US Navy had positioned a handful of vessels a hundred miles off the Burmese coast, but only as a precaution – in case it became necessary to evacuate US embassy staff and other American citizens in Burma at short notice. By chance, in an entirely separate operation, a US fleet was conducting exercises further out in the Indian Ocean. This may have prompted the government to bring forward the next scheduled 'extraordinary' meeting of the BSPP congress and Council of State to 10th September. Faced by the reality of what was happening in 'the parliament of the streets', Dr Maung Maung again seemed ready to yield ground. There was no more talk of a referendum to decide the fate of the BSPP; instead direct, multi-party elections were promised, though no date was set.

But even this was not enough to satisfy those yearning for instant democracy. The demonstrations, mass gatherings and strikes continued, and with them a sense of national carnival, a great political *pwe*. But only for a few more days. By the second week of September, if not well before, Ne Win and his inner circle were already preparing to blow the whistle on the Burmese people's new-found sense of freedom. Just like the Prague Spring of 1968, or the Paris Commune of 1871, the 'Rangoon Spring' was to be brought to a sudden, crashing halt.

After a quarter of a century of severe press censorship and state control of the media, the people's uprising witnessed an extraordinary sunburst of free print expression, once martial law had been lifted. Scores of independent newspapers and pamphlets, all urging the army to withdraw from politics permanently, appeared overnight. Burma's presses, working round the clock, produced striking posters that soon covered every available billboard and wall. Portraits of Aung San, the father of the nation, hung everywhere. In most cases such presses belonged either to the country's official newspapers or to ministries and colleges. The government newspapers were effectively halted by strike action, and with increasing numbers of government workers siding with the protestors, nobody was overly minded to ask too closely to what use the presses were put.

The uprising was markedly successful in other ways. Despite the strikes, which brought most of Burma's industry and transport systems to a halt, for the first few weeks at least essential services – including the provision of electricity and running water, and (temporarily) the supply of foodstuffs to the country's towns and cities – were maintained. In the townships local people's committees, conjured out of the air, assumed many of the responsibilities of government, including, in most areas, the maintenance of basic law and order. Crucially, the Buddhist *sangha*, or monkhood, willingly stepped forward as a moral arbiter that all could respect, settling disputes, preventing excessive retribution and preserving a sense of normative justice.

But the uprising was also a vast, fragmented mirage, and ultimately a failure in its own terms. The rebels failed to commandeer the state broadcasting apparatus, failed to gain control of key ministries, failed to suborn members of the armed forces in meaningful numbers and, especially, failed to furnish the movement with a galvanising, centralised leadership that all could adhere to. The BBC and VOA provided relatively reliable commentaries on events as they unfolded, but did not properly 'belong' to the people. Instead, the only domestic radio station that broadcast in favour of the uprising belonged to the outlawed CPB (Communist Party of Burma).

Opportunistically, the CPB declared its support for the democracy movement. Likewise, the previously captured veteran 'Red Flag' communist leader Thakin Soe issued a supportive statement from his hospital bed. But such earnests only played into the hands of the junta, which wasted no time asserting that the 'disturbances' were, all along, orchestrated by communists determined to wreck the country. This the regime had done before, and would do again, but its message struck home especially with the armed forces' officer class. Demonstrators gathered in their thousands, sometimes tens of thousands, outside City Hall and other state buildings, but, until too late in the day, there was no attempt to storm even one such bastion of power. Throughout the uprising, the Ministry of Defence and state broadcasting buildings were heavily guarded – an exception to the 'return to barracks' pattern – although a trickle of NCOs and junior air-force men did desert their posts and there was a walk-out by ground staff at Mingaladon air-force base. While in themselves these hardly constituted a full-blown mutiny, the sight of some off-duty soldiers participating in democracy demonstrations can only have unsettled their superiors.

Above all, no single, compelling demagogue whom all the people could respect emerged to shape the movement. Min Ko Naing, Moe Thee Zun and other student leaders, much later styled 'the Generation of '88', dominated the colleges and schools, and worked tirelessly organising strike committees and demonstrations, but failed to project themselves convincingly onto the larger stage. Aung Gyi, U Tin Oo and even U Nu added their weight and years to the movement, but none of them had quite the charisma to carry the whole show. Aung San Suu Kyi, who patently did have charisma, came closest, in her Shwedagon address. But as yet she neither wanted to become a national leader, nor had the experience or depth of political understanding to fulfil such a role. Rather, throughout the beginning of September she abided by the position she had adopted on 26th August: she was there to mediate and conciliate if asked, but, sensitive to charges that she was an 'outsider' who had only recently returned to Burma, she still hesitated to adopt a more active role.

It was scarcely surprising that, after decades of oppression, those who craved freedom inside Burma should struggle to find an effective means of gaining their objectives. There was, amongst Burma's core non-communist population, no embedded know-how for mounting an effective challenge against tyranny, for seeing the uprising through to its logical and just conclusion. Rather, tactics and strategy had to be improvised and learned from scratch. In that process, too many opportunities were missed.

As the days ticked off, a kind of anarchy set in. Increasingly there were episodes of violence, some perpetrated by agents provocateurs, others by members of the democracy movement itself. Incidences of looting, robbery and other crimes multiplied. In Moulmein, government officials had to be rescued by the navy to prevent their being lynched. Of the thousands of barricades erected in the streets of Rangoon and other cities, by no means all were intended to hinder or deter potential operations by the regime's strangely quiescent security forces. Those few who did have wealth became apprehensive, and took appropriate measures to defend their property.

That agents provocateurs were at work there was no doubt. From early September the regime, far from striving to maintain order, seemed hell-bent on sowing panic and confusion. Too often looters were allowed to pursue their business as the police stood by and watched. Perhaps in a botched attempt to elicit international sympathy, a compound holding German aid materials was looted by soldiers. Similarly, a warehouse belonging to the UNFAO (United Nations Food and Agriculture Organisation) was ransacked as men in uniforms stood by. Other men, disgorging from army trucks, raided the Foreign Trade Bank, making off with 600 million *kyat*, earmarked (it was later said) for paying the Tatmadaw's wages in advance.

On the same day that Suu Kyi addressed the multitude at the Shwedagon, some 5,000 prisoners, the majority of them criminals, were released from Insein prison alone, without either food or money, following a prison riot that had left fifty dead and a hundred injured. Hundreds of inmates of the city's asylums were also set free, again on government orders. Rangoon's back streets became unsafe after dark, sometimes during the day as well.

On 9th September, Ma San, a known prostitute, was caught red-handed by democratic vigilantes committing arson in Dawbon township. When cross-examined, she confessed that she had been given money and drugs by the 'authorities' to carry out the deed. More sinisterly still, five men were apprehended as they endeavoured to poison the water supply adjacent to a children's hospital in Halpin Road. While two of them remained tight-lipped, under forceful interrogation three 'confessed' that they were MI agents.

The three who admitted their identity were spared, but the two who said nothing were summarily executed with rusty swords. The same fate befell Ma San. Immediately afterwards, Rangoon's citizens were advised to test any water with small fish before drinking it – advice that was heeded by a nervous staff at the German embassy. The army kept a low profile, but Military Intelligence had not been reined in, and unruly revolutionary elements launched a witch-hunt against MI operatives. Scores were seized and killed, usually hacked to pieces with whatever crude weapon was to hand. Had it not been for the intercession of monks, many more would have been butchered. Aung San Suu Kyi, Aung Gyi, Tin Oo and U Nu urged that non-violence should be the hallmark of the uprising, but by mid-September no one could control all the groups and gangs involved. Long years of brutal oppression by the regime inevitably led to individual episodes of bloody revenge.

Arguably, the uprising failed not because some of its participants turned to violence, but because it was, as a whole, not forceful enough. There was a devout, Buddhist reluctance to fight fire with fire, to organise a people's militia that might easily have secured weapons from across Burma's permeable borders, as so many of the country's minority insurgents had demonstrated year in, year out. A few home-made bombs went off, but even those were believed to be the work of government agents. Among Burmans there was as yet no concerted effort to create a guerrilla force that, at the least, might have provided a focal point for ongoing resistance, if the regime moved to reassert its authority. A land once famous for dacoitry seemed no longer to have any dacoits – unless, as those within the democracy movement maintained, the Tatmadaw itself had become a dacoit force par excellence.

It is also arguable that the uprising was doomed to failure from the outset: that it was allowed to happen only because General Ne Win wanted it to; that the Old Man, bolstered by the Machiavellian cunning of his intelligence chief Khin Nyunt, and perhaps of his bullish daughter Sanda Win, deliberately sought to create an atmosphere of such seething unrest and uncertainty that the intervention of the Tatmadaw would be greeted as a welcome respite.

According to this reading, unwittingly or otherwise Ne Win and his associates re-enacted a version of the infamous 'Hundred Flowers Movement' that had gripped communist China in 1957. Mao Zedong and the Chinese PLA (People's Liberation Army) had wrested control of the whole of China in 1949. But, an innately devious man, Mao never felt secure in the top-dog position. Ultimate power induced ultimate paranoia, and much of his time as Chairman was spent identifying and thwarting his enemies, both real and imagined. So it was that in 1956, using the slogan 'Let a hundred flowers bloom', Mao openly encouraged criticism of the Communist Party. Critics, fearful of the consequences, were slow to respond to his uncharacteristically open-minded invitation. But the following year the call was taken up, and with growing enthusiasm. In Beijing, posters demanding a multi-party election appeared on a 'democracy wall'. Then in July Mao launched an 'anti-rightist' campaign that saw half a million urban dissidents packed off to the deep countryside to amend their errant ways through hard labour. 'Coaxing the snakes out of their holes, then striking against them' was Mao's retrospective take.

Towards the end of August 1988 an extraordinary document, purportedly summarising an 'emergency' meeting known to have taken place at Ne Win's Inya Lake residence on the 23rd of the same month, began circulating in Rangoon. The meeting had been attended by, amongst others, Dr Maung Maung, the Defence Minister and Chief of Army Staff General Saw Maung, Khin Nyunt, Sanda Win and (allegedly) Sein

Lwin. According to the 'leaked report', the discussion was chaired by Ne Win and had as its purpose the formulation of an appropriate policy to contain and destroy the democracy uprising, and thus ensure the continuing supremacy of the Tatmadaw. Top of the agenda was the identification and isolation of the movement's student leaders. To achieve this, soldiers masquerading as civilians 'should be sent to all cities to commit anarchic activities and crime. The people and businessmen would then welcome, long for and rely on the protection which the armed forces would bring. The people would then see that the multi-party system is the cause of all the trouble. In order to instil such thoughts in the minds of the people, it is desirable that the state of chaos should be prolonged as much as possible.' Undercover intelligence officers were to encourage dissident students to step forward and offer themselves as leaders. 'In this way a list of all those who are to be destroyed could be made.' Then, at the appropriate moment, Defence Minister General Saw Maung was to stage a *coup d'état*. Student leaders and other trouble-makers ('artists, intellectuals and lawyers') should then be arrested 'according to their photographs' and handed over to the 'torture squads'.

The document was almost certainly a fabrication, and was dismissed as such by the diplomatic community. But as Ambassador Morland observed in his special dispatch of 9th November, whoever concocted it 'had a shrewd idea of Ne Win's strategy'. Its predictions proved unnervingly accurate.

The tipping point came midway through September. On Friday the 16th a student leader, addressing a small rally not far from the War Office, began making unprecedented personal attacks on Ne Win, Dr Maung Maung, General Saw Maung and other regime heavyweights. Suddenly, out of nowhere, a loudspeaker warned him that unless he desisted the army would shoot him. However, this only angered the crowd. Word spread quickly, and soon thousands of demonstrators gathered around him. The 'army' loudspeaker backed off, but the sense of humiliation was reported back to Ady Road.

The following day, Saturday the 17th, General Saw Maung's ministry issued an order that the Tatmadaw fulfil its three cardinal duties: to perpetuate the Union, maintain national unity and safeguard the sovereignty of the state. Simultaneously, protestors camped outside the Ministry of Trade provoked soldiers guarding the building into opening fire and killing one of their number. Again the crowd reacted angrily. The ministry was stormed by several hundred demonstrators, and twenty-four soldiers were seized and forcibly disarmed before being handed over to monks at a nearby monastery.

This latest affront to the Tatmadaw was the last straw. The time had come to strike back. Early in the morning on Sunday the 18th Dr Maung Maung was summoned by Ne Win to Ady Road and dismissed from office, after serving as Burma's president for less than a month. In his place General Saw Maung was appointed chief of state, heading up what began as a nineteen-member emergency cabinet, composed almost entirely of senior army men (the exception was Minister of Health Dr Pe Thein). This formed the nucleus of the State Law and Order Restoration Council, a military junta destined to rule over Burma for the next nine years, usually identified by its unappetising acronym SLORC.

Other appointees to the new ruling body included Khin Nyunt, who retained control over MI and became SLORC's 'Secretary One'; and Lieutenant-General Than Shwe, another Ne Win loyalist, who was already Deputy Chief-of-Staff and now became SLORC's vice-chairman under Saw Maung. Simultaneously the Council of State was dissolved, as was the BSPP, shortly to be streamlined and resurrected as the National Unity Party (NUP).

The Burmese public was informed of these developments only later in the day. At four in the afternoon, when tens of thousands of demonstrators were on the march, radio and television broadcasts were interrupted by a special announcement, promulgating a takeover of power by the 'defence forces'. Emphasis was placed on the 'restoration of order'.

A nationwide curfew lasting from 8 p.m. to 6 a.m. was instituted. For several hours still nothing much happened. As news of the 'coup' spread, crowds swelled in the usual public places, but without any targets to vent their anger on. Not until later that evening did the army come out in any numbers. But when troops did pour into Rangoon, again trucked in from outlying barracks, they went about their business with remorseless precision, opening fire with rifles, Bren guns and machine guns.

It is easier, no doubt, to mow down civilians under the cover of dark, when their faces and individuality are not so clearly visible. Crowds were not asked to disperse: they were dispersed with the bullet. The shootings continued throughout the night. At Rangoon Hospital, doctors and nurses were appalled by the number of children who began filling up the casualty wards. Many had been shot in the back, some between the eyes. But the people did not surrender immediately. The following morning, Monday 19th September, a further march on City Hall was attempted, only to be trapped between carefully emplaced fire points. No sooner had demonstrators fallen to the ground than they were gathered up and removed to a mass crematorium at Kyandaw. There, it was later asserted, not all those thrown into the incinerators were dead; some were just horribly wounded. And where bodies were not hurriedly burned, care was taken to disfigure the faces of the fallen, so that they would not be identified by relatives.

One of the most savage assaults, caught on video by watching diplomats, took place outside the American embassy. Along Prome Road, soldiers sprayed tea-shops and market stalls with gunfire as they drove by in jeeps and armoured vehicles. And what took place in Rangoon was repeated in every other town and city. Troops moved in to break up strike centres, and looted private properties as they went looking for known dissidents.

There were isolated incidents of resistance. Soldiers unlucky enough to be caught on their own or in small numbers were clubbed to death. But military casualties were as nothing compared to those sustained by the civilian populace. Khin Nyunt went on record as saying that the numbers killed amounted to 238 civilians as against twenty-five soldiers and police, but on the civilian side the true figure is likely to have been at least ten times higher.

The operation lasted four days, until the morning of the 21st, when the people's resilience was finally broken. Thereafter government employees, warned that if they did not comply they faced lengthy prison sentences, were coerced back to work, as SLORC endeavoured to rekindle a semblance of normality. Government employees were also obliged to fill in lengthy forms, confessing whether or not they had taken part in any protests, and pledging their future obedience.

Some were happy to return to work. The army backlash had been carried out against a backdrop of sharply rising food prices and petrol shortages, and most had not received any wages or salaries since mid-August. But only a minority concurred with the Tatmadaw's propaganda that it had intervened to 'save the nation'.

Worst affected were the many thousands of students across Burma who had been at the vanguard of the uprising. MI had been busy assembling fat dossiers that contained endless photographs of the young idealists. A witch-hunt ensued. Hundreds were rounded up and incarcerated, some never to be seen or heard of again. Many thousands more decided to flee, leaving their town and city homes for the mountain jungles along the Thai and Chinese borders, where they threw themselves on the mercy of Karen and other insurgents.

The KNU had given the 'people's uprising' only lukewarm support whilst it lasted, using the disruption caused by it to further its own guerrilla operations. Now, however, it welcomed those fleeing Burma's cities, and assisted in the creation of a new body, the ABSDF (All Burma Students' Democratic Front), which survives to this day in the maquis as a staunchly anti-regime grouping committed to securing Burmese democracy by any means. Intensified fighting broke out between the Tatmadaw and ethnic insurgent groups in the Karen and other borderlands. For many students jungle life, with its attendant hazards of malaria and other deadly illnesses, was too much. Some made their way to Thailand, but when SLORC declared an amnesty, many returned home, only to be arrested, interrogated, tortured and imprisoned.

To the dismay of onlookers and commentators around the world, the uprising of 1988 had been systematically smashed. Over a six-month period perhaps as many as 10,000 citizens had been killed by the Tatmadaw and Burmese security forces. It was 1962 all over again, but with the difference that, with twenty-six years' experience of absolute power under their belts, Burma's generals, still guided by Ne Win, were well versed in the techniques of control and oppression. Their hideous juggernaut, temporarily derailed by the events of August and September, was on track again, with a renewed sense of purpose. The people, in as far as they existed at all, existed only to be bullied into submission.

Yet there was an anomaly. Multi-party elections had been promised by Dr Maung Maung. One of SLORC's first actions was to affirm that 'free and fair' elections would go ahead, though still at an unspecified date. While the immediate motive behind this decision must have been to undermine continuing resistance domestically and take the sting out of some at least of the international opprobrium generated by the September coup, its actual logic only became transparent in the days, weeks and months that followed.

XXV

DIGGING IN

I would like every country in the world to recognize that the people of Burma are being shot down for no reason at all.
Aung San Suu Kyi, appeal to the United Nations and other
international bodies, 22nd September 1988

NYO Ohn Myint, the Rangoon University history teacher who had encouraged Suu Kyi to declare her hand, and helped organise her appearance at the Shwedagon, thought that, once her speech had been made, his duties by her were done. He wanted to return to the university and resume his research and teaching duties – not that any classes were being held. He had found some of the students at the front of the rally 'somewhat officious, one or two of them very rude'. He did not think of himself as a politician, and could not foresee such a life for himself. But Suu Kyi would have none of it. When, later the same afternoon, she returned to the compound in University Avenue she asked Nyo Ohn Myint and four of his colleagues to stay on. There was no giving up halfway through, she said. Everyone must continue to make every effort until democracy was achieved, which she believed would be soon.

So Nyo Ohn Myint, along with thirty or forty others who had started camping out at no. 54 (many students among them) stayed – on condition that once the movement was successful, he would be free to decide what he wanted to do next.

That, said Suu Kyi, was the whole point: to promote freedom of choice. Until such time, he was asked to work as Suu Kyi's deputy information officer, amongst other duties. Sometimes she asked him to take notes during meetings; at other times he volunteered as a truck driver.

Yet there was another, sharper exchange a few days later, after the two boys, Alexander and Kim, had left Burma at the beginning of September 1988. In England it was the beginning of the school year. Dr Aris remained in Burma, but he too would be leaving soon. A rumour had started that Suu Kyi herself would join the family exodus, even though her mother needed constant care. Nyo Ohn Myint confronted her. 'Is it true?' he asked. 'Are you leaving us as well?'

'Who told you that?' Suu Kyi answered, clearly piqued.

Nyo Ohn Myint reminded her of her promise, and Suu Kyi exploded. She was, he recalls, 'very very angry'. Her small fists clenched, her knuckles blenched. No, she had no intention of quitting. She had already told everybody that. So why was he asking?

Not for the first time, or for the last, Suu Kyi had allowed a quick temper to get the better of her. It was something else she had inherited from her father. Normally self-possessed almost to a fault, she could, if provoked, suddenly boil over, especially if any slur were cast on her integrity. But she calmed immediately, and did not hold Nyo Ohn Myint's challenge against him. She liked people who spoke their minds, and he was already proving himself a useful member of her team. If he had some of the Burman male's natural impetuosity, she saw no ill in that. Soon afterwards he was promoted her chief press officer.

Dealing with the press was another challenge to which Suu Kyi had to adjust quickly, and she did so impressively. Even though she was still finding her way politically and refining her thoughts, she seemed able to bat any question with effortless ease. Time and again she hit just the right balance between self-assurance and humility, projecting herself as someone who was absolutely clear about her objectives, but who at the same time did not pretend to know the answer to everything and was willing to listen to anyone with a modicum of sense. Equally, she was adept at spotting traps and neatly side-stepping them.

The Shwedagon had given her instant celebrity, on the world stage as much as in Burma, and there was a steady stream of requests for interviews. Even right after the speech she had not come home immediately, but had gone to another house for a prearranged telephone interview with the BBC.

'In my thoughts, I have never been away from my country and my people,' she told the BBC reporter – echoing Eva Perón, made famous for her patriotism by Andrew Lloyd Webber and Tim Rice's hit song of 1975, 'Don't cry for me, Argentina'. But unlike Perón, Suu Kyi's 'wild days', if any, had been few and far between. Again she invoked Aung San's memory. 'From childhood,' she continued, 'I have been deeply interested in the history of the independence movement and in the social and political development of Burma. My father died when I was only two years old, and it was only when I grew older and started collecting material about his life that I began to learn how much he had achieved in his thirty-two years. Because of this strong bond I feel a deep responsibility for the welfare of my country.'

But what shape and direction that responsibility would take was not so obvious on 26th August 1988, even though the main elements of Suu Kyi's commitment and political philosophy were already adumbrated in the speech she had given, among them an insistence that the restoration of democracy in Burma should be accompanied by a 'revolution of the spirit'. One reason why she had agreed to address the Shwedagon rally was the lack of any response to the letter she and Htwe Myint had composed and sent to the Council of State on 15th August. From a longer, more substantive interview that appeared in the London *Times* on 29th August, it is clear that Suu Kyi still saw herself as a mediator between factions – an enabler, but not yet a leader.

'It is my aim,' she said, 'to help the people in Burma attain democracy without further violence or loss of life.' What was offensive to her was the military regime's denial of 'the full enjoyment of human rights', which undermined any notion of 'full independence'. That the people had demonstrated their desire for democracy was overwhelmingly apparent from the uprising that had begun on 8.8.88. It was not a question of what she, Aung San Suu Kyi, wanted, but of what the people wanted; and the people would 'continue with their demands until they get the sort of political system they want'. Nor was it, in her view, just a question of toppling the regime itself. What she wished to promote was a change of heart within the regime, and a commonality of understanding between all sides. There was no need for 'dissension' between the people and the army, provided the army upheld the ideals originally inculcated by Aung San.

The immediate way forward was 'an interim government in which people have confidence', to get the country 'back on an even keel'. Free and fair elections should then follow as a matter of course. But would Suu Kyi herself wish to form a party? 'Not if it is at all avoidable,' she answered. A 'life in politics holds no attraction for me', she said, then added, 'At the moment I serve as a kind of unifying force because of my father's name and because I am not interested in jostling for any kind of position.'

About this there was something of the fairy godmother, the *dea ex machina*. If Suu Kyi waved her magic wand hard enough, all might yet come right. It was a patrician (some might say elitist) stance to take, and not one altogether aligned with the realities of what was happening in Burma. But for Suu Kyi objective moral principles, including the principle of non-violence, meant everything. The real task ahead was to crystallise those principles in such a way that they gave beneficial sustenance to 'her' beleaguered people, the military included.

In early September, amid all the comings and goings and representations of those determined to enlist her active participation, she found time to gather some of her thoughts in an essay, 'In the Eye of the Revolution', extracts from which appeared in the *Independent* on 12th September.* Already there was a shift in her approach, from that of the anxious but elevated onlooker to someone more acutely aware of the scale of the mountain to be climbed. 'There are moments of tragedy, horror, and sheer disbelief,' the essay begins. Then it rehearsed the situation in Burma, but in a less conciliatory manner towards Ne Win's dictatorship than hitherto. For twenty-six years 'the people of Burma have been suppressed by a regime which allowed no freedom of thought or initiative of any kind'. Now, amidst the pandemonium of the uprising, it was the people who strove to maintain order, while the regime engaged only in exercises of destabilisation. Without naming names, a finger was pointed at 'some members of the present regime' whose 'actions seem to be directed solely towards creating chaos and maximum suffering of the people who have rejected them with a unanimity seldom seen in the course of the nation's history'.

While Suu Kyi did not deny that there were some who sought revenge against the regime, the 'majority of the people are more likely to pursue a line of justice tempered by mercy'. Nor was the army itself to be blamed. Rather 'it is being manipulated and misused by a handful of corrupt fanatics whose powers and privileges are dependent on the survival of the present system'. After yet again invoking the spirit of Aung San – 'an upright and honourable man who put the welfare of

*The complete essay is reproduced in Aung San Suu Kyi, *Freedom from Fear* (1991)

his country above his own interests' – Suu Kyi wrote of her own 'uneasy' relationship with the regime. 'There have always been individual members of the government who entertained such strong sentiments of love and loyalty toward my father that they regard his family with warm affection and respect. On the other hand there are those who, while using my father's name for their own purposes, have never practised the principles that he laid down as essential for the good of the nation.' And she added that some such 'harbour strong feelings of jealousy toward our family' and 'see us as a threat'.

Critically, on the matter of forming a political party, Suu Kyi modified her position as given to *The Times* a short while earlier. Repeating that forming a party had no personal attraction for her, she wrote, 'I am prepared to engage in the very kind of party politics I wish to avoid if I am convinced that it would be necessary to uphold the democratic system for which we are all striving at this moment.'

Just as critically, 'In the Eye of the Revolution' showed Suu Kyi moving closer to the more moderate, at least among the dissident students. 'I have found a great majority of them not only brave and resourceful but also receptive to new ideas.' If she had already become an inspiration to them, they were an inspiration to her.

Suu Kyi was changing tack. Although she continued – and always would continue – to believe in the power of moral persuasion, she was beginning to appreciate that there could be no quick fix. Hour by hour almost, as yet more tales of the regime's underhand techniques reached her teeming compound, the reluctant speaker at the Shwedagon was metamorphosing into Burma's principal opposition figure.

The Aung San card might work with the masses, but palpably it was not working with Ne Win, Khin Nyunt, General Saw Maung or even the dithering, turpitudinous Dr Maung Maung. On Tuesday 13th September, together with former General Tin Oo and former Brigadier-General Aung Gyi, Suu Kyi met with an Election Commission, set up by what was left of the BSPP, to seek clarification and confirmation of whatever arrangements were being made apropos the elections promised by Dr Maung Maung three days before. Nothing concrete resulted from the meeting, and the three emergent leaders issued a joint statement indicating that they had little or no confidence in the government.

On the same day student representatives visited Rangoon's foreign embassies. Their mission was to ascertain how much international support might be forthcoming for a self-declared interim democratic government. Not all the embassies responded positively, or could do so without instructions from their own governments. But the students were sufficiently encouraged to push ahead anyway. As well as Suu Kyi, U Tin Oo and Aung Gyi, U Nu and Bo Yan Naing (one of the Thirty Comrades) were invited to an open debate at the Medical Institute Number One, close to Rangoon General Hospital.

The proceedings were relayed by loudspeakers to a large crowd gathered outside on the street. Inside, Moe Thee Zun spoke on behalf of the students, of whom approximately a hundred were present. He urged the seniors to lay aside whatever differences they might have between themselves and join the students in the immediate formation of a rebel administration. But even before a proper discussion could begin, U Nu threw a spanner in the works. He and he alone, he declared, was Burma's constitutionally elected Prime Minister. The others should follow his lead and join the provisional government he had already proclaimed. The 'others', and the students – most of whom belonged to the more radical wing of the student movement – were unimpressed. The octogenarian was just posturing. Nobody believed he had either sufficient support or the nous to see his initiative through.

The meeting ended quickly and untidily, without an agreed agenda being reached. It had three significant consequences, however. Firstly, the students drew up a list of 'nominees' for their proposed authority; among them was Aung San Suu Kyi, even though she had expressed reservations about taking such a drastic step. Secondly, it helped cement relations between Suu Kyi, U Tin Oo and Aung Gyi, who now agreed to act in concert. And thirdly, intelligence that the democracy movement might be coalescing in such a way as to set up a rival government probably advanced the timing of the coup.

On the very morning of the coup, Sunday 18th September, radical students at Rangoon University decided to proceed with their plans regardless, and proclaimed an interim government – a quixotic gesture soon lost amid the violence and killings that followed that night. But that Suu Kyi was now regarded as a potential enemy of the state was evidenced by the concentration of troops that assembled outside 54 University Avenue in the late afternoon.

Around a hundred soldiers appeared outside the gates, along with two jeeps bearing mounted Bren guns. No one was allowed to enter the compound. Anybody attempting to leave was liable to arrest. Temporarily the telephone line was cut.

Nyo Ohn Myint, who had earlier gone to Rangoon University to report on developments there, was among scores trapped inside. Eighteen years later he could still recall the atmosphere of uncertainty that prevailed. 'All through the night we were kept awake by the noise of machine gun fire that raged across the city. And we had no idea whether we would be attacked, or when. It was clear that the regime was exacting bloody reprisals, and we might be next.'

Nyo Ohn Myint wanted to improvise Molotov cocktails to use against the army, should it attempt to force the gates, but Suu Kyi was adamant that no violence should be offered, even in self-defence. 'It is better that I be taken off to prison,' she said. 'It is better that we should all be taken off to prison.' She had already insisted that none of her followers arm themselves in any way, even with *jinglees*. As she subsequently told the *Financial Times*, the only weapon kept inside the compound was a ceremonial samurai sword presented to her father by the Japanese, and the generals would be hard pressed to hold that against her.*

Suu Kyi's position was that to resort to force of any kind, however physically inconsequential, would fatally damage the principles she stood for. Any victory gained by violence could only perpetuate violence, and it was Burma's historic culture of violence that she wished to dismantle. If the Tatmadaw wanted to confront her, then she would meet them face-to-face, unarmed and undefended.

Although he was persuaded by Suu Kyi's arguments, Nyo Ohn Myint was still nonplussed. Like others, he had developed a profound admiration for the Bogyoke's daughter in the short period he had got to know her. She was 'big sister' to him, to his academic colleagues and to virtually everyone else at no. 54. Consumed by anxiety for her safety, his next stratagem was to bundle her over the wall into the adjoining compound, which, as chance would have it, was rented by the Russian news agency Tass. If Suu Kyi resisted, he would knock her out first. 'If we did that,' he said, 'it wouldn't matter if the army came in. They could shoot us all, but still she would be alive.' But, finding no takers for his plan of action, Nyo Ohn Myint gave up the idea.

The siege lasted only two days. The junta did not yet have the bottle

Financial Times, 24th October 1988

to move directly against Aung San's daughter. On Tuesday the 20th the troops in University Avenue thinned out and telephonic communication was restored. Understanding that the immediate danger was past, Suu Kyi sent a politely worded request to the new supremo, General Saw Maung, asking for immediate dialogue – a request that was stonewalled with a vague promise of talks at some unspecified date in the future.

The following day, although tight restrictions had been placed on native Burmese journalists, Suu Kyi – with Dr Aris still at her side – held an impromptu press conference with the handful of foreign reporters who had stayed on in Rangoon during the final moments of the people's uprising. Quizzed for the umpteenth time on how long she intended remaining in Burma, she answered, 'I am going to stand by the democratic movement here all the way. Which is braver or more necessary? To stay or to leave?'

Ask a dumb question, she might have said. Soon enough foreign press-men would learn, on such occasions as they had access to her, to use the opportunity more thoughtfully. Already her commitment was the *sine qua non* of her very existence.

SLORC, anxious to spin some sort of reputation for itself, was serious about holding elections. In its unbridled and inhumane arrogance, it believed, through the newly constituted NUP (National Unity Party), that it could and would win them hands down. What better way to deliver a resounding rebuff to the sustained international chorus of disapproval that greeted its accession to power, and its brutal methods? At the same time SLORC hoped that, by being seen to promote democracy, in however lukewarm a way, it could fast-track economic recovery.

Immediately after the coup nearly every aid and development programme benefiting Burma had been suspended. The USA, Europe and Japan, aghast at the civilian massacres perpetrated by the Tatmadaw, concerted to deny SLORC vital funds. The IMF, the World Bank and the ADB (Asian Development Bank) suspended their Burmese operations. This was grim news for the junta. Burma's foreign debts were massive and its foreign-currency reserves, meagre at the best of times, depleted. But just as parlous was the state of the economy itself. In August and September Burma's limited manufacturing capacity had ground to a halt, as had most other economic activities.

SLORC's solution was to begin auctioning the family silver. One by one Burma's natural resources – its teak, gems, oil, significant deposits of offshore gas and hydroelectric potential – were sold off to the highest bidder. Thailand was the first to cooperate, from November 1988 onwards, but soon China and Singapore, and later India and Bangladesh, joined the jamboree. Efforts were also made to attract investment by Western, Japanese and South Korean companies.

The People's Republic of China was to be of particular significance in the junta's battle for survival. Untroubled by reports of human-rights violations, Chinese officials and entrepreneurs recognised a golden opportunity to acquire some of the raw materials needed for China's fast-track programme towards becoming an industrial super-state 'within a generation'. Providing the Burmese government with modern weaponry to fight its interminable insurgency wars was likewise good for the Chinese arms industry. But Burma's complicity with Chinese expansionism also satisfied China's political ambitions. For a thousand years and more it had regarded South-East Asia as part of its natural provenance. Since the early nineteenth century its influence there had been at best ambivalent. In Burma, Beijing's new post-Mao mandarins could hope to begin redressing the balance in China's favour.

But if China was prepared to provide Burma's military rulers with an indispensable life-raft, the fruits of that policy lay well in the future. In September 1988 there were no guarantees, and the mood of the country was still potentially volatile. General Saw Maung and his colleagues had fewer friends outside Burma even than Ne Win during his years of formal power, so other strategies were considered. These included the holding of a general election, as a means of encouraging inward investment from the world's richer countries. But SLORC was taking no chances. While it was inevitable that, given the Burmese military's past performance, few believed any elections would be free or fair, the junta took immediate and purposive steps to ensure victory for its loyalist creation, the National Unity Party.

The NUP inherited the facilities, and many of the civilian officers, of the disbanded BSPP. It was also rumoured that some of the 600 million *kyat* seized from the Foreign Investment Bank during the first week of September 1988 were placed at the NUP's disposal. But the NUP also benefited from SLORC's wall-to-wall censorship policies, and from the restitution of the *Working People's Daily* as the single permitted national newspaper. Every step was taken to hobble any opposition propaganda. Immediately after 18th September the free press that had blossomed in Burma during the people's uprising was forcibly closed down. SLORC prohibited the publication of any materials – leaflets, pamphlets, and so on – not authorised by itself.

SLORC also denied the basic right of assembly. Gatherings of five people or more were outlawed, on pain of imprisonment. In principle, this ruled out opposition rallies. But – and this was the most startling aspect of SLORC's coercive stage-managing of the electoral process – political parties (oppositional or otherwise) were deliberately encouraged. As of 27th September a law was promulgated facilitating their registration. If parties that did not register were deemed illegal, parties that did were offered significant benefits: much-prized telephone lines, up to seventy gallons of free petrol (at a time of fearsome rationing) and, in many cases, offices.

These measures were designed to create such a profusion of parties contesting the election that the electorate could only become utterly confused, with the NUP reaping full advantage. Nothing else demonstrated so acutely the contempt in which SLORC held the democratic spirit. Nor was the take-up anything less than of Klondike proportions. Within weeks a hundred new parties had registered, some of them just fronts for people who wanted telephones, petrol and offices. The final tally, reached in 1989, was 234. In the great majority of cases, registered parties were little more than clubs, with little or no electioneering capacity.

In the worst-case scenario projected by SLORC, the NUP might not win an overall majority of seats, but no other party would either, thereby giving SLORC the perfect excuse to reassert its authority.

And still no polling date was set, prompting speculation that SLORC would only allow the election to go ahead once it was convinced everything was fully under its control. But the junta had reckoned without the tenacity of Aung San Suu Kyi and those around her. By leaving the democratic door just half an inch ajar, Burma's new rulers – still guided by the manifestly eccentric General Ne Win and his immediate accomplices – had made a gross miscalculation. Far from stemming the tide of obloquy against it, in the free world at least, the junta had merely contrived to perpetuate the shame in which its reputation languished.

XXVI

SQUARING UP

A free-for-all election campaign after the present clampdown looks as likely as a happy ending to Macbeth.
British ambassador Martin Morland, in his annual dispatch to the Foreign Office, January 1989

SHE might so easily have said, 'I've given it my best shot, there's nothing more I can do in Burma. I'm going home to Oxford, to look after my children and my husband and pursue my academic interests.' Guilt would have pursued her for a while perhaps, but not for ever. The world is full of people who have stepped away, and the human psyche is adept at rationalising its activities. But Aung San Suu Kyi was made of sterner stuff. She would not renege on the promises she had made to Nyo Ohn Myint and many, many others. The fragile daughter of Bogyoke Aung San and Daw Khin Kyi had her parents' grit through and through.

Even before SLORC promulgated its Political Parties Registration Law of 27th September 1988, Suu Kyi threw herself into raising a new political party that would contest the promised election. In this important enterprise she joined forces with Aung Gyi and U Tin Oo. Between them they decided the party should be called the National League for Democracy, or NLD for short. The words were carefully chosen. They implied an umbrella organisation rather than an ideological group committed to a particular interpretation of democracy. In that way it was hoped to attract as wide a following as possible. Only then could SLORC's tactics of divide and rule be effectively challenged. As crucially, the term 'national' meant just that. The League was not to be restricted to Burmans alone. It was to be open to members of every one of Burma's numerous minorities – anyone in fact who believed that only through a functional democracy could the country's fortunes be restored.

The NLD was formally registered on 2nd October. By then its outline structure was already in place. Classically, its determining body was to be a thirty-three-strong Central Committee, from which was drawn a twelve-person Executive Committee, charged with the actual running of the party and its election campaign. Aung Gyi was appointed chairman, and U Tin Oo vice-chairman. Aung San Suu Kyi was to be the NLD's general-secretary, with other important positions filled by U Win Tin (one of three secretaries), U Lwin (treasurer), U Aung Shwe (chief campaign organiser), Daw Myint Myint Khin (assistant campaign organiser, with special responsibilities for the NLD's women's membership) and U Aung Lwin (information).

Nominees to both committees were put forward by Aung Gyi, U Tin Oo and Suu Kyi. Because Aung Gyi and Tin Oo had both been senior-ranking military men, it was no huge surprise that, in its first formation, the NLD was top-heavy with former officers who had become disillusioned with Ne Win's regime. Of the twelve members of the Executive Committee, no fewer than eight had been in the Tatmadaw, with the rank of Lieutenant-Colonel or above. If this reflected chairman Aung Gyi's input, and to a lesser extent U Tin Oo's, at the time it seemed sensible. The presence of so many disaffected army men in what immediately emerged as the dominant opposition party underlined the theme that Burma's military had become corrupted. Simultaneously it indicated that the NLD was not 'anti-army' *per se*. Moreover, their shared organisational experience could only be a benefit.

By contrast, Suu Kyi's nominees, and to a lesser extent Tin Oo's, were decidedly civilian. They included, as well as U Win Tin, Daw Myint Myint Khin and U Aung Lwin (a well-known actor and film director), such writers, journalists and lawyers as Maung Thawka, U Ko Yu, U Chan Aye, U Tun Tin and U Win Khet. In addition there was U Khin Maung Swe, a professor of geology from Rangoon University, and U Tin Myo Win, a medical doctor and Suu Kyi's personal physician.

The Central Committee and Executive Committee, however, were only the uppermost storeys of the NLD edifice. Just as critical to its success was the quick build-up of regional and local NLD offices throughout Burma. From its inception the NLD was conceived, and organised, as a mass party, modelled on mainline parties in the Western democracies, but also drawing inspiration from the AFPFL (Anti-Fascist People's Freedom League) of the mid-1940s and after.

Everything depended on efficient networking, where efficiency meant a degree of secrecy, since the constant surveillance, and increasing harassment, of known NLD members by MI and other state-security agencies militated against open recruitment. With astonishing speed, the NLD fanned out from Rangoon, establishing base offices first in Mandalay, Bassein, Prome, Moulmein and other cities, then in the towns and rural districts. NLD activists worked overtime to identify and persuade potential sympathisers to join the League and help create a local infrastructure, and to put in place effective communication channels – the life and soul of any popularist movement.

And it worked. No other party contesting the election set about its task with the same degree of dedicated professionalism – not U Nu's own League, or the former communist leader Thakin Soe's UDP (Unity and Development Party) or even the regime-backed NUP. For once, too, Burma's more senior dissidents had stolen a march on the students. The student population, habitually at the forefront of oppositional politics in Burma, squandered the opportunity to campaign legally against the government. Instead it splintered, setting up a dozen or more often rival bodies: the militant Mandalay-based Organisation of Students and Youth for National Politics, for example, and the ABFSU-inspired DPNS (Democratic Party for a New Society). These paled in comparison with what the 'Suu-Tin-Gyi' troika achieved.

A good many of those politicised students who had avoided detection by MI, and had not fled towards the Thai border, threw in their lot with the NLD, swelling the ranks of its activists. But if, in the necessarily half-lit and furtive world of electoral politics Burmese-style, the NLD prospered, it was not just because it addressed challenges of structure head-on. In Aung San Suu Kyi it had the biggest electoral asset in Burma. On paper she might rank only third in the NLD hierarchy, behind her 'uncles' Aung Gyi and Tin Oo. But as Bogyoke Aung San's daughter, and as the woman who had so convincingly stormed the hearts and minds of a great swathe of the Burmese people at the Shwedagon pagoda on 26th August, she was head and shoulders above anyone else in the national arena.

It helped that Suu Kyi herself took to her latest incarnation, as a political leader, with the utmost commitment, as well as with a distinctive personal style, quite at odds with the laid-back style of former

Brigadier-General Aung Gyi. At 54 University Avenue she settled immediately into a demanding but productive daily regimen. Always an early riser, she spent the mornings in consultation with her fellow NLD Executive Committee associates, assessing reports and determining party strategy. The evenings she kept largely for herself: for spending with Dr Aris, until immigration refused to extend his visa; for reading; and for writing. But in the afternoons she held court in her office, a tiny room at 44 University Avenue, which the League rented as its headquarters, with just enough space for a desk and three chairs.

'A fat person would have had great difficulty squeezing in,' remembered U Win Khet, charged with screening and then priming those who wished to see her. 'Most meetings lasted no more than ten or fifteen minutes, but for most this was honour enough. Most too came because they wanted to help or join the League. Daw Suu Kyi had the gift of giving someone her undivided attention, identifying their core concerns, and then satisfying them with her answers. She sensed what it was her visitors wanted her to say, and then she said it, but never in such a way as to compromise her principles.'

To do this day after day demanded remarkable powers of concentration. In her one-on-one meetings she took her own notes, and quickly learned how to tell her visitors that she had other people to see, without giving offence. But Suu Kyi could be mischievous as well. Win Khet knew for a fact that one of her callers, dressed as a monk, was a captain in the Tatmadaw. 'Then I certainly want to see him!' she insisted. As it transpired, the man had come to University Avenue not to spy on her, but because he too, like countless others, craved personal contact.

Suu Kyi developed an ability to relate quickly and compellingly to virtually everyone. Although she lost none of her poise, she did lose some of the reserve that had previously characterised her manner in front of strangers and half-knowns. Not since she was an adolescent had she been exposed to anything like such a cross-section of Burmese, or in such numbers; but, as those around her have attested, she seemed to thrive on the experience.

Yet she knew that making herself available to her compatriots in Rangoon was only half the battle. If the NLD was to flourish, and democracy stand a chance, then she needed to get out amongst the people, to take to the campaign trail. At the end of October 1988, together with the popular U Tin Oo and other trusted colleagues, Suu

General Ne Win, who seized power in 1961 to become one of the world's most brutal dictators

June Rose Bellamy, also known as Yadana Natmai, photographed in Maymyo in 1952. In 1977 she became Ne Win's fifth or sixth wife, but the marriage lasted only a few months. It ended when the dictator hurled an ashtray at her

Nita Yin Yin May, who worked at the British embassy and relayed information about Suu Kyi and the National League for Democracy (NLD) to the BBC. She was subsequently imprisoned, but eventually became a producer for the BBC World Service in London

Martin Morland, British Ambassador to Burma during the upheavals of 1988

Aung San Suu Kyi flanked by the veteran politician and former Burmese prime minister U Nu (*left*) and her fellow NLD leader U Tin Oo (*right*) during a meeting in Rangoon, October 1988

U Win Khet, a founder member of the NLD and its first Executive Committee, here photographed by the author in self-imposed exile in Thailand, 2005

Nyo Ohn Myint, the Rangoon University history teacher who became one of Aung San Suu Kyi's earliest followers

Tin Hlaing (aka Eva), one of Aung San Suu Kyi's dedicated bodyguards. She became 'a second mother' to him

Win Thein, who courageously walked in front of Aung San Suu Kyi at the Dabubyu showdown in April 1989

Ko Aung, Aung San Suu Kyi's all-purpose helper who assumed responsibility for organising her personal security

The Nobel Peace Prize, awarded to Aung San Suu Kyi in December 1991

56 University Avenue
Rangoon
16 May 1992

At times during the last couple of years when I seemed surrounded by ill-will and unreasonableness the thought of friends and well-wishers did much to sustain me. Memories of shared warmth and laughter, the rare occasions when I heard familiar voices on the radio and the belief that even at the worst of times there is still much kindness and love and goodwill filled my days with joy and hope. What I have learnt from Michael about the enormous generosity with which friends as well as strangers have rallied around has confirmed my faith in the nicer side of human nature. Whatever the future may bring this faith will continue to be my support and stay.

Thank you so very much for all that you have done – that you continue to do – for the cause of justice and peace in Burma and for my family.

Aung San Suu Kyi

A round robin letter written by Aung San Suu Kyi in May 1992 and sent to those outside Burma who had supported her cause from the time she was placed under house arrest

Following her release from the first period of house arrest, in October 1995 Aung San Suu Kyi drove to Pa'an in Karen State, to pay respect to the *Hsayadaw* U Vinaya, one of Burma's most venerated monks

How *Time* magazine depicted Aung San Suu Kyi's release from house arrest, a year later in June 1996

"There, we've set you free as promised!"

Suu Kyi with her two sons, Alexander and Kim, on one of the rare occasions they were permitted to visit her in Rangoon after 1990

Daw San San, whose seat was the first to be declared in the 1990 election, fifteen years later in Thailand. Like many other NLD candidates she was later incarcerated in Rangoon's notorious Insein prison

Dr Michael Aris in Oxford, not long before he was diagnosed with prostate cancer

The widowed Aung San Suu Kyi campaigns in Ch' state, northern Burma, in April 2003, barely a mon' before the Depayin massacre

Poster distributed by the ABSDF (All Burma Students Democratic Front)

Generals Than Shwe, Maung Aye and Khin Nyunt as depicted on the cover of *The Irrawaddy*, immediately after Khin Nyunt's fall from grace in October 2004

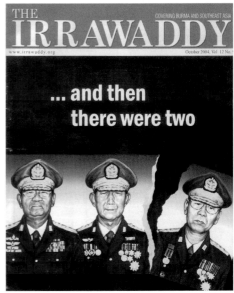

Saturday
Edition

(Republic of Ireland, €1.80) £1.20

Saturday 18
June 2005
www.independent.co.uk
NUMBER 5,825

THE INDEPENDENT

By Peter Popham

The Lady at 60

Already the photographs have that deathly historical look of events long ago and far away, of campaigns and triumphs that belong to another era. The pictures of Burma's general election of 1990, the only time in the past 45 years that the Burmese people have been given the opportunity to vote, were reproduced in the May issue of the Burmese opposition magazine *Irrawaddy*, published in Bangkok. They are unbearably sad.

In *longyi* and white shirts, hair slick with oil, Burmese people young and old crowd around the ballot boxes in the polling stations. A young member of Aung San Suu Kyi's party, the National League for Democracy (NLD), flowers in her hair, smiles proudly before a romantic poster of Suu Kyi, garlanded and beaming, striding into the radiant future with the Burmese flag. In another picture Suu Kyi herself, petite, elegant and composed, marches towards another podium, shadowed by soldiers with automatic rifles.

Aung San Suu Kyi, still a young woman in those grainy election photos, turns 60 tomorrow. And if, as seems very likely, the day passes like all the other days since she was rearrested in May 2003, there will be no party. Suu Kyi has been held in almost complete isolation for more than two years now, first in Rangoon's notorious Insein Prison, then in the dilapidation of her family's lakeside home in the capital's suburbs.

As campaigners protested yesterday outside 50 Burmese embassies around the world, including the one in London, the Foreign Secretary, Jack Straw, added his voice to those condemning Suu Kyi's incarceration, calling her treatment "indefensible". The only visitor she is allowed is the family doctor, once a fortnight. The junta's guards enforce a total ban on visitors. A couple of women help with the cooking and the cleaning. And that is it. No foreign diplomats
CONTINUED ON PAGE 2

Still imprisoned. Still fighting for democracy. Why the story of Aung San Suu Kyi should haunt the conscience of the world

Aung San Suu Kyi celebrated her sixtieth birthday alone, but *The Independent* was one of many newspapers to mark the occasion on its front page

Detail of the royal palace at Mandalay, recreated at huge cost by Burma's military regime to attract tourists and keep alive its dream of retaining undiluted power

Dr Zarni, one time co-founder of the U.S.-based Free Burma Coalition, now a critic of Aung San Suu Kyi and the NLD: a sympton as much as an agent of disarray within the Burmese democracy movement

Kyi made her first upcountry tour, stopping at Mandalay, then visiting Sagaing, Magwe and Pegu Divisions. She addressed rallies in fifty different townships in thirteen days, repeating much of what she had said at the Shwedagon, but – since she was throwing herself into the Burman heartlands – taking care to emphasise what she conceived to be an essential continuity between democracy and Buddhism.

This required no little courage, since the right of assembly was denied by SLORC on pain of imprisonment. Nonetheless, Daw Aung San Suu Kyi's appearances were invariably greeted by thousands, and sometimes tens of thousands. Units of the Tatmadaw attended the rallies as well, to observe proceedings, but for the time being refrained from interfering.

Another potential difficulty was giving advance notice of the rallies, so that people would know where and when to gather. SLORC controlled the Burmese media, and leaflets and fly-posting were prohibited. But the League's nascent infrastructure proved its value, as did the BBC's Burma Service.

A key (though clandestine) player was Nita Yin Yin May, information officer at the British embassy in Rangoon since 1986. A Muslim Burman whose father had worked for the US embassy, Nita May had enrolled at Rangoon University in the mid-1960s, at a time when Mao Zedong's *Little Red Book* was all the rage among politicised students. She then spent the best part of twenty years working as a journalist. Her ambition had always been to work for the BBC World Service, which amongst non-regime Burmese was held as the touchstone of objective reporting.

Nita's position at the embassy enabled her to pass on information to the BBC in a safe and secure way. She established a close relationship with Ma Thanegi, Suu Kyi's personal assistant at 54 University Avenue, who provided Nita with details of Suu Kyi's campaign itinerary, as well as upcountry telephone numbers where she could be contacted for radio interviews. As a result, BBC Burma Service's daily broadcasts, listened to by almost everyone who had a wireless, kept the nation informed in a way that Burmese radio, television and the *Working People's Daily* did not.

This may not have been entirely within the remit of permissible diplomatic activity, but Ambassador Morland, who had an intense admiration for Suu Kyi, turned a blind eye. Later, when Nita was hauled in for harrowing three-day interrogation sessions by MI, to be quizzed not only about her relations with the BBC and NLD but also about the sexual proclivities of other embassy staff, Morland vigorously and effectively protested her innocence. Eventually however, once the ambassador's posting terminated, Nita May was imprisoned at Insein and tortured.

Against the odds, the Mandalay tour was a resounding success. It demonstrated that, despite the September crackdown, large numbers of Burmese were still prepared to brave the prohibition against assembly, enshrined in the infamous Order 2/88. Large crowds turned out for what they believed in and wanted, and this confirmed Suu Kyi's ascendancy. Outside Mandalay, many wore the *kamauk*, a traditional broad-rimmed peasant farmer's hat, good for keeping off the sun. The same hat was also good for obscuring the face from the eyes of prying intelligence types. It became a symbol of the NLD.

The NLD bandwagon was firmly on the road. Another campaign tour was quickly organised, to Moulmein and townships in Mon and Karen (Kayah) states. For the first time, Suu Kyi found herself addressing large gatherings of Burma's minority peoples. Always impeccably turned out, with a flower or two in her elegantly groomed hair, she reached out to her new audiences by wearing appropriate 'ethnic' dress. If she did not disguise her antipathy towards secession in any shape or form, she urged her listeners to embrace democracy and the defence of basic human rights as the only way to validate the Burmese 'Union'.

Back in Rangoon, Suu Kyi worked on a third front: whipping up international concern and support. As early as 24th September she wrote to Amnesty International, the world's best-known voluntary human-rights vigilante body, outlining the atrocities perpetrated by SLORC just a few days before. On 16th October she wrote to Amnesty again, detailing the detention of 'over six hundred men, mostly young students . . . seized by the armed forces as they sat in teashops and eating stalls in Rangoon'. Most, she went on, had been 'taken to the front lines where the Burmese army is engaged in actions against insurgents' as involuntary porters, even human landmine detectors.

Other letters were written by her to the International Commission of Jurists, and to Rangoon's resident foreign ambassadors, urging their governments to table a motion of censure against Burma's rulers at a General Debate of the United Nations General Assembly. Partly as a result of her representations, 'Burma' became a fixture on the international human-rights circuit in a way it had not been hitherto.

Burma's democracy movement, so cruelly crushed by the bullets of a wanton intolerance on 18th September 1988, was being rebirthed even in its death-throes, again in no small measure thanks to Aung San Suu Kyi – with her beauty and her pedigree, a natural draw for the world's free media. Yet as ever black clouds were massing on the horizon, two of them ready to break. The fledgling NLD was about to be spun into internecine confusion; and Daw Khin Kyi's life was drawing to a close.

From the beginning Suu Kyi's opponents in the military and the state-run media attempted to undermine her by insinuating that she was being used by the unscrupulous to further their own ends, despite clear disavowals made by Suu Kyi herself. Even in her Shwedagon speech, referring to 'some veteran politicians', she had seen fit to declare her unwillingness to accept the support of anyone whose 'object is to obtain positions of power for themselves'. In a report published by *The Times* on 21st September 1988, she expanded on this theme. 'There has been speculation that politicians might be influencing my actions,' she said. 'Those who wish to discredit me have implied that I am surrounded by communists.' Whilst it was true that 'veteran politicians of varying political colour are giving me practical assistance', she was only prepared to accept their help 'on the understanding that they are working for the democratic cause without expectation of political advantage or personal gain'.

Persistent insinuations by intelligence chief Khin Nyunt, by elements of the military and by the state-run media that Suu Kyi was being manipulated by communists were predictable and routine. Burma's successive military governments usually did respond to opposition like that, when they were not pointing a finger in the other direction, at the USA and its 'imperialist' allies. Playing the communist card ensured the loyalty and motivation of the Tatmadaw, and cost little or nothing – the more so now, since China was withdrawing whatever remained of its support for the CPB and other insurgents. But in late November and early December, the poison spread to within the NLD itself.

Leading the charge was party chairman Aung Gyi, the former Brigadier-General who had once been Ne Win's right-hand man. The NLD, he began putting it about, had been infiltrated by communists and was at risk of being taken over by them, if it hadn't already been. A purge was needed. Aung Gyi identified eight members of the Central Committee whom, for one reason or another, he deemed suspect. He also alleged that Thakin Tin Mya, formerly a senior figure in the CPB, had become Suu Kyi's principal adviser, even though Tin Mya had been taken into custody by SLORC immediately following the September coup.

Aung Gyi's allegations were not entirely groundless. Many of those who belonged to Burma's oppositional intelligentsia had at some time in their lives toyed with Marxism and Maoism, usually as students in the 1960s and 1970s, and it was from the oppositional intelligentsia that Suu Kyi drew much of her most active support. Among those on the Central Committee, for example, U Win Tin and Daw Myint Myint Khin had both belonged to a Marxist study group in the 1950s, and had been imprisoned after Ne Win's 1962 coup. But the real point was that those fingered as communists by Aung Gyi were, if they were Marxists at all, disillusioned Marxists. They knew enough about what had happened in the Soviet Union and China to know that communism was not the answer, particularly for a country like Burma, with its ethnic and cultural complexities and a deep-seated adherence to the Buddhist faith among a majority of its population.

The picture was complicated by the brief re-emergence into public life of Aung San's older brother and Suu Kyi's uncle, U Aung Than, a one-time leader of the post-war left-leaning Burma Workers' and Farmers' Party. U Aung Than, regarded by the regime as a communist (as indeed Bogyoke Aung San himself had once been), had nothing to do with the NLD, but that did not stop Suu Kyi's detractors from intimating a powerful family connection that was leading her astray.

What distressed Suu Kyi and those closest to her was how Aung Gyi's accusations were minutely echoed by SLORC, and by Brigadier Khin Nyunt especially. Suu Kyi had not greatly warmed to Aung Gyi. She had, however, been impressed by his 'public' letters addressed to Ne Win circulated in the summer of 1988, and had taken on trust his declared commitment to the democracy movement. He had made himself the regime's best-known defector, after U Tin Oo. His chairmanship of the NLD added gravitas to the party's cause. But now it became horribly obvious that Aung Gyi was playing a double-game, though the nature of that double-game was unclear. Either he was positioning for himself, hoping that a party purge would elevate him as a national leader; or – more sinisterly – he was undermining the League on behalf of SLORC.

It was known that Aung Gyi continued on friendly terms with several members of the State Law and Order Restoration Council. Sometimes he would compromise himself by making such utterances as, apropos Sanda Win, 'She is like a daughter to me.' But rather than waste time getting to the bottom of Aung Gyi's opaque machinations, Suu Kyi and U Tin Oo decided to force the issue by challenging his allegations. What were his grounds? Did he have any? The showdown came at a stormy emergency meeting of the NLD's Central Committee on 3rd December. Both sides had their heated say, then the matter was put to a vote. Aung Gyi lost, and had no option but to step down as NLD chairman and withdraw his party membership. Others who were his nominees on the Central and Executive Committees followed him to the door.

Aung Gyi had indeed instigated a purge, but against his expectations (and, probably, the longings of SLORC) he became its victim. Crucially U Tin Oo, who now took on the role of party chairman, backed Suu Kyi and the intellectuals. In the long run, Aung Gyi's ousting strengthened the League, if only because his standing among the people had never been that high, despite his criticisms of Ne Win. In the eyes of many he was damaged goods, an opportunist bent on resurrecting his own career. But, among Rangoon's political elite at least, the episode also begged a serious question about Suu Kyi herself. Had she not been naïve to embrace Aung Gyi in the first place?

Privately, Suu Kyi conceded that she had made a mistake. 'I went wrong,' she confided to U Win Khet, 'but not without a reason. I held a personal grudge against Aung Gyi, but when I started to work for my country I decided to set personal grudges aside.' She would know better next time. On the incalculably steep learning curve she was embarked upon, some misfootings were inevitable.

Suu Kyi's mother died at her home in University Avenue on 27th December 1988, barely three weeks after the rupture inside the NLD. However much this was an event foretold, for Daw Khin Kyi's daughter the loss of the only parent she had known could only induce an immeasurable sadness. They had not always seen eye-to-eye (Suu Kyi's marriage to Dr Aris being a case in point), but whatever differences they had had were long since resolved. The customary strength of the mother–daughter relationship had, in the closing straits of Daw Khin Kyi's life, become a thing of steel. To the end, Daw Khin Kyi retained the better part of her lucidity, and almost certainly went to her grave knowing that her husband's legacy was in safe hands.

One beneficial consequence of her death was that the authorities agreed to allow Dr Aris and his two sons back into Burma on short-stay visas – probably on the mistaken premise that, reunited with her kith and kin, Suu Kyi might see sense, pack her bags and join them on the flight back to England. The family had narrowly missed spending Christmas together; but they could see in the 'Western' New Year together. That Suu Kyi was now committed to remaining in Burma until the promised elections was something that Dr Aris, Alexander and Kim already knew. But it helped that they could see the lie of the land, and gauge Suu Kyi's determination, directly for themselves.

Also allowed back into Burma temporarily was Suu Kyi's surviving brother. Aung San Oo was now an American citizen, and as a rule the regime refused entry visas to émigrés who had surrendered their Burmese nationality. But as the Bogyoke's son, Aung San Oo was granted an exemption, perhaps because SLORC hoped his presence would act as a counterfoil to Suu Kyi. Many knew that brother and sister did not get on. In an excessively male-dominant culture, the aberrant daughter might be cut down to size. But it did not pan out like that. During the lead-up to Daw Khin Kyi's funeral, Suu Kyi and Aung San Oo had of necessity to meet. Relations between them were as frosty as ever. Neither had genuine time for each other's company, despite the shared bereavement. For Aung San Oo, his sister had unforgivably upstaged him on the national stage. For Suu Kyi, her brother had singularly failed to grasp the parental nettle.

The funeral took place on 2nd January 1989. For once there was an agreed stand-off with the regime. In the words of Dr Aris, 'The negotiations and arrangements for the funeral of the widow of the national hero were carried out in exemplary fashion.'

Even so, the marking of Daw Khin Kyi's demise turned into an overwhelming confirmation of Suu Kyi's and the NLD's popularity, for all that Suu Kyi herself urged that politics for once be put aside. Within hours of Daw Khin Kyi's death, thousands gathered outside the gates of 54 University Avenue and stayed there for the duration.

On 1st January, the day before the funeral, a military motorcade descended on Daw Khin Kyi's residence. Ostensibly, SLORC chairman General Saw Maung and first secretary Brigadier-General Khin Nyunt, accompanied by the Minister for Home and Religious Affairs Major-General Phone Myint, had come to sign a book of condolences. In reality they wanted to parley with Suu Kyi. She offered them tea, but what, if anything, transpired during that meeting remains occluded.

Suu Kyi had appealed for 'calm and discipline in sending my mother on her last journey'. The last thing she wanted was for Daw Khin Kyi's funeral to become yet another instance of state-abetted violence. And so it came about. Unusually for a Buddhist, Daw Khin Kyi was to be buried, not cremated – in Burman values, the equivalent of a state funeral. Moreover, she was to be entombed close to the Shwedagon and close to her husband. The four-mile route of the funeral cortège from University Avenue was lined with tens of thousands of wet-eyed well-wishers. For the first time since 18th September Rangoon's citizenry felt safe to turn out in numbers. If SLORC moved against them, it would move against itself, since anything associated with Aung San was holy grail. But among the mourners were hundreds and hundreds of democracy enthusiasts, waving the newfangled NLD flag, of the fighting peacock and the single Star of Burma set on a red ground.

After a short ceremony at the Shwedagon, which General Saw Maung and his SLORC colleagues did not attend, perhaps for fear the crowds would turn upon them, Daw Khin Kyi's body was interred without any untoward incident. Rumours that her corpse would be hijacked by radical students, in the same way U Thant's corpse had once been seized, proved unfounded. A day of potential confrontation had indeed unfolded with 'calm and discipline', helped by a brief appearance of the wanted student leader Min Ko Naing, who, like Suu Kyi, urged everyone to conduct themselves in an exemplary fashion.

And it was that which disturbed the junta most. Rangoon's back streets had been packed with army, police and other security detachments. But no pretext for their intervention presented itself. Instead, the essential ambiguity of Daw Khin Kyi's funeral procession was gifted to the democratic opposition by the people's restraint. The passing of the Bogyoke's widow had turned not just into an expression of their grief, but into a near-balletic expression of their deepest longings. That being so, Aung San Suu Kyi and the NLD had best be dealt with before any election.

XXVII

SUU KYI'S TIGHTROPE

The people adore her. Everywhere she goes, they bedeck her with flowers – roses, jasmine, chrysanthemums.
        Terry McCarthy, reporting in *The Independent*, 2nd May 1989

ALTHOUGH it had yet to announce a date for the election, in February 1989 SLORC issued 'an election law' setting out some at least of the ground rules. Serving members of the armed services were barred from offering themselves as candidates, just as they were barred from joining the regime-backed NUP. Also disqualified were candidates with any connections to 'foreign powers'. Contending parties were prohibited from receiving campaign funds from overseas or having any contact with Burma's various insurgency movements. Only those with full Burmese citizenship were entitled to register as voters. This disenfranchised thousands of ethnic Indian and Chinese, who, though they could legitimately claim to be second- or third-generation settlers, still had only residential status. Candidates had to be aged at least twenty-one, while the minimum voting age was set at eighteen.

These parameters, though they significantly narrowed the size of the electorate, were not overly draconian. But what SLORC singularly failed to clarify, which as the country's *de facto* authority it had a duty to do, was the nature of the elections themselves. It was assumed by all the opposition parties that whoever won the elections would be empowered to form at least a caretaker government while a new constitution was hammered out. But nowhere was this made explicit. Later, SLORC would take the line that the elections were only to a constituent assembly, to draft the new constitution, and were not intended to determine the composition of any government. At the outset, however, there was no breath of this; nor did SLORC endeavour to disburden the contending parties and the electorate of any misapprehensions that arose out of its anomalous and irresponsible reticence.

It might also have been supposed that, with the electoral agenda now apparently set, martial law (reimposed by SLORC on 18th September 1988) would be lifted. But it remained in place. Although the curfew in Burma's towns and cities was slightly relaxed, to between 10 p.m. and 4 a.m., during those hours it was rigorously enforced. Order 88/2 prohibiting assembly was not revoked. Political parties were reminded that they could produce some campaign literature, provided it was first cleared with the authorities, but there were punitive restrictions on what such literature might contain. No implied criticism of SLORC or of the armed forces was to be tolerated.

More disturbingly, in July 1989 SLORC introduced a new system of summary justice that abolished such judicial procedures as had survived the 1962 coup. Burma's criminal courts were replaced by military tribunals presided over by army, air-force and navy officers. Defendants might or might not be allowed legal representation, or to call their own witnesses. These matters were at the discretion of the military tribunal itself. In a majority of cases such basic rights were withheld. Even when they were allowed, they made no difference to a tribunal's foregone outcome. In the majority of cases, too, hearings were short and perfunctory. Little or no distinction was made between charges read out and evidence against the accused. Members of the tribunals themselves often acted as prosecutors, and acquittals – particularly where political charges had been preferred – were virtually unheard of. It was simply assumed that anybody appearing before a military tribunal was guilty. Sentences were stiff, and only the death penalty had to be referred to a regional commander for validation – though surprisingly, the death penalty was seldom applied, at least formally.

Hearings generally followed a period of interrogation that might last days or weeks. The thrust of such interrogations, usually carried out by Khin Nyunt's Military Intelligence, had as much to do with identifying other miscreants as investigating the activities of the individual concerned. The use of torture also escalated. Torture had been a feature of the pre-coup BSPP regime, but now became endemic within Burma's justice system, and assumed many forms. Beatings, food and sleep deprivation, and sometimes drinking-water deprivation, were standard practice. When not being interrogated, detainees were locked up in tiny concrete cells without any bedding and subjected to a barrage of noise, including the cries of other nearby detainees, and to strong electric light around the clock. Their shins were repeatedly hit with iron bars until they bled and the bone showed throug' Detainees were regularly given electric-shock treatment, burned with cigarettes, suspended upside down from a ceiling hook for hours on end or forced to adopt contortionist positions (the 'aeroplane', the 'frog', the 'bicycle') for similar lengths of time. Other forms of gross abuse, some remembered from the period of Japanese occupation, included various types of water torture: prolonged duckings; the constantly wetted towel over the face, making it difficult to breathe; being forced to drink gallons of the stuff; and so forth. Female prisoners faced being raped, while male prisoners might have their genitals mutilated.

Interrogation and torture were used as a deterrent, and to extract confessions and pledges of good behaviour. Individuals were often seized and subjected to Military Intelligence's unholy ordeals, then released without charge. The idea was to cower them into obedience and the avoidance of any further political activity. While some courageously resisted every attempt to make them talk, for others even the initial shock of arrest might be enough to induce submission. What was paramount was to hold out for twenty-four hours if you could, to give your associates time to evade capture. But for as long as they were temporarily detained, no effort was made to inform their relatives of their whereabouts. Families became frantic wondering what had happened to their loved ones – the more so since some of those seized simply disappeared.

At first, in the months following the September 1988 coup, it was mainly students who bore the brunt of SLORC's malevolence. But from the beginning of 1989 SLORC and Military Intelligence directed at least some of their attention towards older activists, nearly always on trumped-up charges, until by the summer monsoons no one opposed to the regime could feel safe.

These were tough conditions for electioneering by any standard. Few diplomats believed there was any likelihood of a 'free and fair' contest. Having called the election, it seemed that SLORC's main aim was to make a mockery of it. Yet the calling and holding of what, if you closed both eyes very tightly, might just pass muster as an election was integral to SLORC's wider programme. By September 1988 Burma's economy was in such dire straits that even Ne Win, Saw Maung and Khin Nyunt recognised that recovery would be impossible without some assistance from the West. Therefore they had to pay democracy lip-service at least. For without assistance, the military's grip on power was tenuous in the extreme. A hungry people was a people ready to explode again at any moment.

SLORC remained committed to economic liberalisation, in however piecemeal and inequitable a fashion. By 1989, as even those within the military elite had become all too painfully aware, the wealth gap between Burma and the other principal states of South-East Asia – Thailand, Malaysia, Singapore, Indonesia, the Philippines, even Vietnam – had become too wide to ignore. Added to which, it was becoming apparent that the economic reforms instituted by Deng Xiaoping in China were beginning to bite. 'To get rich is glorious,' the veteran Chinese communist and (intermittently) right-hand man of Mao Zedong had declared. Chinese entrepreneurs were taking him at his word, transforming the 'Middle Kingdom' in the process. Not that Burma's militocracy wanted a general enrichment of the Burmese people. It did not: such a prospect was scary. National prosperity could all too easily mean heightened expectations of accountability and democracy. But what Burma's military did want was a more generous portion for itself, even if that meant giving limited encouragement to the country's modest entrepreneurial class. And it wanted the wherewithal to perpetuate what had always been the Tatmadaw's heartfelt raison d'être: its championing of 'national unity' in the face of the wayward antics of communist and minority insurgencies.

If SLORC's accession to power had been accompanied by an affirmation of the 'nationwide' election promised by Dr Maung Maung, the junta made no discernible attempt to take this message into Burma's troubled ethnic states. It did not see democratisation – expressed in, say, a genuine union of semi-autonomous federated states – as the way forward. Instead it set its sights on beefing up Burma's armed forces to such a degree that Karen, Karenni, Kachin and other 'rebel' forces would be pulverised into abject submission.

That SLORC's mindset was intransigently 'Burman' was made crystal-clear in June 1989 when, by simple authoritarian fiat, it changed the country's name from Burma to Myanmar, or more properly *Myanmar Naing Ngan-daw* – the 'Union of Myanmar'. At the same time SLORC effected a sweeping 'Burmanisation' of place-name changes. Rangoon reverted to Yangon, Pegu became Bago, Pagan Bagan, Moulmein Mawlamyine, Maymyo Pyin-Oo-Lwin, Bassein Pathein, the Irrawaddy the Ayerwaddy, and so on. Simultaneously many street and market names were changed.

SLORC justified this lexicographical intervention as a cleansing of the country's colonial (that is, British) cartographical heritage. Ironically 'Myanmar', derived from a medieval formulation that reflected Burman hegemonism, was no more (but no less) 'Burman' than Burma (*bama*) itself. But that was not the issue. The Burmese people had grown used to calling the country Burma, and thinking of themselves as Burmese (not Myanmar) people. Amongst the minorities particularly, this latest expression of centralist puissance rankled deeply. More widely, outside as well as inside Burma/Myanmar, it became a point of honour to persist in calling Burma Burma, and Rangoon Rangoon, among those opposed to the nation's unelected rulers, at least when English was the chosen medium.

By June 1989 SLORC had reason to feel more confident, more bullish. The most persistent and dangerous of the state's 'enemies' – the communists – had been seen off. Since independence the CPB had been the biggest thorn in the government's side, tying up disproportionate numbers of its troops. Committed to armed resistance, initially the CPB operated, seemingly at random, in a number of locations: in the Pegu hills and the 'central dry region' as well as in Shan state. Latterly the communists had been restricted to Shanland, but there they had made themselves strong. Up until around 1980 the CPB had enjoyed the unequivocal support of communist China – money, weapons and training. But although, under Deng Xiaoping, China began turning off the tap, Burma's communists were not left high and dry. As an alternative source of income they turned to opium. By 1988 they controlled an estimated 80 per cent of Burma's poppy fields, producing perhaps 1,500 tons of opium per year, ready for smuggling to the Thai borderlands to be refined as heroin by narco-military and business groups. The communists, using both military and business contacts accrued over the years, also controlled much of an illicit cross-border trade in jade, gems and timber in exchange for Chinese manufactured goods to be passed down the line to Mandalay. Yet to maintain its new profile, and defend itself from such warlords as Khun Sa, the essentially Burman CPB had turned to mercenaries drawn from north-eastern Burma's minorities.

The most useful of these were the Wa, a tough hill people who were prepared to fight for the CPB. But in March 1989, sensing that there was a richer prize to be had, the Wa and other 'tribal cadres' mutinied. Eventually the UWSA (United Wa State Army) was formed – ostensibly to protect Wa interests and pressure Rangoon for a separate Wa state within the Union, but really as a means of wresting a significant slice of the narcotics trade for Wa leaders. Simultaneously, Chinese agents promised the Burmese communist leaders a safe haven in the Chinese province of Yunnan if they abandoned their 'struggle'. At the end of 1988 Burma and China had agreed to legalise cross-border trade. To Beijing's irritation, the Burmese communists had also begun trafficking opium into China. The inevitable result was that an insurgency movement that had lasted the best part of forty years collapsed, not least because many younger Burman radicals, uneasy with the CPB's habit of carrying out vicious internal purges, now looked to the democracy movement and the NLD as the preferred option.

The demise of the CPB, and with it the end of any serious communist movement inside Burma, was (mendaciously) hailed as a triumph for the Tatmadaw by the junta. Even so, it brought SLORC signal benefits. Through a series of deals with the UWSA and some other local war-bands, it could reduce troop levels in Shan state and increase the number of units fighting the Kachins, Karens, Karennis and other ethnic insurgents. And the same understandings gave the regime an increased share in the opium industry.

Even more than before, opium became the oil of the Burmese officer class. Opium profits, kickbacks and a burgeoning trade along the Sino-Burman border were important elements in Burma's partial economic recovery post-September 1988. But they were not the only elements. As early as 12th December 1988 Thailand signalled its willingness to normalise relations with Burma by sending its own army chief, General Chavalit Yongchaiyat, on a goodwill mission to Rangoon. Accompanied by a planeload of henchmen, Chavalit was met (and embraced) amid great pomp and ceremony at Mingaladon airport by General Saw Maung. Trade deals were struck, giving Thai commercial enterprises (in which the Thai military usually had an interest) significant access to Burmese fisheries, timber and gems. In return the regime netted in excess of $100 million.

The Thai-Burmese agreements furnished a model for future deals with other of Burma's neighbours and near-neighbours. But there was another outcome to this secretive accord. Thailand began forcibly repatriating some of the dissident students who had fled across the border following SLORC's seizure of power. The Burmese air force, too, was soon spotted enjoying Thai air space during reconnaissance missions against Karen and Karenni targets.

During the people's uprising some of the insurgent armies – notably the Karens, Kachins and Karennis – had taken advantage of the Tatmadaw's preoccupation with quelling unrest in Burman cities by expanding their operations. The Karens would have made more ground had they not been distracted by hostilities with a Mon insurgency force to the south. But once SLORC was up and running, it determined to hit the ethnic rebels hard. At the beginning of 1989 several strongholds belonging to the KNU (Karen National Union) were wiped out. Only the KIA (Kachin Independence Army) managed to withstand ferocious assaults.

This was a foretaste of things to come. Burma's armed forces, estimated at between 150,000 and 175,000 in 1988, would grow to exceed 400,000. A hopelessly outdated and minuscule navy, and an almost equally dilapidated air force, would be enlarged and modernised, as SLORC's procurement officers went about obtaining up-to-date weaponry and other military technology (including electronic surveillance systems) from (amongst other sources) China, Singapore, Israel, Russia and Pakistan.

As the tarantula state revived, Suu Kyi's indignation grew. Just as the idea of sex before marriage had sent a shiver through her moral being when she was a first-year student at Oxford, so now the junta's want of any discernible principle dismayed her to the quick. Yet dismay was a negative attitude, never to be given way to. Its only use was to inspire positive action, and greater effort.

With Daw Khin Kyi laid to rest, Dr Aris and the boys soon afterwards left Rangoon. Suu Kyi's turn came next. Ten days into the Western New Year she set off on another campaign tour, to Irrawaddy District, the sprawling, populous delta province to the west of the capital. It was essential, during the four or five months remaining of the dry season, that she visit as much of the country as possible – to restore a sense of hope to a recently demoralised people, and to propagate the NLD as widely as she could. When the summer monsoons arrived, many villages and even some towns would be all but unreachable.

Campaigning in Irrawaddy District was especially gruelling. The roads were bad and some destinations necessitated travel by small fishing boats, and sometimes bullock carts. But now there was an added hazard. Although local police generally continued to turn a blind eye to the NLD's flouting of Order 88/2, Suu Kyi and her entourage were regularly harassed by SLORC's security services. Soldiers might not break up NLD rallies, but their guns were increasingly cocked as they stood by to watch and observe. Local residents were ordered not to attend. During Suu Kyi's speeches loud music blared from army trucks parked nearby, to drown out her words.

It got worse. Soon residents were ordered not to lean out of their windows or wave flags when Suu Kyi passed by. Stray warning shots were fired. But still the crowds turned out, and in large numbers. No one wanted to miss out on seeing the Bogyoke's daughter in the flesh, or, if they were very lucky, getting close enough to touch her clothes or arms.

Before the month was out, the arrests began. On 21st January 1989 Suu Kyi, by then back in Rangoon, had occasion to write to her husband about a visit to Bassein. 'Here I am, having a battle royal with the notorious Brigadier Myint Aung,' her letter began. The brigadier had called out his men in numbers almost equal to Suu Kyi's well-wishers. Her boat, returning to the town after an outreach visit to nearby villages, was accompanied by other boats laden with soldiers. Bassein harbour, when she reached it, 'was full of troops, most of the streets blocked, sandbagged and barbedwired'.

Overnight Suu Kyi and those members of her entourage still at liberty slept in a 'very comfortable bungalow'. In the morning, however, she learned that a number of NLD supporters had been taken into custody. This prompted Suu Kyi to register a complaint with SLORC's local representative. She would not leave Bassein, she said, 'until I am satisfied there is fair play'. Further, the motor cars that had brought her to Bassein were prevented from taking to the streets. Undeterred, Suu Kyi walked to her next meeting. A captain hurried after her. Before he could speak, she asked whether she was under arrest. When the officer told her she was not, she walked over to 'a couple of sheepish-looking soldiers with guns at the ready' and began talking to them in a friendly manner. As she intended, this produced a sort of pandemonium. Within minutes, the cars were allowed to drive out.

'Myint Aung will get a good run for his money,' she concluded her

letter to Dr Aris. By their bullying tactics, SLORC, the Tatmadaw and
MI were turning the NLD campaign into a major civil-rights movement.
Soon enough, newspapers outside Burma were comparing Suu Kyi to
Mahatma Gandhi and Martin Luther King – two icons whom Suu Kyi
herself increasingly evoked in her speeches.

But the authorities gave Suu Kyi a good run for her money too.
Henceforward the harassment never ceased, and more and more NLD
members and supporters were detained – usually just for a few days,
but long enough for SLORC and its agents to remind everyone where
the real power in Burma lay.

In the early months of 1989 there was another problem confronting the
NLD and Suu Kyi. It was decided to launch an NLD 'Youth Wing', to
give students and other young pro-democracy activists an identity within
the League, even though many of them would be too young to vote in
May 1990. But contact with any student body was fraught with danger.
Some student leaders continued to press for an 'interim government' to
be established immediately, ahead of the elections. Others were
sympathetic to the border-bound ABSDF (All Burma Student Democratic
Front), which urged armed resistance and was closely affiliated with the
Karen National Union, the Karenni National Progressive Party and
other ethnic rebel groups.

This put Suu Kyi on a tightrope. For as long as NLD policy was to
work as best it could within the electoral agenda set by the junta, neither
she nor her colleagues could risk being seen to have any association
with those deemed enemies of the state. Yet to alienate student opinion
risked losing thousands of young activists who, at the grass-roots level,
were doing as much as anyone to build up the League's strength. But
it was not just a matter of political tactics. Suu Kyi felt indebted to the
student movement, which in 1988 had been at the forefront of the
people's uprising. There were also those staunch student followers, still
living in the compound at 54 University Avenue, who courageously
acted as her marshals and bodyguards.

What Suu Kyi wanted most was to draw as many students as possible
into her own, non-violent programme. But she knew that the students
had a mind of their own, and were not always to be gainsaid. By March
she felt it necessary to clarify her position through a series of statements
to the foreign media, which she knew would quickly find their way
back home. In an interview broadcast by Radio India on 25th March

she underlined that neither she nor the NLD had any interest in forming an interim government. Even the scheduled election was of secondary interest. What was important was the 'attainment of basic human rights as soon as possible', because once such rights were achieved, free and fair elections would follow as a matter of course.

In the same interview Suu Kyi neatly deflected a question asking whether the NLD was prepared to hold negotiations with students in insurgent-held border areas – that is, the ABSDF. She replied that neither she nor her party would ever 'desert those students, who are our democracy comrades'. 'Our position,' she added pointedly 'is that they ended up at the border because of the brutal suppression by the government.'

'I don't believe in armed struggle,' she was reported as saying in the *Bangkok Post* the following day, 26th March. 'But I sympathise with the students who are engaged in armed struggle.'

Such statements reflected the NLD's predicament. There was a growing danger that younger members might compromise the League, through exuberance or hot-headedness. March 1989 witnessed a series of potentially volatile demonstrations commemorating the anniversaries of the White Bridge/Red Bridge incident and other atrocities of the year before. At such gatherings, many students proudly wore NLD badges, and were among those seized by MI and the police. Yet Suu Kyi was adamant that the League should not narrow its remit or institute authoritarian rules of its own.

XXVIII

DANUBYU

*In spite of all the difficulties I feel that what I am doing is worthwhile
– the people of Burma deserve better than this mess of inefficiency,
corruption and misuse of power.*
Aung San Suu Kyi, in a letter to Dr Michael Aris, 14th April 1989

THE compound at 54 University Avenue was full of students and other
young people dedicated to helping Suu Kyi and the NLD. Meals were
taken communally, with little attention paid to traditional Burmese
social protocol, whereby elders were looked up to and never challenged.
Suu Kyi herself set the example, talking openly and inviting criticism.
She trusted the young 'because they had no hidden agenda'. Always she
encouraged them to think for themselves and to learn the values of
candour and openness.

'There were no superfluous courtesies' is Min Zin's recollection. Min
Zin was still at high school, but had played a prominent part in the
August 1988 uprising and became a frequent visitor to no. 54. Full of
adolescent fire, to begin with he was sceptical about Suu Kyi, finding
her 'too mild'. But after the September coup he realised that 'she was
on our side', and took note when she gently warned him not to be too
outspoken.

For another high-school student, Tin Hlaing (aka Eva), the Bogyoke's
daughter 'became a second mother, sometimes scolding me to keep my
clothes tidy, but sometimes, if her busy schedule permitted, washing
them for me herself'. Tin Hlaing would also recall how, whenever Daw
Suu Kyi 'started to become emotional' (whether up or down), she would

take time out to play the upright piano acquired by her mother: sometimes Mozart, but more usually Bach, fiercely mathematical music all about restoring composure and retaining discipline.

Much older was Ko Aung, the son of a retired major-general, who had first been introduced to Suu Kyi through Daw Khin Kyi in the early 1970s. Whenever, with or without Dr Aris and her sons, she had visited Rangoon, Ko Aung put himself at her disposal, as baggage-handler, driver and anything else she needed. Born in 1957, he was now a tall thirty-two-year-old with a quick but sure intelligence. Because of his high-ranking father he had not participated in 8.8.88. But from September 1988 onwards he spent more and more time at University Avenue, where Suu Kyi assigned him overall responsibility for 'maintaining security'.

'One morning she came down a little late for breakfast with a piece of paper in her hands,' Ko Aung recounted seventeen years later. 'This was her own translation of Rudyard Kipling's poem "If":

> *If you can dream – and not make dreams your master,*
> *If you can think – and not make thoughts your aim;*
> *If you can meet with Triumph and Disaster*
> *And treat those two impostors just the same;*
> *If you can bear to hear the truth you've spoken*
> *Twisted by knaves to make a trap for fools,*
> *Or watch the things you gave your life to, broken,*
> *And stoop and build 'em up with worn-out tools: . . .*

'She had done it for her student supporters, she said, because she wanted them to understand the importance of self-reliance. Only it had taken her a while longer to finish than she had anticipated.'

And then there was Win Thein, the Rangoon University student lucky to survive the White Bridge/Red Bridge massacre of March 1988. Immediately afterwards he resolved to do whatever he could to bring about justice in Burma. The way forward for him did not become clear until he met Aung San Suu Kyi at Rangoon General Hospital in early June of the same year. Subsequently he went to University Avenue to visit her with a group of fellow students. 'We were all so surprised,' he recalled. 'We were looking for an older leader. Aung San Oo was at the back of our minds, the Bogyoke's oldest son. But he was not interested in his country. Instead there was Daw Aung San Suu Kyi. We didn't expect her to want to become involved, but we were quite wrong. And the strangest thing was we felt immediately we could rely on her completely. Her sincerity and humility overwhelmed us, as it overwhelmed almost everybody who came in contact with her.'

Suu Kyi must also have taken a shine to the broad-shouldered, pleasant-faced Win Thein. He too had physical presence, but did not push himself about. He was a quiet, sober-minded lad whose commitment to Burma's 'second independence movement' was, like her own, beyond reproach. When she decided to declare her hand at the Shwedagon pagoda, she asked if he would join the small group of personal student 'bodyguards' that she needed. He readily assented. On the day itself he stood behind her on the platform, and became even more convinced that Daw Suu Kyi was the right (perhaps only) person who could heal his country's ills. Afterwards he offered his services unreservedly and moved into her compound.

One of Win Thein's keenest memories was how, on the night of 18th September, when it became clear that the military was hell-bent on reasserting itself, Suu Kyi withdrew from the company of those around her and sat for an hour or so by herself, her face furrowed with concern and intense thought. 'I think,' he said, 'that was the moment she grasped just how deep our problems lay.'

He did not need to be asked twice if he would accompany Suu Kyi when she set out on her campaign tours. He was at her side in Mandalay, in Moulmein, in Bassein, and in many other places – not an intimidating figure, but a watchful rock, ready to do whatever the situation required. He was unprepared, however, for what happened at Danubyu, the Irrawaddy river town where, in April 1825, the First Anglo-Burmese War had turned decisively in favour of the British when the Burmese commander General Bandula was struck by a stray rocket, and where, on 5th April 1989, Brigadier-General Myint Aung was ready to resume his duel with Aung San Suu Kyi.

In Burma April is the hottest month. Although nothing is ever truly still, at midday the sun blazes, stationary in the blue empyrean. The burning air is as dry as an old stick of cinnamon. It carries, too, a hint of cinnamon, among myriad other odours that together make up the Irrawaddy basin potpourri: gasoline and diesel, smoking charcoal, acrid durian, tobacco, tea, fried garlic, incense, a trace of jasmine, a hint of juniper. Specks of tamarind. Cement dust. Cicada are at their loudest, and at night the air is full of quick bats and mystifying moths.

Suu Kyi and a sizeable NLD retinue had resumed campaigning in

Irrawaddy District at the beginning of the month, after a brief return to Rangoon. On 4th April they stayed overnight in Yandaung, a smaller township two or three hours from Danubyu. The plan was to drive to Danubyu early the next morning, visit the local NLD headquarters and address a rally in the road outside, then go on by boat in the afternoon to some outlying villages further upriver. They would return to Danubyu for the night, then drive back to Yandaung the following morning. But as soon as Suu Kyi's motorcade of eight vehicles approached Danubyu, it was apparent that a difficult day lay ahead. There were more troops out on the streets than ever before. Some roads had been blocked off with army trucks and barricades.

As Win Thein later learned, Danubyu's inhabitants had been ordered not to come out to greet Daw Suu Kyi on pain of being shot. At the gateway into Danubyu, the NLD motorcade was stopped and told to return to Yandaung. When the drivers refused to turn around, the cars' occupants were ordered to get out. Again, Suu Kyi refused to comply.

After a tight exchange with the Tatmadaw officers present, she and her followers were allowed to proceed. Within moments there was a near-collision between the front vehicle, carrying four of Suu Kyi's bodyguards, and a jeep full of soldiers hurtling recklessly in the opposite direction. Inside Danubyu the streets were deserted, except for soldiers posted at regular intervals along the route. Only when the motorcade reached the NLD office in Danubyu's downtown area were any civilians visible. But, unlike everywhere else Suu Kyi had visited, they held back, not daring a single cheer. In front of the office were scores more soldiers, their weapons at the ready.

The officer in charge was one Captain Myint Oo, under orders from Brigadier Myint Aung. Nobody was allowed to enter the NLD building until Suu Kyi spoke to him, and then only a handful. Captain Myint Oo explained that Danubyu had been placed under martial law, and there was no question of her being allowed to make a public speech. SLORC's Order 88/2 was to be observed to the letter.

Necessarily Suu Kyi compromised. She delivered her speech, but only to a small gathering of NLD supporters inside the office, where she also took an early lunch. In the afternoon she pressed ahead with her programme. On foot, she and her entourage, which had now swollen to around eighty, made their way to Dunubyu's river port, where five small motor boats were waiting. It was a fifteen-minute walk that ordinarily should have taken ten minutes. Along the way, she continued to be harassed by the military. Soldiers shouted abuse and pointed their rifles at her, telling her to go away and not come back. In front of the jetty where the boats were tethered was a squad of more troops: in all thirty of them, ten across and three deep.

Captain Myint Oo was there, and had another exchange with Suu Kyi. He told her to go back and collect her cars and leave Danubyu. But Suu Kyi held her ground. She had every right to get in a boat and go where she pleased. The only way to stop her was to arrest her and put her in prison.

Win Thein watched the captain's face closely. His blood vessels bulged, and there was a manic hatred in his eyes. But, confronted by Suu Kyi's cool determination, he gave way. Perhaps Brigadier Myint Aung had told him to get Aung San Suu Kyi out of town as quickly as possible. By allowing her to board a motor boat he would achieve that end. Before he turned and walked away, he informed her that no boats would be allowed to land at Danubyu after 5 p.m.

'That's all right,' Suu Kyi said. 'We'll be back by then.'

She and her followers climbed down into the boats and, under the full glare of the sun, headed out onto the Irrawaddy. For three hours all went tolerably well. The villages to be visited were within relatively easy reach, and the Tatmadaw was not in evidence – just plenty of police. The people came out to greet Suu Kyi and listen to what she had to say; then the motor boats turned back for Danubyu.

Although it was still well before five o'clock, there were even more soldiers crowding the jetty and its surrounds. Some were wearing the red armbands of 'high specials', commandos who could be relied upon to do the state's dirty work. Win Thein, riding in the third and largest motor boat beside Suu Kyi, sensed that serious trouble awaited them. He added his voice to suggestions that the motor boats should press on and give Danubyu a miss. They could land somewhere further downriver, and the cars could be brought from the NLD office to collect them. But Suu Kyi was impervious to any change of plan. If they did not land at Danubyu, that meant victory for Brigadier Myint Aung, and for SLORC.

As the boats, holding their course, approached the jetty, the soldiers lining it raised their weapons and took aim. Then Captain Myint Oo's voice blasted across the water, ordering the boats not to land.

'Ignore him,' Suu Kyi said, as everyone else fell silent. 'I'll land first. The other boats can follow.'

As Suu Kyi's vessel edged towards the jetty, a company of soldiers advanced at pace towards the landing spot, then took up firing positions, in what seemed a perfectly rehearsed manoeuvre.

Again Suu Kyi said, 'Ignore them.'

Captain Myint Oo, now with a loudhailer in his hands, continued to bark out threats and orders.

It befell Win Thein to jump ashore and pull Suu Kyi's boat in. Suu Kyi quickly alighted onto the slippery stone steps, and the others followed. But at once her party was closely surrounded by soldiers, who began to jostle members of her entourage, pulling at their clothing and shoving them back. Captain Myint Oo was perhaps hoping for a scuffle to break out, so that his men could take stronger action. But, cautioned by Suu Kyi, her followers resisted being drawn into a fight, and in a minute or so the soldiers backed off.

Lone shouts of 'Let Daw Aung San Suu Kyi be!' and 'Long life to Daw Aung San Suu Kyi' rang out from one or two nearby houses as the remaining boats landed and disgorged their passengers.

Once everyone was ashore, Suu Kyi indicated that they should walk in a calm and orderly fashion back to the NLD office, along a street lined with two-storey shop-houses in ill repair, a crumbling mixture of concrete, timber and occasional brickwork, the sidewalks so badly broken as hardly to exist.

Suu Kyi herself led the way. But no sooner had they left the jetty than their path was blocked by three more soldiers. She kept on walking until she was within touching distance of their German Bren guns.

'You really shouldn't bully me so much,' she told the soldiers with the trace of a smile, gently but firmly pushing the barrels of their weapons downwards. 'You must let us pass.'

The three high specials did not attempt to lift their Brens again, but let first Suu Kyi and then the others through.

Had the danger passed? Win Thein, clutching an NLD flag, thought perhaps it had. Even so, he told Suu Kyi that he was going to walk ahead of her. 'I must protect you,' he said. She nodded and let him have his way. They progressed 300 or 400 yards. But, as they approached Danubyu's market (closed for the day by the Tatmadaw), they saw in front of them a company of riflemen kneeling in firing formation.

Win Thein turned quickly and nervously round.

'Just keep going,' Suu Kyi mouthed.

People were no longer calling out from their houses, though somewhere in the distance a baby cried and a motorcycle stuttered. Win Thein moved forward as he had been instructed, aware that Suu Kyi was keeping pace behind him.

A loudspeaker started blaring: Colonel Myint Oo warning them not to advance another pace, his voice climbing towards hysteria. Win Thein looked at the soldiers in front of him and saw fear in their eyes. But he also caught sight of Captain Myint Oo. The man was clearly deranged.

'If you do not go back to your boats,' Myint Oo screamed, 'you will be shot.'

But Win Thein knew what Daw Aung San Suu Kyi wanted and kept walking forward.

Then came Myint Oo's command: the soldiers were to aim and fire. Again Win Thein turned towards Suu Kyi. Again she motioned him forward. But now he saw that the others behind her had come to a halt. If the soldiers were going to shoot Suu Kyi, she did not want anyone else to be killed, so she had told them to stop.

'If Suu Kyi tells me to run,' Win Thein said to himself, 'then I will run. But only if.'

He heard the click of the rifles, and froze. Because he had been at White Bridge, he believed the soldiers would obey their captain's orders.

'At the count of three!' Myint Oo shouted.

Win Thein closed his eyes and waited for death.

'Two!'

But death did not come. Another voice rang out, a voice he did not recognise. He heard movement in front of him. When he opened his eyes, he saw that the soldiers had lowered their weapons. And that Daw Suu Kyi had moved ahead of him.

She had not stopped walking. With less than a moment to spare, a Major had stepped out of the shadows and countermanded Myint Oo's instructions.

Captain Myint Oo was beside himself. Screaming obscenities at the Major, he tore the black operations band from his arm and threw it on the ground.

No one present had any doubt that Myint Oo wanted Daw Aung San Suu Kyi dead, but exactly what took place remains a mystery. The Tatmadaw does not render up its secrets readily. Had the whole episode been an elaborate charade to intimidate Suu Kyi and her retinue, or had Brigadier-General Myint Aung really intended her assassination should she not back down? Had someone urgently contacted SLORC in Rangoon to report what was happening in Danubyu, and had this, in the nick of time, brought the situation under control? Did the unidentified Major intervene off his own bat, or was he too following orders? Had either Brigadier Myint Aung or Captain Myint Oo exceeded theirs? Or had the 'Danubyu Incident' been orchestrated by SLORC itself all along? All that is known is that, later that night, Captain Myint Oo was summoned to Myint Aung's quarters. He may or may not have been dressed down, just as Myint Aung may or may not have been reprimanded by his own seniors. But neither lost his job or suffered demotion, or appears to have sustained any other career penalty.

Far less ambiguously, word of Aung San Suu Kyi's facing down of the Tatmadaw at Danubyu quickly became the subject of the Burmese people's whispered tea-shop conversations, once it had been reported by the BBC and VOA. It confirmed her absolute commitment to her people, and raised her to new heights in their love. It may also have opened Suu Kyi's eyes to the depths of her own fortitude and courage, so that it may not be too much to call Danubyu Aung San Suu Kyi's Rubicon. Now there could be no turning back, of any kind. The regime knew it, the people knew it, and she knew it.

Refusing to be intimidated, Suu Kyi had given Brigadier Myint Aung a better run for his money than he could ever give her. In the process she had made a fool of him. The soldiers having lowered their weapons, Suu Kyi and her followers passed through their line and made their way to the NLD office, another spacious bungalow that had been lent to the League by a well-wisher. There they spent the night. Until the early hours the building was surrounded by troops, but by daybreak these had melted away. Danubyu appeared to be returning to normal. Its inhabitants were out on the streets again, and after an early breakfast Suu Kyi went out to meet them. Then, at 8.30 a.m., the NLD roadshow climbed into its vehicles and headed back, first for Yandaung, then for Rangoon.

Suu Kyi laughed and joked with her fellow passengers on the journey home, making light of what had happened, just as a week later she wrote laconically to Dr Aris, 'Alas, your poor Suu is getting weather-beaten, none of that pampered elegance left as she tramps the countryside spattered with mud, straggly-haired, breathing in dust and pouring with sweat.' She needed, she said, 'a few months in grey, damp Oxford to restore my complexion!' But she was more shaken than she was ready to let on to anyone around her, or to her family in England.

Back in the capital, she hot-footed it to the British ambassador's residence in Signal Road. She needed to make sure that the diplomatic community and particularly the BBC knew about Danubyu, in case the regime was serious about eliminating her. She knew that Ambassador Morland would pass on her account to his information officer, the ever-dependable Nita May, who in turn would see to it that the BBC was alerted. Equally she needed to talk Danubyu through with someone who could fully understand where she was coming from.

In Burma, deprived of the company of Dr Aris, Alexander and Kim, as of her mother, Suu Kyi necessarily had to play the part she assigned herself from dawn to dusk. However alone she might sometimes feel, she was never actually alone, except when she slept, or retreated to her study to read, write or cogitate. Instead she was perpetually surrounded by those whose expectations of her she feared she might not rise to. Ambassador Morland, on the other hand, with a surfeit of concerned understanding, but also a sharp, educated humour, gave her an opportunity to lower her guard, if only for an hour or so.

She also needed to rest her voice. With so much speechifying it had become hoarse. By the time she reached Danubyu even talking was painful. But within days she was back campaigning, braving the dust, the bullock carts and April's ferocious heat. With the rainy season in the offing, there was not a moment to be lost. She left Win Thein behind, however, insisting that he get some rest after the ordeal he had been through. Yet further ordeals awaited him. Two months later, in June, he would be picked up by MI and hauled before a military tribunal. He spent the next fourteen years in prison, first at Insein, then at Taungoo. His original sentence was three years, but was extended when he was caught circulating a human-rights report critical of SLORC amongst his fellow prisoners. A year after his release in 2003 he made his way to Thailand, where – his admiration for Daw Aung San Suu Kyi undiminished – he became one among thousands of political refugees eking out a precarious existence in the edgy border town of Mae Sot.

XXIX

THE DOOR SLAMS SHUT

What I mean by defying authority is non-acceptance of unlawful orders meant to suppress the people. There's nothing violent about it. It's no more violent than is necessary in banging the keys of a typewriter.

Aung San Suu Kyi, addressing a rally
at the Sule pagoda, 10th July 1989

As the rains arrived, Burma's students participated in more and more gatherings and demonstrations that contravened Order 88/2, and SLORC made more and more arrests. But even well before the rains, as early as 24th March 1989, just ahead of Armed Forces Day, Min Ko Naing (Paw U Htun) – chairman of the All Burma Federation of Student Unions – was apprehended, interrogated, tortured and charged before a military tribunal with creating disturbances. Not released until 2005, he would, like Win Thein and countless others, miss out on what should have been the most productive period of his life, held in custody 'without seeing anything, studying anything or reading anything'.*

Min Ko Naing's arrest was doubly significant. After Aung San Suu Kyi, he was the most charismatic figure opposed to the regime. But his detention also indicated that the junta was now prepared to incarcerate even the most prominent among those within the democracy movement. Although Moe Thee Zun, chairman of the student-based but legally registered DPNS (Democratic Party for a New Society), evaded capture, hiding out in monasteries and safe houses before being forced to take

*In an interview with *Irrawaddy*, 15th November 2005

sanctuary within the Thai border area at the end of April, other student leaders were not so fortunate. DPNS vice-chairman Thet Tun and treasurer Kyi Myo were taken in on 8th April. Two weeks later it was the turn of Aung Din, the ABFSU's number three.

The regime also turned its attention to non-students, picking off the leaders of some of the smaller registered parties. Ominously, on 19th June the actor and NLD Executive Committee member U Aung Lwin was grabbed in a Rangoon street by a gang of MI plain-clothesmen, beaten on the spot, then handcuffed and driven away face-down in the back of an unmarked truck.

On 4th July Suu Kyi lost an even more highly valued 'uncle' and colleague, the journalist U Win Tin, also on the NLD Executive Committee. Initially the charge brought against the fifty-nine-year-old journalist centred on alleged contacts with known communists, but subsequently this was dropped and an ordinary criminal charge preferred. U Win Tin had, Brigadier Khin Nyunt asserted at a press conference, offered hospitality to a fellow NLD member whose companion had had an abortion. Since abortion was (and remains) illegal in Burma, Win Tin was accused of aiding and abetting a criminal practice and given three years' hard labour at Insein. His sentence was later extended by twelve years, and by the end of 2006 he was still behind bars, despite two heart attacks and other serious ailments and several promises of an 'early' release.

If the severity of U Win Tin's punishment was a consequence of direct and personal criticisms that he had made of General Ne Win, the length of his detention has been seen as an attempt to wound Aung San Suu Kyi. But, as Danubyu has already proved, if SLORC thought she could be intimidated into silence or flight, SLORC was mistaken. Those around Suu Kyi warned that it must be her turn next. But for her, personal liberty was a minor consideration. All the same, her campaign had become more urgent, more importunate. Since March SLORC had been detaining NLD members, moving steadily up the party's hierarchy. Now her comments were more barbed and she was more outspoken in her condemnation of the junta. If she was going to go down, as seemed inevitable, she would speak her mind first.

Under relentless provocation, Suu Kyi abandoned her previous policy of refraining from *ad hominem* attacks. It was time to name and shame the principal aggressor. From June onwards she denounced Ne Win at her rallies. 'He is the one who lowered the prestige of the armed forces,' she said bluntly. 'I call on you all to be loyal to the State. Be loyal to the people. You don't have to be loyal to Ne Win.'* Specifically she charged the ageing dictator with derailing Aung San's legacy. 'My father didn't build up the Burmese Army in order to suppress the people,' the *Christian Science Monitor* reported her as saying on 13th June. 'Everybody knew from last year that the main culprit is Ne Win.' By the end of the month she was openly referring to him as a 'megalomaniac' who would do anything to hang on to power.

Both sides were upping the ante. In Rangoon people joked that Sanda Win, who, like her father, never went anywhere without a pistol, had challenged Suu Kyi to a duel. Suu Kyi declined, saying, 'Let's just walk down a street unarmed together, and see which one of us is still alive when we reach the other end.' By mid-June Burma's jails allegedly contained upwards of 2,000 political prisoners. At the end of July Amnesty International would put the figure at 6,000.

Order 88/2, prohibiting assembly, was invoked with increasing frequency as SLORC moved to uphold and intensify press restrictions. On 14th June, after repeated warnings issued by the Home and Religious Affairs Minister, General Phone Myint, that the 'Law for the Registration of Printers and Publishers' and other directives that militated against any kind of press freedom must be rigorously upheld, Colonel Thura Pe Aung, director-general of the national police, convened a compulsory meeting of more than 800 printers and publishers and read them the riot act. 'Decisive action,' the Colonel said, would be taken against any and every offender who 'slandered' either the junta or the armed forces, in however small a way, regardless of whether they had or had not infringed the letter of the law.

Soon afterwards, in a nationwide trawl for 'subversive literature', including posters, the raids on Burma's publishing houses and printing presses began, adding to the number of political detainees. Yet this onslaught against freedom of speech was only part of the wider offensive against civil rights and liberties, which culminated on 16th July. SLORC issued revised orders affecting its system of military tribunals. Now even junior officers were permitted to arrest protestors and other dissidents and administer one of three sentences: three years' hard labour, life imprisonment or execution.

*   *   *

* *Time* magazine, 14th August 1989

Through the *Working People's Daily* and other state media organs, the junta maintained its venomous personal attacks, depicting Aung San Suu Kyi as no better than a prostitute who had three (maybe four), foreign husbands, with whom she practised 'all the wifely duties'. She was also, the regime alleged, a corrupter of the youth who flocked around her. During one notably creative press conference held by the SLORC Information Committee on 22nd June, a junta spokesman insinuated that Aung San Suu Kyi indulged in dark profanities. It was recalled, accurately or otherwise, that back in December she had described the Buddha as 'an ordinary person like us' during one of her speeches – hardly a blasphemy. More recently she had criticised SLORC's decision to rename Burma Myanmar. Putting these two things together, the junta spokesman declared as a matter of incontrovertible fact that Aung San Suu Kyi had welcomed a suggestion by one student that a better shift from B to M would be to rename the Buddha *Moatta*, the Burmese word for testicle.

There were no depths to which SLORC's propaganda hacks would not stoop to discredit the woman who, within the space of sixteen months, had emerged as the most coherent challenge to continuing military rule in Burma. But the junta's calumnies were brushed aside by Suu Kyi with a smile or a laugh, and few people took them seriously. All they signified was the tiny-minded spite of Burma's rulers. Her rallies, inside and outside the capital, continued to be attended by hundreds, thousands and sometimes tens of thousands of supporters, in spite of the summer rains and repeated warnings that those disobeying Order 88/2 would be harshly dealt with.

Special warnings had been issued ahead of the *Thingyan*, the great water festival celebrated by nearly all Burmese at the time of the Burmese New Year – a moveable feast that in 1989 fell on 17th April. By tradition, the entire country took a four-day holiday, during which everyone gathered in the streets to douse everyone else with water, using cups, basins, cans, hosepipes or whatever else was to hand. By tradition too, the water festival was an occasion when people were free to speak out against those who governed them, without fear of reprisal.

SLORC was nervous that this year the *Thingyan* might get out of hand and develop into pandemic anti-regime riots. Yet it was unimaginable that the *Thingyan* should be cancelled, even though by definition it contravened Order 88/2. Instead SLORC promulgated 'rules' defining what was and was not acceptable behaviour. Unfazed, the NLD went ahead with its own arrangements, inviting Burma's finest troupes of actors and musicians to perform outside its headquarters in Rangoon. Because political satire was to be high on the agenda, the NLD insisted that this should be a 'non-public' entertainment, to which only NLD members were invited. It did not want to give SLORC an excuse for levelling accusations of inciting or coordinating unrest.

MI got wind of what was planned. On the morning of 13th April soldiers were posted outside 46 University Avenue. When the performances began – in all twenty-eight troupes had gathered – seven NLD members were arrested. The festivities went ahead regardless, as the 'audience' swelled to 2,000. After a while the soldiers either withdrew or stayed to watch and enjoy the performances. A cultural victory for the NLD perhaps, but in the week that followed a further thirty NLD members, mainly students, were detained.

Suu Kyi always protested vigorously about these and other arrests. She constantly urged SLORC to allow freedom of peaceable assembly, though always without any response. None of her letters to SLORC, or to its various ministries, received an answer. Instead the arrests intensified, and the junta reiterated its draconian provisions. This in turn encouraged Suu Kyi, U Tin Oo and other NLD leaders to characterise SLORC's orders as 'unlawful commands', fit only to be disregarded. It also encouraged the NLD leaders to align themselves even more closely with the student movement. Up until late June 1989 the NLD had deliberately held off 'commemorating' the anniversaries of the brutalities committed against students the year before, although as individuals no NLD member was told not to attend such gatherings. On 21st June that changed. On the morning of that day a crowd of youngsters gathered at Myenigon Circle, a Rangoon roundabout where at least three students had been shot by the Tatmadaw the year before. Aung San Suu Kyi and U Tin Oo decided to make speeches at a nearby NLD office, in Sanchaung township, and attend a religious ceremony held in honour of the dead.

At Myenigon Circle, truckloads of soldiers drove past. Using a loudhailer, an officer shouted out, 'Animals, get back!' Then Aung San Suu Kyi arrived on the scene. Before she could lay a wreath on the spot where one of the students had died, her car was surrounded by security types. Against her will and under armed escort, she was taken to the nearest Law and Order Restoration office and warned flatly not to create 'any further disturbances'. Her detention there lasted barely fifteen minutes, but demonstrated that even the Bogyoke's daughter should not consider herself immune to arrest. Undeterred, Suu Kyi called a press conference. 'Unless there are human rights and democratic freedoms, I don't think these elections are going to be the kind of elections we want,' she said. 'If the military resorts to arms every time anniversaries are held for students who died during the pro-democracy movement, the shedding of blood will never end.'

Immediately afterwards she left Rangoon, to campaign for a few days in Pegu. And immediately afterwards Secretary One Khin Nyunt and other junta heavyweights began issuing statements that, regardless of the outcome of the May 1990 elections, SLORC would remain in power at least until the elected 'parliament' had determined a new constitution – the first time the regime had offered any clarification as to the nature of the elections.

Back in Rangoon on 26th June, Suu Kyi held a further press conference. The NLD, she announced, would be holding mass meetings to commemorate four more anniversaries: the first on 7th July, in memory of the 1962 destruction of the Student Union Building at Rangoon University; the second on Martyrs' Day, 19th July; the third on 8th August, marking the beginning of the 8.8.88 people's uprising; and (most provocatively) the fourth on 18th September – the date of SLORC's military coup.

Of the four, Martyrs' Day – forty-two years on from the assassination of Aung San and his cabinet – was the most momentous. In a profound way, the ongoing tussle between Aung San Suu Kyi and General Ne Win was about who had the greater claim on the Bogyoke and his legacy. For Ne Win, still the ultimate controller of the Tatmadaw, Aung San was the source of whatever legitimacy his rule enjoyed. For Suu Kyi, her father's heritage had been systematically perverted by the dictator of Ady Road. Even so, in the pursuit of non-violence, Suu Kyi was prepared to compromise. At a major rally of NLD supporters held at the Sule pagoda on 3rd July attended by more than 10,000, she yet again urged SLORC to 'thrash out existing misunderstandings' by holding discussions with representatives of the opposition parties. But answer came there none – except the arrest of NLD Executive Committee member U Win Tin the following day.

On 6th July Suu Kyi addressed further massed rallies in two other Rangoon townships, Pazudaung and Bothathuang. But the 7th July anniversary commemoration came to nothing. The army and the police simply sealed off Rangoon University. A ceremony was held at the NLD headquarters in University Avenue, but was sparsely attended. Army trucks were everywhere. Some arrests took place, but none of NLD members. The day did not pass off without serious incident, however. A bomb exploded across the Rangoon river in Syriam, killing two oil refinery workers and badly injuring a third. Before any thorough forensic investigation could take place, SLORC insinuated that the ABFSU was probably responsible, and promptly detained three of its senior officials. Cynics believed that the bomb had been planted by MI.

A second bomb detonated at City Hall on 10th July, killing three and injuring four. The same day Suu Kyi addressed another gathering at the Sule pagoda, this time estimated at 30,000. But the crowd, as always seemed to happen when the NLD was involved, behaved with impeccable restraint. From SLORC's perspective, it seemed that another people's uprising was in the offing, adding yet greater significance to the planned Martyrs' Day commemoration rally.

A head-on collision between the NLD and SLORC now seemed certain. On 16th July, just three days before Martyrs' Day, Suu Kyi insisted that the League would proceed with its programme, whatever the regime threatened. Wreaths would be laid at the Martyrs' Mausoleum, close to the Shwedagon pagoda, and many thousands would attend. She fully expected there to be further arrests – her own and those of other NLD Executive Committee members included.

Caught in a cleft stick, SLORC panicked. On the one hand, in defence of the Tatmadaw, the junta could not be seen to deny the principal annual tribute to Bogyoke Aung San. On the other, it knew too well that any such gathering would double as an anti-government protest. A fresh order – 89/2 – was issued. Individuals were entitled to pay their respects at the Mausoleum on the 19th, but any group of five or more would be deemed hostile to the state. Marching in procession, gathering en masse, chanting slogans and 'inciting trouble' were strictly prohibited.

From the evening of the 18th Rangoon's streets began filling with units of the Tatmadaw, brought in from outlying barracks. The city teemed with thousands of troops armed with automatic rifles and fixed bayonets. Ominously, soldiers so deployed included battalions of the 11th and 22nd Light Infantry Divisions, both of which had been used to crush the 8.8.88 protests. Coils of barbed wire were stretched across Rangoon's main thoroughfares, and loudspeaker trucks announced a new, daytime curfew for the 19th, lasting from 6 a.m. to 6 p.m.

Simultaneously, MI began a night-time sweep of the capital, arresting hundreds of those deemed potential troublemakers, scores of NLD followers among them. Chillingly, Rangoon's hospitals were advised to ready themselves for an influx of casualties.

As 19th July dawned, Rangoon was bristling with junta firepower. A bloodbath equivalent to that of August 1988 was in the offing. Meeting for an early breakfast, the NLD Executive Committee decided to call off the scheduled Martyrs' Day commemoration march and rally, instead issuing a statement that it 'had no intention of leading our people straight into a killing field'. Suu Kyi added a personal statement. SLORC's preventative actions, she said, only showed that 'we have a fascist government in power'.

At the last moment, and for the most honourable of reasons, the Martyrs' Day commemoration march, from University Avenue to the Shwedagon, was cancelled. Notwithstanding, some several hundred demonstrators, mainly students, opted to protest. None was killed, but many were seized by the Tatmadaw.

Suu Kyi decided that, come hell or high water, she would honour her father's memory at the Martyrs' Mausoleum the following day, in a purely private capacity. It would be a family affair. A week beforehand Alexander and Kim had arrived in Burma to spend the summer holidays with their mother. Dr Aris too had planned to fly out. Instead he found himself in Scotland, attending the funeral of his father John Aris. Suu Kyi was, however, determined that her sons should accompany her to pay their respects to their famous grandfather.

SLORC was minded otherwise. The time had come to silence the Bogyoke's daughter.

In the early hours of 20th July 1989 the junta sealed off University Avenue, relying on a dozen-odd truckloads of soldiery to do the job. Barbed wire was strung across each end of the road, and troops were posted outside both the NLD headquarters at no. 44 and Aung San Suu Kyi's compound. No one was allowed in, and no one was allowed out.

Inside the compound there was some consternation at first light when it was realised that no. 54 was under siege. But Suu Kyi, already awake, insisted everyone remain calm. Breakfast should go ahead as usual. She had been expecting the Tatmadaw to make a move, though what that move would be remained uncertain. She tried putting a call through to

Dr Aris in Scotland, only to discover that Burma's international lines were suspended. She also tried leaving her residence, to go to the Martyrs' Mausoleum, but was turned back at gunpoint.

Any minute she could be taken away to Insein, or some other prison. She even had a small bag of personal belongings ready to take with her. Yet all morning nothing happened. The soldiers remained outside in the road, apparently on a watching brief only. If Alexander (then aged sixteen) and Kim (twelve) were frightened, as they had every right to be, they strove not to show it. Yet something needed to be done about them. To their mother's relief, Ma Thanegi, her personal secretary and sometime NLD spokesperson, who had been staying overnight, volunteered to play cards and a board game with them.

Lunch was taken at the usual early hour, then everyone settled back down again into the waiting game. Another three hours passed. But at a little after four in the afternoon, two Tatmadaw officers presented themselves at the gate and asked to come inside. Suu Kyi was told she had been placed under house arrest. Henceforward she was not to leave the compound, was not to have any contact with her NLD colleagues and was only to receive such visitors as the regime allowed. She would be permitted to retain the services of a maid and a cook, but other than that everyone except her sons was to leave.

She was given no choice, except – by insinuation – the choice to leave the country forthwith, taking Alexander and Kim with her. It was a *fait accompli*. If she did not cooperate, the compound would be stormed, with certain loss of life.

In case there was any doubt, the telephone lines into no. 54 were cut – it is said with a pair of scissors.

Why, Suu Kyi asked, since so many NLD members had already been imprisoned, should she not receive the same treatment? But the officers remained adamant. They were following orders.

Not wishing to endanger the lives of her followers, Suu Kyi resigned herself to the inevitable. She gathered the forty-odd students and others present in the compound on the porch outside and explained the situation to them. They should, she said, leave at once, in an orderly fashion and return to their homes. But the trucks were still waiting in University Avenue. All forty-odd, including Ma Thanegi, were arrested as they walked along University Avenue and were taken away, to serve jail sentences ranging from a few months to several years. The regime's initial pretext was that none had registered the compound as their place of residence, though for those given longer sentences other charges were soon trumped up.

Once no. 54 had been cleared of Suu Kyi's followers, the Tatmadaw moved in. Soldiers and intelligence officers conducted a minute search of her property. Every drawer and cupboard was ransacked in the hope of finding incriminating evidence. Sacks of papers were carried off. Suu Kyi watched on impassively, the shadow of a smile on her face. The soldiers could turn the whole place upside down ten times and still they would not find what they were looking for.

All over Rangoon arrests were taking place. Among scores of NLD members apprehended on the 20th were several of Suu Kyi's Executive Committee colleagues, among them Daw Myint Myint Khin, Maung Moe Thu and U Thaw Ka. The League's chairman, and Suu Kyi's closest political ally, was also placed under house arrest. In the early morning U Tin Oo had attempted to visit no. 54, as he did most days, but had been turned away by the Tatmadaw. When he returned home he found that his house too was surrounded by soldiers. Yet strangely no effort was made to detain every member of the NLD Executive Committee, which, fearing what was to come, Suu Kyi and U Tin Oo had expanded by an additional four seats on 16th July. Nor was the NLD itself outlawed.

On 21st July SLORC fielded a spokesman, Colonel Kyaw San, to provide an explanation of the detention orders. Under the provisions of the State Protection Law, Aung San Suu Kyi and U Tin Oo were to be confined to their residences for a minimum of one year 'because they have violated the law by committing acts designed to put the country in a perilous state'. He went on to cite various statements each had made that were either derogatory of the regime or undermined the 'prestige of the armed forces'. Their activities, Colonel Kyaw San implied, were treasonous. Yet neither Suu Kyi nor U Tin Oo was formally charged. Later SLORC would claim that this had been in their own interests, since treason carried the death penalty.

To suggest, however, as SLORC soon did, that in July 1989 it was guided by some benign impulse in its attitude towards Suu Kyi was purest bull. If Ne Win and his gang stopped short of eliminating the Bogyoke's daughter, it was because they sensed that the people's fury would know no bounds. It was their own skin, not hers, they wanted to protect.

PART FOUR

THE POLITICAL MADONNA

XXX

EGG ON THE GENERALS' FACES

The Prince of Wales – what was his name? – had to abdicate because he married a foreigner, Mrs Simpson. That is our law too.
General Saw Maung, explaining SLORC's decision to bar Aung San
Suu Kyi from standing for election, January 1990*

PLACING Aung San Suu Kyi under house arrest did not remove her from public life, as SLORC had hoped. It iconicised her. Abroad, she became the world's best-known prisoner of conscience; at home, a political madonna – the focus of a people's hunger for temporal salvation, and a symbol of a nation's enduring disrepair.

The junta's problems began immediately. Dr Aris first got wind of his wife's detention from radio reports while still in Scotland. At once he asked to be allowed to go to Rangoon and, if nothing else, collect his sons. SLORC, believing that Aris might cajole his wife into leaving with him, readily assented. From the outset Suu Kyi was informed by the military that though she might not be free to leave her compound to continue her work with the NLD, she was free to leave the country, on condition she did not return. Yet so badly managed was Aris's visit that it generated nothing but adverse publicity for SLORC. Even before then, on the morning after the day of her detention, Suu Kyi herself struck back at the regime. The only way she would leave Burma, she said, was if she was taken to Mingaladon airport in chains. Since she had retained her Burmese passport, and had no other, she could not be deported – unless some third country

Daily Telegraph, 15th October 1991

agreed to accept her against her will. Suu Kyi then repeated her demands that she be treated the same as other NLD prisoners and be taken to Insein prison. When SLORC again refused to remove her from the compound, she started a hunger strike on 21st July 1989. She would take no food, only liquids – water and fruit juices.

It was as well Dr Aris was on his way. However much she might explain and justify her decision, for Alexander and Kim it was upsetting to watch their mother put herself in jeopardy so wilfully. Their father's presence would be a boon to them as well as to their mother. But SLORC, fearful that Aris would liaise with what remained of the NLD's Executive Committee on his wife's behalf, determined that his liberty too should be constricted. When his plane touched down, to the consternation of Aris's fellow passengers it was at once surrounded by soldiers. Indeed, the whole airport was awash with the Tatmadaw.

Aris was led away to an emptied VIP lounge. The British embassy, concerned about the fate of Alexander and Kim, both of whom held British as well as Burmese passports, had sent one of its own officials to meet Dr Aris. But no meeting was permitted. Instead, an army colonel politely informed Aris that while he was welcome to stay with Daw Aung San Suu Kyi for two weeks, he would only be allowed out of her residence except under armed escort. He was forbidden, on pain of immediate deportation, to have contact either with the staff of any embassy or with the NLD. But these restrictions were not conveyed to the British embassy man. All the embassy knew was that Aris had been driven away from the airport by the Tatmadaw. It did not even know that he had been taken to University Avenue.

Over the next three weeks repeated requests for consular access to Aris were brushed aside. No information as to his whereabouts was provided. As a result, there were fears for his well-being. In Aris's own words, 'For twenty-two days I effectively disappeared from sight. Nobody knew what had happened to me.' Inadvertently, SLORC had handed the foreign press a dinner ticket. All the ingredients were there: a secretive and ruthless tropical dictatorship; a respected Oxford academic gone missing; his beautiful wife under house arrest; his white-knight mission to comfort her and rescue their sons . . .

Several days in, news of Suu Kyi's hunger strike leaked out, and her picture was splashed across the front of the Asia-Pacific edition of *Time* magazine. By their own cack-handedness, the generals had turned their most effective opponent into a cover girl. Nor had the junta bothered to inform Suu Kyi herself that her husband was on his way. When he arrived at no. 54 on 24th July, the third day of her hunger strike, both she and their sons were taken by surprise. But at once the quick-thinking Suu Kyi saw there was another point to be scored. Since she had not been informed, she thought it more appropriate that Michael stay in the second, smaller villa, inhabited by her aunt Daw Khin Gyi.

The matter was soon resolved by a Tatmadaw officer, who begrudgingly 'informed' Suu Kyi of the authorities' decision. Aris moved across to join his wife and the family was reunited. Notwithstanding, SLORC's propagandists tried to make hay where none existed. Some months later it was put about that, far from being pleased to see Dr Aris, she had turned her back on him and walked away – proof, if proof were needed, that their marriage was on the rocks. Yet whatever tensions may have crept into their relationship (natural in any marriage of nineteen years' standing) soon evaporated. The extraordinary circumstances in which Suu Kyi and Michael now found themselves reaffirmed and strengthened the bond between them. SLORC's determined efforts to pretend otherwise only cast the generals in an even worse light.

Mentally, Suu Kyi was as resolute as ever, to the point of obduracy, but physically her hunger strike began to take its toll. Since it was clear the regime would not budge apropos sending her to Insein, and since with each day that passed it would be more hazardous for her if the junta did relent, Dr Aris – by temperament averse to involving himself directly in anything halfway political – took it upon himself to mediate between Suu Kyi and her captors, while encouraging her to be less inflexible (just as, when he returned to England, he began assiduously rallying support for her outside Burma).

What good would it do if she went all the way? The democracy movement would be left rudderless. Persuaded by Michael, Suu Kyi softened. She would not insist on going to jail, but would end her hunger strike if she were given firm assurances that those NLD members and others who had been incarcerated for opposing the regime were not maltreated. Dr Aris put this to the Tatmadaw officers who regularly came to the compound. At the end of the month he found himself addressing a collection of top brass at Rangoon's City Hall.

Neither General Saw Maung nor Khin Nyunt was present, but cameras were. Doubtless the session would be played back at Ady Road. Steeling himself, Dr Aris reiterated Suu Kyi's conditions. As on every other occasion, he was treated courteously before being escorted back to University Avenue. Two days later, at midday on 1st August 1989, an officer arrived to tell Suu Kyi that the regime acceded to her demands. By then her hunger strike had lasted twelve days. Unable to stand, and having lost one-tenth of her bodyweight, Suu Kyi ended her fast. Doctors were called and an intravenous drip applied.

Aris had come up with a classic face-saver. Whether he or Suu Kyi believed that SLORC, already renowned for its bad faith, would abide by its word is not known. There is scant evidence that political prisoners were treated any more leniently than before. A week later, as students attempted to commemorate the first anniversary of 8.8.88, there was a fresh intake of detainees at Insein and other penitentiaries. Still, it was a victory of sorts. As at Danubyu, Suu Kyi had demonstrated that she was not going to be bullied into doing, or not doing, anything. Once again it was clear that SLORC dreaded any circumstance whereby it might be held responsible for the loss of Aung San's daughter's life.

Over the following days Suu Kyi recovered her vitality and began regaining her lost weight. This was an incalculable relief to Dr Aris and the two boys. Her hunger strike was an unsettling passage that stuck in all their minds. Sooner or later they would have to return to England, for the start of the school and university year – September at the very latest. Each was apprehensive about what SLORC might get up to in their absence. Although the Tatmadaw took it for granted that it was entitled to come and go as it pleased, and at all times soldiers were posted inside the compound as well as at its gate, these provisions were not carried out in an unfriendly fashion. Some officers as well as NCOs were almost apologetic in their demeanour. Yet whether they would continue in the same mode once Suu Kyi was left alone was imponderable. Probably the junta was merely anxious that when they returned to Oxford they would not take with them disparaging reports.

Although Dr Aris's visa expired on 5th August, SLORC agreed to extend it until 2nd September, so that he could accompany Alexander and Kim back to England that day. Two further concessions were made. Dr Aris requested that once he had left Burma, Aung San Suu Kyi be permitted to receive letters and parcels containing books and personal effects from him. Then, on 12th August; he was at last allowed contact with a British embassy official. The meeting took place under supervision at a military guest house on Inya Lake. Aris confirmed that his wife had indeed gone on hunger strike, but was now eating properly. The next day newspapers in Britain and elsewhere ran stories that the 'hunt' for Dr Aris was over: he was at his wife's side, under armed guard.

There was now something almost surreal about the atmosphere at 54 University Avenue. Because Suu Kyi was unable to continue her political work, she had so much more time for her family. The last three weeks of August became a parody of an Oxford summer vacation spent at home. The boys – adolescents who needed daily exercise – were permitted to roam about the garden, though always under the watchful eyes of the Tatmadaw. Sometimes too, under armed escort, they were able to go sightseeing in Rangoon. Yet SLORC, determined to keep turning the screw, had another unpleasant surprise in store. No sooner had Dr Aris, together with Alexander and Kim, returned to England than the Burmese embassy in London informed Dr Aris that his sons' Burmese passports had been revoked. They were no longer entitled to consider themselves Burmese citizens, and would not be granted entry visas on their British passports.

This did not prevent Dr Aris himself returning to Rangoon at the end of the year, on 16th December, to spend his Christmas vacation with Suu Kyi. The junta continued to hope that he would persuade her to leave with him, that the absence of her children might finally push her into doing what the generals wanted her to do. Aris, however, made no attempt to get her to change her mind. He already knew, and inwardly applauded, the depth of her commitment to her fellow Burmese. Instead, the couple took advantage of the generals' misconceptions and quietly enjoyed each other's company. Later, Aris would write that the two weeks he and Suu Kyi spent together at the end of 1989 'are among my happiest memories of our many years of marriage'. They were 'wonderfully peaceful'. Rather than give Suu Kyi at once all the presents he had brought in his suitcase – from himself, Alexander and Kim, and from other members of her 'English' family – he gave them to her one by one, day by day. But one gift must have meant more than any other. Aris was able to tell Suu Kyi that an Oxford colleague, John Finnis, Professor of Law and Legal Philosophy, had agreed to put her name forward for the Nobel Peace Prize. What the outcome would be was in the lap of the gods. Much would depend on what other candidates emerged, what happened in Burma over the coming months, the support that could be mustered and how strong a case for Suu Kyi could be mounted. But for now she could rest assured that her husband would leave no stone unturned to help her realise her political aims.

Both before and after the anniversary of 8.8.88 MI busied itself rounding up hundreds of the regime's opponents. In scenes reminiscent of the worst excesses of Stalin's Soviet Union, young men and women were seized in tea-shops, dragged off their bicycles or out of buses, or taken away from their homes in the dead of night. On the day itself, the army was out in force in all of Burma's principal urban centres. Rallies and gatherings were small and ineffectual. There was no repeat of the previous year's unrest.

With Suu Kyi under guard night and day, the regime felt confident about allowing the elections to proceed, although it was not until early November that a date was set: Sunday, 27th May 1990. As astrologers were quick to note, 9s were everywhere: 2 + 7 = 9, and then the 4th week of the 5th month in the year '90. Surely this meant the Old Man was still pulling the strings? Collectively, Ne Win, Saw Maung, Khin Nyunt and army chief Than Shwe believed that through the National Unity Party they could secure an outright victory. They must also have felt bolstered by the Chinese government's successful suppression of dissidents. On 4th June 1989 a month-long mass democracy rally in Beijing's Tiananmen Square had been abruptly ended when the People's Liberation Army moved in with its tanks, killing thousands. But still Burma's generals were taking no chances. Colleges and high schools remained closed. The night-time curfew continued to be enforced and the media remained gagged, except as a propaganda outlet for the NUP, and for the junta.

Security at Burma's ports and border crossings was tightened to weed out foreign journalists. Until Burmese dissidents began organising effective news networks, the outside world largely depended on Rangoon's diplomats for information about what went on in Burma. Diplomats were sometimes invited to 'domestic' press conferences, and the larger embassies had staff skilled at 'decoding' Burmese media product, spotting contradictions and reading between the lines. One well-attended press conference was given by Secretary One Khin Nyunt on 5th August. He reiterated the charge that the NLD had been infiltrated by communists. Targeting Aung San Suu Kyi, he accused her of conducting a secret correspondence with Bo Kyaw Zaw, one of the Thirty Comrades who had subsequently joined the CPB. Though he was unable to produce any decisive evidence, Bo Kyaw Zaw's daughter, Daw San Kyaw Zaw, was immediately afterwards taken into custody. Yet barely a month later, on 9th September, Khin Nyunt gave another press conference. Now he asserted that the NLD, Suu Kyi and U Tin Oo were at the heart of a 'rightist' conspiracy that involved 'powerful' foreign governments, Although he refrained from naming specific countries, the BBC, VOA and All India Radio were denounced for disseminating lies and untruths.

Khin Nyunt wanted to warn diplomats not to meddle in Burma's affairs. Soon afterwards he published *The Conspiracy of Treasonous Minions Within Myanmar and Traitorous Cohorts Abroad*, a fulsome (though inconsistent) expression of his conclusions. Among those identified as enemies of the state was Stephen Solarz, the US congressman who in September 1988 had attempted to mediate between Burma's contending factions. Despite or because of its bombastic title, the book failed to become a bestseller. But it was not all just sound and fury. From August onwards, the number of military tribunals dispensing summary justice proliferated. Throughout the period leading up to the election political arrests continued, even though not quite on the same scale as during June to September 1989. As fast as the largest student party, the DPNS, could elect new leaders to replace those who had been detained, so they in turn were taken away. SLORC also moved to finally silence U Nu. In December he found himself in jail, and his League for Democracy and Peace barred from fielding any candidates.

In the same month the NLD's chairman U Tin Oo, put under house arrest at the same time as Aung San Suu Kyi, was transferred to Insein prison and given three years' hard labour. Then, in January 1990, Suu Kyi was informed that she had been disqualified from putting her name forward as an electoral candidate. Previously Khin Nyunt had invoked a clause in the 1947 constitution prohibiting anyone married to a foreigner from becoming Burma's President, for all that the same constitution had been suspended by Ne Win in 1962. Now the same restriction was arbitrarily applied to constituency candidates, specifically to prevent anyone voting for Aung San Suu Kyi personally on 27th May 1990. If SLORC had its way, the NLD would not win even one seat.

But the junta badly underestimated the organisational strength of the NLD, its capacity to survive and its popular appeal. The maltreatment of Aung San Suu Kyi, U Tin Oo and other senior members merely stirred the League's rank-and-file to redouble their efforts to win the electoral contest, if that were possible. Knowing how likely it was that SLORC would strike against them, well before their house arrests Suu Kyi and Tin Oo had made provisions for the NLD to function under an alternative leadership. So long as the entire Central Committee was not apprehended, there would be continuity. U Kyi Maung, a former colonel who had been among U Tin Oo's nominees to the Executive Committee, took over as acting chairman. That the NLD held together during the difficult months leading up to the election was in large measure due to his unstinting labours and cool commitment.

Suu Kyi and U Tin Oo, together with their colleagues, had also worked together drafting a party manifesto. As soon as the election date was promulgated, this was released, on 6th November 1989. There was of course no likelihood of its being referred to, let alone reproduced in part or in whole, in the *Working People's Daily* or any other state media organ. Notwithstanding, copies were widely distributed. If nothing else, it served as a manual for party workers. The challenge was to offer specific policies while at the same time – since the election was being fought in the absence of any formal democratic constitution – addressing broader framework issues. But that gave the NLD the opportunity to show its whole hand. A document of just over 3,500 words when translated into English, the manifesto offered a blueprint for both Burma's short-term and long-term future.

Taking some liberties, the manifesto asserted that 'all the people of Burma are anxious to establish a firmly united "Union" . . . with equal rights for all ethnic nationalities who cherish democracy'. The NLD promised that, under a new constitution that would be brokered in consultation with all other democratically elected parties, the executive, the legislature and the judiciary would be separated. National sovereignty was to be invested in the Pyithu Hluttaw – parliament – to which all other bodies (including the army) would become accountable. Simultaneously, and crucially, the manifesto offered the 'ethnic nationalities' a greater degree of autonomy than the 1947 constitution had allowed. The minorities were to have 'the right to self-determination with respect to . . . politics, administration and economic management in accordance with the law'. In this way the NLD hoped to put an end to 'armed conflict' that had already lasted 'for more than forty years'.

The manifesto expressly welcomed economic liberalisation and the growth of a market economy, although individual clauses offered special protection for the interests of Burma's peasant farmers. Education, healthcare and social welfare were given priority consideration. It did not, however, promise the earth today. Many of the pledges made by the NLD were qualified by the caveat 'as circumstances permit'. Overall, Burmese voters, if they voted for the NLD, could look forward to something radically different, and radically better. For at the heart of the manifesto, reflecting Aung San Suu Kyi's personal crusade, was a determination to uphold human rights and liberties.

The message was bright, but getting it across to voters – even when the military and the Tatmadaw did not directly interfere – was fraught with difficulties. In the sticks, village headmen, either because they were in cahoots with SLORC's local representatives or feared reprisals by SLORC once the election was over, too often assisted the National Unity Party at the NLD's expense. NLD workers had to go about their work furtively, speaking to voters individually or in small groups, explaining the League's policies and how the ballot paper should be filled in when the day came.

There were problems too with the electoral registers in Rangoon and some other cities. In another blatant attempt to affect the outcome of the election, from the end of 1989 SLORC began cleansing those townships that had put up most resistance to the regime in August 1988 and at other times. Tens of thousands were forcibly relocated to half-finished, shoddily constructed satellite townships miles from where they lived and worked. In many cases there was neither running water nor electricity, and no provision had been made for voters to re-register. SLORC trumpeted this as slum clearance, but the reality was that those concerned were disenfranchised.

Yet there was one slither of hope. On 9th January 1990, contradicting some of the public utterances made by Secretary One Khin Nyunt, head of state General Saw Maung went on air to reassure the nation. 'An election has to be held to bring forth a government,' he said. 'That is our responsibility. But the actual work of forming a legal government after the election is not the duty of the Tatmadaw. We are saying it very clearly and candidly right now.'

The subtext of Saw Maung's address was that SLORC had deluded itself into believing the NUP would win a clear-cut victory. Crates of champagne began arriving at Ady Road.

A week before polling day a vicious cartoon appeared in the *Working People's Daily*. A scruffy-looking Eurasian boy, wearing jeans and a dirty T-shirt and identified as one of Aung San Suu Kyi's sons, declared himself to be 'of mixed race'. On either side he was flanked by Burman lads, dressed in smart *longyis*. 'We are genuine citizens,' their legend ran, 'genuine nationals.' Being racist through and through, the generals could not imagine how any true Burman could take an alternative view. However, to the astonishment of Rangoon's diplomats, and around sixty foreign journalists permitted to enter Burma for the occasion, the election was indeed conducted fairly and openly.

On the evening before, 26th May, the curfew was temporarily suspended. On polling day itself the Tatmadaw largely kept off the streets. Even those soldiers patrolling University Avenue outside Suu Kyi's compound were replaced by plain-clothesmen. There were isolated scuffles at some of the 18,190 polling stations, and one or two country stations were just too far – more than a day's journey – for all its registered voters to attend. But, contrary to expectation, neither the army nor military watched as the electorate cast its votes. If anything the boot was on the other foot. On 27th May the NLD was out in force, riding through Burma's streets in trucks and vans, encouraging the populace to vote ... and vote for the League. NLD members were also out in force at many polling booths. But most voters needed no prompting. The people of Burma were up early that morning. Often dressed in their finest, they queued for however long it took, then filled in their ballot papers. Some, apprehensive that they might be photographed exercising their democratic right, delayed. But when their neighbours returned home and told them how it was, they too turned out.

Although it had made a provision that the final election result would not be declared until 14th June, perhaps through sheer ignorance of electoral procedures SLORC permitted individual constituencies to announce their results as and when they were ready. This was a huge miscalculation. The first result came at Seikkan township in Rangoon, won handsomely by NLD candidate Daw San San. That the seat had been captured by a woman was propitious. For many voters the NLD meant first and foremost Aung San Suu Kyi, the Bogyoke's daughter. And Daw San San's triumph set the pattern.

In all, there were 492 constituencies, though this number was reduced to 485 when seven constituencies close to insurgency areas were suspended for 'security reasons'. The NLD captured a staggering 392 seats, out of the 447 it contested – a shade over 80 per cent of the overall total. But the true measure of its success was even greater. The seats it did not contest were mainly in the 'ethnic' states. In those, 'minority' parties, banded together under the umbrella of the UNLD (United Nationalities League for Democracy) – sympathetic, if not actually allied, to the NLD – did equally well, winning sixty-five seats, with the Shan Nationalities League for Democracy becoming the second overall biggest winner, with twenty-three seats gained. The regime party, the NUP, netted close on 20 per cent of votes cast, but because a first-past-the-post system had been adopted, this resulted in a miserable ten seats only. More upsetting still for the junta, even some of those constituencies where military inhabitants were predominant – Dagon township in Rangoon, for example – fell to the NLD. The secrecy of the ballot had been maintained, and it was clear that many soldiers and their families had voted for the opposition. Even the NUP leader, U Tha Khaw, formerly a BSPP minister, standing in Hmawbi township, was defeated.

Another loser was former Brigadier-General Aung Gyi, the NLD chairman until his ousting in December 1988. That his United Nationals Democratic Party fielded 247 candidates – the third-largest entry in the contest – was perceived as evidence that he now enjoyed the clandestine backing of SLORC. His final tally, however, was just one seat won.

The student parties scored a handful of victories in college townships, and 'independents', of uncertain political loyalty, another six seats. The turnout was put at 72.6 per cent of those eligible to vote. When irregularities in the electoral registers are taken into account, the actual figure was probably higher. One in eight votes was declared invalid, usually because ballot papers had been spoiled. In all there were 2,300 candidates, representing ninety-three parties, the vast majority of which, fielding only a handful of candidates, lost out altogether.

Well before 14th June the outcome of the election was known to all, making redundant any formal declaration of the result. There could be no mistaking the magnitude of the NLD's success. It was not just a landslide, it was a nationwide earthquake. Suu Kyi's League had triumphed. Yet it had fought the election under the most arduous conditions. Later, regime apologists and others would endeavour to diminish the NLD's achievement by claiming that voters had no idea what they were voting for when they went to the polls, or that most were minded to vote against the existing regime, rather than for democracy – and democracy's best exponents – in particular. But what such critics ignored, quite apart from the charismatic appeal of Aung San Suu Kyi, was the selfless hard labour put in by NLD activists and party workers in the weeks and months leading up to the election.

There would have been even less ambiguity, had SLORC tolerated opinion polls and other instruments (such as freedom of the press) for gauging the mood and wishes of the Burmese people in the electoral run-up. By the same token, SLORC might have grasped the extent of its own unpopularity and taken whatever evasive actions it deemed appropriate. But because the junta's position was essentially one of blind intolerance, by allowing the May 1990 election to proceed, it scored the mother of own goals.

But that did not mean SLORC would meekly abide by the result. If any tensions had arisen among Burma's seniormost ruling generals – Saw Maung, Khin Nyunt, Than Shwe and, still above the rest, Ne Win – the junta now closed ranks. The champagne at Ady Road (not just a metaphor, but a physical actuality) might have to wait for another day, but Aung San Suu Kyi and the NLD could go to hell.

XXXI

SOLDIERS AT THE GATE

Some have asked me: when are you going to transfer power? I cannot say when. I cannot see into the future. I have to handle the situation as it comes. I cannot tell whether I will drown tomorrow.
General Saw Maung, in a radio broadcast, 18th October 1990

WITH so many soldiers and their families having apparently polled against the regime, it is possible that one more big push by the democracy movement, on the same scale as 8.8.88, might have carried the day, though the cost in lives could have been great. But this did not happen. Playing for time, a badly shaken SLORC adroitly resisted pressure to convene the people's assembly that had been promised, and then took steps to further damage the NLD.

For a few days after 27th May 1990 nothing very much happened at all, except that the night-time curfew resumed and soldiers again appeared on Burma's streets. The *Working People's Daily* and the state's broadcasting services were strangely reticent about the election. Having proposed that the final result be called on 14th June, the junta had fortuitously bought itself a breathing space. But even before that date the tame NUP lodged complaints with the Electoral Commission that the NLD had resorted to underhand means to secure its victory. While such complaints were never formally upheld, investigation of them bought the regime yet more time.

For its part, second-guessing what Aung San Suu Kyi might have wished, the NLD opted to remain 'within the law', however much the law (as defined by SLORC) rankled. The League's caretaker chairman,

U Kyi Maung, who had done so much to secure the NLD's electoral triumph, requested 'dialogue' with the junta. It was only when the most evasive of responses was given to his repeated entreaties that the League decided to hold a two-day meeting of all those NLD candidates who had won seats, at the Gandhi Hall in Rangoon's Kyauktada township, set for 28th July. By then, the first anniversary of Aung San Suu Kyi's house arrest, 20th July, had come and gone. Although her original detention order had been for one year only, there was no sign of her release. A crowd of protesters attempted to gather in University Avenue, but was quickly dispersed. Instead, her followers had to content themselves with wearing Aung San Suu Kyi T-shirts and badges, and fly-posting her printed portrait when no one was looking.

Had the NLD not won the election, or if the margin of victory had been much smaller, it is possible she would have been set free. But the sheer weight of the mandate given to her party decided the generals' minds for them. A day before the 'Gandhi Meeting', as it would become known, SLORC finally declared its hand. On 27th July it issued Order 90/1, in its way as infamous as Order 88/2. SLORC's authority, it proclaimed, was based on its recognition by foreign governments, by the United Nations and by other international bodies. It was therefore not obliged to surrender power, to the NLD or anyone else. There would, however, be a cumbersome transition to civilian rule, beginning with a National Convention that would devise 'guidelines' for a new constitution. Only when such guidelines had been approved by the army could the Convention proceed to draft an actual constitution, which would then be put to the people in a referendum. And so on. No time-frame was suggested, nor was the participation in the Convention of NLD or any other newly elected 'MPs' guaranteed. Instead, delegates would be selected by SLORC.

It was as though the election had never happened. Even Khin Nyunt's pre-election assertions, that the contest was to choose members of a Constituent Assembly, not a parliament, now appeared a dead letter. However, it was Khin Nyunt who took the lion's part in explaining the new package to the nation, and it is probable that it was primarily his inspiration.

The NLD's elected candidates were incensed. But when they met at Gandhi Hall, together with UNLD MPs, there was division within their ranks. Some wanted immediate, strong action – at the least a demand that SLORC step down forthwith. Others preferred to play along with the junta, in the hope that the NLD would be given a larger rather than a smaller part to play in the forthcoming constitutional process. In the street outside large numbers of NLD supporters, most of them wearing Aung San Suu Kyi badges, waited expectantly. But when, after two days, the 'Gandhi Hall Declaration' was issued, it struck many as a toothless compromise. While calling for the immediate release of Aung San Suu Kyi, U Tin Oo and all other political prisoners, as regards SLORC it urged only 'frank and sincere discussions'.

The junta was not out of the woods yet, however. As August loomed, so did the second anniversary of 8.8.88. Now it was Burma's monks, and in particular the monks of Mandalay, who took the lead in challenging the regime. In the country's second city, thousands of brown-robed *pongyi* set out in the early morning to collect alms. Nothing unusual about that, except that on 8th August 1990 they set out as a single body, accompanied by hundreds of students, many of whom had taken refuge from MI in Mandalay's monasteries.

The trouble started when one student unfurled a peacock flag. When soldiers attempted to seize him, a scuffle broke out. Suddenly students and monks alike were being roundly beaten by the Tatmadaw. Then shots rang out. Two monks and two students were killed. Scores more were wounded.

The Buddhist *Sangha* reacted angrily, the more so when the state media reported that only one monk had been slightly wounded. All over Burma, when soldiers or members of their families attempted to offer alms, the monks turned their begging bowls upside down. From 27th August the *Sangha* refused to perform religious rites for the military, including funerals – no laughing matter, since even soldiers believed that the intercession of monks increased their chances of a better life in their next reincarnation. Simultaneously stories spread that the left-side pectorals of many stone and marble Buddha images had begun to 'swell and weep'. One inference was that while SLORC might deal as it pleased with its political enemies, it provoked Burma's religious orders at its peril; another, that since the left-hand breast was associated with the female principle, the Buddha himself was lamenting Aung San Suu Kyi's 'imprisonment'.

For a month or two SLORC let the situation ride, then retaliated. As ever, the junta preferred force to reasoned argument or appeasement. Towards the end of October the Tatmadaw stormed 350 of Burma's monasteries, 133 of them in Mandalay alone. Armed troops moved into their prayer halls and dormitories, seizing those monks suspected of being most anti-regime and grabbing student dissidents living in the monasteries for sanctuary. By a further state order, the existing *Sangha* was dissolved and a new '*Sangha* union', controlled by the Ministry for Religious and Home Affairs, established. All monks had to register with this, or disrobe. Further, each monk was required to give an undertaking not to oppose either SLORC or the Tatmadaw.

Burma's oldest, proudest and most independent institution had been emasculated. Again SLORC justified its actions by raising the spectre of communist infiltration. Yet the junta's attention had not been wholly diverted by the country's 'troublesome priests'. In September it resumed its campaign against the NLD, arresting several more of its leaders, including acting chairman U Kyi Maung and U Chit Khaing, another former colonel who had become number two on the Executive Committee. Both were given ten-year prison sentences on bogus charges of inciting unrest and disclosing state secrets. Also rounded up and put in jail were forty-odd elected NLD MPs. While it might have stretched SLORC's resources to have arrested all 392 of the NLD's successful candidates, there was method in its piecemeal approach. The idea was not to destroy the NLD in one go, but to keep thinning out its most effective members, until hopefully it collapsed of its own accord. And certainly the man who now took on the responsibilities of acting NLD chairman, former Brigadier-General U Aung Shwe, was distinctly less capable than his predecessors and struggled to hold the League together.

In time, other MPs could either be picked up individually or in batches – unless of course they renounced their NLD ties altogether, in which case the authorities might leave them alone. But here again SLORC miscalculated. While even at this early stage some successful NLD candidates began to waver, most remained committed to the democratic cause and loyal to Aung San Suu Kyi.

Through an oversight perhaps, or because he had not played a conspicuous part in the NLD's national campaign, SLORC had neglected to fully rein in Suu Kyi's cousin and contemporary, Dr Sein Win. The son of Bogyoke Aung San's eldest brother U Ba Win, Sein Win too had been educated abroad, though in Germany, not England. Before the election, he had been given the responsibility of looking after the NLD's accounts. Like many other NLD members, he had been held in detention, but only briefly. Sensing that MI was now hot on his tail, Sein Win fled

Rangoon. Together with seven NLD MPs, and with the express backing of another 250 following a conference in Mandalay, he made his way to Manerplaw, close to the Thai border in Karen (Kayin) state.

As well as being the main stronghold of the Karen National Union (KNU), Manerplaw was the headquarters of the Democratic Alliance of Burma (DAB), a broad federation of anti-regime groups that included, as well as all the main ethnic insurgency movements (except the KNPP), the militant ABSDF. While holding back from condoning armed resistance, Dr Sein Win made contact with the principal leaders of the 'Burmese Revolt', including the Karen strongman Saw Bo Mya, who was chairman of both the DAB and the KNU.

Largely as a result of his meetings in Manerplaw, on 18th December Dr Sein Win set up the National Coalition Government of the Union of Burma (NCGUB). At the same time U Win Khet, one of the few original NLD Central Committee members still at liberty, created what he called the NLD-LA (National League for Democracy – Liberated Area) along the Thai border. Both bodies would transfer out of Burma once the Tatmadaw intensified its campaign against the KNU. Win Khet moved to Thailand, to establish the NLD-LA in Mae Sot. But Dr Sein Win eventually went much further afield, taking the NCGUB's headquarters to Washington, the better to lobby the UN and the US government to take firm action against the regime.

In the long term these were significant developments. The NCGUB declared itself the legitimate government of Burma, based on the 1990 election result and its membership of elected representatives. As 'a government in exile', however, it did not overplay its hand. Dr Sein Win, loyal to his cousin, insisted that its role was to act as an interim body only. Once the junta stepped down, it would disband in favour of the whole elected people's assembly. As significantly, the creation of the NCGUB, the NLD-LA and the NCUB (National Council of the Union of Burma, another solidarity front), provided forums beyond the physical reach of the junta for the NLD and its affiliated parties to continue the struggle for Burmese democracy. The same forums – a confusing Aladdin's cave of acronyms – promoted international awareness of Burma's plight and encouraged the spawning of a plethora of pro-Aung San Suu Kyi activist organisations around the world. These would include the Burma Action Group (later renamed the Burma Campaign UK) in Britain, and in the USA the Free Burma Coalition.

These developments, however, lay mainly in the future. By the end of 1990, SLORC had several reasons to congratulate itself. Although the suspension of development aid by the USA and the European Union remained in force, and President George Bush, Sr was busy persuading Congress to impose a ban on Burmese imports, Japan had broken ranks. Total, the French-based oil giant, was tendering to develop the 'Yandana' pipeline, which would take gas from Burmese reserves in the Andaman Sea to a fuel-hungry Thailand. Other Western brand names, including PepsiCo. Inc., were also showing an interest in taking advantage of Burma's new 'open door' trading policy. A major weapons-supply deal, valued at an estimated $1.4 billion, had been struck with China, giving SLORC (amongst other hardware) its first advanced MiG fighter jets. And politically all the evidence was that the house arrest of Aung San Suu Kyi was paying handsome dividends. The NLD had not yet been smashed, but for sure it had been knocked to the ground.

Soon enough it became an offence to wear an Aung San Suu Kyi T-shirt or badge, or even to own her photograph or picture. Mere possession of such items was enough to rile MI, as was the bare utterance of her name. Instead, people began referring to her more simply as 'The Lady' – though even that could be enough to arouse suspicion. It was a code that too many understood. Yet SLORC's attempts to erase her from the national consciousness were counterproductive. They were merely one more step towards her beatification. Imprisoned in her lakeside residence, and for the time being allowed no visitors, 'The Lady' could do no wrong. Much better to have left her alone and waited for her to make some bad mistake, as everyone does sooner or later in politics.

What the rest of the world called 'house arrest', the junta called 'restricted residence'. Yet this did not explain the large signs erected outside 54 University Avenue advising drivers 'Do Not Slow Down' and 'No U-Turns'. Nor did it explain the permanent presence of soldiers at her gate, or why pedestrians loitering anywhere near it were liable to be seized and beaten on the spot. Or indeed, why the number 54 itself had been carefully removed.

And it went on. Having failed to release Daw Aung San Suu Kyi on 20th July 1990, SLORC also failed to release her on 20th July 1991. Instead, three weeks later, on 10th August, the 'law' – never anything other than the arbitrary dictates of a small gang of ill-educated ageing soldiers desperate to preserve their ill-gotten power – was retroactively amended to allow the 'government' to detain anyone, in whatever manner, for up to five years without preferring charges or bringing them to trial.

Suu Kyi herself took such setbacks on the chin. Being under house arrest was hardly a holiday, but it did not compare to being tortured and imprisoned amid the lethal squalor of Insein and other jails, as happened to droves of her NLD colleagues and followers. Enduring it, for however long – perhaps indefinitely – was the least (not the most) she could do for her country. In a curious way too house arrest, and the progressively tight restrictions to which she was subjected, were not unsuited to her moralising temperament. If, in the English proverb, sticks and stones can break no bones, in Burmese Theravada Buddhist lore the abnegation of the self is the highest ideal to which a human may aspire.

Prior to 20th July 1989 Buddhism had been present in Suu Kyi's life as part of her cultural inheritance, but seldom seemed to dominate her mindset. She had performed Buddhist rites at her marriage and, during a family visit to Rangoon, had seen to it that Alexander and Kim went through 'novitiation' ceremonies. Campaigning for the NLD, she made a point of attending local pagodas and monasteries, lighting joss-sticks before famous Buddha images and making other offerings. But few had considered her an especially devout or religious person.

Under house arrest her faith deepened. Buddhism became both a solace and a means of further training and enriching her intellect. She was fortunate that her mother had built up a small library of Buddhist books. Dr Aris, when he visited 54 University Avenue at the close of 1989, discovered that his wife had begun learning and reciting the *sutras* – those prayer-like incantations that are the audible backbone of Buddhist monastic practice. She had also, he noted, taken to meditating.

Meditation following the *Vipassana* method – mental concentration through controlled, conscious breathing – was used by many Burmese prisoners. It had been urged upon Suu Kyi by U Tin Oo, who had himself used it during his spell of imprisonment in the 1980s. Under house arrest, *Vipassana* meditation became a core element in the strict regimen that Suu Kyi adopted. It was how she began each day. Always regular in her habits, she rose at 4.30 a.m., well before dawn. After meditating, she listened to her short-wave radio, picking up the BBC's World and Burmese services, and sometimes VOA; and later, from July 1992 onwards, the DVB (Democratic Voice of Burma), an external broadcasting station funded by the Norwegian government and staffed by Burmese émigrés. Next she exercised, using a 'Nordic Track' that Dr Aris had bought for her. Only then did she treat herself to a light breakfast.

The remainder of the day was divided between 'study', household chores and, until it became sorely out of tune and its wires began to break, playing the piano – Bach being, like meditation, another form of self-discipline. Later on she prepared another light meal, from foodstuffs purchased for her by the single 'maid' who was the only non-military person she was normally permitted to have any contact with, other than her ageing aunt, Daw Khin Gyi, who continued to live in the compound's smaller house. After another session with the short-wave radio she turned in early, to sleep as best she could.

During the first months of house arrest, Suu Kyi spent some hours tending the garden, but desisted when she observed her guards taking photographs of her. She was, she believed, entitled to her privacy. As a result the compound became overgrown with tropical foliage. Water-snakes, abounding in Inya Lake, could be heard slithering through the unkempt grass. Other, often voluntary privations followed. True to his word, Dr Aris sent her a regular supply of books and other goods. A particular boon was when the publishers donated a set of the *Encyclopædia Britannica*, and had it shipped to Rangoon at their own expense. But then Suu Kyi learned that the Tatmadaw's cameras had again been busy. When parcels were brought to her gate from the British embassy, they were carefully opened and their contents photographed. The reason? To shame her in the *Working People's Daily*. Photographs appeared of a Jane Fonda callisthenics video, and of a quality lipstick. While so many of her fellow Burmese struggled to fill their stomachs, the 'Western fashion girl' continued to live a life of decadent debauchery, the inference was. At once Suu Kyi announced she would receive no more parcels. SLORC retaliated by confiscating her correspondence. The last letter Michael received from his Suu in 1990 was dated 17th July, requesting copies of two Indian literary epics, the *Mahabharata* and the *Ramayana*, both of which she had read before, but wanted to reread. After that, nothing. Like others who wrote to her, Dr Aris had no idea whether the letters he continued to send were getting through. More disheartening still, though not unanticipated, the regime refused Dr Aris a further visa, even for a short visit. Years would go by before he saw her again.

In a bid to make Aung San Suu Kyi directly beholden to them, the generals prevented any money being sent, to cover her living expenses.

If she needed food, let SLORC buy it for her; they would pay her utility bills as well. But Suu Kyi would have none of that. Instead, she began selling off pieces of her furniture, even a bathtub and her air-conditioning equipment. Her liaison officers apparently cooperated, telling her they were being sold in a market and giving her the proceeds. In fact Suu Kyi's furniture was deposited in an army warehouse – ready to be returned to her when and if her 'restricted residence' was lifted. She hung on to her short-wave radio, though. The BBC and VOA were the only means she had of following, however incompletely, events as they unfolded, both in Burma and in the wider world beyond. Those guarding her were under strict instructions not to 'talk politics' with their prisoner, so that even the results of the 1990 election became known to Suu Kyi only once they were known in London and Ohio.

To tease her custodians, she peppered the downstairs walls of her residence with choice quotations from Gandhi, Nehru and other political luminaries, including of course her father, Aung San. Soldiers and liaison officers who came into the house would look at them and smile, but say nothing. Mostly they treated her with the respect due to the Bogyoke's daughter – there was none of Captain Myint Oo's Danubyu wrath. Similarly, Suu Kyi treated her immediate captors well. It was not the fault of the ordinary soldiers around her that she was not allowed out, that she had to experience the constant anguish of enforced separation from her husband and sons, or that her health was beginning to suffer – because of her meagre diet her vision dimmed, and spinal osteoarthritis (spondylosis) set in. Rather, the problem swung too far the other way. The cornerstone of Aung San Suu Kyi's emerging Buddhism was *metta*, loving-kindness, or empathetic care towards all sentient beings, particularly human beings. She may have had no great affection for General Ne Win, but she could still feel, and practise, a commonality with less exalted military men. If the Tatmadaw was ever to be returned to the ideals ordained by her father, then now was as good a time as any to begin the process.

She talked to the soldiers, asked about their families, smiled back at them, laughed, made jokes. For their officers, answerable to their seniors, this was disquieting. The men had to be replaced, and then replaced again. Nobody served at 54 University Avenue too long.

It was a strangely ascetic existence for a woman who was married and a mother. No. 54 had become a hermitage infested by the military, and

Aung San Suu Kyi its increasingly venerated solitary. As Suu Kyi herself discovered from crackling reports picked up on her wireless, far from being forgotten she was becoming a global icon. While not neglecting his academic duties, Dr Aris networked tirelessly on her behalf. And in 1991 his efforts bore wondrous fruit.

The first two honours to be bestowed upon Aung San Suu Kyi came early in the year. Her Oxford college, St Hugh's, made her an Honorary Fellow. Then she was awarded the Rafto Prize – established in 1981 to commemorate the life of Professor Thorolf Rafto, a Norwegian economic historian and outstanding human-rights advocate. Yet estimable as these distinctions were, they were but a prelude to what followed. Next came the news that Aung San Suu Kyi had won the Sakharov Prize for Freedom of Thought, awarded by no less a body than the European Parliament.

Andrei Sakharov had been the best-known Soviet dissident of the Cold War period. A brilliant physicist, he helped the USSR develop its first hydrogen bomb in the early 1950s, and was the youngest ever member of the Soviet Academy of Sciences. In the 1960s, however, he became disillusioned with the Kremlin's nuclear weapons programme, and began campaigning instead for nuclear disarmament and civil rights. By 1985, when the European Parliament voted to create a human-rights award, Sakharov was in his sixth year of internal exile. It seemed only appropriate to name the prize after him.

Previous recipients included Nelson Mandela and Alexander Dubček, the leader of the Czech uprising of 1968. It was auspicious too that Sakharov himself had been awarded the Nobel Peace Prize, in 1975. On the morning of 14th October 1991, the Nobel Peace Prize Committee, at a press conference in Oslo, announced the winner of the most prestigious award of all, in any category.

Dr Aris, who had taken up a visiting professorship at Harvard University in September, issued a press statement of his own that same day. 'I am informed . . . that my dear wife Suu has been awarded the Nobel Peace Prize,' he wrote. 'Many will now for the first time learn of her courageous leadership of the non-violent struggle for the restoration of human rights in her country. I believe her role will come to serve as an inspiration to a great number of people in the world today.'

'The pride and joy which I and our children feel at this moment,' Aris went on, 'is matched by sadness and continuing apprehension. We, her family, are denied any contact with her whatsoever, and know nothing of her condition except that she is quite alone. We do not even know if she is still kept in her own home or if she has been moved elsewhere.'

The Nobel Prizes, all six of them, were the inspiration of Alfred Nobel, a Swedish industrialist, credited with (amongst other money-spinning ventures) the invention of dynamite – the Nobel family company was called Nitroglycerine Inc. By the terms of his will (he died in 1896) he set up a fund (fifty-five million Swedish kroner) to reward, and therefore promote, the work of outstanding scientists and writers. But he added a Peace Prize for those who contributed most to the 'confraternity of mankind', whether as individuals or organisations. By an anomaly – in 1896 Sweden and Norway had a common throne – 'peace laureates' were to be chosen not by the Swedish Academy, but by a committee appointed by the *Storting*, the Norwegian parliament.

The Peace Prize was first awarded in 1901, to the founder of the International Committee of the Red Cross, Jean Henri Durant. By 1991 more recent recipients included Albert Schweitzer (1953), the Office of the United Nations High Commission for Refugees (1955), Martin Luther King, Jr (1964), Amnesty International (1977), Mother Teresa (1979), Lech Wałęsa (1983), Desmond Tutu (1984) and the Fourteenth Dalai Lama (1989). That two American presidents (Theodore Roosevelt and Woodrow Wilson), as well as Henry Kissinger, accused of war crimes in some quarters, had also won the prize devalued it to a degree: critics claimed that it validated a specifically 'Western' political agenda. But in a broader, more balanced view it was, and is, a club eminently worth belonging to. Each year a hundred names or so are proposed – a tough field to come through. Candidates may be nominated by the Nobel Peace Prize Committee; by members of the *Storting* itself, and of other national assemblies; by previous winners; by members of the International Court of Justice and some other international human-rights organisations; and by professors of law, political science, history and philosophy at recognised universities. They may also be nominated by national leaders, as happened with Aung San Suu Kyi: Václav Havel, President of the Czech Republic, was her eventual sponsor. While the sifting of names and final selection process are secretive, it is likely that in Aung San Suu Kyi's case special consideration was given to the appalling catalogue of human-rights abuses documented by Amnesty International and others rights groups. As Nobel Peace Prize winners go, Suu Kyi was fast-tracked. Even Nelson Mandela, the champion of the anti-apartheid movement in South Africa, given a life sentence in 1960, was not awarded the prize until 1993.

The award ceremony was held at Oslo's City Hall on 10th December 1991 – International Human Rights Day. Amongst many distinguished guests were the King and Queen of Norway, eight previous winners of the prize, members of the *Storting* and a bevy of senior diplomats. Not present was any representative of the Burmese government. Proceedings began with the Norwegian Chamber Orchestra playing the Preludium from Edvard Grieg's *Holberg Suite* under the baton of Iona Brown. The chairman of the Nobel Peace Prize Committee, Professor Francis Sejersted, then delivered an encomium. The original citation had characterised Aung San Suu Kyi as 'one of the most extraordinary examples of civil courage in Asia in recent decades'. Sejersted now added his own appraisal. She had, he said, 'built a policy marked by an extraordinary combination of sober realism and visionary idealism'. He compared her to Gandhi, while not neglecting the example of her father, Aung San. 'Aung San Suu Kyi,' he went on, 'brings out something of the best in us. We feel we need precisely her sort of person in order to retain our faith in the future. That is what gives her such power as a symbol, and that is why any ill-treatment of her feels like a violation of what we have most at heart.'

Sejersted's speech concluded, two Burmese musicians, U Tun Aung and U Mya Maung, performed a traditional Burmese air, 'Loving Kindness and the Golden Harp'. It was then Alexander Aris's turn to speak.

Ordinarily the recipient of the prize would have taken the podium to make an acceptance speech. As that was clearly impossible, Suu Kyi's elder son, flanked by Dr Aris and his brother Kim, spoke on her behalf, reading a text his father had helped him prepare. 'Firstly,' he quite properly commenced, 'I know that she would begin by saying that she accepts the Nobel Prize not in her own name but in the name of all the people of Burma.' But while Alexander did not shirk from fleshing out the state of fear in Burma, he evoked his mother's insistence that the only true way forward was through reconciliation. 'I know that if she were free today,' he said, 'my mother would in thanking you also ask you to pray that the oppressors and the oppressed should throw down their weapons and join together to build a nation founded on humanity in the spirit of peace.'

Towards the close of the ceremony, Alexander and Kim were presented with the Nobel Peace Prize diploma, a gold medal, and 'a document indicating the amount of the Prize' – some six million Swedish kronor, equivalent to roughly one million US dollars. The orchestra then played

Johann Pachelbel's Canon in D major, and the hall quietly emptied.

That it was Alexander (not Michael) Aris who gave the acceptance speech added to the solemn drama of the award ceremony, and did not go unnoticed by the world's media. Still a teenager, he had had neither the opportunity nor the inclination to develop himself as a public speaker, least of all on so prestigious a stage. But if his delivery was halting, that too reflected courage and reminded his audience that it is, above all, the young who have most to lose at the hands of tyranny.

By 10th December the United Nations General Assembly had already passed the first in a long line of resolutions condemning Burma's military junta; and the UN Secretary-General, Javier Pérez de Cuéllar, had made a personal statement calling for Aung San Suu Kyi's release. Now, other heavyweight bodies repeated the same demands, including the European Parliament, the White House and individual governments.

Had SLORC not placed Suu Kyi under house arrest, it is improbable that she would have been given the Nobel Peace Prize in 1991, and perhaps in any other year. While the junta dismissed her as a 'trouble-maker', and responded with its usual callous force when a celebratory crowd gathered outside her compound, it had unwittingly set her on the highest pedestal imaginable. The troubles of Burma were under international scrutiny as never before, even if media coverage remained sporadic and selective.

XXXII

FAMOUSLY ALONE

When I was under house arrest, here on my own, I would come down at night and walk around and look up at his photograph and feel very close to him. I would say to him then: 'It's you and me, father, against them.'

Aung San Suu Kyi, in Fergal Keane, 'The Lady Who
Frightens Generals', *The Sunday Times*, 14th July 1996

SINCE October 1991 and the winning of the Nobel Peace Prize, Aung San Suu Kyi has been feted with scores more awards and accolades, none of which she has been able to accept in person. In 1992 she became the recipient of the Simón Bolivar Prize, given by UNESCO; in 1995, the Jawaharlal Nehru and Gandhi Awards were given to her; in 1996 followed the Empty Chair Award, at the launch of 'Women of the Year' in London; in 1997, the Pearl S. Buck Women's Award; in 2000, at the behest of Bill Clinton, the Presidential Medal of Freedom – the highest honour that may be bestowed on a foreigner by the US government; and in 2006 the Franklin D. Roosevelt Four Freedoms Award. Several cities have given her their freedom, including Rome, Oxford, Dublin, Edinburgh and (getting in on the act before any of the rest) tiny Giugliano in Italy, in 1993. Universities too have queued up to give her honorary degrees or membership – among them the Universities of Thammasat (Bangkok), Toronto, Brussels, Prague, Melbourne, Natal and Cambridge. As early as 1992 the Student Union of the London School of Economics made her its honorary president, while by 2006 Suu Kyi's alma mater, St Hugh's College, was naming its 'full moon' summer ball after her. *Time* magazine, the BBC and the *New Statesman* are just some of the media organisations that have conducted polls among readers, listeners and viewers in her favour. In John Boorman's somewhat forgettable 1995 movie *Beyond Rangoon*, Suu Kyi, or an actress purporting to resemble her, figures somewhere near the heart of the 1988 uprising, though not as prominently as the obligatory American heroine, a higher-minded Barbarella played by the glamorously perspirational Patricia Arquette. Richard Shannon went some way to restoring the balance with his one-woman play *The Lady of Burma*, first performed (by Liana Gould) at the Old Vic in London in November 2006. Nor has Suu Kyi been ignored by popular musicians. Rock groups as disparate as U2, R.E.M. and Coldplay have dedicated tracks and songs to her, as have individual performers such as Bono, Damien Rice and former Beatle (Sir) Paul McCartney.

It has all become a bit of a bandwagon, made almost comic by Suu Kyi's declared distaste for anything that even vaguely hints of a personality cult. Where she has been able, she has always indicated that her acceptance of honours is on behalf of the Burmese people, not herself. But in the perennial search for the ultimate embodiment of human goodness, she has been seized upon, not so much by Hollywood or Rockwood, but by a plethora of more-or-less interconnected august institutions, whether governmental, inter-governmental, supra-governmental, academic or rights-voluntarist. If, in the modern, mass, visual-image-led perception of heroes and heroines, she has yet to attain the pure iconic status of Che Guevara, the beneficiary of a single photograph and the enduring mascot of the anti-capitalist brigade, she has become revered by thousands who have neither visited Burma nor directly experienced the deadpan stare of its military dictatorship.

Although there can be no questioning Aung San Suu Kyi's fortitude and obstinacy for justice, she is more interesting than the hype allows. The announcement of the Nobel Prize in October 1991 was accompanied by the publication of *Freedom from Fear*, a collection of writings by and about Suu Kyi compiled and edited by Dr Aris. Prior to publication, the manuscript had been selectively circulated and probably influenced the deliberations of the Nobel Peace Prize Committee. Václav Havel, who had nominated her for the prize, furnished a foreword. 'She is an outstanding example of the power of the powerless,' he wrote.

It contained most of what Suu Kyi had already published – her short life of her father, *Let's Visit Burma* (though this was now given the more politically correct title 'My Country and People'), and the 'Indian' essays written before and after Simla. There was also a sampling of her letters and speeches, including her Shwedagon address. Aris himself contributed an introduction, summarising Suu Kyi's biography up to the time of her house arrest. Appended at the end were four 'appreciations', two of them of a personal character, by Ma Than É and Ann Pasternak Slater, and two of them by academics, Josef Silverstain and Philip Kreager. If, of necessity, *Freedom from Fear* had a mixed-bag potpourri feel about it, at its core were two relatively new essays written by Aung San Suu Kyi after her return to Rangoon in March 1988. 'In Quest of Democracy' and, prompting the book's title, 'Freedom from Fear' – adumbrated her political philosophy.

As Aris explains, it had been Suu Kyi's intention to compose an entire volume of essays, provisionally entitled *Essays in Honour of Bogyoke Aung San*. Either house arrest put a stop to this project, or Aris only had the texts of the two essays included. The phrase itself, 'freedom from fear', was not her own, but was ultimately derived from a congressional address given by President Franklin D. Roosevelt on 6th January 1941 in the wake of Japan's attack on Pearl Harbor a month earlier that propelled the United States into the Second World War. Roosevelt's line was that the Axis powers had put democracy itself in jeopardy, but if Americans truly cherished what he called 'the four freedoms', then Germany and Japan would be defeated.

Roosevelt's other 'freedoms' were freedom of speech and expression, freedom of worship and freedom from want. By 'freedom from fear' he meant, quite specifically, a 'world-wide reduction in armaments' – once the war was over, of course. But by Aung San Suu Kyi it was developed into something much broader. For her, 'freedom from fear' means not just the removal of the oppression that causes fear in people's minds, but a change in their mindset when confronted by oppression. As crucially, she urges freedom from fear in the minds of the oppressors. Only if the 'fear of losing power' among Burma's power-holders is overcome can a peaceable transition to democracy and a respect for human rights be achieved.

Aung San Suu Kyi rules out force as a means of achieving transition. Its use only institutionalises violence – or causes, as she puts it, 'an Animal Farm syndrome where the new order after its first flush of enthusiastic reforms takes on the murky colours of the very system it has replaced'. Instead, she urges that 'the quintessential revolution' should be:

that of the spirit, born of an intellectual conviction of the need for change in those mental attitudes and values which shape the course of a nation's development. A revolution which aims merely at changing official policies and institutions with a view to an improvement in material conditions has little chance of genuine success. Without a revolution of the spirit, the forces which produced the iniquities of the old order would continue to be operative, posing a constant threat to the process of reform and regeneration.

But where, or how, was this 'revolution of the spirit' to be found or centred, especially when 'There is nothing new in Third World governments seeking to justify and perpetuate authoritarian rule by denouncing liberal democratic principles as alien'? Aung San Suu Kyi's solution is twofold. On the one hand, by regularly evoking the memory of her father (albeit an idealised memory) and of the 1940s independence struggle, she insists that the principles of liberal democracy are already embedded in Burmese history. On the other, and equally damaging to the 'traditionalist' position taken by her opponents in the junta, she seeks to demonstrate that not only are democracy and Buddhism (the bedrock of Burmese culture) wholly compatible, but that the one is, at the very least, latent in the other. Otherwise why, after 'a quarter-century of narrow authoritarianism under which they had been fed a pabulum of shallow, negative dogma', should the Burmese people have responded with such alacrity and enthusiasm to the calls for a democratic uprising in 1988?

While Aung San Suu Kyi acknowledges the prominent part played by Burmese monks during the upheavals 'in their customary role as mentors', she contends that the 'timeless values' expressed by them were not confined 'to any particular circle'. Rather a 'traditional knowledge', far deeper than the 'traditions' of Ne Win's military regime, 'went right through Burmese society from urban intellectuals to small shopkeepers to doughty village grandmothers'.

Aung San Suu Kyi locates her 'true' tradition in specific Buddhist precepts and practices: in a theory of kingship that requires the ruler to govern for their people, and with their assent, outlined in such instruments as the 'Ten Duties of Kings', the 'Seven Safeguards against Decline' and 'Four Assistances to the People'. While she concedes that kingship itself may not be the most appropriate form of government in the modern age, the ten rules that Buddhist kings are bound by – 'liberality, morality, self-sacrifice, integrity, kindness, austerity, non-anger, non-violence, forbearance and non-opposition (to the will of the people)'– provide a matrix of responsibility and accountability that apply to authority at all times. 'By invoking the Ten Duties of Kings the Burmese are not so much indulging in wishful thinking,' Aung San Suu Kyi writes, 'as drawing on time-honoured values to reinforce the validity of political reforms they consider necessary.' Further, 'The people of Burma view democracy not merely as a form of government but as an integrated social and ideological system based on respect for the individual.'

Through such arguments and assumptions, Suu Kyi takes on the junta at its own game. Yet in both essays her overview is reinforced by other joists. Both contain fulsome references to Mahatma Gandhi and to the United Nations' Universal Declaration of Human Rights, signed up to by Burma in December 1948. Her political thought, too, is couched in a markedly 'liberal' style of discourse, acquired during her long years in Oxford. And that perhaps is the real measure of her written achievement, of her contribution to the moral end of political philosophy: the merging of four distinctive strands: a version of Buddhism, Gandhian non-violence, the UN rights programme and Anglo-Saxon liberalism. Here is a package that is at once universalistic and trans-cultural, and ostensibly tailored to the traditions, needs and aspirations of a particular people.

Yet Aung San Suu Kyi's vision is also idiosyncratic – quite apart from its obvious indebtedness to the places and cultures with which she is most familiar: Rangoon, Delhi, Oxford, London, New York, Bhutan, Tokyo and Simla. If her appraisal of Buddhism as a source of political correctitude is unusual (for many, Buddhism is a deliberate shunning of the temporal world), then so too is her reading of history. 'The Emperor Ashoka,' she writes, 'who ruled his realm in accordance with the principles of non-violence and compassion is always held up as an ideal Buddhist king.' But although Ashoka, the most celebrated of India's rulers, did indeed, in the middle of the third century BC, preside over something like a Buddhist utopia (if the pillar inscriptions that Ashoka himself left behind are to be believed), his 'empire' was the outcome of a long series of bloody wars. Ashoka had been a formidable warrior.

A similar observation might be made of Bogyoke Aung San, who took to the gun before he took to the ballot box. More generally, where democracy does exist, usually it has been preceded by armed conflict of some kind, the American War of Independence being a prime example. As the histories of Europe and South America in the nineteenth century also testify, whole nations can sometimes be mobilised under circumstances of extreme adversity, but, under responsible leadership, prosper thereafter.

Aung San Suu Kyi's 'revolution of the spirit' seems to take the very concept of revolution to a higher level – one reason why she is widely admired in actual democracies where secularist materialism may create a vacuum of the spirit. Whether it was the most appropriate package for a country as backward and authoritarian as Burma was, in 1990, is another matter. Yet despite the gloomiest predictions of some Burma-watchers, the five years that followed offered just sufficient evidence of change for hope to be rekindled.

At about the time Suu Kyi learned that she had received the Nobel Peace Prize, Burma's formal head-of-state, General Saw Maung, began exhibiting unambiguous signs of dementia. Although still only in his early sixties, his speech was slurred and his behaviour unpredictable. It was reported in the *Bangkok Post* and *The Far Eastern Economic Review* that, on 21st December 1991, he threatened to kill onlookers with his revolver during an official tournament at the army golf course in Rangoon. He then proclaimed, 'I am King Kyansittha' – a Pagan period monarch well known to Burmese for outfoxing death many times. At other times he asserted that there had been sightings of Jesus Christ in Tibet. On 21st January 1992, during a long, rambling televised address, he told his audience that 'martial law is no law at all', then reassured them that Burma was ruled 'with wisdom', not 'black magic'. He was after all, he reiterated, King Kyansittha.

Insiders were little surprised when on 23rd April, Radio Burma announced Saw Maung's resignation on the grounds of 'ill-health'. Probably he had suffered a stroke six or seven months before. But because, as ever, SLORC was less than forthcoming with details, rumours soon spread that he had been slowly poisoned. Almost certainly Saw Maung had been removed from office some weeks before, for barely did SLORC have time to reorganise itself than a tranche of new policies was promulgated.

Encouraged by favourable omens (an earthquake along the Chinese border, and the first flowering of a rare bamboo in fifty years), General Than Shwe took over as SLORC chairman. The stolidly uninspiring General Maung Aye was promoted to vice-chairman and Commander-in-Chief of Burma's armed forces. It was generally assumed, perhaps because there was little evidence to the contrary, that Ne Win continued to exert final power from behind the scenes, though it is just as credible that the longed-for waning of the Old Man's influence began with Saw Maung's 'resignation'.

Both Than Shwe and Maung Aye were known to be Tatmadaw hardliners, and both preferred to keep a low profile. The same could not be said of Brigadier-General Khin Nyunt, who retained his position as Secretary One, but who now, in terms of public relations, took it upon himself to play the role of SLORC's main mouthpiece.

To some Khin Nyunt was known as the 'Prince of Darkness', complementing Khun Sa, the 'Prince of Death'. Born in 1937, the man who had moulded MI into a tropical KGB had wanted to be a movie actor before joining the army. Always meticulous about his appearance, he was better-looking than the rest of the junta. Though people said he had 'the cold eyes of a killer', he could, when so minded, exude charm. More often than not diplomats and other foreign dignitaries were taken in by his quick-thinking, vivacious personality. Everybody sensed that much of what he said was pure spin, but because it was said with panache, the temptation to take him at face value was often too strong to resist. But more than that, because Khin Nyunt seemed to make all the running, especially when compared to his media-unfriendly colleagues, it was soon believed that he, and not Than Shwe, was the real master of Burma.

Ever since Mikhail Gorbachev broke the mould of Soviet politics, Westerners especially were on the lookout for someone they 'could do business with' in Burma, a man who would work within the regime to bring about reform. For a while it seemed that Khin Nyunt was that man. That he himself actively encouraged such a view was auspicious. By supporting him, and by turning a blind eye on his past misdemeanours, it seemed possible that real progress might be made.

The reality was somewhat different. Though there was little love lost between MI and the army proper – Tatmadaw officers resented the fact that many intelligence officers had never put their lives on the line for the 'defence of the Union' in the same way they had – it is barely credible that SLORC, so soon after its inception, acted in anything but concert. Nor was Than Shwe a mere figurehead, as Saw Maung had been. Though he lacked flamboyance and was a devoted family man, he had a shrewd head dedicated above all to preserving the military's ascendancy. Once the immediate danger of continuing large-scale unrest had receded, in 1990, the junta, still guided by Ne Win, collectively determined policy. Individual policies may indeed have been devised by Khin Nyunt, but without the backing of Than Shwe and Maung Aye, they would have come to nothing.

The same policies were cleverly integrated, expressive of the sort of malign intent that characterises any totalitarian government that survives. Central to SLORC's strategy for retaining power was the ongoing expansion and modernisation of Burma's armed forces. This was done not to counter any external threat (there was none), but to put greater pressure on the ethnic insurgents, and to provide the junta with added manpower in the event of another uprising amongst the Burman people.

New, complementary approaches evolved to contain both insurgency and more purely political opposition. Disregarding the DAB – that loose confederation of minority pro-federal and armed pro-democracy factions – and the ABSDF, SLORC began offering apparently generous 'ceasefire' terms to individual insurgent groups, having first softened them up with an escalation of its military campaigns. Among the first to accept was the PNO (Pa'o National Organisation) in Shan state, in March 1991. More significantly the bulk of the Kachin Independence Army soon followed suit. Pursuing its policy of divide and conquer, the regime picked off other 'rebel' armies one by one. The terms offered varied between groups. Most were allowed to keep their weapons, at least for the time being. The regime also gave promises of economic assistance. But there were no real guarantees against the regime reneging on its promises of greater autonomy for those minorities who, after decades of fighting, agreed to 'come into the fold'. Nor did the ceasefire approach work in every case. The KNU (Karen National Union) particularly was to prove a tough nut to crack. But SLORC could claim that it was at last making headway in 'resolving' the deepest and most long-standing of Burma's problems.

Towards political dissidents, SLORC was less accommodating. Month in, month out, arrests and other kinds of harassment continued. Those political parties (including the NLD) that had come into being during the run-up to the 1990 election were systematically undermined by new decrees, which effectively gave SLORC the power of veto over their leaderships. Parties that refused to comply were threatened with immediate liquidation. Most simply packed up without bothering to contest the issue. Conversely, SLORC continued to hold out the promise of actual (as it saw it) democratic reform. A National Convention (or Constituent Assembly) for drawing up a new constitution, originally proposed by Khin Nyunt in 1990, was still very much 'on the cards'.

In the case of the NLD, Aung Shwe's leadership was confirmed by the junta, but only after the League agreed, under duress, to dismiss its titular chairman, U Tin Oo. Aung Shwe was not a collaborationist, but SLORC sensed that he did not have the metal to mount a sustained challenge to its rule. With U Tin Oo still in jail, and Aung San Suu Kyi under house arrest, the best that Aung Shwe could hope for was to keep the NLD in being. Yet the downward path of compromise was steep and slippery. When, at last, a date was set for the first meeting of the National Convention, in January 1993, the NLD had to decide whether to attend or be outlawed altogether. Some thought it should attend, others that it should not, and the party was split as badly as it had been by Aung Gyi's 'apostasy' in December 1988.

The problem with the National Convention was that, from the start, it was nothing but a Kafkaesque sham. Its composition bore only ironic resemblance to the election results of May 1990. Of 702 delegates, only ninety-nine were elected 'MPs'. Of these, a mere eighty-one belonged to the NLD – once the NLD, under Aung Shwe's tutelage, had decided that it was better to be a part of the 'process' than left stranded outside it. The rest were hand-picked by SLORC. Often such delegates had little or no political experience. The minorities were represented more or less proportionately to their share of the population, but again the regime did its utmost to pack the benches. Noticeably, some minority delegates were drawn from those who had recently negotiated ceasefire deals, and so were expected to be 'tame'.

But it was not just the composition of the Convention that was fixed. So was its entire agenda – as delegates rapidly discovered once the first session was under way. Khin Nyunt arrived to give an opening address, in which he did little other than extol the Tatmadaw. He then handed over to Lieutenant-General Myo Nyunt, chairman of the Convening Committee, and left. Myo Nyunt at once made it clear that the first requirement of any new parliament was that the army should have 25 per cent of the seats, chosen by the Chief-of-Staff, and that any new constitution should make no provision for the Tatmadaw to be held accountable to any body other than itself. Further 'guidelines', he intimated, would be provided in due course. Delegates were divided into 'working groups', with little or no contact permitted between them. They were also prohibited from having contact with anyone outside the Convention. Instead they were 'housed' in segregated army dormitories in a barracks close to where the Convention was being held. Soon enough, SLORC furnished '104 basic principles' that delegates could discuss within their groups, but not in the conference hall itself. Any comments and suggestions were to be submitted to the Convening Committee in written form, but not otherwise circulated.

The Convening Committee took no notice of whatever bits of paper came its way. But that did not expedite matters one iota. Instead, the Convention was regularly 'suspended' almost as soon as it had gathered. Among the pretexts given was that its members needed to return to their farms to tend the harvest. And so it became obvious that SLORC had no real interest in framing a new constitution, even one wholly articulated by itself. Rather, the real purpose of the Convention was to demonstrate that a 'democratic process' was under way, no matter that it might take for ever to complete.

This the junta needed to do to contain dissent at home, to appease its critics abroad and to clear the way for Burma's admission into ASEAN (Association of South-East Asian Nations), the increasingly influential regional trading bloc whose existing members included Thailand, Malaysia, Singapore, Vietnam, Indonesia, Brunei and the Philippines. In essence, the National Convention was nothing other than one part of a wider programme of window-dressing aimed at convincing the international financial community especially that the junta was serious about reform, and that Burma was therefore a safe place to invest in. For unless the dollars kept coming in the Tatmadaw would run out of funds and the whole house of cards would come tumbling down again.

On the economic front, again the omens looked favourable. Not only Total, but now Unocal, the American oil giant, came in on the Yandana gas pipeline project. Other Western companies were also entering into joint ventures, among them BAT (British American Tobacco) and Hewlett-Packard, as well as PepsiCo., Inc. The China trade was picking up nicely, and a tranche of international consortiums were busy building luxury hotels for a planned boom in tourism. The private-sector jobs market too was expanding.

On the streets of Rangoon and Mandalay, visitors were greeted with the sight of kids in jeans, and to the sound of Western rock music blaring out from upgraded tea-houses and newly opened discotheques. Yet the ugly truth was that 'economic liberalisation' – and with it an attempt to nurture a larger, but quiescent middle class – was accompanied, and significantly funded, by a quantum leap in opium production. Although exact figures were hard to come by, it was estimated by the DEA and other agencies that the area of land under poppy cultivation had grown by 80 per cent between 1988 and the end of 1991. Heroin manufacture had more than doubled, to 182 tons per annum. Eventually even Khun Sa and half his Mong Tai army would be bought out by

SLORC, in 1996. Despite repeated requests for his extradition by the USA, Khun Sa settled comfortably in Rangoon, investing his ill-gotten fortune in 'legitimate businesses', including the hotel trade.

Nor was there any reduction in the level of human-rights violations. The opposite, in fact. Not just the laying of the Yandana pipeline, but other infrastructure projects – new roads, new rail tracks, new bridges – were completed through forced labour. More and more young boys were recruited into the Tatmadaw, and as often as not soldiers helped themselves to what they wanted in remote villages, including girls and women. Thousands of young, mainly ethnic Burmese girls, especially from Shan State, were being sold into prostitution, mainly in Thailand; and in Burma's prisons torture remained routine.

No one suffered more than the Muslim Rohingyas of Arakan. There SLORC intermittently pursued a policy as close to ethnic cleansing as made no difference. Mosques were destroyed, belongings confiscated, and lands earmarked for redistribution among Arakan's Buddhist population. As a result, and for the second time since 1962, there was a mass exodus of 250,000 refugees to Bangladesh. As one Rohingya refugee was quoted as saying in *The Independent* (15th February 1992), 'at least now we can die in peace'.

On the other side of Burma, refugees continued pouring into Thailand. Tens of thousands ended up in ill-resourced refugee camps. Hundreds of thousands more entered the kingdom as migrant workers. Unable to bring the KNU to the ceasefire table, the Tatmadaw launched a major offensive against Manerplaw – 'Operation Dragon King' – at the end of 1991. Capturing a nearby hill ('Sleeping Dog Mountain'), the Burmese used Israeli mortars and its improved air power to reduce much of the town to rubble. Well dug in, the Karen soldiers held out and Manerplaw was not, this time round, overrun. But for miles around, Karen villages were burned to the ground. Those inhabitants who did not escape to Thailand were either killed or taken away in chains to join SLORC's labour gangs, and the younger women raped.

By March 1992 it was clear that the assault had failed. With the rainy season ahead, Manerplaw would have to wait another year. But this did not prevent the junta declaring a temporary 'unilateral' ceasefire immediately after Saw Maung's resignation. Simultaneously (on 27th April) it agreed to the repatriation of 200,000 Rohingyas from Bangladesh under the supervision of the United Nations. Further, some hundreds of political prisoners were released on 25th April, among them U Nu.

General Than Shwe himself said (untruthfully) that he was prepared to open talks with the NLD.

SLORC used Saw Maung's departure to give itself a cosmetic facelift. The *Working People's Daily* was renamed *The New Light of Myanmar*, although its content and blatantly pro-regime editorialising remained unchanged. The trick was to do just enough to keep optimists interested. Burma's universities, closed since the preceding December, were reopened. Selected foreign journalists were told they could have visas. But, as everyone knew, the real litmus test was whether Aung San Suu Kyi's house arrest would be lifted – and of that there was no sign. Questioned by foreign press-men, Khin Nyunt explained that her confinement was for 'Daw Suu Kyi's own safety'. He avoided using her full name, as Aung San was best left out of it. Yet, just to show how decent and reasonable it could be, SLORC now said that her husband and sons were welcome to visit her.

A year earlier, on 27th March 1991, coinciding with his birthday, Dr Aris had been called to the Burmese embassy in London. Hoping he would be granted a visa to visit Suu Kyi, he was instead told that he could write to her on condition that he encouraged her to leave Burma. Aris politely but firmly told embassy officials that they knew as well as he what his wife's response would be, then resigned himself to not seeing her for the foreseeable future. When, at the end of April 1992, SLORC changed its mind, he wasted no time making travel arrangements. He arrived in Rangoon on the afternoon of 2nd May. He was driven straight to University Avenue from the airport, after being told that, as on his previous visit, he was not at liberty to leave the compound or contact anyone without the regime's permission. By 17 May he was back in Bangkok, where he gave a press conference at Dom Muang airport. He read out a prepared statement, asking those present to understand 'the delicacy and the sensitivity of my situation'. He dreaded being trapped into giving an answer that might compromise Suu Kyi. Nonetheless he did his best to satisfy his audience's curiosity. His wife was, he said, 'in good health, but not particularly robust'. More importantly, her 'spirits remain as ever indomitable'. But there was no question of her leaving Burma. Indeed, they had hardly discussed the matter.

'In the nearly two and a half years since I last saw Suu,' Aris said, 'things have not been easy for her, but in the days we spent together she repeatedly pointed out to me that others have suffered much more than she has. So she does not want to complain.' 'Hers is an austere and disciplined life,' he added. Under house arrest, his wife spent her time 'reading politics, philosophy, literature, Buddhist writings and listening to the radio'. She had also, 'with her own hands', sewn curtains for every room in the house. There was no truth in a rumour that she had been removed from 54 University Avenue, nor that she had been hospitalised for a while. She had very little money – everything she won from the Nobel and other prizes went into a fund for promoting the education and health of the Burmese people – but enough to survive.

If, knowing his statement would be widely reported and picked up by SLORC, Aris had a political message, it came towards the end. Suu Kyi kept 'an open on mind' on government intentions. With strong emphasis he said, 'Please mark my words, she is prepared to give the authorities the benefit of the doubt.' But even in this there was nothing new. All along she had pressed for 'dialogue' with the junta, believing that if only the two sides started talking to each other, a way forward would emerge.

Alexander and Kim followed their father to Burma, each staying with their mother for a week. To a degree, the family had broken up. Having finished his secondary education at King Edward's School in Bath, Alexander (now nineteen) had enrolled at an American university and spent his vacations with his father. Kim (four years younger) was still at boarding school in Oxford. During his holidays he was looked after mainly by his aunt, Dr Aris's sister Lucinda Phillips and her husband Adrian.

In some quarters there had been real hope that a genuine 'thaw' was under way, and that Aung San Suu Kyi would indeed be released, as Bill Clinton, other heads-of-state and the UN General Council repeatedly demanded. But as the months slipped by, nothing seemed to happen. Then, in November 1992, Dr Aris received a brief handwritten letter from Suu Kyi asking him not to attempt to come back at Christmas as she had 'insufficient money to receive them'. This was her way of saying that she was not minded to accept any favours from her captors. On 1st December *The Times* reported that Aung San Suu Kyi was back on hunger strike, and quoted Aris as saying, 'Suu Kyi is doing what she believes is right. I stand by her; I support her in her decision; I completely understand it. I believe I am doing right in revealing to the world what I know of her condition. The alternative of doing nothing is unthinkable.'

As it turned out, there was no truth in the story. But Dr Aris, worried sick for his wife, had no way of knowing that. As he told a local reporter a few days later, when he visited his sister Lucinda in Warminster, 'In a situation so dark and remote, I fear it will be impossible to follow the course of events in the days ahead.'* Whether, though, Aris would have been granted another visa was doubtful. Among those denied access to Suu Kyi were a UN human-rights rapporteur, Dr Yozo Yokota, and (in February 1993) seven fellow Nobel Peace Prize winners. Called the 'laureate mission', and sponsored by the Montreal-based International Centre for Democracy and Democratic Development, the group comprised the Dalai Lama, Betty Williams, Mairead Corrigan, Desmond Tutu, Adolfo Esquivel and Oscar Arias Sánchez, as well as a representative from Amnesty International. Refused visas to enter Burma, they instead convened in Bangkok, where they held a press conference on 14th February

Khin Nyunt held a press conference in Rangoon the same day. He refused point-blank to field any question relating to Aung San Suu Kyi. But then there was no need. A month earlier Colonel Kyaw Win had categorically stated SLORC's position. 'We cannot release her,' he said, 'because we are afraid that unscrupulous elements might manipulate her and destabilise the situation. The next government will have to consider the release of Aung San Suu Kyi after a peaceful transfer of power.'† Since SLORC had no intention of transferring power, peacefully or otherwise, this suggested that Suu Kyi could well remain under house arrest indefinitely. Periodically SLORC revised the term of her sentence in accordance with its own, changeable 'laws'. On 21st January 1994 the junta announced that the total period of Aung San Suu Kyi's house arrest could be as much as six years, with another year added if three of SLORC's ministers so chose. But since SLORC had been arbitrarily prolonging her arrest since 1989, this meant nothing. Yet less than four weeks later, on 14th February 1994, and without any clear reason being given, the junta allowed a US congressman (Bill Richardson), the UNDP Rangoon resident (Jehan Raheem) and a *New York Times* reporter (Philip Shenon) to call on Aung San Suu Kyi at 54 University Avenue.

Suu Kyi had been permitted to attend the funeral of an uncle, in January 1992. That apart, this was the first time in more than four years that she had contact with anyone except her minders, her family,

---

* *Wiltshire Times*, 4th December 1992
† *The Times*, 13th January 1993

her maid and her doctor. Since Richardson, Raheem and Shenon were accompanied by officials and their meeting was taped, Suu Kyi assumed that it might be a prelude to the dialogue she had been seeking, and conducted herself accordingly. Told by Congressman Richardson that it was his view that Khin Nyunt 'should talk to you', Suu Kyi unhesitatingly riposted, 'I've always said he should talk to me.' If anyone was being inflexible, it was the regime, not herself. Yet her political principles remained intact, whatever ploys the junta used to make her abandon them. Instead of talking about 'freedom from fear', Suu Kyi now expatiated on 'confidence'. The success of any economic or political system, she told her visitors, was down to everybody having confidence – the people in the government, and the government in the people. 'It's no use,' she said pointedly, 'setting up a National Convention if nobody has any confidence in it.'

When elections are held, and the results ignored, the 'people feel cheated', so confidence becomes impossible. Quizzed by both Richardson and Raheem about her views on using development aid as a 'carrot', she at once asked where the stick was. If economic reform was all the United States was after, she was not interested. First there must be dialogue, followed by political reform. But she also used the opportunity to reiterate her personal ambition, or lack of it. Asked by Richardson, 'What would be your vision for Burma, if you were in power?', she answered quickly, 'It's not *my* vision. We must *not* emphasise this personality business. I'm quite happy to be a figurehead ... [but] I'm not Burma.' There were plenty of 'very able people' in the NLD who could take care of the future, if only they were allowed.

The subtext of Suu Kyi's responses was that SLORC had no good reason to fear her for what she was, but had everything to gain by talking to her and other NLD leaders. Yet the giveaway was in Richardson's opener. If Khin Nyunt's name had popped up so quickly, it was because he had set the meeting up and had briefed Richardson, Raheem and Shenon beforehand. Suu Kyi must have thought that good news, since it suggested that SLORC might finally be interested in listening to what the NLD had to say. But the generals were in no hurry to accommodate her or her party. After the three men left, her companionless life under house arrest resumed. For many months there was no further movement, and no further visitors.

But then, on 20th September 1994 and again on 28th October, she was taken to a state guest house to meet her principal antagonists, Than

Shwe and Khin Nyunt. The details of whatever exchanges took place have never been fully divulged, by either side. Soon afterwards, however, SLORC used the meetings to insinuate that 'dialogue' had indeed been instigated, prompting Suu Kyi to smuggle out a disclaimer that was subsequently published by Amnesty International. 'There has not been and there will not be any secret deals with regard to either my release or to any other issue,' she wrote.

Before the meetings took place she was visited by U Rewata Dhamma, her Buddhist mentor of old, who had agreed to act as an intermediary during a visit to Rangoon. But – contrary to speculation – it is unlikely their conversation had much political content. Rather, the junta may have felt that the ageing monk would make her realise where her best interests lay, where others had failed.

Again months went by without any change. Then, out of the blue, on the afternoon of 10th July 1995 – ten days short of six years from the beginning of her detention, and twenty-one days after her fiftieth birthday – a white limousine pulled into 54 University Avenue. The guards saluted smartly. Inside was Rangoon's chief of police. Minutes later Aung San Suu Kyi was politely informed that her house arrest was over.

Yet again SLORC was unforthcoming about the reasons behind its decision, though that did not prevent the international media fingering a specific cause. Japan, it was reported, had made any further grant of development aid conditional on her release. Doubtless some such behind-the-scenes leverage was involved. That the junta, in its bid to attract tourists on the same scale as Thailand, had already declared 1995/6 'Visit Myanmar Year', and had started negotiations to join ASEAN, also entered the reckoning. It is unlikely, though, that SLORC would have taken such a step unless it was convinced that the NLD was so weakened that Aung San Suu Kyi no longer had a platform for her 'trouble-making'. The regime's confidence was further boosted by the final storming of the KNU stronghold of Manerplaw in January 1995 following the emergence of the pro-regime DBKA (Democratic Buddhist Karen Army) born of divisions within the KNU's ranks, though fighting with the KNU, and with the Karennis, continued. Or it may just have been a supreme example of the kidology associated with Khin Nyunt. 'We've let her go, so what more do you want?'

XXXIII

FREEDOM ON A LEASH

Khin Nyunt expressed the belief that the SLORC had broad public support, and observed that the Burmese people smile a lot. I said that it has been my experience, in a lifetime of studying repressive societies, that dictators often delude themselves into believing they have popular support, but that people often smile not because they are happy, but because they are afraid.

Madeleine Albright, US ambassador to the United Nations,
in a press statement, 11th September 1995

THE evening of the day her house arrest was lifted, Aung San Suu Kyi received three more visitors: U Aung Shwe, caretaker leader of the NLD, and U Tin Oo and U Kyi Maung, both of whom had been released from prison some while before. These were the most important of her 'uncles', and immediately they discussed how to revive the League. In Suu Kyi's own words, 'we simply decided to pick up where we had left off six years ago, to continue our work. It remains in my memory as a quiet day, not a momentous one.'*

Her tone was similarly undemonstrative when she told foreign journalists about her first telephone conversation with Dr Aris. It would be days before lines into no. 54 were restored, so to speak to her husband she had to go to the residence of a British diplomat. 'He said "hello" and I said "hello" and then we talked about his plans.'† 2,171

---

* Aung San Suu Kyi, *Letters from Burma* (1997)
† *The Sunday Times*, 16th July 1995

days of detention had forged her self-control into an instrument of steel. Speaking to an impromptu press conference at no.54, she told reporters, 'I look upon these past six years as having been a chance to experience the kind of life that not many people have.' With equal sangfroid, when an army truck came by to return her furniture, Suu Kyi refused to take it in until such time as she had the money to repay what she had previously received. As it happened, that time would not be far away. Although Suu Kyi had made over all the prize moneys she had received to a specially created Burmese education trust, she kept the earnings from *Freedom from Fear* for herself, as being the sweat of her own brow; some of these could now be fed through to her.

The people of Rangoon were not so restrained. Within hours a crowd began collecting outside her gate. University Avenue had been cleared of soldiers, though they were at once replaced by MI types, identifiable by their cameras, sunglasses and unsmiling faces. Many of Suu Kyi's former student helpers – those whom she called 'my new sons' – hurried to her residence to offer their services afresh, among them Tin Hlaing (Eva), who, seven years before, had stood by her side at the Shwedagon pagoda. Like the others, he was a young man now, in his mid-twenties, but had lost none of his devotion to 'The Lady by the Lake'.

By the morning of 11th July the crowd outside had swollen to several thousand. Suu Kyi's instinct was to go out into the street and mingle with her well-wishers, but Tin Oo and Kyi Maung urged caution. Though it was clear to them that she had lost none of her mental strength, she was not in good physical condition, and was frailer than ever; they feared she would be crushed in a surge of adoration. Instead, following her press conference, a table that Suu Kyi sometimes used for writing was taken outside and pushed against the gate. Moments later, to the thrill of those gathered outside, the Bogyoke's daughter's head and shoulders appeared above them. Cheers broke out. It was true. She was still alive, and she was free to talk.

Aung San Suu Kyi spoke for little more than ten minutes. She thanked her supporters for their steadfast loyalty, then told them that SLORC had asked her to assist in the process of 'national reconciliation'. Democracy was still achievable, she said, provided people were prepared to stand up, but be patient as well. Everything had to be done 'step by step'. For herself, she fully expected to be party to a 'dialogue' with the regime, along with other NLD leaders, but people were not to rely on her alone.

The crowd did not disperse, but was still there the next day, and the day after. Each morning for a week Suu Kyi climbed up on the table and repeated her message. A microphone and two loudspeakers were found, so that those sitting or standing away from the gate could hear her words. But still the people kept coming. Because it seemed she would have to do this indefinitely, it was decided that her 'gate-side' talks would be held at the weekends only, with U Tin Oo and U Kyi Maung joining in. Otherwise they would not have sufficient time for the important task of rebuilding the party.

Out of this arrangement grew an extraordinary fixture in Rangoon's weekly calendar. Every Saturday and Sunday people of all sorts assembled outside no. 54 and waited for Aung San Suu Kyi to appear: teachers and students, tradesmen and artisans, taxi-drivers and lawyers, grandparents and infants, and the ordinary poor, all willing to brave the attentions of Military Intelligence. Soon hawkers homed in: stalls sprouted up, selling water and fruit juices, grilled meat and noodles, jellied pig's blood, betel nuts and cheroots. Soon too foreigners could be spotted in the crowd, tourists and embassy wives and others who wanted to see for themselves the Nobel Laureate perform. And Suu Kyi, always impeccably presented with her trademark flowers (jasmine or orchids) in her hair, did perform. A metal letter-box was hung on the gate for written questions to be left any time during the preceding week. Clutching a sheaf of papers as she stood up, Suu Kyi answered as many as she could as best she could, whether they were about gardening or literature, food or other domestic matters, as well as political issues. Adopting an informal manner, she laughed and joked and refused to take anything too seriously. Like her father, she took it upon herself to be the nation's teacher, but in a manner much lighter than the Bogyoke had ever managed.

U Kyi Maung helped out with stories about a fictitious 'nephew', a young man prone to both accidents and narrow scrapes, who clearly belonged, though he never spelled it out, to MI. Of those who attended every weekend, some came back to hear Kyi Maung's next episode. But there was no doubting the star attraction. Through her informal roadside addresses, Aung San Suu Kyi created a uniquely warm rapport with her followers. If she lifted their spirits, they lifted hers. Within weeks of her release she seemed to have recovered her original vitality, and something more perhaps. By Burmese standards, her upbringing may have been privileged, her years in distant Oxford rarefied, but she found the common touch, and thrived upon it.

Before long video-tapes of Aung San Suu Kyi appearing above her compound gates were circulating throughout Burma, for the benefit of those who could not make it to the capital. Inside the compound too, where (in her slightly quaint phrase) the 'general public' was not permitted, a festive holiday mood prevailed at the weekends. 'Friends and colleagues start arriving and it is very much like a family gathering,' Suu Kyi wrote:

Some of the visitors come laden with food. The wife of U Kyi Maung ... generally brings a large supply of steamed glutinous rice with both sweet and savoury accompaniments such as tiny, crisply fried fish and grated fresh coconut. After the public meeting we sit out in the garden in small groups, drinking hot green tea, eating glutinous rice and exchanging news. An outsider witnessing the animation of the conversation and hearing the gales of laughter bursting out intermittently from each group would not guess that most of the people present worked together every day, voluntarily and without pay, under circumstances which were far from easy.*

By around 7 p.m. on Sundays the 'weekend' was over, and the NLD leadership began preparing for the hard work of the week ahead. For several months Suu Kyi scarcely ventured outside the compound. On 19th July, the anniversary of Aung San's assassination, she attended a formal ceremony at the Martyrs' Memorial and laid a wreath on her father's tomb. In October she travelled by car to Thamanya, close to Pa'an in Karen (Kayin) state, to pay her respects to U Vinaya, a *Hsayadaw* (holy teacher) and one of Burma's most venerated monks. But these excursions apart, for the sake of marshalling her energies most efficiently, and to avoid provoking any breach of the peace, Suu Kyi preferred to let the world come to her. There was no election campaign to be fought, and the NLD was best rebirthed in Rangoon. Upcountry rallies could wait awhile.

As in 1988 and 1989 there was a constant stream of visitors to University Avenue, so that again Su Kyi had to rely on secretaries and aides to manage her schedule. Within days, no. 54 was once more the hub of political opposition in Burma, though without quite the same predominance of student activists. Conversely, with Burma opening its doors in the generals' expectations of an inflow of tourist dollars, there were many more foreigners who requested meetings and interviews with

*Aung San Suu Kyi, *Letters from Burma* (1997)

the Nobel Prize winner. These included, as well as diplomats, rights activists and women's groups, a legion of journalists. With her photogenic beauty, Suu Kyi was an obvious choice not only for news outlets, but also such fashion magazines as *Elle, Marie Claire* and *Vogue*. She was not just the Western media's favourite political pin-up girl, but an outstanding example of what womanhood could achieve in a country that was, because of the ascendancy of the Tatmadaw, soaked in the will of men.

Cultivating the foreign media was an integral part of Suu Kyi's daily work, the more so since SLORC continued to maintain draconian censorship in Burma. Although she fiercely believed that any political change must come from within the country, she knew the value of the pressure that foreign governments, the United Nations and other international bodies exerted on the regime. She was also committed to a trans-cultural understanding of human affairs. In the 1997 Pope Paul VI Memorial Lecture, delivered on her behalf by Dr Aris at the Royal Institution in London on 3rd November the same year, she wrote that 'whatever our race or religion, we can all learn to agree on certain basic values essential to the development of human society'.* Significantly, she was the first non-Christian, as well as the first Asian, invited to give the address. But while such platforms offered Suu Kyi opportunities to expand her ideas in detailed seriousness, more routine encounters with the press often exasperated her. 'Why,' she asked Debbie Stothard, an Anglo-Malay activist whose Alternative South-East Asian Network (ALTSEAN) is dedicated to promoting awareness of human-rights violations in Burma, 'do I have to keep repeating myself?'

Stothard explained that that is just how it is with the media. Getting a political or humanitarian message across is no different from brand imaging. Repetition and presentation are of the essence. Trained in television, she helped Aung San Suu Kyi adapt to the video camera, while acknowledging that she brought her own special qualities to the task:

Once she learned to look the lenses in the eye, she was a natural. Just because she knew exactly what she wanted to say, she said it with maximum clarity, maximum effect. She responded to questions without hesitation, and she had the knack of presenting her views as simple common sense. Simultaneously her

*Aung San Suu Kyi, 'Heavenly abodes and human development', CAFOD, 1997

intrinsic sobriety was leavened with glimpses of that charm which stays in the memory of anyone who has known her off-camera.

But there was another talent Suu Kyi had up her sleeve. She knew how, if she were so minded, to make instant bridges with those who visited her. Interviewed for the *Irish Times* by Katherine Smyth at the time she was given the freedom of Dublin, Aung San Suu Kyi made a point of recalling how Michael Collins, a key figure in the Irish independence movement, 'was a great hero for my father and for a lot of our [own] independence leaders'.

On a previous occasion, in early August 1996, a young American came to see her. David Eubank was a former Green Beret in the US army turned missionary, working out of Thailand to bring relief to Karens, Karennis and other displaced and dispirited minorities. For half an hour he found himself alone with Suu Kyi. 'I knew she was not a Christian,' he wrote to fellow missionaries shortly afterwards, 'but when I met her I felt God's presence. She exudes faith and told me her favourite scripture was John 8.32, "you shall know the truth and the truth shall set you free".'* Deeply inspired by Aung San Suu Kyi, Eubank has remained on the Thai-Burmese border ever since, stressing the need for reconciliation between non-Burman and Burman Burmese in his jungle sermons, and often putting his own life at risk.

Was this ability to empathise with her collocutors opportunist, or an expression of her own deepening spiritual convictions? Through her life experiences Suu Kyi had a broader background than most of the Burmese around her, or – for that matter – most of the foreigners who came to her door. She was well bred and well read, and sought to share such advantages with others, where sharing also meant listening. She could, however, give anyone she suspected of insincerity, or seeking to take advantage of her, short shrift. Although the sulks and tantrums that had sometimes marked her behaviour during her Oxford years belonged to the past, she could still, as she confessed to Alan Clements, let anger get the better of her.

Clements was another American who sought out Aung San Suu Kyi. A generation older than Eubank, his 'Burmese' credentials were impeccable. A convert to Buddhism, from 1980 he had spent five years living as a monk in Mahasi Monastery in Rangoon. Even during the

---

*Letter circulated by David Eubank on 10th August 1996

isolationist years of Ne Win's BSPP regime, some foreigners were given 'monastic visas' to train as *pongyi*. By coincidence the Mahasi was the same monastery where U Tin Oo retreated after his release from his first spell of imprisonment, in 1981. Returning to California, Clements founded the Burma Project, dedicated to exposing and ameliorating human-rights abuses, and published an account of the military regime's misdeeds: *Burma: The Next Killing Fields?* (1991).

Returning to Burma, Clements proposed, through U Tin Oo, that he conduct a series of taped 'conversations' with Suu Kyi. She agreed, with the proviso that Clements include interviews with U Tin Oo and U Kyi Maung. The result, published by Penguin Books in 1997 as *The Voice of Hope*, contained the fullest statement to date of Aung San Suu Kyi's mature convictions. Although the question-and-answer format militates against definitive coherence – their conversations sometimes double-back on and repeat themselves – Clements is sufficiently immersed in Burmese affairs to dig beneath superficial platitudes. Yet from the outset there is a palpable sense of shared values. An authority on Burmese Buddhism, Clements assists Aung San Suu Kyi to adumbrate her own religious and spiritual world view. His interrogation of her is searching, but never hostile.

'We are still prisoners in our own country,' Suu Kyi tells him. The solution – at odds with received notions of Buddhism as a fatalistic faith – is for people to adopt 'self-responsibility'. Again, 'Engaged Buddhism is active compassion.' As always, she emphasises the importance of *metta*, 'loving-kindness'. All dictatorships must collapse sooner or later, and non-violence is one way to hasten, not delay, their end. Compassion should be extended even to the perpetrators of violence. A murder is one thing, the murderer another. 'I've always felt that if I had really started hating my captors, hating the SLORC and the army, I would have defeated myself.' But it is not just a matter of replacing military with civilian rule. Maintaining one's own dignity and mental equilibrium is of equal importance. 'My highest ambition,' Suu Kyi says, 'is very much a spiritual one: purity of mind.' And this involves humility. 'If you contemplate your own death it means that you accept how unimportant you are.' That, however, is not the same as resignation. In Aung San Suu Kyi's view, Buddhist precepts, rightly understood, demand selflessness, even self-sacrifice.

In all, *The Voice of Hope* contains thirteen conversations with Aung San Suu Kyi, and one apiece with U Tin Oo and U Kyi Maung. They were taped over an eight-month period between November 1995 and June 1996, and then transcribed by Clements. But if sitting down with an informed, sympathetic and trusted interlocutor for two or three hours every three or four weeks suited Suu Kyi's busy workload, she herself was engaged in writing projects. Even under house arrest she had composed some lectures and prize acceptance speeches, which were either taken away by Dr Aris or smuggled out of her compound. After July 1995 she was at greater liberty to fulfil such tasks. But a more interesting commission was presented to her by Nagai Hiroshi, an editor of the Japanese newspaper *Mainichi Shinbun*. Beginning in October 1995, for a year Suu Kyi filed a weekly diary column that generated another book, *Letters from Burma*, again published by Penguin Books, in 1997.

The *Letters* are Aung San Suu Kyi's most polished literary performance. They demonstrate that her youthful ambition to pursue an authorial career was not misplaced. Although each of the fifty-two brief chapters focuses on a different aspect of Burmese life, and of Suu Kyi's experiences as a dissident, they are knitted together by the steady portrayal of Burma as a place of 'charm and cruelty'. The result is a fragrantly understated polemic, elegiac rather than satirical, as Suu Kyi contemplates cultural ideals and cultural memories, contrasting them with the actualities she finds around her. Whether her subject matter is rain, babies, children, visiting friends, festivals or the price of an egg, there is invariably an opening for an adverse comparison.

Writing about tea-making leads Suu Kyi to the phrase 'pouring water', a euphemism for the backhanders demanded by corrupt officials. Roof repairs – a topic brought about by the dilapidation of her own house through six years' enforced inattention – becomes an opportunity to extol Burmese womenfolk, 'to whom the international media pay scant attention', but 'who play an essential role in our endeavour to repair the roof of our nation'. If there is an obligatory chapter on the Burmese seasons, this too is put to effective use. Suu Kyi tells us first about the comforts she derives from thick woven Chin blankets, long used by her family during the cooler months, and of a Japanese quilt given to her parents as a wedding present. But then, 'as I lie on a good mattress under a mosquito net', she evokes the harsh conditions at Insein prison, where 'my political colleagues are lying in bleak cells on thin mats through which seeps the peculiarly unpleasant chill of a concrete floor'.

Written in English before being translated into Japanese (and

subsequently several other languages), *Letters from Burma* reaches out
to a worldwide readership, not least because it skirts round the intricacies
of Buddhist theology. However, its pages tell an urgent story. If the book
begins with a quietly joyous description of Suu Kyi's visit to the *Hsayadaw*
of Thamanya in Karen state, it progressively addresses fresh setbacks
encountered by the NLD. Although SLORC had intimated to Aung San
Suu Kyi that her release from house arrest was 'unconditional', it remained
intolerant of opposition, however peaceable the opposition's methods.
Nor did the junta evince the slightest inclination to enter into any genuine,
substantive dialogue. The quarter where Suu Kyi most wanted to put
her proven communication skills to good use was denied her. Instead
there was just the phoney dialogue of the National Convention.

Any sense of a truce between Aung San Suu Kyi and SLORC was
dispelled within weeks of her new-found freedom. At her very first
meeting with journalists she made it plain that she would continue the
struggle for democracy. As her access to, and appreciation by, the
international press blossomed, she urged foreign companies not to invest
in Burma until its political climate changed. Similarly she discouraged
tourists from visiting Burma if their only purpose was sightseeing, until
such human-rights violations as forced labour, forced relocation and the
detention of political prisoners ceased. 'It is true that many hotels have
come in,' she told the *Singapore Business Times* in April 1996, 'but
what progress has there been in the fields of health and education?' For
its part the regime, dismayed by the popularity of her weekend rallies
in University Avenue, as well as by the publicity she attracted overseas,
soon began issuing disparaging statements about 'Mrs Michael Aris' in
The New Light of Myanmar. Cartoons caricatured her as a withered
hag boring street urchins to death. She was up to her old tricks again,
inciting unrest, plotting with Burma's external enemies and undermining
SLORC's best efforts at national renewal.

Proof of the regime's allegations seemed forthcoming in September
1995. Returning to Washington after talks in Rangoon with both Aung
San Suu Kyi and Khin Nyunt, the USA's ambassador to the United
Nations, Madeleine Albright, roundly condemned the junta in a statement
issued on the 9th. Yet, having so recently released her from house arrest,
the generals recognised that the Bogyoke's daughter needed to be
handled with kid gloves, at least for the while. Rearresting her would
only give substance to her claims that Burma was neither good to invest

in, nor good to visit. When, in October, a reconstituted NLD Central Committee reinstated Aung San Suu Kyi as party general-secretary and U Tin Oo as vice-chairman, SLORC's Election Commission, tasked with vetting the leaderships of all registered parties, objected, but no stronger action was taken. That Aung Shwe, already approved by the Commission, stayed on as chairman possibly defused a confrontation.

The following month, however, the gloves came off. Guided by Suu Kyi, Tin Oo and Kyi Maung, the NLD announced that it was withdrawing its handful of representatives from the National Convention. In five months there had been no movement whatsoever towards meaningful debate, and the Convention was denounced for what it was – a sham. Nonplussed, SLORC responded by 'expelling' the NLD from the Convention, but everyone knew the true sequence of events.

At the end of December Suu Kyi and her colleagues were prevented from attending a Karen New Year ceremony in Rangoon. Suu Kyi herself was taken to a military headquarters and told that her freedom did not mean she was free to travel anywhere she pleased. Simultaneously Secretary One Khin Nyunt convened a press conference. 'Adopted sons and daughters of the colonialists,' he said, as though nothing had changed since 1945, 'are attempting to cause the disintegration of the Union and the loss of independence.'* Already SLORC had begun arresting NLD activists for distributing video-tapes of Suu Kyi's roadside speeches.

More arrests followed a private celebration of Independence Day held by the NLD at no. 54 University Avenue on 4th January 1996. Among several Mandalay-based entertainers invited to attend were two comedians, U Par Par Lay and U Lu Zaw. Having performed sketches that satirised the junta, no sooner had they left the compound than they were picked up by MI and taken off to Kachin state for three years' hard labour. Nor, when Suu Kyi decided she should visit Mandalay for the first time since 1989, were the authorities any better disposed. On 13th March she and an entourage were checked at Rangoon station. Officials who were clearly not railway employees told her that a last-minute fault had developed with her carriage and that the rest of the train was full.

Barely a month went by before SLORC again flexed its muscle, and in a most unchivalrous manner. It is a Burmese custom to free caged

*The Times, 29th December 1995

birds and release captured fish into lakes and rivers on the first day of the new year. In 1996 the Burmese New Year fell on 16th April. Suu Kyi decided to make a women-only event of it. Her intention was to proceed from University Avenue to a pond near the Shwedagon pagoda. However, the regime got wind of this, and on the 15th NLD officers were given formal warnings not to attend. On the day itself, University Avenue was sealed off with barbed wire. SLORC's excuse was that the procession would contravene standing orders against public gatherings.

Forced to cancel the fish-releasing ceremony, Suu Kyi decided instead that she and her fellow NLD members should see in the New Year at her compound, chanting Buddhist *sutras*. But even in this she was obstructed. Most worryingly, posted round the barricades in University Avenue were, as well as soldiers and MI types, a number of civilians, each with a handkerchief tied round their wrists.

These were members of the Union Solidarity and Development Association (USDA), created by SLORC in September 1993 with General Than Shwe taking the position of chairman. Although ostensibly set up as a social self-help organisation, it was designed as, and fast became, a main instrument of the junta's coercive control. In essence the association functioned as the mass party in a one-party state. Membership conferred some benefits and 'privileges' that in most other countries would pass for basic civil rights. Farmers who joined were exempt from forced labour. Civil servants, on the other hand, had to join unless they wished to lose their jobs. When the USDA staged rallies, non-attendance could result in fines and imprisonment. Where Burma's public education system was failing horrendously, USDA children were offered courses in English, even on how to use a computer. But such state-sponsored 'relative elitism' apart, there was a darker side to the Association. Some younger male members were given paramilitary training. As a result, SLORC had at its beck and call thugs in all parts of the country to do its dirty work for it.

The handkerchiefs worn by USDA members in University Avenue were not in any sense a badge or uniform. They were to identify their wearers as loyalists as and when trouble broke out – for the object of the exercise was to incite mischief. A shove here, a kick there, leading to a brawl, whereupon the Tatmadaw or the *Lon Htein* could move in. But on 16th April those NLD members who had come to the barricades declined to be drawn into a fight. Showing their usual restraint, they accepted that most of them would not that day be allowed to visit Suu

Kyi's compound. Instead, Suu Kyi herself came from the other direction and greeted her supporters across the barbed wire.

In the regime's scheme of things, the USDA provided the perfect foil to the NLD. Its rehearsed marches and enforced public celebrations of SLORC's 'achievements' looked good on Myanmar TV and in *The New Light of Myanmar*. But as well as being a dubious propaganda tool, the USDA was effective at the village and township level, where its members could harass and bully NLD supporters, either directly or by withholding 'favours'. Locally, USDA members were also encouraged to gather signatures for petitions objecting to the 1990 election result, leading to the unseating of more than a handful of NLD MPs. The term 'socialist' may have been dropped from Burma's official name, 'The Union of Myanmar', but in reality the country remained totalitarian.

Yet all the while the NLD was recovering something of its former strength. Although many of its regional offices remained closed on SLORC's orders, those that were still open sprang back into life. The League was prohibited from using fax machines or distributing flyers and pamphlets, but even so old communication networks were revived.

By May 1996 the Central Committee felt sufficiently emboldened to call a party conference in Rangoon. The date chosen was the 27th, the sixth anniversary of the 1990 election. As early as the 21st SLORC intervened, arresting two prominent NLD leaders, the League's foreign media coordinator U Aye Win and U Win Htein, a former army captain. Over the next few days no fewer than 258 arrests were made, including 238 elected MPs, as delegates began arriving in the capital. Notwithstanding, fourteen delegates managed to attend, and the conference ended with a declaration that unless SLORC released all of its political prisoners and called the parliament that had been elected in 1990, the NLD would itself draft a national constitution.

The seizure of U Aye Win (sentenced to five years in jail) was indicative of the difficulties in which the junta found itself. Largely because of Aung San Suu Kyi's coverage in the foreign media, and of her cousin Dr Sein Win's lobbying in Washington, there was now a strong feeling on Capitol Hill that the USA should impose tougher sanctions on Burma, other than the embargo on selling arms that had been in place since 1988. Although President Clinton responded cautiously, Congress soon passed legislation prohibiting further investment in Burma by US companies and prohibiting visas to SLORC members and their families. With similar measures being adopted by the European Union, Burma risked being isolated economically at a time when the regime was struggling to control spiralling inflation. Only China's continuing support, and ASEAN's decision to admit 'Myanmar' into its ranks in July 1997, spared the nation from economic meltdown and the unrest that would have ensued.

Still, SLORC refused to contemplate either dialogue or compromise with Aung San Suu Kyi. Instead it used every means at its disposal to disparage both the NLD and its *de facto* leader. Although most of those elected representatives who had been apprehended before the May conference were released, following pressure from the United Nations, fresh arrests continued. One hapless victim of SLORC's malice was Leo Nicholls, an Anglo-Burman who for many years had acted as honorary consul for Denmark, Sweden, Norway and Switzerland. He had also been on close terms with Daw Khin Kyi, and was regarded by Suu Kyi as an 'uncle'. His crime was to have allowed Suu Kyi to use his fax machine for sending instalments of *Letters from Burma* to Japan. He was given a three-year prison sentence, but the harsh conditions at Insein killed him within two months, raising a storm of protest abroad.

Nicholls's death dismayed Suu Kyi. But nothing the junta could do dented her resolution, nor that of her followers. When SLORC threatened those attending her weekend talks in University Avenue with twenty years' imprisonment, the crowds just grew bigger. SLORC responded from September by sealing off University Avenue from Friday evening until Monday morning. Undeterred, Suu Kyi, U Tin Oo and U Kyi Maung went out to nearby road junctions and addressed their followers there. In early November this led to a nasty incident. A USDA mob of around 200 young men, watched by the Tatmadaw, was waiting for them and attacked their car with stones and sticks, breaking its windows and injuring Tin Oo.

Such incidents fuelled concerns about Suu Kyi's safety. But in an interview with a *Times* reporter published on 3rd September, she commented, 'If the army really wants to kill me they can do it without any problems at all, so there is no point in making elaborate security arrangements. It is not bravado or anything like that. I suppose I am just rather down to earth and I just don't see the point to this worry.' But it was becoming an uphill battle. An attempt to convene an NLD congress in September 1996 was thwarted by an even greater number of temporary detentions – between 800 and 1,000. Although as yet no move was made to put Aung San Suu Kyi back under house arrest, no. 54 was intermittently under military blockade. Suu Kyi continued to hold NLD Executive Committee meetings at her residence and to receive visitors. The latter, though, were now routinely screened by MI, who stopped visitors at her gate, checked through their belongings and took their names. Even some diplomats were denied access to the Nobel Laureate.

In December, amid a wave of student unrest centred on the Rangoon Institute of Technology, Suu Kyi was temporarily confined to her house 'for her own safety'. At the (Western) New Year, the NLD suffered a further setback. Following a meeting of several ethnic-minority leaders at Mae Tha Raw Tha on the Thai border, which (inter alia) declared its support for the democratic movement, all communication between the League and the 'ceasefire groups' was outlawed.

Efforts to rebuild the NLD stalled – the more so as the regime proved partially successful in its attempts to lure some elected MPs away from the League. By early 1998, of the 392 NLD candidates who had won seats in the never-to-be parliament, 112 were either no longer 'active' or had fled abroad. A further forty languished in prison. Notwithstanding, in May the League managed to stage something resembling a congress, though this was marked by discontent among some delegates, who openly questioned the non-confrontational strategy of the party leadership. Yet again calling on the junta to implement the 1990 election result, the congress issued an ultimatum. Unless there was substantive progress within sixty days, it would simply convene the elected parliament itself. But this only prompted the junta to intensify its own campaign. More NLD offices were closed down and more NLD members held in detention. In September the League countered by instigating CRPP, the 'Committee Representing the People's Parliament', but this was powerless to achieve anything meaningful inside Burma.

Suu Kyi meanwhile was subjected to further harassment. Twice, in July and August 1998, she found herself trapped inside a motor car for several days as she attempted to drive outside Rangoon, her way blocked by the Tatmadaw. She insisted on her right to move forward, the army insisted she turn back. On the first occasion, after five days, soldiers forcibly removed her driver from her vehicle on 29th July, restrained Suu Kyi and drove her back to University Avenue. On the second, as she headed westwards for Bassein, she held out for six days, having prepared extra food and water. But when the supplies ran out and the soldiers at the road block refused permission to replenish them, there was little option but to turn back.

At times the lengths to which the junta would go in its efforts to contain and humiliate Aung San Suu Kyi were near-farcical. But in one respect at least it was not farcical at all. Two weeks after being set free from house arrest, Suu Kyi had been visited by Dr Aris and her younger son Kim. Dr Aris and his stepmother Evelyn, who had assumed the responsibilities of chairing Prospect Burma, an educational trust supported by Suu Kyi's prize money, were also given permission to stay with her for Christmas and the New Year at the end of 1995. But no further entry visas were granted to her family. In January 1999 Aris telephoned Suu Kyi to tell her that he had been diagnosed with prostate cancer. Worse, the cancer had already spread to his spine and lungs. The prognosis was grim. Barring a miracle, he would be dead within a matter of months. Still, though, the junta would not grant him a visa.

XXXIV

THE SADDEST THING

My poor old husband. He is the most indulgent husband that ever was.
I don't know what they mean by saying I am his puppet. They know
very well that is not the case.

Aung San Suu Kyi, in *The Sunday Times*, 9th June 1996

IN November 1997 the military regime gave itself a facelift. The supreme
governing body of Burma was no longer to be called the State Law and
Order Restoration Council (SLORC), but the State Peace and
Development Council (SPDC). Characteristically, the junta did not rush
to explain this change in nomenclature, leading some to speculate that
it had been brought about at the instigation of Ne Win: it was after all
his magic number nine years since SLORC had seized power in 1988.
Others believed it was the inspiration of Lieutenant-General Khin
Nyunt, or of one amongst several US public-relations companies that
the regime had intermittently employed to soften its image. Some smart
detective work by the *Far Eastern Economic Review* correspondent
Bertil Lintner exposed two American PR companies that were paid
handsomely to window-dress the regime's activities, Jackson Bash and
Jefferson Waterman International. According to Lintner, before either
of these became involved, a former human-rights activist, Lest Wolff,
had been hired by SLORC for US $10,000 a month.

It is unlikely that Ne Win had much to do with it. In his late eighties
and plagued by the infirmities of age, his main preoccupation was the
raising of a new pagoda close to the Shwedagon, to immortalise (or,
quite literally, cement) his place in the nation's history. More probably

the switch from SLORC to SPDC finally marked the Old Man's political
eclipse, although Khin Nyunt faithfully continued to visit his fortified
residence by Inya Lake in the early mornings. Already Ne Win's boots
were being amply filled by Senior General Than Shwe, an equally reclusive
figure similarly addicted to fortune-tellers and superstition.

Born in Mandalay Division in 1933, Than Shwe was a low-level
postal worker before joining the Tatmadaw in 1953. But he rose rapidly
through the ranks after completing a course in psychological warfare.
As a commander, he made a name for himself in Shan and Kachin states,
using brutal methods to suppress ethnic insurgency. His intolerance of
Burma's minorities did not deter him from marrying a Pa'o, Kyaing
Kyiang – as far as is known, the only woman in his life. While prominence
in Ne Win's BSPP gave him the reputation of a regime conservative, in
power Than Shwe revealed an instinct for manipulative statecraft,
especially when it came to controlling (and, if necessary, eliminating)
rivals. An unglamorous figure – his squashed-frog facial features scarcely
make him a dictator to adore – he is nonetheless rumoured to consider
himself equal to the greatest of the Burman kings, with an ambition to
found a new dynasty through one of his many grandsons. His daughters,
it is said, insist on being treated as royals.

The introduction of the SPDC was accompanied by the sacking of a
handful of lesser ministers on the grounds of 'excessive' corruption, to
make room for a new generation of aspiring brigadiers. But at the top of
the tree the pecking order was undisturbed. General Maung Aye continued
as army chief and Khin Nyunt as intelligence chief. Nor was there any
conspicuous change to government policies. Health and education services
went on being starved of funds while yet more money was thrown at the
armed forces. And for most of Burma's minority peoples there was no
improvement in living conditions, despite the fifteen-odd ceasefires concluded
by the end of 1996. More often the opposite, in fact. The Tatmadaw
regularly encroached on demilitarised areas, especially when they contained
valuable resources or lay in the way of new roads, rail-lines and other
infrastructural projects. Elsewhere in conflict zones, whole villages were
razed and their inhabitants either dragooned into labour gangs or relocated
to less hospitable habitats. Like the National Convention (which stopped
meeting some months after the NLD walk-out), the ceasefires were little
more than a painted cloak to divert attention from the regime's undiminished
rapacity, now manifest in a tranche of 'state-owned' enterprises in which
the Tatmadaw had a controlling share.

It was, however, the SPDC's callous handling of Aung San Suu Kyi in her latest predicament that, in the early months of 1999, dominated foreign media coverage of Burma. In place of compassion, which might have been extended to any woman with a terminally ill husband, the junta exhibited only petty-minded vindictiveness. Though normally an undemonstrative individual, Than Shwe was known to fly into a rage at the mere mention of her name.

Michael Aris desperately wanted to pay Suu Kyi a final visit – for, as they both knew, if she left Burma to visit him she was unlikely to be allowed back in. But his application for a visa was repeatedly rejected. Even after British Foreign Office officials intervened to plead his cause, the answer was no. Hoping that, in desperation, Suu Kyi would up sticks at the last moment and board a plane for Bangkok, the regime monitored her phone calls (as indeed it had since 1995) and began cutting her off whenever she was on the line to Dr Aris. When the junta learned that he had been hospitalised, it claimed that the reason he should not come to Burma was that caring for him would overburden Rangoon's medical facilities. More probably, the regime feared the disturbances that might erupt if Aris was given a Rangoon funeral. As British officials advised, the money and means were available to fly him out in a medical aeroplane – and with him all the support equipment he might need. But Senior General Than Shwe and his belted colleagues were unswayed. Aung San Suu Kyi's personal plight meant nothing to them. All that mattered was the satisfaction of their collective lust for absolute control. Had the newfangled State Peace and Development Council contained any woman ministers, the outcome might have been different. But there were none, just as there had been no women ministers in the old-fangled SLORC. Women ministers were an abomination, and a reason why democracy was to be avoided.

For a decade Michael Aris had fretted for the survival of his Suu; but it was his death (not hers) that occurred in the early morning of 27th March 1999, drawing to a close, as Maurice Chittenden put it in *The Times* the following day, a 'love that tyranny could not crush'. Because of the seriousness of his condition, Aris had been given a bed at the Churchill Hospital off Oxford's Headington Road shortly after his cancer was diagnosed. His medical team did all they could for him, but when, just a few days before he died, it became obvious he could not survive, he was transferred to Sir Michael Sobell House, a hospice within the grounds of the Churchill. By chance or otherwise, the day of his death, cloudless and bright, was his fifty-third birthday.

During his final illness Aris received a string of visitors: members of his family, university colleagues, old friends and admirers, among them HRH The Prince of Wales. The two men knew each other through the Dalai Lama. The heir to the English throne also arranged for Aris to be brought by ambulance to Sandringham in Norfolk. There Charles readily agreed to become Patron of a Centre for Tibetan and Himalayan Studies – a project most dear to Aris's heart, but which he narrowly failed to live long enough to see come to fruition.

A funeral service was held at Oxford Crematorium on 31st March. Despite invitations being restricted to family and close friends, a large number turned out. It was an impressively organised 'inter-faith' event. Michael's twin brother Anthony gave a preamble, then prayers and plainsong were offered by Benedictine monks from Worth and Ampleforth Abbeys – a reminder that Dr Aris had been raised a Catholic. His sons Alexander and Kim recited the Lord's Prayer, and then Dr Peter Carey, Aris's long-standing Oxford friend and colleague, gave the principal address in the form of a personal appreciation. 'Michael's deep throaty laugh, his benign and avuncular presence and great scholarly knowledge of Asia as well as of the contemporary world,' he said, 'all meant that meetings with Michael were always a rare combination of delight and enrichment.' In particular he recalled a meeting in June 1996, 'in the garden of 15 Park Town – last minute instructions before a visit to Rangoon, my first in forty years. The complete works of Shakespeare, and the *Shorter OED* – stuffed into a canvas hold-all with loo rolls on top. Personal for University Avenue. You must do this, but be careful! God speed. And so one departed on yet another adventure, Michael's blessing warm on one's back. Le Grand Meaulnes in Rangoon!'

After Dr Carey had finished, Buddhist monks offered their prayers, followed by the timeless Vajrayana chant, *Om mani padme hum* – 'Behold the jewel is in the Lotus'.

Tributes flowed in from around the world, including from President Clinton. 'I want to reaffirm to Michael's family and to all the people of Burma,' he said in a statement issued by the White House on 28th March, 'that the United States will keep working for the day when all who have been separated and sent into exile by the denial of human rights in Burma are reunited with their families, and when Burma is reunited with the family of freedom.'

Inevitably, reactions to Dr Aris's death centred on his relationship with Aung San Suu Kyi. 'Married to a cruel destiny' (*The Independent*, 29th March) was typical of the sort of headline that appeared in Western newspapers. Only in a second, more elaborate commemorative event, billed as 'A Celebration of the Life and Work of Michael Vaillaincourt Aris', held in the spacious circular hall of Oxford University's Sheldonian Theatre on 18th September, and lasting two hours, did the true measure of the man emerge. Again, tributes were presented – from the UN Secretary-General Kofi Annan (for whom Aris was 'an exemplary citizen of the world') and the Dalai Lama. One amongst several distinguished speakers, Sir Marrack Goulding, Warden of St Anthony's College, where Aris had become a Fellow in 1989, drew attention to the many 'compartments' in Michael's life: not just his personal support for Suu Kyi, but his constant behind-the-scenes agitation on behalf of the Burmese democracy movement; his uncomplaining shouldering of the responsibility for bringing up their sons when she could no longer look after them; his towering contribution to Tibetan and Himalayan studies; his role in the opening up of Bhutan; his enlightened understanding of Buddhism; his excellence as a teacher; his attentive care for his students; and a voluminous correspondence whose recipients included, *inter alia*, the Carmelite nuns of Lisieux. Typically, Goulding said, only those who knew Aris well had any idea of the range of his activities. But perhaps, the Warden suggested, that range was only possible because he did compartmentalise. It was the only way to manage what for most would have been Protean demands on their time.

To mark his lifelong love of music, especially chamber music, the Oxford University Chamber Orchestra performed pieces by Vivaldi, Bach and Johann Pachelbel, as well as, heartbreakingly, Vaughan Williams's *The Lark Ascending*, with Priya Mitchell playing solo violin. But Suu Kyi could not be kept out of it for long. One of Aris's Tibetan students, Karma Phuntsho, spoke on her behalf, recalling the spiritual debt that both owed to Dilgo Khentse Rinpoche, a Tibeto-Bhutanese lama who had taught them that the happiness of the individual is insignificant compared to that of the many, and so the one should be subordinated to the other. Amongst several readings of poems, one stood out, a 'love song' by the Sixth Dalai Lama (Tsangyang Gyatso, 1683–1706) that Aris himself had translated. A nephew, Julian Phillips, recited:

If my mind could move to religion
As it always goes to her
Then in just one life and one body
I would attain buddhahood.

In the last of the speeches, the podium was taken by Robin Christopher, who had known Suu Kyi since his student days and was now British ambassador to Indonesia. 'Mine is a story of friendship,' he began, 'a friendship born of a common affection for a particular Burmese girl.' At their wedding in 1972 he had been one of those who, on the floor of the Gore-Booths' Chelsea living room, drew the 'holy thread' around Suu and Michael – the white string that in Buddhist ritual binds humans together, and to the Buddhahood. Because of that bond, 'despite separation and solitude, Michael flowed with warm-heartedness, good humour and hope – above all, hope.' Even on his deathbed, Aris had exalted in the release from prison of the East Timorese freedom fighter Xanana Gusmao.

Another speaker, Professor Per Kværne – a fellow Tibetologist from Oslo University – was pleased to announce, $2 million had been raised for 'The Michael Aris Memorial Trust for Tibetan and Himalayan Studies' – which meant that his dream of a centre could go ahead, housed at the Oxford University Faculty of Oriental Studies. That the histories and cultures of Tibet, Nepal and Bhutan should be accorded full academic status in the West, and thereby be subjected to the rigours of modern scholarship, was what Aris had devoted his academic life to, both before and after his wife's return to Burma. As a further mark of respect for his achievements, Oxford's Bodleian Library would house the many Tibetan books and manuscripts he had accumulated, as 'The Michael Aris Collection'.

Along the way Aris had caused some upset, with his own book *Hidden Treasures and Secret Lives: A Study of Pemalingpa (1450–1521) and the Sixth Dalai Lama (1683–1706)*, first published in Simla just as Aung San Suu Kyi was becoming embroiled in the Burmese democracy movement. In it Aris exploded two deeply held Tibetan myths. The first concerned 'treasure texts', supposedly written by Padmasambhava, an eighth-century mystic, but buried in caves and rocks by him to await discovery in 'more propitious times'. Pemalingpa was a 'treasure-discoverer' who claimed to have found Padmasambhava's writings, but who was shown by Aris, on conclusive documentary evidence, to have been a charlatan. Similarly a 'secret life' of the Sixth Dalai Lama, purporting to reveal him as something other than a womaniser, was exposed by Aris as equally bogus. Many of his Tibetan and Bhutanese associates were shocked and offended by Aris's 'findings', and by his audacity in printing them. Some wondered whether his interest in Tibetan Buddhism had not been cavalier all along: for was it not a tradition among Western historians to relentlessly debunk? But Aris stuck to his guns. He had as much respect and empathy for the Buddhist Path as any Westerner alive, but he did not believe that either the Buddhist or Tibetan cause was helped by subscribing to patently ridiculous medieval falsehoods. As it happened, relations with the Tibeto-Bhutanese community were restored in 1994, with the publication of the beautifully illustrated *The Raven Crown: The Origins of Buddhist Monarchy in Bhutan*, of all Aris's writings the most accessible to the non-specialist.

The pursuit of truth for truth's sake, particularly where 'truth' had a moral or humanitarian colouring, was a conviction Dr Aris shared with his wife. Their marriage, like any other marriage, was full of physical and emotional incident – at least when circumstances permitted them to be together. But there was too a profoundly cerebral aspect to their relationship, common among 'Oxford couples'. What set them apart was the Buddhist dimension. Suu Kyi had been born and raised in the Buddhist faith; Aris came to it as a young man, not through her so much as through the six years he spent tutoring the Bhutanese royal family. Prior to that, he had sometimes read Buddhist texts under his desk at Worth School during lessons he found boring. As he was the better scholar, he could sometimes act as her mentor. When Suu Kyi was first placed under house arrest and began meditating, it was Aris who helped her find her way. On a visit to Rangoon in 1989 he presented her with a copy of *In This Very Life*, by Hsayadaw U Pandita, whom he knew personally, and who later became one of Suu Kyi's principal Buddhist mentors. His book, both an introduction to and manual of *Vipassana* meditation, had been written in 1984, after conducting a retreat in Barre, Massachusetts. It made U Pandita the best-known Burmese Buddhist master in the West. Its instruction emphasises *sila*, moral discipline. *Sila* is not the product of meditation, he urges, but the framework without which meditation is purposeless.

Aris himself was known to meditate sometimes, but whether he was a Buddhist in any strict sense is uncertain. He was not someone who either gave himself, or welcomed, labels. Yet his knowledge of Buddhism and its many different schools and sects enabled him to be accepted as a kindred spirit by Buddhist scholars in South-East Asia, the Himalayas and China. The regime in Rangoon, however, took none of this into account, and persistently refused to acknowledge Aris's dominant character trait, his all-encompassing sincerity. Instead he was vilified in *The New Light of Myanmar* and other propaganda outlets as a colonialist, an imperialist and a stooge of the CIA – the same epithets that were applied to Aung San Suu Kyi. For a while he was described as an Indian, thereby making him a black, not a white, *kala*, which for chauvinist Burmans was worse. Either way, he had made of his Burmese wife, whom as a foreigner he had no right to marry, a whore-slave, and through her sought to suborn the Burmese state.

Laughable as all this was, in his efforts to support Suu Kyi, which also meant supporting the Burmese democracy movement, Aris had always to tread carefully. If he involved himself overtly in any political action, the regime would take it out on her. Everything had to be done softly-softly behind the scenes. In the hectic weeks surrounding the announcement of the Nobel Peace Prize and the publication of *Freedom from Fear*, he wrote to his family, 'I want to try and keep the focus very firmly on Suu in all this, and don't want her image diluted or complicated by our efforts.' Surprisingly perhaps, the regime did not at the time seize upon *Freedom from Fear*, and Aris's contribution to it, as an excuse to deny him any further entry visa. If, from 1996 onwards, Aris was permanently banned from visiting Rangoon, the reason given was that he had carried the texts of some of Suu Kyi's speeches out of Burma the previous year. All along, the junta's interest in him was as a bait to lure Suu Kyi out of the country.

That Aris was devoted to Suu Kyi is beyond question. In 1997 he gave a lecture at London's Royal Geographical Society. He talked specifically about Suu Kyi, and the time they had spent together 'on honeymoon' in Bhutan. Sharing with a packed audience the photographs he had taken of her riding ponies in the hills around Thimphu, his eyes steadily moistened. However compartmentalised his mind, she was a constant in his thoughts.

Once Alexander and Kim had grown up and left home, the house at 15 Park Town was again divided in two, the ground and first floors being rented out as a separate dwelling. Aris moved into the top floor, turning it into something of a shrine to his wife. The books she had been reading at the time she received the telephone call telling her that

Daw Khin Kyi had had a stroke were kept on display. The walls were decorated with the certificates of the many prizes she had won. Above his bed was a vastly enlarged photograph of her. 'Don't touch my wife, but watch my knife,' he would sometimes chuckle, quoting a Burmese saying. But his humour masked a lasting passion.

Suu Kyi was equally devoted to Michael, and her two sons, though not with the same sentimentality. For many years *The Sunday Times* Colour Magazine had run a diary-type column for guest contributors, entitled 'A Life in the Day of'. Suu Kyi's turn came in 1996. Describing her average daily routine at 54 University Avenue, she began the final paragraph with the simple statement, 'I dream about my family all the time.' Yet she went on to say, 'but there are a lot of people here who need to be cared about and loved and looked after. They've become my second family.'

For some, it was incomprehensible that a woman should put any sort of political consideration 'before' her loved ones – a censure most often voiced by other women. When *Vogue* magazine ran a profile of Aung San Suu Kyi in October 1996, it was far from flattering. The writer, Barbara Bradley, who normally worked for the *Christian Science Monitor*, tracked down Maria Aung Thwin, the wife of Michael Aung Thwin, one of Suu Kyi's fellow research scholars at Kyoto University in 1985/6. Bradley reported 'Mrs Aung Thwin' as telling her apropos Aung San Suu Kyi: 'she asked, very indirectly, my opinion about whether it were right for her to choose her country over her children. And I said, "Well, Suu, if it were me, I would of course choose my family ..." She said it was a dilemma for her, but in the end her conclusion was that she would choose her country.' Bradley also quoted Mrs Aung Thwin as saying, 'It also seemed to me like she didn't have a husband. She never once mentioned she missed him, and it seemed that the farther she was from him, the better it was for her.'

Bradley might have observed that as a Filipina, raised in a Catholic country with a strong Marian tradition, Maria Aung Thwin's response was somewhat predictable. She could also have learned that between Michael Aung Thwin, the Hawaii-based historian accused by some of being a regime apologist, and Suu Kyi little love was lost. But there was more to Bradley's piece than this. She had wanted to write a biography of Aung San Suu Kyi, but abandoned the idea after interviewing Aung San Suu Kyi in Rangoon. 'In public, Suu Kyi exudes warmth and

openness,' she wrote, 'but she shields her private life fiercely and will
no longer allow journalists to meet her husband.' The implication was
that Suu Kyi gave the orders, and Aris followed them. Quite mistakenly
too, on both counts, Bradley reported how 'After the first two and a
half years [of house arrest], Aris visited three times a year (finances,
not visa restrictions, prevented him from going more often).'

Noting 'something of a clinical quality to Suu Kyi's resolve', Bradley
described the room in which, in 1995, the Nobel Laureate received her,
as 'crammed with artifacts from her political life . . . Pinned to the wall
behind her hangs a huge textile stencil of her father – the same portrait
that served as her backdrop when she launched her political life at
Shwedagon Pagoda. Gracing another wall are old sepia photographs of
her parents but none of her husband and sons. It is a political museum
and points to where her future lies.' Yet at the time the reception room
at no. 54 was used mainly for NLD business. Suu Kyi had plenty of
photographs of Michael, Alexander and Kim, but she kept them upstairs
in her private space, away from prying eyes.

Where Bradley failed, another American journalist, Barbara Victor,
succeeded, at least in producing a first, slim biography: *The Lady:
Burma's Aung San Suu Kyi*, published in 1998. Curiously, Maria Aung
Thwin's comments about Suu Kyi, and the choice between family and
country, are produced verbatim. Yet they are ascribed by Victor to
Maureen Aung Thwin, the historian's sister and, as it happens, a
prominent activist who has consistently given her support to Suu Kyi,
making it unlikely she would ever tell a story that reflected badly on
her heroine. Victor managed, however, to go one step further along the
Aung Thwin trail. The historian himself is quoted as saying, apropos
Aung San Suu Kyi in Kyoto, 'She was her father's daughter and often
expressed her role as guardian of his honor and memory in very
authoritarian ways.' Not surprisingly perhaps, since Suu Kyi was
researching her father's life at the time, but the real killer follows:
'According to Aung-Thwin, she once told him, with a twinkle in her
eye, "It is my destiny to rule Burma." When Michael Aung Thwin
pointed out that "having a famous name was certain to make her ascent
to power much easier" she balked at the notion of using her father's
name to further her own ambitions. "I will do it myself," Aung San
Suu Kyi answered.'

That Suu Kyi's ambition was quite so vaulting in 1985–6, when she
was studying in Kyoto, is uncorroborated by any other evidence or

testimony that I have been able to discover. Like Bradley's *Vogue* feature, Victor's biography appears hastily prepared and under-researched: amongst its shortcomings are a belief that Suu Kyi was born at 54 University Avenue, and a failure even to allude to the Danubyu incident of May 1989. Both Barbaras give credence to a view of Aung San Suu Kyi as an essentially self-serving individual who single-mindedly sacrificed her family on the altar of political ambition.

In her defence, Victor's *Lady* was written and published well before Dr Aris's death. The press coverage produced by that event might have made her reconsider her take on Suu Kyi's marital relations. It might also have led her to Robin Christopher, who knew both Suu and Michael as well as anyone outside their immediate families. In March 1999 his duties as British ambassador to Indonesia prevented him attending Aris's funeral, but immediately afterwards he managed to fly to Rangoon, to offer Suu Kyi what comfort he could. He arrived in the middle of a Buddhist ceremony being held in Aris's memory at no. 54, dispelling any notion that he was unmourned in Burma. While Suu Kyi, in the best stoical tradition, projected an immaculate calm for as long as the compound was crowded with guests and well-wishers, it was clear to Christopher, when they spoke in private over the two days that followed, that she was in considerable distress.

Inevitably they talked about the regime's refusal to allow Dr Aris to die in Rangoon. In Christopher's own words:

Suu said it was an agonising decision for her not to go to be with him. She had discussed it all with him by telephone and he was insistent that she should stay in Burma. It was a joint decision. Two factors were decisive: that it was clear that, by refusing Michael's visa to come to Burma, the regime wanted her to leave and that they would never allow her to return; secondly, and more importantly for her, that the regime would take the opportunity of her absence to round up more of her followers and feel less constrained about how they were treated. Much of her time was devoted to providing support for the families of those imprisoned and doing everything she could to try to ensure that those detained were properly treated. Many families were dependent on her. If she left the country she knew that many of those who had made great sacrifices for her would die in a new crackdown by the regime. She could not leave them. And Michael did not want her to do so.

It was not just a matter of the 'democracy jihad', a phrase touted by Michael Aung Thwin in his academic papers. It also welled from deep within Burmese culture. When, as Prince Sakyamuni, the Buddha set off from the palace he had grown up in to seek enlightenment, he left behind him a wife and a newborn son. What may appear to Westerners an act of callous abandonment was to Easterners high self-sacrifice, later made good by the Buddha's welcoming of his son into the first *Sangha*, or order of Buddhist monks.

In both cultures the family is cherished, but in different ways. The problem for Suu Kyi's family was that it belonged to both. In so far as the Oxford household conformed to the Western stereotype of the nuclear family, it was always likely that Suu Kyi's detention in Rangoon would create emotional as well as practical upheaval. Whereas for Dr Aris, sharing her outlook as she shared his, any 'problems' were containable, the same did not apply to their sons. Both of them suffered. Alexander, the more introverted and serious-minded of the two, withdrew from Washington University and spent a year brooding back in England, before returning to America to enrol in a Burmese studies course at Northern Illinois University, De Kalb. Kim, always more extrovert as a boy, but also less disciplined, failed to make his way through college, and instead became involved in heavy rock and recreational drugs.

In time each made good. After graduation, Alexander met and married a Burmese émigré and settled in the United States. Kim stayed in Oxford, and started a family, earning a living as a decorator. Quite possibly either or both might have encountered difficulties along the road to adulthood, regardless of who or where their mother was. What neither Suu Kyi nor Dr Aris anticipated in 1988 was just how long the 'second struggle' for Burmese independence would take, and therefore how long the disruption to their family life would last. A few months perhaps, a year or two, and then, one way or another, everyone would be reunited. It was unthinkable that victory in so important and just a cause should be deferred indefinitely.

XXXV

THE WIDOWED ROAD TO DEPAYIN

As long as even one person remains in Burma who is not going to give up, then I am not going to leave that person and abandon the cause for my own peace of mind.

Aung San Suu Kyi, 'Never Say Never',
in *The Nation*, 17th February 1998

FOLLOWING his cremation, Dr Aris's ashes were taken to Dumfriesshire, Scotland, and there placed beneath a prayer-wheel at Samyé Lin, a Tibetan centre that Michael had himself helped to create with his twin brother Anthony. In a rare instance of compassion, Kim was given permission by the regime to visit Rangoon, to offer his mother comfort. He brought with him the young child he had had with his partner Rachel, giving Suu Kyi a chance to experience the joy of being a grandmother at first hand. A month later Alexander flew out on a similar mission. Suu Kyi had seen neither of her sons for three years, and was struck by how much Kim especially had changed. Now that he was fully grown and in his twenties, she would not, she confided, have recognised him had they passed each other in the street. It was, however, possibly the last time she would see either of them. As her political work resumed, the SPDC refused further entry visas.

A year before, Suu Kyi had told Steven Gan of the Bangkok *Nation* that her aim was still to reach an understanding with the junta. 'All sides have to realise that the impasse is not doing anybody any good,' she said. 'Ten years is not much compared to the length of time which other countries had to struggle for democracy. So I do not think there is any cause for too much despair or disappointment at this stage. It is quite normal for authoritarian regimes to be intractable for long periods. One just perseveres.'* Yet the more she persevered, the less light there seemed to be at the end of the tunnel. Sometimes she was humoured by the generals, but more usually she was checked by them, until, on the night of 30th May 2003, Than Shwe moved decisively against her.

Week in, week out, she gave her all to the cause. Michael's death was no reason for her to slacken her efforts. Scarcely a day passed when meetings were not held at 54 University Avenue. She continued too to give interviews to foreign journalists, either at her residence or, when it worked, by telephone, as a way of sustaining international pressure on the regime to mend its ways. In June 1999 there began an extraordinary series of six extended interviews in *Asiaweek*, a regional magazine comparable to *Time* or *Newsweek*. Similarly, her pen was kept busy writing messages and speeches. Even if she was not free to venture outside Rangoon, and had no access to Myanmar's state-controlled media, others could deliver her words for her, at home or abroad.

As early as 9th April a video-taped address by Aung San Suu Kyi, pre-recorded with the help of ALTSEAN's Debbie Stothard, was played at the fifty-fifth session of the UNHCR (United Nations Commission on Human Rights) in Geneva. Drawing attention to the fact that 150 elected members of parliament were now in prison, Suu Kyi declared that it had 'come to the point when the activities of the regime are tantamount to criminal activities' – an unusually strong condemnation for her to make. This was followed in May by an address to the Hague Peace Conference. 'A conference on peace is tantamount to a conference on one of the basic necessities of life,' she said. 'In fact one could say that peace is life itself.' Soon after came a message, disseminated by the NLD, for 'Women of Burma Day' – 19th June, her fifty-fourth birthday:

According to a number of psychologists, women are better able than men to cope with crisis situations. We should use this ability to bring about peace and progress to our country, and to better the condition of peoples the world over. There is a great need for our women of Burma to use their capabilities to bring democracy and human rights to our country. It is no longer possible even for housewives to keep out of politics, because politics has invaded the traditional domain of housewives. The root cause of upward spiralling commodity prices,

*The Nation, 17th February 1998.

greatly increased charges for electricity and rising costs of education and healthcare is a political one.

More followed – carefully worded messages to World Voices and the Burma Campaign UK, to the Australian Parliament, to the Inter-Parliamentary Union, to the World Conference on Religion and Peace (held that year in Jordan) and to the Montreal-based International Centre for Human Rights and Democratic Development (ICHRDD), which on International Human Rights Day, 12th December 1999, gave two of her compatriots its John Humphrey Freedom Award: Min Ko Naing, the student leader who was still in prison, and Dr Cynthia Maung, an infinitely resourceful Karen who had created, almost out of nothing, a clinic for the tens of thousands of Burmese refugees in Mae Sot. Nor did the passing of the millennium go unmarked by Suu Kyi. In a video-tape smuggled out to Hong Kong, where it was played at a democracy rally outside the Legislative Council Building on 31st December, she expressed her personal wish that the new millennium bring with it freedom from fear, and freedom from want:

In a country like Burma, want and fear stalk us all the time. People wake up in the morning wondering which of their friends have been taken into detention by the authorities. People wake up in the morning wondering where their next meal is going to come from. They wake up in the morning wondering what the future of their children will be and worrying about it. Want and fear go together where there are no human rights and where there is no justice.

Suu Kyi was steadfast in her objectives and how she thought them best achieved: through non-violence and dialogue with the oppressors. Her hymnal hardly changed, except through increments to its contents. A fresh theme for the new millennium was the alarming spread of HIV infection inside Burma, which the government tried to brush aside, but the World Health Organisation and other international medical agencies monitored as best they could. Seemingly incapable of defeat, Suu Kyi with her calm delivery, absolute composure and brilliant eyes promised only victory. Detached from the hurly-burly of politics, she did not need a new script every day to keep her followers mesmerised. It was her unwavering constancy that guaranteed her appeal.

Myanmar's state media went on vilifying Aung San Suu Kyi, but in other respects for a year or so the SPDC left her more or less alone.

Generals Than Shwe, Maung Aye and Khin Nyunt were confident that they had her under control. Any trouble and they closed down yet more NLD offices, and arrested yet more of its members. But by the end of April 2000 the junta was on heat again. On the 28th Aye Tha Aung, one of the League's senior leaders, was taken into 'temporary detention'. As well as being a member of the committee of parliamentary representatives, Aye Tha Aung had a brief to liaise with Burma's ethnic minorities. Despite the ceasefires of the mid-1990s, large portions of the country's uplands were still in upheaval, with continuing fighting in several borderland areas. Days later *The Mirror*, a government newspaper as waspish as *The New Light of Myanmar*, accused Aung San Suu Kyi herself of a number of 'crimes', including treason. She was, the daily asserted, 'power-crazy'. Determined to 'block foreign aid and investment', she was 'attempting to foment disunity'. Since there was 'evidence that Daw Suu Kyi has contacts with dissidents and armed terrorist groups', she and 'her accomplices could face the death penalty or life imprisonment.'*

It was not armed terrorists that Aung San Suu Kyi had contacted, however, but the United Nations. In another video message to the UNHCR, this time for its fifty-sixth session, recorded at the beginning of the month, she had condemned the SPDC's human-rights and social records. At the end of the month the SPDC was playing host to the economic ministers of China and South Korea, as well as ASEAN. The meeting was billed as the 'biggest diplomatic event' to be held in Burma/Myanmar since the SPDC was formed in 1997. Behind the scenes, some ASEAN ministers asked searching questions about Aung San Suu Kyi and the junta's treatment of her. At the same time one of Japan's biggest companies, Toyota, announced that it was discontinuing its Burmese operations. It seemed appropriate therefore to slander Aung San Suu Kyi as an unprincipled rebel, by way of damage limitation.

For now, the SPDC was only sabre-rattling. For a few days University Avenue filled with troops, then they melted away, leaving behind the usual contingent of Military Intelligence. But the explicit threat to her life only goaded Suu Kyi into greater action. When ASEAN convened its seventh regional forum in Bangkok on 20th July, ministerial delegates were individually presented with a twenty-minute video in which Suu

*Associated Press report, 2nd May 2000

Kyi urged Burma's South-East Asian partners to collectively pressurise Than Shwe to introduce democratic reforms.

A month later, together with a dozen of her closest associates, Suu Kyi decided the time had come to attempt a break-out from Rangoon. However, her convoy of just two vehicles got no further than Dala, a suburb to the south of the capital, before running into a police road block. In a replay of the stand-offs of 1998, Suu Kyi remained inside her car for nine days, refusing to turn back.

What ensued was darkly farcical. As word of Aung San Suu Kyi's latest manoeuvre in her 'war of endurance' against the SPDC got out, the USA, Britain, France and Norway, as well as the European Union, demanded that she be allowed to travel freely around Burma. The SPDC responded by saying that Daw Suu Kyi and her companions were merely holidaying in Dala, and that every amenity was being afforded them. Local authorities had even provided a state-of-the-art portable bathroom and beach umbrellas. To prove its case, the regime released photographs purportedly showing NLD members in Dala carrying shopping bags, and lazily washing themselves under an outdoor shower. There were no photographs of Aung San Suu Kyi herself, though. She remained resolutely inside her vehicle, halted in a notoriously malarial marshland. When word of this got out, the regime explained the dozens of soldiers surrounding her as being there 'for her own protection'. The area was infested not just with mosquitoes, but with 'armed terrorist insurgents' – an entirely spurious claim, of course.

The head-to-head lasted nine days, before 200 *Lon Htein* forced her back to University Avenue, reportedly in an ambulance, on 2nd September On the 3rd soldiers entered her compound, swept through her residence and took away armfuls of documents. Undeterred, on the 15th Suu Kyi announced before a gathering of 300 supporters at the NLD headquarters (now located in the Shwedagon Road) that in a few days' time she, U Tin Oo and others would board a train for Mandalay. 'As I am not legally restricted in any way, we have decided that it is time for us to make this clear. I shall travel outside Rangoon in the next few days. This will be an organised trip and will be done openly.'

Her supporters cheered, but this second re-enactment of an earlier confrontation had far more serious consequences. When, on 21st September 2000, Suu Kyi arrived at Rangoon station, the entire building had been sealed off and was swarming with soldiers. Only she, U Tin Oo and their entourage were permitted to enter. This time there were no fabricated excuses about some last-minute technical hitch. Suu Kyi was to return immediately to University Avenue under armed escort.

Outside the station, dozens of young NLD supporters had already been arrested and taken away. Suu Kyi herself was manhandled into a waiting security van and driven to no. 54. For the second time since coming back to Burma she was under house arrest, though the SPDC failed to make any formal announcement of its order. U Tin Oo and five other NLD Executive Committee members were even less fortunate: they were carted off to Insein. Eleven weeks later, in far-away Washington, and in the closing straight of his eight-year Democrat administration, Bill Clinton conferred upon Aung San Suu Kyi the Presidential Medal of Freedom, on 7th December. For all Burma's ruling generals cared, he might as well have sneezed.

The black comedy lasted throughout 2001 and into 2002. Not for the first time, the regime gave out that Aung San Suu Kyi's latest spell of house arrest was for her own protection, to prevent her being used by 'criminal and terrorist elements'. However, the SPDC found itself under pressure, too. Nothing it did could make the economy work to its satisfaction, and a chorus of disapproval during a 'new millennium' meeting of the UN Security Council raised the spectre of further sanctions. As inflation, accompanied by escalating food shortages, soared, there was a serious and ongoing danger of rice riots amid threats by Japan as well as Western donor nations to cut off all development and even humanitarian aid. Nor, when George Bush, Jr took over as President on 18th January 2001, was there any prospect of the United States relaxing its 'tough' stand on Burma: the arch-exponent of democratisation as an export commodity had arrived in the White House.

Twelve years on from SLORC's September 1988 coup, Burma's generals still found their grip on power precarious. Yet the ruling triumvirate – Than Shwe, Maung Aye and Khin Nyunt – continued to resist even the notion of actual, constructive reform. In their own way, they were as stubborn as Aung San Suu Kyi herself. Instead they strung 'the international community' along, promising much and delivering only what they absolutely had to. Khin Nyunt was in his element. Under the leadership of Secretary-General Kofi Annan, the United Nations regularly dispatched two senior representatives to Rangoon: its human-rights inspector Paulo Sérgio Pinheiro, and special envoy Razali Ismail. Keen to foster visa diplomacy, Khin Nyunt was always on hand to greet them and assure them that the SPDC was preparing to reintroduce democracy. Sometimes they were even permitted to go and talk to Aung San Suu Kyi, either in her compound or at a government guest house. More rarely, Khin Nyunt himself would visit her, for 'secret' discussions, though everybody knew soon enough they had taken place. But 'The Lady' herself remained under house arrest. The SPDC wanted her release, Khin Nyunt intimated, but only when it was 'safe' for her.

To maintain the interest of potential donors and investors, the regime depended on cosmetic gestures. At the beginning of 2001 the vilification of Aung San Suu Kyi in *The New Light of Myanmar* abruptly ceased. Quickly spotted by Rangoon's resident diplomats, this was passed on to their governments. Also in January of that year an EU delegation was permitted to visit Burma for the first time in four years, in an attempt to resolve the 'deadlock' between the SPDC and the NLD. To show that it meant business, a few days before the delegation's arrival the SPDC released U Tin Oo and other NLD leaders from military imprisonment, placing them under house arrest instead. A month later, American diplomats were allowed to interview Suu Kyi. And so it went on: endless (though carefully rationed) talks, month after month, leading nowhere. Meanwhile Suu Kyi endured her second spell of house arrest with the same gallantry as she had endured the first. Paulo Sérgio Pinheiro, Razali Ismail and others invariably reported that she was in good spirits after their meetings with her. She was not about to crack, even though, during the course of 2001, she became embroiled in a civil lawsuit with her own brother, Aung San Oo.

For years, brother and sister had not been on speaking terms. One theory put forward in the media was that each disapproved of the other's choice of spouse. Never one to cherish Suu Kyi, or even pay lip-service to the principled stand she had taken against the dictators who ruled the country he himself had long ago abandoned, Aung San Oo decided to challenge her for at least half-possession of no. 54 University Avenue. As Daw Khin Kyi's elder son, surely he had as much right to the property as his difficult little sister? Under Burmese Buddhist law, property should be divided equally amongst the deceased's children. But there was a fly in the ointment. According to another law, vigorously upheld by the regime in other cases, no foreigner was allowed to own Burmese land. Aung San Oo had taken out US citizenship in the 1980s, and now ran a moderately successful computer engineering business in San Diego.

Ordinarily the military authorities would simply have instructed the

Rangoon Division Court, where the case was to be heard, to give whatever ruling suited it best. But Aung San Oo v. Aung San Suu Kyi put the regime on the spot. The petition was a clear opportunity to further humiliate Daw Suu Kyi. Yet to allow her brother to have his way, at a time when the SPDC was 'talking about talks' with the NLD, risked unnecessary international censure. The solution was to let the case drag on indefinitely – allow it to hang over Daw Suu Kyi's head like the Sword of Damocles, but not let it actually drop. For then there would be the problem of where to keep her under house arrest when she no longer had a house that was all hers.

In a first hearing, Aung San Oo's petition was thrown out by Judge Soe Thein on a technicality: initially he should have applied for an 'administration' order only. But Aung San Oo was allowed to lodge a second, amended petition in April. After further hearings, Aung San Oo's petition was amended yet again. Now he was asking just for 'an appropriate share' in the house. When Suu Kyi's lawyer raised the matter of foreigners being disqualified from owning property, Aung San Oo changed tack again. He wanted half the two-acre site by Inya Lake (valued by one commentator at $2 million) to set up a charity. If necessary he was prepared to hand it over to the state. But he wanted his entitlement to be recognised, in one form or another.

The last proposition especially prompted speculation that Aung San Oo and the regime were in cahoots. That seems not to have been so, even though, six years down the line, judgement was still pending. But what was his motivation? Bitter sibling rivalry? Or was his wife Lei Lei, a businesswoman with interests in Rangoon, the driving force behind the litigation? – as *Time* magazine and other media outlets suggested.* Whatever his actual reason, Aung San Oo's action made for riveting copy. At the same time it cast him in the most unglamorous light. If Aung San Suu Kyi declined to have anything to do with him, was it not perfectly obvious why?

Nonetheless, it must have hurt her. Apart from her sons, who were barred from seeing her, Aung San Oo was the only close blood relative left alive. It would have been so easy to resolve the dispute with a brother she got along with. But that brother, Aung San Lin, had been dead for half a century. Instead she was isolated. Her telephone was again cut, and armed guards were stationed outside and inside her gate.

Time, 18th December 2001; earlier, AFP newswire, 27th June 2001

The Tatmadaw had even moved into a house across the road, the better to maintain its surveillance. To add insult to injury, when Daw Khin Gyi, her mother's elder sister, died in early April 2001 aged ninety-three, she was barred from attending her funeral at the Yayway Cemetery. Aung San Oo was free to fly in and out of Rangoon, but Suu Kyi could not even step out into University Avenue.

And so it went on, into 2002. In January she was accorded another meeting with Khin Nyunt, to talk about 'reconciliation'. But immediately afterwards a planned visit by Razali Ismail was postponed until 19th March by the regime. When 19th March approached, the visit was postponed again. At least this time the SPDC's excuse was half-based in fact. A plot to overthrow the SPDC had been uncovered, the government announced, and it was now busy tidying up. Incredibly, the ringleaders were identified as members of General Ne Win's family. Sanda Win's husband and three of their sons were arrested. For good measure, both Ne Win and his malevolent daughter were placed under house arrest. There was no insinuation that the Old Man himself was involved, but when the details leaked out, many were overjoyed that at last he was tasting a drop or two of the medicine he had concocted forty years before. Whether Ne Win saw it that way was another matter. At the age of ninety-one he was already on his deathbed and had only a few more months to live. His demise, on 5th December 2002, went virtually unreported by the Burmese media. There was no public (let alone state) funeral.

And then, suddenly, the thaw began, or what was presented as such. Razali Ismail was allowed to return to Burma in the last week of April. A series of high-level discussions followed. On the 25th Razali met first with NLD representatives, then with Aung San Suu Kyi, then with Senior General Than Shwe. Six days later Suu Kyi herself, accompanied by other NLD leaders, held talks with the SPDC; and five days after that, on 6th May, her house arrest was lifted.

In an official statement, regime spokesman Colonel Hla Min proclaimed 'a new page for the people of Myanmar'. Using whatever, undisclosed leverage was available to him – shortly afterwards Japan, Burma's biggest donor of aid, cancelled Burma's debts – Razali had, it seemed, pulled it off. Now the way was open for genuine dialogue between Burma's opposing factions. There would be a new constitution, and the NLD would be licensed to play an active role in national reconstruction.

But once again it was an illusion. Whatever pledges Khin Nyunt had given the UN special envoy went unfulfilled. In an apparent show of good faith, several hundred political prisoners had been released over the preceding months, but as many remained in detention. As in 1995, there was no dialogue. The junta was simply playing for time, hoping to impress the outside world with an act of ostensible magnanimity. As for Aung San Suu Kyi, she could go hang. All she needed was enough rope and she would do the job herself. Now categorised as a 'visitor to Myanmar', despite her Burmese passport, either she 'behaved' or 'faced the consequences', *The New Light of Myanmar* warned.

Suu Kyi's second spell of house arrest had lasted nineteen months, but did nothing to impair her resolve. During the second half of 2002 she waited patiently for the SPDC to open its doors for negotiations. But in any meaningful sense they remained shut. 'We shall recommit ourselves to allowing all our citizens to participate freely in the political process, while giving priority to national unity, peace and stability for the country as well as the region,' Colonel Hla Min had said in his statement of 6th May, but these were empty words.

She worked hard in University Avenue, holding 'democracy workshops' for students and women's groups, organising practical support for political prisoners and their families, and receiving a renewed flow of visitors. As always, it was paramount to maintain pressure on the junta by making sure Burma was not forgotten by the outside world. On 2nd August she again met Razali Ismail. Two months later it was the turn of Australian Foreign Minister Alexander Downer. Australia had always been less critical of the junta than other 'Western' nations, but when Downer spoke to journalists at the end of his trip to Burma, on 2nd October, he was downbeat. The SPDC had been unable to give him any indication as to when reforms would be introduced, or what form they might take. Aung San Suu Kyi, he said, now 'doubted' that the regime was capable of change.

But defeat remained a stranger to her vocabulary. In late December she opted to test the junta by resuming her campaign outside Rangoon. Apart from any other consideration, the NLD sorely needed rebuilding in the provinces. She fully expected that she would be prevented from leaving the capital, but owed it to her people at least to try. Her target was Arakan (Rakhine state). To her surprise, no attempt was made to hinder her convoy of three motor cars as it drove north out of Rangoon into Pegu Division. Only when she and her entourage reached Arakan did the problems begin. In several towns and cities the army was out in force. Trucks and barbed wire were placed across her route, and people were warned not to attend her rallies.

This established a new pattern, quite different from 1998, when she had found herself unable to leave Rangoon. Patently the junta had concluded that creating incidents within the capital only fuelled outside censure. Much better to harass Daw Suu Kyi in the sticks, beyond the view of diplomats and other foreigners. But ominously there was now another element. The SPDC had been working hard to build up the USDA as an antidote to the NLD. In the early months of 2003, whenever she embarked on her outreach programme, Suu Kyi and her followers found themselves being taunted by USDA members who were clearly spoiling for a fight.

It was a two-faced game that the junta played. When she returned from Arakan, through the NLD Suu Kyi used National Day on 4th January to urge the commencement of talks – a plea repeated on Union Day, 12th February. There was no response. On the other hand, to maintain appearances, the regime permitted her to receive some unlikely visitors: a Japanese Deputy Foreign Minister on 20th January, for example, and, more encouragingly still, two representatives of Amnesty International eleven days later. On 19th March Paulo Sérgio Pinheiro, the UN human-rights envoy, paid her a second call – though the effect was immediately nullified on the 24th when Pinheiro withdrew his mission from Burma. Interviewing a political prisoner at Insein in what he thought were 'secure' conditions, he discovered a microphone taped underneath his table.

The authorities kept the kid gloves on when Suu Kyi became involved in a squabble with a cousin, Soe Aung, whom her NLD bodyguards had physically prevented from entering the 'family' property at no. 54. On 21st February Suu Kyi was obliged to appear at a local court. Found guilty, she could have been sent to jail for seven days, but instead the judge imposed a fine of 500 *kyats* – $50 at the official exchange rate, but a mere fifty cents at the black-market rate. On principle Suu Kyi refused to pay. Whether the compound belonged to her or her brother, or to them both, might be the subject of painfully protracted litigation, but certainly it did not belong to any cousin, least of all one whose negative feelings about the NLD were well known to her. Instead, her lawyer lodged an appeal with the West Rangoon District Court. Within hours, the fine was suspended pending a further ruling. Some observers were surprised by such leniency, but to have sent Aung San Suu Kyi to prison for so trivial a matter would have provoked uproar.

As soon as she stepped outside Rangoon, life assumed an entirely different complexion. When, at the beginning of March 2003, she took her bandwagon to Tenasserim (modern Tanintharyi Division), another contretemps exploded in Myeik (old Mergui). Traders in the market there seized two men found carrying pamphlets and cartoons lampooning 'The Lady'. Since these were now prohibited by the regime in its efforts to foster the appearance of a changing climate, the men were taken to the local SPDC office. But when NLD representatives tried to ascertain what had happened to the culprits, they found their way blocked by fire engines and were threatened with arrest.

It was in the north, in what had once been called Upper Burma, that the real trouble brewed. From early April 2003, Aung San Suu Kyi began visiting Chin, Kachin and Shan States. The SPDC might not be able to unify the nation, but, by going into the heartlands of the minorities, she wanted to demonstrate that the NLD could. Because of increasing levels of intimidation by the USDA, she took with her, as well as senior party colleagues, some twenty or so NLD Youth bodyguards. As in Arakan, people were warned not to attempt to see her or take part in any NLD rallies, but as often as not they turned out in their thousands, sometimes tens of thousands. Conversely, everywhere her entourage went, they were trailed by MI and regime photographers. Her every move was being watched, her every word recorded. When they could, USDA members surrounded her motor car, shouting ribald slogans and threatening to smash its windows.

The first trip, to Chin state, lasted twelve days. On 6th May – the first anniversary of her release from house arrest – she set out for Kachin state on an even longer journey that would encompass, as well as Shan state, Sagaing and Mandalay Divisions. By the 9th she was outside the Kachin capital of Myitkyina, a thousand miles and more from Rangoon by road. There, an ugly episode took place. Several hundred USDA stood before her as her car attempted to cross a bridge into the city. Once more, the vehicle was threateningly surrounded. On the 14th she reached Longin (Lonkin), and five days later she was in Bhamo (Bhamaw), where even torrential mountain rains did not deter her followers from gathering to greet her. Then it was on to Mogok, home to Burma's largest ruby mines, and on again, to Kyat Pyin and Thabagyin. In the hottest part of the year, it was as gruelling an itinerary as any Suu Kyi had undertaken in 1989. Approaching her fifty-eighth birthday, she seemed to have twice the energy of supporters half her age. Yet even she needed some respite. Photographs and video-tapes taken of her in Kachin and Shan states reveal drawn features, bags beneath her eyes. She still joked with her colleagues – the generals wore more make-up than she did, she quipped, probably with the heavily pomaded Khin Nyunt in mind – but her laughter was rarer and thinner than before. Worryingly for those around her, the strain was getting to her.

It was proposed, and Suu Kyi agreed, to rest up in Mandalay for a couple of days. But there would be no going back to Rangoon until she had visited all the places she had promised to see. This dismayed the junta. Than Shwe had monitored Aung San Suu Kyi's near-triumphal progress through Upper Burma with mounting anger. Too many people simply ignored the orders to stay away. Instead they lined her route, lighting candles if she was scheduled to pass by after dark. More disturbingly still, everyone seemed to know when to expect her. The NLD was clearly in a stronger condition than Than Shwe's sycophantic minions had led him to believe.

It was time to act.

In a last-ditch effort to persuade Suu Kyi to terminate her tour, the state media broadcast a statement saying that the NLD must 'accept' that many Burmese did not support the League – meaning of course the USDA, most of whose members had no choice in the matter. Nothing more specific was said – officially Aung San Suu Kyi's tour did not exist – but the implicit threat was there all the same. Her bodyguards reacted by beefing up their numbers, with further volunteers from the NLD's Mandalay youth wing. Then, at 9 a.m. on 29th May, an enlarged convoy (ten motor vehicles and ten motorcycles) headed out westwards from the former capital into Sagaing Division. Ahead went an eleventh vehicle, a 'scout car', designed to provide advance warning of any military road blocks or unfriendly USDA mobs. Reasonably enough, 'security' was now a matter of burning concern.

The convoy bypassed Sagaing itself, though at a bridge outside the city hundreds of supporters had gathered to shout 'Long live Aung San Suu Kyi' and 'Long live U Tin Oo' (who was riding in a separate vehicle). At noon they came to Myinma, a smaller township where Suu Kyi presided over the reopening of an NLD office. By three o'clock they were on the road again, reaching the larger township of Monywa at dusk. There, the authorities had shut down the electricity supply to inhibit Monywa's inhabitants from coming out to greet Suu Kyi. Notwithstanding, people poured onto the streets with candles, again shouting 'Long live Daw Aung San Suu Kyi' and 'Long live Ba Ba U Tin'. Suu Kyi's motorcade then made its way to a house belonging to U Tin Soe, a former soldier and NLD elected member. Early the next morning she addressed a huge crowd before visiting the Zawtika monastery, whose abbot Suu Kyi had been hoping to meet. But the abbot was nowhere to be seen. Officers from Burma's Northwest Command had arrived earlier and 'invited' him to spend the day elsewhere.

Suu Kyi climbed back into her car and the convoy headed off for Butalin, where she was due to open another NLD office. Only now, instead of ten motorcycles accompanying her, there were hundreds. Anyone who owned one, or could borrow one, wanted to follow her. As with a queen bee on the move, the swarm around her grew and grew. But at Zeedaw village, close to Northwest Command's headquarters, the swarm was cut back down to size, from perhaps 800 to fewer than 400 individuals. A police road block ordered all those from Monywa to return home, where some received a severe beating.

But why were only half sent back? Why was the entire procession not stopped, or thinned down further, so that it only included Aung San Suu Kyi's immediate entourage?

Suu Kyi's convoy was shadowed by police and MI in their own vehicles. Leaving Butalin in the late afternoon of 30th May, the NLD continued heading northwards. Eventually the road would circle back eastwards, towards Shwebo. But Shwebo would not be reached until tomorrow. The plan was to rest overnight at Depayin.

Suu Kyi stopped at Saingpyin village to meet U Win Myint Aung, another MP-elect, to thank him and his family for their support. By the time she set off again, darkness had fallen. Because the highway was in bad repair the going was slow, the line of vehicles a long black snake studded with lamplights. Dutifully it stuck to the right-hand side of the road and there was no overtaking. The last thing anyone wanted was an altercation with the traffic cops. But Depayin was not so far away now, just three or four miles, and with it the prospect of cooler interiors and dinner.

The first sign that something was amiss was when the scout car, sent ahead to confirm that there were no problems at Depayin itself, failed to come back. The second sign was when two motorcycles, dispatched to find out what had happened to the scout car, similarly failed to return. The third sign was that for a while no oncoming traffic had been encountered. And the fourth sign, just past a junction with a dust track leading to Kyee village, was two men dressed as monks. Wearing red scarves on their upper bodies, they were standing in the middle of the road ahead, illuminated by the headlights of Suu Kyi's car, which was at the head of the pack.

Ko Tun Zaw Zaw, the bodyguard seated next to Suu Kyi's driver, got out to ask the monks what they wanted. The monks replied that they had heard Daw Suu Kyi was on her way and wanted her to give them a speech. Would she get out of the car too and speak to them? They had, they said, been waiting a long time. Most politely Tun Zaw Zaw told the monks that no such thing was possible, but if they cared to be in Depayin early next morning . . .

Suddenly four trucks packed with thuggish-looking men wearing white armbands roared up from behind the convoy on the left-hand side of the road and screeched to a halt. At first they shouted the usual well-rehearsed USDA taunts: 'Relying on external forces, axe handles – we do not want holders of negative views!' and 'We do not want people who do not support the USDA!' (An 'axe handle' was a euphemism for someone in the pay of a foreign interest.) But on the other side of the road were candle-holding villagers from Kyee, who had come out to cheer 'The Lady' as she passed. Some of these began taunting back, 'We the people do not want you!' In a trice, the men jumped down from the trucks. In the glare of the convoy's headlamps it was plain to see that they were armed – with iron bars, clubs, stakes, bamboo bats and knives. It was also clear that they were unusually psyched up.

As the thugs chased the villagers away, Tun Zaw Zaw asked the monks to intervene. They just shrugged; there was nothing they could do. The thugs were turning on the motorcade, on Suu Kyi's car at the front particularly, and on U Tin Oo's four behind. This in itself was horrific, but simultaneously hundreds more ruffians, armed with the same weapons, sprang out from the bushes that lined the far, left-hand side of the road.

The NLD bodyguards knew what to do. Climbing off their motorcycles or out of the cars, they formed two defensive rings around Suu Kyi and U Tin Oo. The outer ring was made up of Mandalay youth, the inner

ring of those who had come from Rangoon. But to little avail. The
thugs meant business this time. With frenzied brutality they began
clubbing and stabbing those in their way. Once they had their victims
on the ground, they pounded their heads with stones. The trucks,
revving their engines, ran down some of those attempting to flee.

'Are you the death-defying force of the *kala* woman?' they screamed.
'If so, prepare to die.'

And many did die. The attackers, it is believed, numbered 2,000 – a
numerical advantage that enabled them to pursue those running for
cover into the surrounding bush and hack them down if they caught
them. The bodies of the fallen were stripped of cash and other valuables.
'If you don't want to die,' one conscience-stricken assailant told an NLD
female youth member, 'just lie down and pretend to be dead. If you
move we will have to continue beating you until you stop.'

Other women were not so fortunate. Their long hair was tied around
their hands to prevent them hitting out, then their heads were repeatedly
smashed on the ground.

U Tin Oo was dragged from his car and taken away with a severe
head injury. Those that could fled on their motorcycles towards Depayin,
but were stopped by another crowd of ruffians, close to an irrigation
works. More killings ensued. Even early next day the carnage continued.
Some who had managed to hide were shot at by police when they
returned to the road to pick up their motorcycles.

By then Aung San Suu Kyi was under arrest. From the back seat
where she was sitting she had told her driver, Ko Kyaw Soe Lin, not
to drive off. She insisted on remaining with her 'people', whatever the
consequences. When, just behind her, the rear window of the car was
shattered, causing cuts to her neck, she must have feared the worst. But
Kyaw Soe Lin, determined to save her life, jammed his foot down on
the accelerator and the car shot forward. Nor did he take his foot off
when they reached the irrigation works. He sped towards the mob,
which scattered to left and right as Suu Kyi passed through.

Shots rang out behind them, but missed their target. They did not
get very much further, however. Outside Yeoo township, beyond the
Depayin turn-off, the car was stopped by the Tatmadaw.

This time there were none of the niceties of house arrest. Aung San
Suu Kyi was put in jail. The truth about Burma had finally caught up
with her. It is a place where the victims of violence, not its perpetrators,
are punished.

XXXVI

BACK TO MANDALAY

Standing on a high place in Pyinmana – the balcony of the railwaymen's flats – and looking out across the derelict rolling-stock, the scorched brick and twisted girders, one saw a glitter of fire, an encrusted brilliance of towers and turrets, that arose shining over the edge of the town. Even at a mile's distance there was no doubt that this was some gaudy pretence, but of such a magnitude that a visit, even in this murderous sunshine, was not to be avoided.

Norman Lewis, *Golden Earth* (1952)

IN the immediate aftermath of Depayin – Burma's 'Black Friday' – the SPDC made predictable noises about Aung San Suu Kyi being placed under 'protective custody'. The grim reality was that the generals had tried to kill her. But, too afraid to do so with their own or the army's hands, they had gone down the road of plausible deniability, depending on a thousands-strong gang of criminals and other hastily recruited toughs, whose assembly in the countryside along the Monywa 'circle road' on a hot summer night was nothing if not orchestrated.

Within hours of the massacre other NLD leaders were either arrested or confined to their homes in many different parts of Burma. The party's offices in Rangoon and Mandalay were sealed off. Simultaneously the country's universities were shut down. Refusing to divulge where Aung San Suu Kyi had been taken, or even whether or not rumours that she herself had been badly injured were true, the junta tried its level best to play down the whole incident. Yes, there had been a 'brawl' in Sagaing Division, and four had been killed, as well as fifty injured. But it was no more than that. As for Daw Suu Kyi, the SPDC belatedly announced that it had received intelligence that 'assassins' had entered the country. It was the government's duty to put her out of harm's way.

The actual figures were quite different. At least seventy had been killed on the night of 30th May 2003, and a hundred injured. A further hundred had been detained by MI and the police, while as many as yet another hundred were unaccounted for, raising the prospect that fatalities were far higher than even the NLD feared. Both at Kyee village and at the disused irrigation plant outside Depayin, within hours the authorities were busy removing the evidence: bodies, bloodied clothing and discarded weapons. The corpses were hurriedly buried between the foundations of the buildings at the irrigation site. Local hands hired to do this work were made to sign papers denying any knowledge or involvement. But later, on 31st May, four of the bodies were dug up again, washed and photographed. It was these, the regime claimed, who were the only dead of Depayin. Yet despite every effort to round up all those who had escaped the carnage, there were just too many witnesses to what had happened.

That scores survived was down to the darkness and the density of the bush – waist-high shrubs and taller, enveloping tamarind trees. There many hid until dawn, too petrified to move. A few kept on going until they reached some kindly village. Some, fearing to go home, fled to Thailand, where, over the coming weeks and months, a picture wholly different from the one painted by the regime emerged. Four such witnesses gave key testimonies to the Thai Senate's Standing Committee on Foreign Affairs five weeks later, on 5th July. Others offered statements to human-rights organisations, including Amnesty International. The most damning indictment came not from any NLD member, but from someone who had operated on the other side.

Identifying himself as Kyaw Lwin, he said he was a Rangoon-based 'spare', a truck driver's assistant. Although the Nissan ten-wheeler he co-drove was registered privately, 'in truth it is the property of the Military Intelligence in Yesagyo'. His 'normal' business was to transport goods from the capital to Monywa. At the end of May he made what he thought was a routine trip north, alongside the first driver, 'Ko Nyo'. On the 28th the Nissan, together with nine other trucks, was requisitioned by the Northwest Army, and then kept parked at the Command's headquarters outside Monywa.

Both drivers were seconded. When darkness fell on the 30th, an army captain 'dressed in civvies climbed into the front compartment. Communication accessories were put on the truck. Then about fifty persons boarded the back compartment. Some were in monks' robes, others in civvies. After that the back of the Nissan was covered with a canvas cloth and orders were given to drive off.' An hour and a half later the Nissan approached Kyee village. The massacre had already begun. 'I saw a noisy crowd where people were being thrashed mercilessly,' Kyaw Lwin testified. 'The captain made the driver keep the headlights on and ordered the men in the [back of the] truck to get down and join in thrashing the people in the crowd.'

Kyaw Lwin remained in the driver's compartment, along with Ko Nyo and the captain, watching as the beatings were 'delivered relentlessly and savagely'. He had never seen anything like it in his life. 'There were people running, shouting, screaming and falling on the ground with blood all over them.' Soon some of the bodies were carried over to the truck. Beside him, the captain was speaking on a radio telephone, saying, 'Yes, General, yes, yes.' The officer then ordered Kyaw Lwin to lift the bodies into the truck. 'At the same time I saw him fire three or four times into the crowd at the front.' Some of the bodies, Kyaw Lwin thought, were still alive.

Once the Nissan was full, it had to be driven back to Monywa. At Ahlone, another village, it was ordered to stop, and the bodies were removed and dumped by the roadside. Lightened of its human cargo, the truck then returned to the parking lot at the Northwest Army headquarters. One by one the other trucks came back, then all the drivers were invited into a small hall. 'There was food and liquor ready prepared for us . . . We ate. Then we were given 30,000 *kyat* each.' The Nissan, however, was taken away 'by someone else' and not returned until the following evening. Kyaw Lwin and Ko Nyo were told to wash the blood-stains from the back, before returning to Rangoon.

Kyaw Lwin's eye-witness account was corroborated by others. Another 'insider' witness, a member of the USDA interviewed by American-sponsored Radio Free Asia in September, described 'how scores of bodies' arrived at a Monywa crematorium over the course of two nights and were burned unceremoniously. He also related how Burma's Deputy Home Minister, Brigadier Myint Maung, had arrived in Monywa a few days before the massacre, and immediately afterwards told those USDA members involved to stick to the official version, of just four killed in a scuffle. But Kyaw Lwin knew this to be untrue, even as he knew that female NLD youth members seized at Depayin were raped in an empty storage hall at the irrigation plant. 'We, the whole town, knew that it was a premeditated attack,' he said. 'But the authorities are trying to cover it up by arresting and killing those who witnessed it.'

It was naïve of the SPDC to think that, with thousands involved, no one would talk, or that none of the massacre's intended victims would escape. That the mob had been concealed only on one side of the road also lessened the impact of the ambush. The trail of meetings and requisitions and hirings, of weapons provided and barrels of strong alcohol given to the impossibly large gang before the assault, led inexorably towards the door of Senior General Than Shwe. Each fresh witness statement and report was vigorously denounced by the junta as a fabrication of Burma's external enemies, meaning the United States. But even the circumstantial evidence was just too strong. For why else had the regime isolated Aung San Suu Kyi, U Tin Oo and other NLD leaders, and stopped anyone going to Depayin for several weeks? Nor was there, or has there been, any indication that the authorities have attempted to bring the perpetrators of the Depayin 'brawl' to book.

An outrage so awful, and on such a scale, could not be covered up, any more than the horrors of 8.8.88 could be. It was, however, the treatment of Aung San Suu Kyi that attracted the lion's share of media attention. For ten days her condition and whereabouts were a mystery, until on 9th June UN special envoy Razali Ismail gave an assurance that she was in 'good health and in good spirits'. He had persuaded Khin Nyunt that it was in the junta's interests to allow him at least a short telephone conversation with her. But he was unable to divulge where she was being held, if indeed he knew.

The SPDC stuck to its story that Aung San Suu Kyi was being detained for her own safety, even though a British Foreign Office minister, Mike O'Brien, asserted on 19th June (Suu Kyi's fifty-eighth birthday) that she was being held under a 'most draconian' 1975 law that allowed for virtually indefinite detention without any means of appeal. Two days later, a team sent to Burma by the International Committee of the Red Cross (ICRC) was denied access to her. Challenged by Japanese Deputy Foreign Minister Tetsuro Yano on whether Aung San Suu Kyi had been taken to Insein prison, Khin Nyunt issued a flat denial. But he was lying. As released inmates and prison warders themselves confirmed,

Insein was exactly where 'the Lady' was being detained. A special,
two-room wooden isolation cell had been hastily constructed within the
prison grounds, close to the women's block. Its single window looked
out directly onto the prison gallows. And she still wore the same clothes
she had been wearing on the night of 30th May.

To staunch any more such stories leaking out from Insein, at the
beginning of July Suu Kyi was transferred to a secret location more
distant from the capital. The junta's attitude towards her was not
softening, however. The state media launched a fresh vilification campaign
accusing her of being 'wilful and hard-headed'. On a strict understanding
that they did not reveal her whereabouts, Red Cross officials were finally
permitted to interview Suu Kyi face-to-face on 28th July. Repeating
what Razali had said about her being in good spirits, head of mission
Michel Ducreaux told reporters that her meeting with himself and a
Red Cross colleague had lasted 'about half an hour, and we were alone.
It was a very decent place and the conditions were also very decent.'
His statement did little to assuage international censure. UN
Secretary-General Kofi Annan repeatedly called for Aung San Suu Kyi's
unconditional release – as did George W. Bush, amongst other world
leaders.

For several years a group of US congressmen, led by Republican
Senator Mitch McConnell and Democrat Representative Tom Lantos,
had been pressing the White House for stronger unilateral sanctions
against Burma. On 28th July 2004 President Bush signed a Burmese
Freedom and Democracy Act, which augmented the measures introduced
by Bill Clinton in 1997. The Act banned all Burmese imports and any
further investment in Burma by American companies. It froze assets
belonging to either the Burmese government or junta members and their
families held by American banks and other financial institutions, and
prohibited entry visas being granted to the same individuals. It also cut
off any American technical and financial aid destined for Burma through
the World Bank and the IMF. But in so far as such measures, broadly
copied by the European Union in October 2004, were designed to
influence the policies of the SPDC, they had little impact. Genuine
democratic reform remained bottom of the junta's agenda, as did the
release of Aung San Suu Kyi.

However, she did not remain in jail, or what the government called
a 'military guest house'. Instead she was returned to house arrest. At
the beginning of September 2003 rumours began circulating that Aung

San Suu Kyi was on hunger strike. Whilst these subsequently proved unfounded, she was suffering from an acute gynaecological disorder, in addition to a chronic stomach ailment (possibly an ulcer) of several years' standing. On the 17th she was removed to the private Asia Royal Cardiac and Medical Centre in Sanchaung Township, Rangoon, where she underwent surgery. While the details of this have not been made public, it is thought that she may have had a hysterectomy. Ten days later she was discharged. Instead of being taken back into military custody, she was allowed to return to her residence at 54 University Avenue in order to 'recuperate'.

And there she has remained ever since, under house arrest, more isolated than at any previous point in her life. Once again her telephone lines were cut, as the Tatmadaw and MI bedded down outside her gate, and inside the compound. It is not even known whether she still enjoys the benefit of her short-wave radio. No visits – whether by her sons, friends or (with one exception) representatives of the United Nations, ICRC or other international bodies – have been permitted.

The exception was Ibrahim Gambari, the UN's Nigerian-born Undersecretary-General who was briefly allowed access to Aung San Suu Kyi in May and again in November 2006. During their second meeting (11th November), which took place at a state guest house, Suu Kyi told Gambari that she was 'in good health' but 'required more medical visits'. Unusually, the regime permitted her photograph to be taken. Well turned out as ever, in a lilac blouse and *longyi*, Suu Kyi appears drawn and and unusually thin.

The request for 'more medical visits' coincided with press reports that she had not been seen by her personal physician, U Tin Myo Win, since late August 2006. This was doubly a cause for concern. Tin Myo Win had been trying, without success, to get permission to test his patient with ultra-sound. Despite her protestation to the contrary, Suu Kyi's health may not have been that good when she saw Gambari the second time. Secondly, Tin Myo Win was her only regular contact with the civilian world (as well as with the NLD) other than her ageing live-in maid, who buys her food and other necessities. The regime responded to Gambari's request to allow Tin Myo Win to bring ultra-sound equipment to 54 University Avenue, but refused to consider granting visas to Alexander and Kim to visit their mother.

The conversion of Aung San Suu Kyi's detention from military custody to house arrest three years before had raised hopes that she would shortly be set at liberty again – hopes that have periodically resurfaced. An apparent relaxation of security arrangements along University Avenue in January 2006 was heralded as a sure sign of her imminent release – until it was appreciated that some road barriers had been removed merely to ease Rangoon's growing traffic congestion. Yet the permitted if increasingly irregular continuance of Dr Tin Myo Win's visits points to the junta's own ongoing dilemma. What the generals must dread more than anything else is Aung San Suu Kyi's death from anything other than unambiguously natural causes. Were she to be looked after by regime medics, no one would believe her demise to be anything other than induced, and then all hell might break loose. Robbed of their venerated icon, the oppressed people of Burma might just, finally, throw all caution to the winds and have the generals' guts for garters. Whereas Suu Kyi has always urged 'national reconciliation', others inside as well as outside the NLD have talked openly of arraigning Burma's dictators for their 'crimes against humanity' – a threat that sits uneasily on the generals' minds.

But there is the other reason why the junta has not (so far) got rid of Aung San Suu Kyi once and for all. She remains the ultimate bargaining counter. So long as the regime can maintain the tantalising prospect of her possible release, then it retains the whip hand over the so-called 'international community'. Move too assertively, too aggressively against the junta, and her sainted blood might trickle into Inya Lake.

Thus has been created an immaculate tragedy, at once national and individual – curiously exacerbated, since 9/11, by the world media's intensive (though understandable) focusing on the 'war against terrorism'. Are the trammels of a third-rate, majoritively non-Christian, non-Muslim South-East Asian state not of the utmost inconsequence? Yet the deep agony of the multi-ethnic, multi-cultural Burmese people endures, as does the symbolic, but also personally real, anguish of the people's principal protagonist. Like the unwitting heroine of some remorseful nineteenth-century opera, 'The Lady by the Lake' sings a piteous aria. But it is, too largely, an aria unheard. The 'new world order' – that much-trumpeted evanescence of the Clinton era – is already being consigned to history.

In every sense we may think of, Aung San Suu Kyi has become the perfect hostage. Her principled stand against a modern tyranny has been adroitly turned against her by her unprincipled captors. Kept in captivity, in part brought about by her own intransigence, the songbird's freedom has a price that no one can, or any longer dares, pay. The latest apostle of non-violence is imprisoned by her creed.

And so Burma has sunk deeper and deeper into the mire. With Aung San Suu Kyi and the NLD finally contained, in a lengthy keynote speech delivered before a phalanx of top-ranking officials and carefully selected foreigners at the Pyithu Hluttaw on 30th August 2003, Prime Minister General Khin Nyunt (as he had now become) outlined what he provocatively called the SPDC's 'Road Map to Democracy'. The National Convention, suspended since 1996, was to be revived. The new constitution was finally to be drafted and put before the people in a referendum. There would then be 'free and fair' multi-party elections to a parliament, followed by the building of a 'modern' nation under the guidance of elected ministers. Yet Khin Nyunt also used the occasion to denigrate both Aung San Suu Kyi and the NLD. 'As long as a political force in the country is acting in harmony with the collaborators of neo-colonialism from abroad who are trying to find ways of bringing down the existing government,' he said, 'and as long as that political force continues to maintain a negative attitude or refuses to change its methods, it will result in a situation where the golden land that we all hope for will remain in the distance.'*

Clearly, free and fair multi-party elections still did not apply to the League. But if some felt that the NLD's exclusion was an acceptable price to be paid for reform, when the Convention met it was subject to the same restraints as in 1993. The junta had already determined the new constitution's principal ingredients, and delegates were hand-picked for their loyalty to the regime. Even then, the process quickly stalled. Not for the first time, the Convention was suspended on the grounds that delegates were better off employed gathering in the post-monsoonal harvest. Several start–stops followed, with no demonstrable progress. In October 2005, Paulo Sérgio Pinheiro told the UN General Assembly: 'The Government's "roadmap" to democracy has no time frame and no scale. The destinations are hazy, the road-signs keep shifting and the journey time between each place is anybody's guess. The loose mention of a referendum and political elections has not yet been clarified. The

*The full text of Khin Nyunt's speech was published in *The New Light of Mynamar*, 31st August 2003

political transition process has become a long and winding road with no clear end in sight.'

A year later the Convention met again but with no palpable sense of urgency. It was fourteen years since the junta had first intimated a return to semi-civilian rule. In 1947 it had taken Bogyoke Aung San's provisional administration just six months to draw up a working democratic constitution. Even in Iraq, the most problematic of all problem territories, a deal was hammered out in the space of eighteen months, between the ousting of Saddam Hussein on 9th April 2003 and the adoption of the Iraqi constitution on 13th October 2005. But, under the tutelage of Burma's military commanders, fourteen years were evidently insufficient.

For Khin Nyunt, the master operator alleged to have once purchased a PhD from a commercial company in Ohio, time was running out. On 19th October 2004 it was announced that, aged sixty-four, he had retired for 'reasons of ill-health'. But that was the usual euphemism. In reality he had been carted off to Insein prison on Than Shwe's orders. A huge purge followed. MI was systematically dismantled, and hundreds of its officers also taken into custody. While the foreign media bemoaned the 'reformist' Khin Nyunt's ousting by army 'hardliners', something rather more complex had occurred. At the heart of the matter was a long, smouldering feud between MI and the Tatmadaw. Regular soldiers felt that Khin Nyunt's intelligence apparatus had grown too powerful. It was known that some of its energies were spent assembling dossiers on the generals themselves. Khin Nyunt's removal from his many positions within government was accompanied by raids on his home and MI offices up and down the land. Truckloads of documents were seized and incinerated.

In July 2005 Khin Nyunt was arraigned in court on charges of corruption and given a forty-four-year prison sentence, quickly commuted to house arrest. Stories that he had been injected with brain-scrambling drugs to prevent the 'Prince of Darkness' ever enjoying a comeback were unfounded. More plausibly it has been said that amongst his personal papers was a diary in which was recorded a flattering appreciation of Senior General Than Shwe – hence the relative leniency of his punishment. But in sidelining a potentially dangerous rival, Than Shwe sought also to restore Burma's extensive surveillance system to its rightful owners, the Tatmadaw and the police Special Branch. For months afterwards MI operatives were hunted down. A few escaped to Thailand, where they were accorded a less than enthusiastic welcome by other political refugees.

Yet the removal of Khin Nyunt did not spell the end of 'his' Road Map. A week after his arrest, in an apparent show of confidence, Than Shwe made a state visit to India. There he assured his hosts that the National Convention would continue its work.

It took the SPDC a while to rebuild its intelligence-gathering capacity. In May 2005 Rangoon, and to a lesser extent Mandalay, were rocked by a series of explosions that left up to seventy dead. The worst-affected targets were a shopping mall and a trade hall in the capital. At a press conference held on 15th May, the regime's Minister of Information Brigadier Kyaw Hsan detailed a wide-ranging conspiracy against the government that implicated pretty well all its enemies: separatists in Shan State, Karen and Karenni rebels, Muslim insurgents in Arakan, the ABSDF, former MI types, the NLD, unnamed foreign powers, and so on. No one took him seriously, other than to surmise that the bombs were probably planted by the regime itself, as a means of reminding the Burmese people of the need for a strong, authoritarian state. This theory was also unlikely. The shopping mall was frequented by Tatmadaw families, and at the time Thai manufacturers were displaying their wares at the trade hall. Relations with Thailand had entered a phase of almost unprecedented harmony, based on state-to-state trade agreements, and there was no sense in putting this in jeopardy. Rather, the SPDC was clearly rattled by what had happened and by its inability to identify the actual perpetrators.

But if Rangoon had become unsafe for the junta, it had already prepared a contingency plan. In November 2005 it surprised nearly everyone by announcing that Burma's capital was being transferred forthwith to a new city being built near Pyinmana, on the banks of the Sittang river in the southernmost part of Mandalay Division.

Diplomats had known about Pyinmana and the closely guarded construction site being developed there for two or three years, but few thought the SPDC would really repot itself. Pyinmana, though on a main north–south trunk road and an important rail junction, enjoyed few other obvious advantages. But it was within the Burman 'heartland', and had once served as General Aung San's headquarters. By relocating there, Than Shwe was reasserting a specifically Burman history of Burma. Tellingly, the name given to the new capital was Nay Pyi Daw – 'The

Place of Kings'. There would be many statues of Burma's former monarchs, and (eventually) a replica of the Shwedagon. Suspicions that the Senior General was seeking to revive the monarchy in his own name were sharpened in November 2006 when a video-tape of his daughter Thandar Shwe's wedding that had taken place in Rangoon the preceding July was released. The marriage ceremony shown was extraordinarily lavish.

Overnight civil servants and other government employees were ordered to head north, with or without their belongings. Those who refused faced not only the sack, but fines and prison sentences. Yet when they reached Nay Pyi Daw, the city was barely half-built. Neither houses nor offices were finished, and water and electricity supplies were, at best, eccentric. Caught off-guard, the foreign press, though not allowed anywhere near the new capital, had a field day, as it strove to explain the inexplicable. Most entertainingly, Jan McGirk, filing for *The Independent* on 8th November, wrote of a 'xenophobe's Xanadu' and of a 'martial Milton Keynes'. Nay Pyi Daw was either a 'secret dream scheme' for establishing a 'command centre in the jungle', much closer to the insurgencies of Shan and Karenni (Kayah) States, or 'Escape City'.

Inevitably, speculation turned towards the occult. Astrologers, fortune-tellers, clairvoyants and palmists, usually with their stalls parked immediately outside a pagoda, are a part of everyday life in Burma. Most families own a little fat book that tells its users what dates are auspicious and inauspicious according to their birth dates. Like Ne Win before him, Than Shwe is widely supposed to be addicted to the forecasts of his own private astrologer, though what passes between them is necessarily a state secret. More publicly, one of Burma's leading astrologers had lately cast a grim prediction that Rangoon was doomed to destruction, in which case the shift to Nay Pyi Daw might well be an unrivalled example of a self-fulfilling prophecy – if by 'destruction' was meant the ending of Rangoon's capital status.

For critics eager to make hay at the regime's expense by hinting at military heads turned loco by archaic soothsaying, such prognostications, regurgitated in newspapers and on the Internet, locked smartly into another, only marginally less irrational explanation. The generals had taken to the hills for fear of an American-led seaborne invasion – just as they were supposed to have called the 1990 election to discourage the Seventh Fleet from steaming into the Andaman Sea. Utter nonsense of course: with its cruise missiles, bunker-busters and satellite surveillance, the USA (even if it had any such intention) would have found Nay Pyi Daw the choicer target. By corralling themselves and their loyalists into a purpose-built administrative complex surrounded by a *cordon sanitaire* replete with landmines, the junta would simply be helping the nominated aggressor by limiting the scope of 'collateral damage'.

It was even suggested that the generals were running away from Aung San Suu Kyi: true at some contorted psychological level perhaps, but unnecessarily expensive. More cost-effective, surely, to have spirited her away to some mountain dungeon – though the thought of good clean upland air prolonging her life would have been a deterrent.

What commentators missed was how the move to Pyinmana/Nay Pyi Daw resonated with the past. For centuries it was virtually *de rigueur* for a new dynasty to create a new capital – the last, and best-recorded, instance being King Mindon's creation of Mandalay.

George Orwell, describing Mandalay in *Burmese Days*, found it a 'rather disagreeable town' whose five 'main products' all began with P: 'namely, pagodas, pariahs, pigs, priests and prostitutes'. Well before the early 1930s, when Orwell published his novel, it played second fiddle to Rangoon in every respect. But for twenty-five years during the latter half of the nineteenth century, the 'Golden City' was a fulcrum of both ceremonial and political drama.

King Mindon began building Mandalay in 1857, to reassert the prestige of the throne (badly dented by the loss of Lower Burma to the British). With its imposing citadel and many pagodas it was designed to enshrine the values and traditions of the Burman people. The old capital, Amarapura, had become too squalid for habitation, and was especially vulnerable to attack from the Irrawaddy. But the transfer from the one city to the other was badly planned and took weeks to complete. An enormous procession of elephants, bullock carts and wheel-barrows wound its way up the river's eastern bank. Many had to go by foot, making the journey several times to bring all their belongings from Amarapura. And when they did reach Mandalay, they found the city only half completed. Inside the moated citadel even the King's palace was still under construction, and Mindon himself had to spend his first few months in Mandalay living in a temporary structure.

Then as now, a new capital was a luxury the nation could ill afford. Like Nay Pyi Daw, Mandalay was only made possible by the use of forced (or slave) labour. And other sorts of inhumanity prevailed. Even the peaceable King Mindon acceded to the demands of his Indian astrologers that men, women and children be buried alive in the foundations of the citadel, to ward off evil spirits. Above all it was imperative that a pregnant woman be interred. The theory was that, their spirits joined in death, the mother and her child would become a composite demon of such dread potency that no enemy would dare approach where the body and its foetus lay.

But the potency of the human sacrifices lasted only so long. Mindon's successor as 'Lord of the Universe', King Thibaw, was powerless to resist the advancing Prendergast, and Mandalay was demoted to the status of mere provincial city.

Whether an equivalent fate awaits Nay Pyi Daw of course remains to be seen. It seems improbable, at least in the foreseeable future. Militarily, 'Myanmar' has no serious aggressors. For years the USA has urged the United Nations to close ranks against the SPDC, whose violations of human rights are comparable to the Konbaung monarchy's. Progress appeared to have been made in December 2005, when, in the wake of a fiercely critical report prepared by the US law firm Piper Rudnick Gray Cary, and commissioned by Nobel Laureate Desmond Tutu and former Czech President Václav Havel,* the UN Security Council agreed by consensus to a formal discussion on Burma – thus putting Burma on the UNSC 'agenda'. But nothing came of this apparent breakthrough. On January 12th 2007 a draft resolution proposed by the USA and Britain calling for immediate reform in Burma was vetoed by fellow Security Council permanent members China and Russia. Bolstered by increasingly close and lucrative trading ties with India, Bangladesh, ASEAN, Japan and South Korea as well as (overwhelmingly) with China itself (the main supplier of weapons and technology to Burma), the regime could finally flick two fingers at the West. Sanctions, however well intentioned, had singularly failed in their objectives.

By 2007, Burma's military government appeared to be more secure than at any other time since Ne Win's 1962 coup. The economy still lurched, Shan state was in a turmoil of fighting factions, and insurgency wars continued, though with the Karen and Karenni rebels pegged right back against the Thai border. But overall the junta had reason enough to feel pleased with itself. The move to Nay Pyi Daw should not

*Threat to the Peace: A Call for the UN Security Council to Act in Burma, 20th September 2005

therefore be interpreted as a flight of any kind, but as an expression of Burman atavism.

By the same token, Aung San Suu Kyi's heroic opposition to the regime looked in tatters. Fears that her third term of house arrest might be permanent were exacerbated on 18th January 2007, a week after the failure of the US-UK draft resolution at the UN Security Council. *The New Light of Myanmar* reported that the Burmese government had acted 'considerately' in not sending Daw Suu Kyi to prison for the rest of her life for not repatriating her Nobel and other prize moneys, and paying taxes on them. To all appearances the NLD was a spent force too, though overseas activists claimed that the League continued to enjoy an extensive underground existence. Although Suu Kyi's cousin, Dr Sein Win, kept the democracy flag flying as head of the émigré 'elected' government in Washington, there were increasing desertions from the cause, both outside and inside Burma. Many NLD MPs had either quit politics altogether, or been bought off by the regime.

A notable defector was Ma Thanegi (never to be confused with the redoubtable Ma Than É), Suu Kyi's one-time aide and close companion. On 29th October 2001, to the stunned silence of her audience, she voiced her disillusionment during a panel meeting at the Carnegie Endowment for International Peace in Washington. Aung San Suu Kyi's natural idealism, she said, had become an obstacle to progress in Myanmar. Because she was 'beautiful and charming', she had commandeered the international press. Ma Thanegi also used the occasion to lambaste US policy. Sanctions, she said, had cost 100,000 women and children their jobs – as though child labour were a thing to be extolled.

Similar criticisms were levelled at Suu Kyi and the NLD in October 2004 by Dr Zarni (aka Maung Zarni), a founder of the US-based Free Burma Coalition. Amongst other successes, the FBC had persuaded PepsiCo., Inc. to close down its Burmese operation, by encouraging American students to boycott Pepsi's soft drinks products. In a lengthy report entitled 'Common Problems, Shared Responsibilities: Citizens' Quest for National Reconciliation in Burma/Myanmar' co-authored with May Oo, Dr Zarni launched a sustained invective against Burma's democratic movement. To the fury of Aung San Suu Kyi's supporters, he urged constructive engagement with the SPDC. When, subsequently, he surrendered his 'green card', that allowed him residence in the USA, and was spotted making trips home to Burma (where, as well as seeing his family, he held talks with mid-ranking military leaders), it was assumed that he had been 'turned' by the regime.

The problem with constructive engagement is, and always has been, the junta's inability to demonstrate good faith. It simply does whatever it pleases whenever it can, the prime example being its dismissal of the 1990 election result. But that is not to say that every criticism levelled at Aung San Suu Kyi should be ignored, otherwise any concern for Burma becomes a Stalinist parody of democracy. While the ridicule directed at her by Burma's state media may be dismissed as (often sexist) malevolence, other objections do carry some weight. Because of the 'male chauvinist' character of Burma's tyrants, her political body language may not always have been best suited to the task of winning over her adversaries. One hand is open and says 'Come talk with me!' But the other persistently wags the admonitory digit: 'You naughty, naughty boys!' In the Burman proverb, she 'carries fire on one shoulder and water on the other'. Again, her admirable insistence on the path of non-violence may also be miscued. Force, or the threat of force, is the language Burma's dictators best understand.

Velvet revolutions do not invariably succeed. More specifically, Aung San Suu Kyi's support for economic sanctions against Burma, and her disapproval of tourism for tourism's sake, are seen by some as doctrinaire. Western embargoes have helped drive the regime deeper into the embrace of China – a nation-empire relatively untutored in the pursuit of human rights. As disturbingly, by depriving the regime of opportunities to engage in 'legitimate' business activities, sanctions may even have prolonged the regime's reliance on narcotics as a source of revenue.

In this context, comments made by Dr Richard Jones, a director of British-based Premier Oil plc, are pertinent. Premier Oil acquired extraction rights to a sizeable gas field in the Gulf of Martaban from Texaco in 1996, and farmed the field until 2003, when 'for business reasons' (and not, Dr Jones insists, because of pressure from the Burma Campaign UK) it sold its interest to the Malaysian company Petronas Nasional Bhd. For seven years Jones was site manager. He followed ethical employment practices of the sort advocated by Global Compact, a voluntary code to which Premier Oil formally subscribed in 2002. Amongst other benefits, he provided his workforce with 'fair wages, company housing and health insurance, as well as a pension scheme'. Taken together, in his view these constituted a 'model' for progressive employment patterns, unlikely to be matched by any Chinese enterprise. He was impressed by Suu Kyi's 'personality' and 'obvious commitment to the highest principles' when he met her, but thought that 'she and her party were just naïve about a lot of things.'*

Dr Jones conceded that some of his operation's profits were going straight into the generals' private pockets, but 'some facts you had to live with'.

One alternative scenario to Aung San Suu Kyi's strategy of highest principle runs as follows. The 'liberal' West should have exploited to the hilt the chance to invest in Burma after 1988 – not just for the sake of profit, but by way of setting better examples of employment and business practice inside Burma. Similarly with tourism. Once the doors of 'Visit Myanmar Year' (1995/6) were opened, we should have gone there in our millions. If only by a process of osmosis, Burma must surely have changed. Limiting contact plays into the junta's hands.

Another instance of 'counterproductive sanctions' may be the USA's and EU's policy of denying places at their universities and colleges to the children of regime members. Surely much better to give the grandsons and granddaughters of General Than Shwe and his ilk a decent liberal education than see them packed off to Beijing? Equally hard to justify is Burma Campaign UK's decision to blacklist the publishing company Lonely Planet, for issuing a travel guide to Myanmar/Burma. As it happens, the guidebook in question is upfront about the tourism issue. 'Should you go?' the cover asks. 'See inside for details.' Inside the reader finds an approving text box on Aung San Suu Kyi, and a disapproving text box on General Ne Win. Perhaps travellers and users (who include many non-tourists as well as tourists) should instead rely on indigenous, regime-approved guidebooks? Any book that honestly adds to our knowledge about Burma should be welcomed. But Lonely Planet is a brand name, and by attacking it Burma Campaign UK enhances its own profile.

These are instances where rightly principled positions have turned into inflexible dogma – a charge sometimes levelled at Aung San Suu Kyi herself. As it is, neither economic sanctions nor the discouragement of tourism have been sufficiently encompassing. Western enterprises, if they are determined, find ways of investing in Burma, often through subsidiaries in Singapore and other Myanmar-friendly nations. Each

*Author interview, October 2005

year hundreds of American, British, French and other Western tourists savour the beauties of Mandalay and Pagan and the Irrawaddy, only dimly aware of the momentously lost opportunity when the results of the 1990 election were dishonoured.

Whether an NLD-led democratic government would have done the trick we may never know. The divisions between Burman and non-Burman Burmese run deep. Teddy Buri, an engagingly urbane Karenni Catholic who stood as an NLD candidate in 1990 and won his seat, told me in 2005 how he could never entirely trust either the League or its leader. There were three grounds for his scepticism. Aung San Suu Kyi might die, and there were no guarantees that the NLD would not then become 'Burmanised'. Or a majority within the NLD might impose its Burman will. And thirdly, Aung San Suu Kyi 'might herself become a tyrant'. 'But remember,' he cautioned, 'whenever you get two Burmese together, the result is invariably three parties.'*

It would simply be dogmatic to assert that an NLD government in 1990 would have mended all Burma's woes. The difficulties of that country may just be too great for any one person to resolve, at least in his or her own lifetime; or for any one determined league or party. But the possibility was there. What needs to be acknowledged, and continuously applauded, is Aung San Suu Kyi's phenomenal ability to inspire others, not just in Burma, where her presence has underpinned the democracy movement since August 1988, but around the world. Without her kind, we are all impoverished. In the Manichaean scheme of things, which sees the human condition as a permanent contest between good and bad, virtue and decay, and to which every culture in one way or another subscribes, her significance reaches far beyond one beleaguered South-East Asian nation. Never let go of hope. Or, as even Dr Zarni – because of his fervent longings for a better Burma, typecast as an 'anti-Suu' – put it to me, 'Fifty years hence, there will be a statue of her in every Burmese township.'†

The triumph of failure? The cynic in me questions such optimism, if optimism it was. Either way, what happens in the intervening fifty years is what matters now. Too many young, as well as many older, Burmese lives depend upon it.

---

* Author interview, 2005
† Author interview 2004

ACKNOWLEDGEMENTS

ONE of the satisfactions of writing a biography is that research contacts may become friends. Donna Jean Guest, who long held Amnesty International's Burma/Myanmar brief, provided the insider's ongoing encouragement any writer engaged in a long-haul project needs. As importantly, during a period when US foreign policy entered one of its darker phases, she persuaded me, just by being herself, that the flame of decent American liberal idealism burns brightly yet. I owe an equivalent debt of gratitude to Martin Morland, Britain's ambassador in Rangoon during the upheavals of 1988. Both read a draft manuscript and offered many helpful comments. I must, too, express particular thanks to Patricia Gore-Booth, the widow of Lord Gore-Booth, another British envoy to Burma. For whatever reason, she put her trust in me. My earnest hope is that her trust has not been misplaced.

One former ambassador to (amongst other nations) Indonesia, Sir Robin Christopher, and one former ambassador to Thailand and Vietnam, Derek Tonkin, gave generously of their time and thoughts. Sir Michael Holroyd, amongst contemporary biographers the best there is, lent encouragement when it was needed most: at the outset. Of the many Burmese encountered, Ma Than É – ninety-seven when I met her at her retirement home in Oxford – slew me most. The firmness of her parting handshake and the clarity of her mind and memory are indelibly imprinted. Aye Chan and Angeline Naw generously shared work-in-progress with me. And then there is Dr Zarni, a well-known dissident living outside the country of his birth who has enraged other expatriates with his criticisms of Aung San Suu Kyi and the NLD. His contentious but challenging views cautioned me to take nothing for granted.

Special thanks are likewise due my erstwhile co-agent Barbara Gorna, and continuing main agent Peter Cox, of Redhammer Management. Barbara, in a moment's inspiration, redirected an interest in, and concern for, Burma's beleaguered minority peoples towards Aung San Suu Kyi herself. Peter turned that deflection into two years' vastly stimulating work. I am also greatly indebted to my editor at Hutchinson/Random House, Paul Sidey – old friend and peerless professional; to his assistant Tess Callaway; to my painstaking copy editor Mandy Greenfield; and to Roger Walker.

From the start I elected to listen to anyone prepared to talk to me, regardless of their political affiliation. Those other helpers and informants who can be named (and there are very many who cannot be, non-Burmese as well as Burmese) are (in roughly alphabetical order): Abel Tweed; Dr Shankar Acharya; Bo Aung Din; Bo Kyi; Vicky Bowman (another former ambassador to Burma); Aung Kyaw Zaya; Professor Michael Aung Thwin; Aung Zaw; Aung Zaw Oo; Saw Ba Thin Sein; Joan Bird; Dr Peter Carey; Professor John Carroll; Marie-Pierre Champagne; Baroness Cox; Dr Cynthia Maung; Professor Frank Dikotter; Andrew Dilnut; Doh Say; Faith Doherty; Dave Eubank; Eva (Tin Hlaing); Patricia Herbert; Noriko Horsley; Guy Horton; Htoo Htoo Lay; Dr Julie Jack; Dr Richard Jones; Jue Jue; Hick K; Malavika Karlekar; Ko Aung; Wendy Law Yone; Bertil Lintner; Mahn Robert BaZan; Maung Too; Min Zin; Dr Kosuke Mizuno; Jenny Morland; Moses Soe Moe Naing; Professor Kei Nemoto; Nerdah Mya; Nita Yin Yin May; Nurul Islam; Nyo Ohn Myint; Michael Reilly; Ben Rogers; Daw San San; Josef Silverstein; Martin Smith; the staff of the library at SOAS; Soe Aung (not the Soe Aung referred to in Chapter XXXV); Dr Margaret Stearn; Debbie Stothard; Hirokuni and Keiko Sugahara; Professor Robert Taylor; Teddy Buri; Than Win Htut; U Kyaw Win; U Tin Moe; U Win Khet; Dr Win Naing; Win Thein; Dr Justin Watkins; Yongyut Losupakarn; Bill Young; Kirsten Young; Zaw Min; Zin Linn; and Zoya Phan.

Although this book is dedicated to Nat and Sugar Yontararak, and to Khun Supinya, another valiant South-East Asian freedom fighter, the underlying debt is, as ever, to wife Kimiko Tezuka-Wintle: in her own, Yamanashi way as steadfast as Suu Kyi.

SOURCES/FURTHER READING/WEBSITES

WHAT follows is not intended to be an exhaustive bibliography, but a 'first base' for anyone wanting to explore the themes and subject matter of this book further. Unless otherwise indicated, the titles listed have been published in the UK and/or the USA.

Aung San Suu Kyi

Aung San Suu Kyi has published seven books. Her brief biography of her father, *Aung San* (1984), reflects a perennial admiration for the founder of the modern Burmese nation felt among a majority of Burman and some other of the Burmese peoples. *Let's Visit Bhutan* (1985), *Let's Visit Burma* (1985) and *Let's Visit Nepal* (1985) are introductory guides of no vast distinction, though ably enough compiled. *Freedom from Fear* (1991, revised and expanded 1995), edited with an Introduction by Dr Michael Aris, a Foreword by Václav Havel and four appraisals by Ma Than É, Ann Pasternak Slater, Josef Silverstein and Philip Kreager, contains the texts of *Let's Visit Burma* and *Aung San* as well as early essays and addresses, including the Shwedagon speech of August 1988. *Letters from Burma* (1997), with an Introduction by Fergal Keane and line drawings by Heinn Htet, collects fifty-two articles contributed by Aung San Suu Kyi to the *Mainichi Shinbun* during the course of 1995–6 and is a gem. *The Voice of Hope: Conversations with Alan Clements* (1997), originally published in French as *La Voix du Déti* (Paris 1996), is the fullest exposition of Aung San Suu Kyi's mature political and social views. Some other essays and speeches have appeared in print, notably 'Heavenly abodes and human development', published by CAFOD in 1997. The author benefited greatly from transcripts of unpublished speeches and messages made available to him by Debbie Stothard at ALTSEAN. He was also fortunate in being given access to an unpublished memoir of her mother (Daw Khin Kyi) written by Aung San Suu Kyi during the period of her first house arrest. The first biography of Aung San Suu Kyi appeared in Japan, though the title of Yoshikazu Mikami's *Aung San Suu Kyi: Toraware no Kujaku* (Tokyo 1991) is intrinsically difficult to translate. The Japanese word 'kujaku' means both peacock and peahen: 'Captured Peahen' strikes the wrong note, but the sense of a caged bird is spot on. Barbara Victor, *The Lady: Burma's Aung San Suu Kyi* (1998) is the first biography in English. While its political heart is in the right place, its attention to detail is sloppy. Ang Chin Geok, *Aung San Suu Kyi: Towards a New Freedom* (1998) and Bettina Ling, *Aung San Suu Kyi: Standing Up for Democracy in Burma* (1999) are mainly lightweight hagiographies. By contrast Gustaaf Houtman, *Culture in Burmese Crisis Politics: Aung San Suu Kyi and the National League for Democracy* (1999) is a serious and valuable academic essay that *inter alia* explores Aung San Suu Kyi's evolving thought in its Buddhist context, and can be downloaded from the Internet by googling the name of its author. Bertil Lintner's earlier *Aung San Suu Kyi and Burma's Unfinished Renaissance* (1992) is non-biographical, but gives a political overview written by a seasoned Burma-watcher. *Les Prix Nobel: The Nobel Prizes 1991* (Stockholm 1991) contains official documentation relating to Aung San Suu Kyi's Nobel Peace Prize. Lisa Brooten, 'The Feminisation of Democracy Under Siege: The Media, "the Lady", and U.S. Foreign Policy', *NWSA Journal* Vol. 17 No. 3 (2005) stands out as a thoughtful feminist critique amidst a burgeoning supply of academic journal literature. *The 60th birthday of a national heroine* (Seoul 2005) in English and Korean contains little of substance, but indicates Aung San Suu Kyi's trans-national appeal. Where I have drawn upon contemporaneous press and other media coverage is detailed in the accompanying footnotes. Here, I would like to draw attention to Timothy Garton Ash's fine essay, 'Beauty and the Beast in Burma', based on an interview with Aung San Suu Kyi and published in the *New York Review of Books*, 25th May 2000. With regard to Dr Michael Aris, I greatly benefited from a video recording of his 1999 Oxford memorial service.

Aung San

Aung San's major speeches and writings can be found in Josef Silverstein ed., *The Political Legacy of Aung San* (revised edition 1993). Another useful source is Mya Han ed. and Thet Tun trans., *The Writings of General Aung San* (Rangoon 2000). Aung San, *Burma's Challenge* (1946) is all that the Bogyoke published in book-form during his lifetime. Aung San Suu Kyi's introductory biography of her father is mentioned above. While Aung San still awaits a major biography, Angelene Naw, *Aung San and the Struggle for Burmese Independence* (Chiang Mai 2001) is well-researched and readable. Dr Maung Maung ed., *Aung San of Burma* (The Hague, 1962) contains individual memoirs and anecdotes, as does the Burmese-language Bo Tun Hla, *Bogyoke Aung San* (Rangoon 1955). The most satisfactory account of Aung San's assassination is Kin Oung, *Who Killed Aung San?* (Bangkok 1996).

The Historical Background

There is no adequate, contemporary and up-to-date account of Burmese history in its entirety that the author is aware of. D.G.E. Hall, *Burma* (1950) is brief and outdated, but is a good read nonetheless, and can be supplemented by F. Tennyson Jesse, *The Story of Burma* (1946). Thant Myint-U, *The Making of Modern Burma* (2001), written by U Thant's grandson, is seminal. Reeling back in time, Michael Aung Thwin is currently the most celebrated historian of early Burma. His books include *Myth and History in the Historiography of Early Burma* (1998) and *The Mists of Ramanna: The Legend That Was Lower Burma* (2005), which challenges the view that Theravada Buddhism was vouchsafed the Burmese people by the Mons. Ronald Latham's translation of *The Travels of Marco Polo* (1958) is widely available as a Penguin Classic. The colonial period is chronicled in G.E. Harvey, *British Rule in Burma 1824–1942* (1956). An eye-witness account of the First Anglo-Burmese War is given in Major J.J. Snodgrass, *The Burmese War 1824–1826* (1827). A.T.Q. Stewart, *The Pagoda War: Lord Dufferin and the Fall of the Kingdom of Ava, 1885–6* (1972) provides a narrative for the Third Anglo-Burmese War. E.C.V. Foucar, *They Reigned in Mandalay* (1946) details the excesses of King Thibaw and Queen Supayalat. Courtney Anderson, *To The Golden Shore: The Life of*

Adoniram Judson (1987) is a biography of the first Christian missionary to Burma. A memoir of Judson's convert Ko Thah Byu can be found in the Rev. Francis Mason, *The Karen Apostle* (The Religious Tract Society, no date, but *circa* 1842). Sir J. George Scott, *The Burman: His Life and His Notion* (1910) is a colonial portrait that contains interesting material on Burmese beliefs and superstitions. Aspects of the colonial legal system are explored in Maurice Collis, *Trials in Burma* (1937). About Burma during the Second World War there is a huge literature, mainly of individual war memoirs, the pick of the bunch being John Masters, *The Road Past Mandalay* (1961) and Field-Marshal Sir William Slim, *Defeat Into Victory* (1956). By far the best overall account of the Burma campaign is Louis Allen's classic *Burma: The Longest War 1941–1945* (1984). John Latimer, *Burma: The Forgotten War* (2004) is as voluminous but less successful. Barbara W. Tuchman, *Stillwell and the American Experience in China 1941–1945* (1972) presents the same campaign from an American viewpoint. Christopher Bayly and Tim Harper, *Forgotten Armies: The Fall of British Asia 1941–1945* (2004) looks at it in the context of the British empire at large. The standard life of Earl Mountbatten is Philip Ziegler, *Mountbatten: The Official Biography* (1985). The aftermath of war is examined in John McEnery, *Epilogue in Burma 1945–1948: The Military Dimensions of British Withdrawal* (1990). U Ba Than, *The Roots of the Revolution* (Rangoon 1962) overstates the role of Aung San's army in the defeat of the Japanese, but at least gives us a Burman's view. As regards the gaining of independence and its aftermath, U Nu's autobiography, *Saturday's Son* (1975), is rather more of a delight than Ba Maw's self-serving *Breakthrough in Burma: Memoirs of a Revolution, 1939–1946* (1968). Hugh Tinker, *The Union of Burma: A Study of the First Years of Independence* (1957) and Frank Trager, *Burma: From Kingdom to Republic* (1966) are ground-breaking works of scholarly importance. Robert H. Taylor, *The State in Burma* (1987) offers a narrative of the changing structures of government in Burma from the early nineteenth century up until the eve of 1988. A comparison of 'state-building' in Burma with state-building among other South-East Asian nations might have spared Taylor's blushes when the meltdown occurred shortly after publication, but his early chapters are good.

Contemporary Burma/Myanmar

A convincing, even essential account of the background to the 1988 uprising is Bertil Lintner *Burma in Revolt: Opium and Insurgency since 1948* (1994). The same author's *Outrage: Burma's Struggle for Democracy* (1995) furnishes a commendable early take on the uprising itself. A blow-by-blow account of the uprising is contained in an Amnesty International report, 'Myanmar (Burma): Prisoners of Conscience: A Chronicle of Developments Since September 1988' (November 1989). Mary P. Callahan, *Making Enemies: War and State Building in Burma* (2003) covers much the same ground more academically. Maung Maung, *Burma and General Ne Win* (Rangoon, 1969) is a sycophantic biography of Ne Win that nonetheless has its moments. Inge Sargent, *Twilight Over Burma: My Life as a Shan Princess* (1994) tells the moving story of a European woman married to a Shan prince who disappeared shortly after the 1962 coup. Harriet O'Brien, *Forgotten Land* (1991) recalls Burma under Ne Win through the eyes of a diplomat's daughter. Andrew Selth, *Burma's Armed Forces: Power Without Glory* (2002) is the best guide to the growth and style of Burma's armed forces. *The Military Balance* (IISS annual) can be relied upon for updated estimates of Myanmar's battle order. Christina Fink, *Living Silence: Burma Under Military Rule* (2001) tells it from the other side, a chilling survey of what a majority of Burmese are forced to endure. James Mawdsley, *The Heart Must Break: The Fight for Democracy and Truth in Burma* (2001) is the compelling account of the ordeal of a Western rights activist imprisoned by the junta. *Inked Over, Ripped Out: Burmese Storytellers and the Censors* (Chiang Mai 1994) by Anna J. Allot exposes the extent of the regime's assault on freedom of expression. Monique Skidmore, *Karaoke Fascism: Burma and the Politics of Fear* (2004) is a passionate and readable evocation of life in post-1990 Rangoon, but gets some of its facts plain wrong. *The White Shirts: How the USDA is Set to Become the New Face of Burma's Military Dictatorship* (Thailand 2006), compiled by the Network for Democracy and Development, is a valuable study of The Myanmar's Union Solidarity and Development Association. The regularly updated Lonely Planet guide *Myanmar (Burma)* contains useful basic information about contemporary Burma.

The Minorities

The most authoritative guide to the tortuously complex world of Burma's ethnic peoples is Martin Smith, *Burma: Insurgency and the Politics of Ethnicity* (1991, revised edition 1999) although some readers will find Bertil Lintner's *Burma in Revolt* (see above) an easier read. Lintner's *Land of Jade: A Journey from India through Northern Burma to China* (Bangkok 1990) moves elegantly through the northern peoples. A few years later Shelby Tucker undertook a similar journey, only in reverse, travelling on foot from China to India: *Among Insurgents: Walking Through Burma* (2000) is a memorable account of a journey underpinned by the author's sense of Christian solidarity with the Kachins. Christian solidarity similarly informs Benedict Rogers, *A Land Without Evil: Stopping the genocide of Burma's Karen people* (2004); and, from an earlier generation, Eugene Morse, *Exodus to a Hidden Valley* (1975). Earlier still, Ian Morrison, *Grandfather Longlegs* (1947) relates the life and death of Major H.P. Seagrim, and his efforts to sustain a Karen guerilla force during the Second World War. Martin Jelsma, Tom Kramer and Pietje Vervest eds., *Trouble in the Triangle: Opium and Conflict in Burma* (Chiang Mai 2005) attempts to untangle the complex history of war and narcotics in Shan state. *Khun Sa: His Own Story and His Thoughts* (Bangkok, no date) is an intriguing collection of photographs and press pieces about the most notorious of the drugs warlords and can be found in some Thai bookstores. Pascal Khoo Thwe, *From the Land of Green Ghosts* (2002) is the beautifully written story of how a young Padaung escaped from Burma and became his people's first student at Cambridge University. Inevitably, Burma's minorities have attracted the attention of anthropologists – at least when they have been allowed to go there. (Sir) Edmund Leach, *Political Systems of Highland Burma* (1954, revised 1964) is a classic study centred mainly on the Kachins. Two books by Melford Spiro – *Burmese Supernaturalism* (1967) and *Anthropological Other or Burmese Brother? Studies in Cultural Analysis* (1991) – also deserve mention, although the latter is, as its title suggests, distinctly theoretical.

Other Literature

Very little Burmese literature of the modern or of any other period has been translated into English. Three travel books about Burma, however, commend themselves: Norman Lewis, *Golden Earth: Travels in Burma* (1952); Andrew Marshall, *The Trouser People: A Story of Burma in the Shadow of the Empire* (2001), which retraces the footsteps of the nineteenth-century traveller and orientalist Sir J. George Scott; and Emma Larkin, *Secret Histories: Finding George Orwell in a Burmese Teashop* (2004). Some readers may also enjoy Ma Thanegi, *The Native Tourist: A Holiday Pilgrimage in Myanmar* (Bangkok 2004). There are a handful of 'Burmese' novels that can be recommended, most obviously George Orwell's *Burmese Days* (1934), but also Michio Takeyama, *The Harp of Burma* (*Biruma no tategoto*, Tokyo 1946, trans. 1966); Daniel Mason, *The Piano Tuner* (2002); Amitav Ghosh, *The Glass Palace* (2002), a solid saga about several generations of an Indian family living in Burma and their roller-coaster fortunes; and (a fine piece of 'witness fiction') Karel Van Loon, *The Invisible Ones* (*De Onzichtbaren* 2003, trans. 2006).

Human Rights

Since 1988 there has been a deluge of reports detailing human-rights violations in Burma published by a widening array of rights agencies. Amnesty International alone has issued almost 150 over an eighteen-year period. Taken together, these constitute a damning indictment of Burma's military regime. Rather than single out individual reports I would point the concerned reader in the direction of some of the principal agencies involved through their websites:

ALTSEAN (Alternative ASEAN Network): www.altsean.org
Amnesty International: www.amnesty.org (search Burma)
Assistance Association for Political Prisoners: www.aappb.org
Burma Border Consortium: www.tbbc.org
Burma Campaign UK: www.burmacampaign.org.uk
Burma Project (Open Society Foundation): www.soros.org/initiatives
Free Burma Coalition: www.freeburmacoalition.org
Human Rights Watch: www.hrw.org
Women's League of Burma: www.womenofburma.org

Other websites

An invaluable source for news about Burma is Burmanet, which assembles a composite of press pieces every weekday, at www.burmanet.org. Another good source of Burma news is *The Irrawaddy* magazine, online at www.irrawaddy.org. Internet coverage is also provided by the Democratic Voice of Burma (radio and television station): www.dvb.org. Those interested in the military regime's version of events can go to *The New Light of Myanmar*: (www.myanmar.com/newspaper/nlm/index.html or the *Myanmar Times* (www.myanmar.com/myanmartimes). Prospect Burma is an educational trust originally established with Aung San Suu Kyi's Nobel and other prize moneys, and can be accessed on www.prospectburma.org.

INDEX